W. H Woodbury

A Shorter Course with the German language

W. H Woodbury

A Shorter Course with the German language

ISBN/EAN: 9783743394209

Manufactured in Europe, USA, Canada, Australia, Japa

Cover: Foto ©Paul-Georg Meister /pixelio.de

Manufactured and distributed by brebook publishing software (www.brebook.com)

W. H Woodbury

A Shorter Course with the German language

A SHORTER COURSE

WITH THE

German Language.

BY

W. H. WOODBURY, A. M.

AUTHOR OF "NEW METHOD OF LEARNING TO READ, SPEAK AND WRITE
THE GERMAN LANGUAGE," "ELEMENTARY GERMAN READER,"
"ECLECTIC GERMAN READER," "GERMAN-ENGLISH AND
ENGLISH-GERMAN READER,"
"NEW METHOD FOR GERMANS TO LEARN ENGLISH," OR
"Neue Methode zur Erlernung der englischen Sprache," &c.

TENTH EDITION.

NEW YORK:
IVISON, PHINNEY & CO, 48 & 50 WALKER STREET.
CHICAGO: S. C. GRIGGS & CO., 39 & 41 LAKE ST.
BOSTON: BROWN, TAGGARD & CHASE. PHILADELPHIA: SOWER, BARNES & CO.,
AND J. B. LIPPINCOTT & CO. CINCINNATI: MOORE, WILSTACH, KEYS & CO.
SAVANNAH: J. M. COOPER & CO. ST. LOUIS: KEITH & WOODS. NEW
ORLEANS: BLOOMFIELD, STEEL & CO. DETROIT: F. RAYMOND & CO.

1862.

PREFACE.

This "Shorter Course" with German is designed as a response to the oft-repeated call for something less elaborate than the author's larger work. Its aim, therefore, is simply and rigidly *practical*.

The plan differs not materially from that which characterizes the author's English Course for Germans, published in 1848: the exercises throughout being alternately English and German.

The details of the method, therefore, need not here be pointed out; as a glance at the following pages will convey a better impression of the leading features of the course, than any amount of statement and specification.

With this brief prefatory note, with sincere thanks for the favor shown to his previous productions, and with the hope that the present one will not be less deserving of regard, the author commits the work confidingly to the public.

New-York, June, 8, 1852.

WOODBURY'S GERMAN SERIES.

WOODBURY'S NEW METHOD
OF
LEARNING TO READ, SPEAK AND WRITE GERMAN
Price, $1. 25.

WOODBURY'S
SHORTER COURSE WITH GERMAN.
Price, $0. 75.

WOODBURY'S
ELEMENTARY GERMAN READER.
Price, $0. 75.

Woodbury's
ECLECTIC GERMAN READER.
Price, $1.

WOODBURY'S
GERMAN-ENGLISH AND ENGLISH-GERMAN READER
Price, $0. 25.

Woodbury's neue Methode
zur Erlernung der englischen Sprache.
Preis $1.

Fasquelle's French Series.

FASQUELLE'S FRENCH COURSE.
Price, $1. 25.

Fasquelle's Colloquial French Reader.
Price, $0. 75.

FASQUELLE'S TELEMAQUE.
Price, $0. 75.

INDEX TO THE LESSONS.

Less. I. German Alphabet.

Less. II. Sounds of the letters. 1. Vowels. 2. Umlauts. 3. Diphthongs. 4. Consonants. 5. Compound consonants.

Less. III. Current hand.

Less. IV. 1. Definite article. 2. Gender of nouns. 3. Pres. sing. of haben.

Less. V. 1. Interrogative conjugation. 2. Pres. sing. of loben.

Less. VI. 1. Cases. 2. Position of genitive. 3. Dative, how rendered. 4. Decl. of def. art. 5. Agreement of art. with noun. 6. 7. 8. Forms of decl. of nouns. 9. Paradigm.

Less. VII. 1. Dative with prepositions. 2. Conj. of verbs.

Less. VIII. 1. Demonstrative pronouns. 2. & 3. Decl. of dieser, jener, &c.

Less. IX. 1. Indef. art. 2. Poss. pron. 3. Decl. of indef. art. and poss. pron.

Less. X. 1. Interrog. prons. 2. Decl. of Wer and Was für ein. 3. Was für separated. 4. Welch and was für in exclamations. 5. Was for Warum. 6. Jemand, Niemand, Etwas, Nichts. 7. Was for Etwas. 8. Decl. of Jemand. 9. Gar, or Ganz und gar.

Less. XI. Adjs. of old Decl. Forms of the adjective. 1. Used predicatively. 2. Three forms of declension. 3. When inflected according to the old declension. 4. Rejection of e before l, n or r. 5. Endings of old decl. in the nominative. 6. Adjs. qualifying Etwas, &c.

Less. XII. 1. Adjectives inflected according to the new declension. 2. Endings of new declension in the nominative.

Less. XIII. 1. Adjective inflected according to the mixed declension. 2. Form of words requiring an adjective to be in the mixed decl. 3. Endings of the mixed decl. in the nominative.

Less. XIV. Speaking and writing German.

Less. XV. 1. Preps. with the dative. 2. Preps. with the accusative. 3. Preps. with the dat. or acc. 4. Preps. and def. art. contracted.

Less. XVI. 1. Negative conjugation. 2. Position of Nicht. 3. Sondern and Aber. 4. Nicht wahr? 5. Nouns of the new decl.

Less. XVII. 1. Articles and pronouns in the feminine gender. 2. Declension of feminine nouns. 3. Appellations of females. 4. Adjectives in the old declension. 5. Adjectives in the new declension.

Less. XVIII. 1. Formation of diminutives. 2. Use of diminutives. 3. Formation of compounds. 4. Gender of compounds.

Less. XIX. 1. Gender of nouns. 2. Appellations of persons. 3. Masculine. 4. Feminine. 5. Neuter. 6. Having two genders. 7. Generic names of animals.

Less. XX. 1. Plural of article, possessive and demonstrative pronouns, &c. 2. Adjectives in the plural. 3. Old declension. 4. Present plural of Haben and Sein. 5. Nouns of the old declension ending in e, el, en, er, chen and lein. 6. Nouns not ending in e, el, &c. 7. Nouns having more than one form for the plural.

Less. XXI. 1. Adjectives of new declention. 2. Nouns of new declension. 3. Feminine nouns. 4. Nouns of old and new declension. 5. Nouns following the old decl. in the singular and the new in the plural. 6. Declension of proper names. 7. Feminine proper names ending in e. 8. Masculine nouns adding ens. 9. Use of the article. 10. Connected view of all declensions.

Less. XXII. 1. Comparison of adjectives. 2. Umlaut. 3. Irregular. 4. Uninflected form. 5. Superlative with am. 6. How declined. 7. Superlative combined with Aller. 8. Compared by means of Mehr. 9. Je— besto. 10. Position of subj. and verb.

INDEX TO THE LESSONS.

Less. XXIII. 1. Adject. used substantively. 2. 3. 4. Terminations dropped. 5. Old and new decl. 6. Used adverbially. Superlative with Aufs and Zum. 8. Eitel and Lauter. 9. Formed from nouns. 10. Sentences used adjectively. 11. Following a noun. 12. Derived from names of countries. 13. From names of persons.

Less. XXIV. 1. Gen. of pers. prons. 2. Pers. pron. used reflex. 3. Refl. pron. Sich. 4. Sich translated by a pers. pron. 5. Pers. and refl. prons. used as reciprocal. 6. 7. Use of the pron. of the second pers. sing. 8. 9. Use of the second pers. plur. 10. Third pers. sing. for the second. 11. Third pers. plur., for the second pers., sing. or plur. 12. Prons. referring to neuter appellations of pers. 13. Gender of prons. referring to inanimate objects. 14. Adv. substitued for a pron. and preposition. 15. Use of Es, as grammatical subj. 16. Position of the grammatical subj. 17. Various uses of Es.

Less. XXV. 1. Absolute possessive pron. 2. Used substantively. 3. Inflection of Kein and Ein. 4. Meinesgleichen, &c.

Less. XXVI. 1. Pres. rendered by the perf. 2. By the fut. 3. Use of the imperf. 4. Position of infinit. and partic. in compound tenses. 5. Perf. in referring to past time. 6. Use of the fut. 7. Verb repeated, or auxil. omitted. 8. Conj. of Haben. 9. Idioms with Haben.

Less. XXVII. 1. Form of infinit. 2. Root. 3. Pres. particip. 4. Perf. particip. 5. Formation of pres. indic. 6. Formation of imperf. 7. Formation of perf. and pluperf. 8. Formation of the futures. 9. Conj. of Lieben.

Less. XXVIII. 1. Relat. pron. 2. Forms of the genitive. 3. 4. Position of the verb in relat. sentence. 5. Relat. and princip. sentence. 6. Conjunctions. 7. Der, Die, Das as relative. 8. So as a relat. 9. Use of Wer. 10. Use of Was. 11. Welcher in the signification of "some". 12. Adv. substituted for a pron. and preposition. 13. Omission of the copula. 14. Use of the relat. with pers. prons. 15. Inversion of relat. and antecedent.

Less. XXIX. 1. Determinative pronouns. 2. Der for derjenige. 3. Derselbe instead of a personal pronoun. 4. Solcher instead of a demonstrative or personal pronoun. 5. Eben. 6. 7. Selbst.

Less. XXX. 1. Der as demonstrative. 2. Use of das and dieß. 3. Man.

Less. XXXI. 1. Können. 2. Dürfen. 3. Mögen. 4. Sollen. 5. Wollen. 6. Müssen. 7. Lassen. 8. Conj. of. 9. Form of perf. and pluperf. 10. Collocation. 11. Omission of the main verb. 12. Form of second and third persons.

Less. XXXII. 1. Sein. 2. Conj. 3. Werben. 4. Conj.

Less. XXXIII. 1. Irregular verbs. 2. Form of infinitive. 3. 4. 5. Formation of imperfect tense, and perfect participle. 6. Irregular in the present tense. 7. Formation of the second and third persons. 8. List of irregular verbs.

Less. XXXIV. Haben as auxiliary. 2. Sein as auxiliary. 3. Haben or Sein.

Less. XXXV. 1. Infinitive without zu. 2. 3. Rendered by our present participle. 4. As subject of a verb. 5. After particles. 6. Used passively. 7. Um with infinitive. 8. After Wissen.

Less. XXXVI. Present participle. 2. Used predicatively. 3. Perfect participle after Kommen. 4. With Gehen. 5. Used imperatively. 6. Future participle. 7. Imperative. 8. Indicative, and Sollen, used as, 9. Dadurch daß.

Less. XXXVII. 1. Compound verbs. 2. 3. 4. Position of the particle. 5. Prefixed to a verb not accented on the first syllable. 6. Signification of.

Less. XXXVIII. Adverbs. 1. With verbs of rest. 2. With verbs of motion. 3. Hin and Her separated from Da and Wo. 4. Hin and Her, defined. 5. How translated. 6. Da, Hier, &c., compounded with preps. 7. Formation of adverbs.

Less. XXXIX. 1. Collocation of subordinate sentence. 2. Correlative words. 3. Obgleich, &c. 4. Aber, &c. 5. Inversion of subject and verb. 6. Conjunction omitted in translation. 7. Position of adverbs

INDEX TO THE LESSONS.

with adjectives. 8. With verbs. 9. Adverbs of time and manner.

Less. XL. Compound verbs. 1. Unaccented particles. 2. 3. Unaccented, or accented. 4. Augment.

Less XLI. 1. Subjunctive as potential. 2. Rendered by the indicative. 3. As imperative. 4. Conj. of subjunctive. 5. Formation of subjunctive; of regular verbs. 6. Of irregular verbs.

Less. XLII. 1. Conditional. 2. Imperfect and pluperfect. 3. Condition not expressed. 4. Conditional used Interrogatively. 5. Conj. of Haben and Sein.

Less. XLIII. 1. Reflexive verbs. 2. Rendered by intransitive or passive verbs.

Less. XLIV. 1. Impersonal verbs. 2. Omission of Es. 3. Geben. 4. Fehlen, &c. 5. Impersonal and reflexive.

Less. XLV. Passive. 1. Formation of. 2. Worden. 3. Used impersonally. 4. Paradigm.

Less. XLVI. 1. Def. art. omitted in translating. 2. Supplied in translating. 3. 4. Indef. art. omitted. 5. Dergleichen, &c.

Less. XLVII. 1. Proper and common nouns. 2. Date. 3. Nouns of weight, &c. 4. Art. 5. Ein Paar. 6. Mann.

Less. XLVIII. 1. Prepos. with the gen. 2. 3. With gen. or dat. 4. Halb, &c. 5. Um—willen. 6. Halben, &c., compounded. 7. Anstatt. 8. Adjectives governing the genitive. 9. Adject. governing the accus. 10. Adject. followed by prepos.

Less. XLIX. 1. Verb governing the gen. 2. Used passively. 3. Reflex. with the gen. 4. With impersonal verbs. 5. With transit. verbs. 6. Verbs followed by prepos. 7. Genitive omitted in translation. 8. Genitive used adverbially.

Less. L. 1. Verbs governing the dat. and accus. 2. Governing the dative.

3. Dative with leid thun, &c. 4. Passive verbs with dative. 5. Verbs governing dat. or accus. 6. Dative with adject. 7. Dative instead of the genitive or a poss. pron. 8. Remote reference. 9. Position of dat. and accus. 10. Dative with von, bei, &c.

Less. LI. 1. Declens. of zwei and drei. 2. Of vier to zwölf. 3. Cardinal numbers used substantively. 4. Hundert, &c. 5. Fractional numbers. 6. Halb. 7. Halb in compounds. 8. Suffixes er and ling.

Less. LII. 1. Aller. 2. Ander. 3. Noch. 4. Einander. 5. Beide. 6. Einiger. 7. Etwas. 8. Irgend. 9. Jeder. 10. Keiner, e, es. 11. Kein, not a, &c. 12. Eigen. 13. 14. 15. Viel and Wenig. 16. Meist with art. or poss. pron.

Less. LIII. An.

Less. LIV. 1. Auf. 2. Aus.

Less. LV. 1. Bei. 2. Durch. 3. Für.

Less. LVI. 1. Gegen. 2. Gegenüber. 3. Entgegen. 4. In.

Less. LVII. 1. Mit. 2. Nach. 3. Nach Hause.

Less. LVIII. 1. Ob. 2. Ohne. 3. Seit.

Less. LIX. Ueber.

Less. LX. Um.

Less. LXI. 1. Unter. 2. Von. 3. Vor.

Less. LXII. 1. Zu. 2. With names of persons. 3. Zu Hause.

Less. LXIII. 1. Aber. 2. Als. 3. Als omitted. 4. Also. 5. Auch.

Less. LXIV. 1. Bald. 2. Bis. 3. Da. 4. Daß.

Less. LXV. 1. Dann. 2. Denn. 3. Doch 4. Eben. 5. Ehe. 6. Erst. 7. Etwa. 8. Gar. 9. Immer. 10. Ja. 11. Je.

Less. LXVI. 1. Nicht. 2. Noch. 3. Nun. 4. Schon. 5. So.

Less. LXVII. 1. Sonst. 2. Vielleicht. 3. 4. Wie. 5. Wohl.

Less. LXVIII. Titles of address.

GENERAL INDEX.

LESSONS.

Aber ſondern, distinguished . 16. 3.
Accusative, 6. 1. With prepositions 15.
 Acc. or dat. with preps. 15. With verbs 50. 5. Acc. or gen. with adj. 48. 8. 9.
 With verbs . . . . 49.
Adjectives, predicative and attributive 11.
 Old Decl. 11. New Decl. 12. Mixed Decl. 13. Comparison of, 22. Used substantively. 23. 1. Used adverbially. 23. 6.
 With the gen. 48. 8. The dat. 50. 6.
 The acc. . . . . 48. 9.
Adverbs, Formation of, 38. 6. 7. 23. 6. 7.
 Position, 39. 7. Nouns, used as, 49. 8.
Allein, ... 63.
Aller, prefixed to superlatives, 22. 7. Applied to number and quantity . 52.
Als . . . . . . 63.
Am, 15. 4. With the superlative 22. 5.
An, ... 15. 3. 53.
Ander, ... 52. 2. 3.
Anderthalb, ... 51. 7.
Anſtatt, 48. 7. With infinitive . 35. 5.
Article, forms of, 4. 9. Decl. 6. 4. 9. 3.
 Contracted with preps. 15. 4. Rules for the use and position of . . 46.
Auch, ... 63.
Auf, 15. 3, 54. With superlatives, 23 7.
Aufs, with superlative, . . 23. 7.
Auxiliary verbs, of tense, 27. 7. 8. 34.
 Omitted, 28. 13. Of mode. 31. Infinitive instead of participle, 31. 9. Main verb omitted . . . . 31. 11.
Bald, ... 64. 1.
Bei, ... 15. 55.
Beide, Beides, . . . 52. 5.
Bis, ... 64. 2.
Capitals, Rules for, 4. Note, 11. 6. 23. 1.
Cardinal numbers . . . 51.
Cases . . . 6. 48. 49. 50.
Collocation of words . . . 39.
Comparison of adjs. . . . 22.
Comparative, Decl. of, 22. 6. Irreg. forms of, ... 22. 3.
Compounds, formation of, Adverbs, 38. Consonants, 2. V. Nouns, 18. 2. Verbs separable, 37. Inseparable . . 40.
Conditional mode . . . 42.
Conjugation of verbs, regular 27. Irregular . . . . 33 and P. 178.
Conjunctions . . . . 39.
Da, 64. In Compounds . . 38.
Dann, ... 65.
Daß, ... 64.
Denn, ... 65.

LESSONS

Doch, ... 65
Dative, ... 50.
Declension, adjective, article, noun, demonst. and poss. pronouns . 21. 10
Demonstrative pronouns, . 8. 30.
Der, . . . 4. 28. 7. 29. 2. 30.
Derjenige, ... 29.
Determinative pronouns . . 29
Diminutives, 18. Gender. 18. 2. 24. 12.
Diphthongs, ... 2. III.
Drei, Declension of . . 51. 1.
Dürfen, ... 31. 2.
Eben, ... 65.
Ehe, ... 65.
Ei, termination, . . 21. 4. b.
Eigen, ... 52. 12.
Ein, ... 9. 4. 25. 3.
Einander, ... 52. 4.
Einige, etliche, . . . 52
En, suffix in forming adjectives . 23. 9.
Entgegen, ... 56. 3.
Erſt, ... 65.
Es, ... 24. 15.
Etwa, ... 65.
Etwas, ... 52.
Feminine, adjective, article, noun, demonstrative and possessive pronouns 17.
Frau, Fräulein, . . . 68.
Future tenses, use of, . . 26. 6.
Ganz, not declined . . 51. 6.
Gender, ... 4. 21.
Genitive, position of, 6. 2. With prepositions 48. 1. Adjectives 48. 8. With verbs, 49. Used adverbially, 49. 8.
Haben, Conjugation, 26. As auxiliary 34.
Halb, ... 51. 6.
Halben, halber, 48. 4. In compounds, 48. 6
Heißen, ... 35.
Heit, suffix. 21
Her and Hin, . . . 38. 2. 3.
Herr, ... 68.
Hier, in compounds . . 38. 2.
Hin, ... 38. 2. 3.
Hundert, . . . 51. 3. 4.
Immer, ... 65.
Imperative, ... 36. 7.
Impersonal verbs. . . . 44.
In, as prep. 56. As termination, . 18.
Indicative used as imperative . 36. 8.
Infinitive, ... 35.
Interrogative conjugation . . 5.
Interrogative ordinal number . 51. 13
Interrogative pronouns . . 10

8

GENERAL INDEX.

	LESSONS.
Irgend,	52. 8.
Irregular verbs,	33. P. 178.
Ja,	65.
Je,	65.
Jeder,	8. 3. 52. 9.
Jeglicher,	52. 9.
Kein,	52. 10, &c.
Keit, suffix	21.
Können,	31. 1.
Lassen,	31. 7.
Lein, diminutives in,	18.
List of irr. verbs	178.
Man,	30. 3.
Mancher,	8. 3.
Mit,	57.
Mixed declension of Adj.	13.
Mögen,	31. 3.
Moods, Conditional, 42. Infinitive, 35. Imperative, 36. 7. Subjunctive	41.
Müssen,	31. 6.
Nach,	57.
Negative Conjugation	16.
Nicht,	66.
Noch,	66.
Nouns, Gender of, 21. Declension, (Old) 6. 6. (New) 16. 5. Of measure, quantity, &c.	47.
Numerals,	51. 52.
Ob	58.
Ohne, 58; with infinitive	35. 5.
Ordinal numbers	51.
Paradigm of Haben, 26; Sein and Werden, 32. 41. 42. Passive	45.
Participles, formation of, 27. 3. 4. Declension and comparison of, 27. *Obs.*	
Past part. for imperative, 36. 5. Future participle	36. 6.
Passive verbs	45.
Perfect tense	26. 5.
Personal pronouns	24.
Plural, nouns having two forms	20.
Possessive pronouns, (conjunctive) 9. 2. (absolute)	25.
Prefixes, of verbs, separable, 37. Inseparable, 40. Separable and inseparable	40. 2.
Prepositions	15. 48.
Pronouns, demonstrative, 8. 30. Determinative, 29. Interrogative, 10. Reciprocal, 24. 5. Reflexive	24. 2. 4.
Proper names	19.
Quantity, weight, &c. Nouns denoting,	47
Reciprocal pronouns	24. 5.
Reflexive, pronouns, 24. 2. 4. Verbs	43.
Relative pronouns	28.
Schon	66.
Sein, as pronoun, 9. 5. Verb	32.
Seit	58.
Selber, selbst	29. 6.
Sentence, construction of, principal, 26. 4. Subordinate	28. 3.
So	66
Sollen, 31. 5; as imperative	36. 8.
Some	52. 6. Note.
Subjunctive mood	41.
Tausend	54. 4.
Tenses, how formed, 27. 5. &c. - How used	26.
Ueber	59.
Um, 60. Um — willen	48. 5.
Umlaut	2. II.
Unter	61.
Verbs, auxiliary, of mode, 31. Of tense, 32. 3 34. Compound, separable, 37. Inseparable, 40. Impersonal, 44. Irregular, 33. Passive, 45. Reflexive, 43. Regular	27. 41. 5.
Viel	52. 13.
Vielleicht	67.
Von	61.
Vor	61.
Vowels	2. I.
Was	10. 28. 10.
Was für ein	10.
Welcher	10. 28.
Wer	10. 28. 9.
Werden	32. 3.
Wie	67.
Wissen, with infinitive	35. 8.
Wo, in compounds	38. 6.
Wohl	67.
Wollen	31.
Worden	45. 2.
Zu	62.
Zufolge	48. 3.
Zwei, when declined	51. 1.

Empfehlungen.

Aus dem „New-Yorker Demokraten".

Fasquelle's Neue französische Grammatik. — Diese Grammatik ist nach Woodbury's berühmtem gramatikalischen Plane entworfen, welcher durch seine Vorzüglichkeit zum Erlernen einer Sprache durch Lehrer oder durch Selbstunterricht eine solche Anerkennung gefunden hat, wie noch kein Entwurf dieser Art. Deutsche, welche die französische Sprache erlernen wollen, und nur einigermaßen mit der englischen Sprache vertraut sind, werden durch die Benützung dieses Buches einen doppelten Vortheil gewinnen, indem sie während der Erlernung der französischen Sprache sich zugleich in der englischen vollends ausbilden.

Woodbury's Plan ist deßhalb so ungemein nützlich, weil er sich mehr mit dem praktischen Theile der Sprache, als mit dem trockenen und ermüdenden Theoretischen beschäftigt und beide Wesenheiten der Sprache auf eine solche angenehme und faßliche Weise verschmilzt, daß der Lernende jede gelernte Lection sogleich anwenden kann, und sohin die Theorie unter dem Gewande der Praxis sich aneignet.

Die einzelnen Lectionen sind auf eine solche ausgezeichnet praktische Art abgetheilt, daß der Schüler nach dem Durchgehen einiger derselben sogleich in den Stand gesetzt wird, selbstständige Sätze zu bilden, und dieselben in Conversation anzuwenden.

FROM THE "NEW-HAVEN PALLADIUM."

Fasquelle's New French Course. — This work is regarded by students in French as possessing qualities not found in any other, and there are none which so effectually and naturally blend the analytic and synthetic systems as this one now before us, which is substantially Woodbury's New Method.

FROM THE "ZION'S HERALD AND WESLEYAN JOURNAL."

This grammar is before all others that we have yet seen, for its thorough practical and idiomatic course of instruction. In fact, it seems to us scarcely capable of an improvement. We are glad to learn that it is rapidly making its way into our schools and academies.

FROM THE "NEW-YORK EVANGELIST."

Woodbury's neue Methode zur Erlernung der englischen Sprache. — The title of the work gives the reader an accurate idea of its object—it is a grammar and chrestomathy for the acquisition of the English language by Germans. Its great merit, and it is very great, lies in its admirable perspicuity. The precise difficulties which a German would experience in learning our language have been detected by close observation and long practice; and these are met and removed with a skill and in an order that may lay claim to true philosophy. The idioms of the two languages—the different force of letters in pronunciation, the difference of grammatical construction, and of the general usage of words, are clearly defined, and illustrated by such varied and perspicuous examples, that the student cannot fail of the right impression. It is a work of evident and long attention to the subject; and we are not surprised that it has acquired sufficient popularity in Germany to be republished there. For the purpose of learning the German it is also highly useful, and might profitably take the place of many a larger grammar.

FROM REV. R. ALLYN, PRINCIPAL OF EAST GREENWICH ACADEMY, R. I.

The philosophy upon which the "METHOD" is founded is the method of nature, and therefore best adapted to a rapid acquisition, a thorough knowledge, and a ready use of any language. As the German is full of the treasures of literature, its worth to a scholar is immense. To all who wish to learn it *well*, and at the same time rapidly and pleasantly, this book is worth more than their money.

FROM THE "CATTARAUGUS CHRONICLE."

There is every thing in having the right kind of a book. It is 25 years since we had our initiation into the German Language, and what obstacles did we not find in our way for want of such a book as the one now before us! We now say to teachers and students get Woodbury's *New Method* with *Germar*, if you would have a pleasant, plain, practical and thorough introduction to reading speaking and composing this interesting language.

WOODBURY'S SHORTER COURSE.

LESSON I. Section I.

German Alphabet.

German	English.	Pronunciation.
U a	a	ah
B b	b	bay
C c	c	tsay
D d	d	day
E e	e	e (as in prey)
F f	f	eff
G g	g	gay
H h	h	hah
J* i	i	i (as in pique)
J* j	j	yote
K k	k	kah
L l	l	ell
M m	m	emm
N n	n	enn
O o	o	oh
P p	p	pay
Q q	q	koo
R r	r	err (as in error)
S ſ s (21. S.)	s	ess
T t	t	tay
U u	u	o (as in do)
V v	v	fow (as in fowl)
W w	w	vay
X x	x	ix
Y y	y	ipsilon
Z z	z	tset.

* J, before a consonant, answers to I; as in Immer, Igel; before a vowel, to Y as in Jahr.

SOUNDS OF THE LETTERS.

UMLAUTS.	DIPHTHONGS.
Ae or ä, Oe or ö, Ue or ü.	ai, au, ei, eu, äu.

COMPOUND CONSONANTS.

ch, ch;	ck, ck;	sch, sch;	ss, ss;	st, st,
tsay-hah;	tsay-kah;	ess-tsay-hah;	ess-ess;	ess-tay

sz, sz;	tz, tz.
ess-tset;	tay-tset.

LESSON II.   Section II.

SOUNDS OF THE LETTERS.

I. *Vowels.*

1. A, a sounds like *a*, in *ah, car.* Ahn, Arm, Aal,* Blatt.*
2. E, e sounds like *e*, in *tete, very.* Mehr, Erz, Heer,* Herr.*
3. I, i sounds like *i*, in *pique, pin.* Ihr, Dir, Mit, Trink.
4. O, o sounds like *o, oo*, in *no, door.* Mohr, Mond, Boot.*
5. U, u sounds like *o*, in *do.* Uhr, Hut, Pur, Nun, Murren.†
6. Y, y sounds like *i*, in Ihr, &c., (see 3 I). Ysop, Styx.

II. *Umlauts.*‡

7. Ae, ä sounds nearly like *e*, Aepfel, Gärtner, Bäcker, Spät.
8. Oe, ö sounds as in Römer‖, Oel, Pöbel, Tödten, Röhre.
9. Ue, ü sounds as in Für, ‖ Uebel, Müller, Güte, Füllen.

III. *Diphthongs.*

10. Ai, ai (or ay) sounds nearly like *ay* in *aye.* Hai, Aai, Mai.
11. Au, au sounds like *ou* in *out.* Haus, Maus, Laut, Brauer.
12. Ei, ei (or ey) sounds like *i* in *die.* Bein, Rein, Kein, Pein.
13. Eu, eu sounds nearly like *oi* and *oy* in *oil, boy.* Heu, Eule.
14. Aeu, äu sounds nearly like eu. Käufer, Aeugeln, Bäumen.

---

* A vowel, when doubled, is thereby lengthened: followed by a double consonant, it is shortened.

† Dissyllables, unless otherwise noted, are accented on the first.

‡ Umlaut signifies changed or modified sound. The Umlauts are produced by a union of e with a, o, u, respectively. Except when they are capital, the e is usually expressed by two dots, thus; ä, ö, ü (instead of ae, oe, ue).

‖ For ö and ü, there are in English no corresponding sounds. Römer and für, for example, might, perhaps, be understood, if pronounced ray'mer, and fear, but this is by no means correct. The French *eu* in *peur* answers pretty nearly to ö, and *u* in *vu*, to ü.

IV. *Consonants.*

15. 𝕭, b, f, h, k, l, m, n, p, q, x sound like *b, d, f, h, k, l, m, n, p, q* and *x*.
16. ℭ, c, before e, i and y in the same syllable sounds like z (*ts*): otherwise, like *k*; Ceber, Civil', Special, Copal'.
17. 𝕲, g, at the beginning of a syllable, sounds like *g* in *gig*: but never as in *gin*, &c. After n in the same syllable it sounds like our *g* hard in like position; Gar, Angst, Bringen, Gellen, Ringel, Bang. Otherwise its sound approaches, usually, that of the Greek χ, or ch (see 26 ch); Tag, Regnen, Magd, Leipzig.
18. ℌ, h, in the midst or at the end of a syllable is silent, but serves to lengthen its vowel; Mehr, Lohn, Thun, Muth.
19. 𝔍 j, sounds like *y* consonant; Jahr, Jude, Januar, Jubel.
20. ℜ, r is uttered with a trill or vibration of the tongue, and with greater stress than our *r*; Rohr, Reim, Brod.
21. 𝔖, s, at the beginning of a syllable followed by a vowel, has a sound between that of *z* and *s*; Sohn, Sage. Otherwise it sounds like *s*; Gas, Dieses. At the end of a word s, instead of f, is employed.
22. 𝔗, t sounds like *t* in *test*; Text, Art. Where in English *t* sounds like *sh*, t has the sound of *ts* (z); Station, station, Nation, nation.
23. 𝔙, v sounds like *f* in *fit*; Vetter. In foreign words v sounds like w; Venedig, Valois.
24. 𝔚, w has a sound between that of *w* and *v*; Welt, Wasser. After a consonant in the same syllable it sounds like *w*; Schwer, Zwei.
25. ℨ, z sounds like *ts*; Zahl, zahm, Zinn, Pelz, Zahn, Zimmer.

V. *Compound Consonants.*

26. Ch, ch, in primitive words, followed by f, sounds like *k*; Dachs, Achse. Otherwise ch has its guttural sound; Nach, Hoch*, Tuch, Nachschrift (compounded of nach and Schrift). In foreign words ch retains its original sound; Character, Chaise.

---

* To aid in producing this sound take, for experiment, the above word hoch: pronounce ho precisely like our word ho! observing, only, to give as full and distinct a *breathing* at the *close* as at the beginning; thus, *hoh,* hoch. When not preceded by a, o, or u, a slight hissing sound of f or sch naturally attaches to the ch; as in Hecht, Reich, Ich.

27. Sch, sch sounds like *sh*; Schnur, Schild, Schiller, Schule, Schiff, Schwere, Schutt.
28. ß (though compounded of ſ and z) sounds like ſſ and occurs only at the end of a syllable; naß, Fuß.
29. tz (compounded of t and z) sounds like z, and, like ß, is used only at the end of a syllable; Platz, Stutzen.

EXERCISE 1.   Aufgabe 1.

Vowels.   Umlauts.   Diphthongs.

(a) Altar, Ball, Bank, Sand, Lamm, Hand, Mann, Acker, Baar, Fall.
(e) Meer, Messer, Keller, Erde, Erbe, Ekel, Eben, Edel, Fett, Besser.
(i) Bitte, Distel, Finden, Finne, Flinte, Himmel, Hinten, Hirn, Hirt.
(o) Bohle, Bolus, Bombe, Bord, Born, Bote, Brod, Forst, Folter.
(u) Ufer, Und, Bund, Mund, Hund, Rund, Huhn, Huld, Gulden, Rund.
(y) Hymen, Hydra, Hymne, Hyper'bel, Pyrami'de, Symbo'l, Tyrann'.
(ai, ei) Hain, Heil, Main, Mein, La'ib, Leib, Pair, Mai, Bei, Pein, Beil.
(au) Bau, Baum, Laub, Staub, Haut, Faul, Faust, Sauer, Mauer.
(äu, eu) Säufer, Läute, Leute, Häute, Heute, Läufer, Beutel, Neuen.
(ä, e) Ehren, Aehre, Heben, Bär, Feder, Fälle, Fehler, Gäter, Geben.
(ö) Oefen, Börne, Dörren, Blöde, Blöken, Oel, Oehr, Töpfer, Tröster.
(ü) Uebung, Ueben, Tümpel, Tülle, Mühle, Münster, Nüsse, Nüster.

EXERCISE 2.   Aufgabe 2.

Consonants.   Double Consonants.

(C) Cadett', Cäsur', Cedern, Cider, Classe, Coder, Cymba'l, Lection.
(G) Gabel, Geben, Geist, Gaul, Gift, Girren, Glas, Singen, Talg.
(H) Haar, Hebel, Hiob, Hobel, Huf, Heiland, Hohl, Hohe, Hoheit.
(J) Ja, Jammer, Jubel, Je, Junker, Just, Jeder, Jäger, Jener.
(R) Rab, Rahm, Reben, Reis, Rind, Rohr, Rolle, Rost, Ruder, Rype.
(S) Saat, Säbel, Sand, Seele, Sehr, Seife, Sieb, Sinn, Sold, Spann.
(T) Tadel, Taub, Teig, Teller, Tinte, Titel, Todt, Torf, Trank, Trost.
(V) Venus, Verbum, Verse, Voll, Border, Vorfall, Vieh, Viel, Viper.
(W) Waare, Webe, Wahn, Weber, Wind, Wolle, Wurst, Wieder, Wille.
(X) Xantippe, Text, Mixtur', Axiom', Axthelm, Hexerei', Hexa'meter.
(Z) Zahlen, Zitter, Zettel, Zauber, Zeiger, Zelt, Zent, Zettel, Zeuge.
(Ch) Chaos, Wachs, Weich, Flachs, Milch, Wichse, Chor, Chur, Christ.
(Sch) Schachtel, Fischer, Schade, Schau, Busch, Schwager, Schwach.
(ß ſſ) Messer, Meßner, Schießen, Haß, Messe, Lassen, Paß, Sassen.
(tz z) Trotz, Fitze, Milz, Blitz, Azur, Schanzer, Schatz, Scherz, Zehe.

Wechsel der Jahreszeiten.

Wie schön ist der Wechsel der Zeiten,
Wie schwindet mit ihnen das Jahr!
Wie herrliche Freuden bereiten
Und bieten den Menschen sie dar!

Lesson III. Lection III.

A a, B b, C c, D d, E e, F f, G g, H h, I i, J j,
K k, L l, M m, N n, O o, P p, Q q, R r, S s, T t,
U u, V v, W w, X x, Y y, Z z, St st

a b c d ff g h i j k l m n
o ö p q r s ß t u v w x y z
ä ö ü ck sch ss st sz tz

Exercise 3. Aufgabe 3.

Arnd Bürger Lange Müller
Hegel Liszt Göthe Heine
Leßing Jacob Kant Leipzig
Wenzel Wanner Götz Pfeffel
Schmidt Richter Schiller Tieck
Uhland Winkler Zimmern Eschiland
... Schelling Aa, Ca, Ua, Ä, Ö, Ü
... Leiden St ü Mächten bittre Blick

LESSON IV. Section IV.

DEFINITE ARTICLE IN THE NOMINATIVE SINGULAR.

1. The definite article in the nominative singular, has a distinct form for each gender; ber masculine, bie feminine and bas neuter.

GENDER OF NOUNS.

2. Some nouns denoting inanimate objects are called masculine or feminine,* and some denoting animate objects are called neuter; as

MASCULINE, ber Winter,† the winter; ber Stahl, the steel;
FEMININE, bie Brigg, the brig; bie Rose, the rose;
NEUTER, bas Kind, the child; bas Schaf, the sheep.

3. PRESENT SINGULAR OF haben.

Affirmatively. *Interrogatively.*

ich habe, I have; habe ich? have I?
Sie haben, you have; haben Sie?† have you?
er hat, he has; hat er? has he?

Bier, *n.* beer. Brauer, *m.* brewer. Brob, *n.* bread. — Glas, *n.* glass. Glaser, *m.* glazier. Gold, *n.* gold. — Ja, yes. — Leber, *n.* leather. — Mehl, *n.* flour. — Nein, no. — Ober, or. Sattler, *m.* saddler. Schmied, *m.* smith. — Und, and. — Was, what. Wein, *m.* wine. Wer, who. See Vocabularies, pp. 190, 230.

EXERCISE 4. Aufgabe 4.

1. Wer hat das Gold? 2. Der Brauer hat das Gold. 3. Hat der Brauer das Glas? 4. Nein, der Glaser hat das Glas, und der Brauer hat das Brob. 5. Haben Sie Mehl ober Brob? 6. Ich habe das Brob, und der Schmied hat das Mehl? 7. Hat der Brauer Bier ober Wein? 8. Er hat Bier, Wein, Mehl und Brob. 9. Hat der Sattler das Leber? 10. Ja, er hat das Leber, der Schmied hat das Bier, der Glaser hat das Mehl, Sie haben das Glas, und ich habe das Brob.

EXERCISE 5. Aufgabe 5.

1. What has the saddler? 2. He has the leather. 3. Has the glazier the gold? 4. No, he has the glass, and the smith has

---

* This is true of nearly all languages. Many words however, though denoting the same objects, are regarded in different languages as being of different genders. Thus, for brig, the French, *le bric*, is masculine, while the German, bie Brigg, is feminine. For "head," the German, ber Kopf, is masculine, the French, *la tete*, is feminine, and the Latin *caput*, is neuter.

† All nouns, and the pronoun Sie, of the second person, begin with a capital.

the gold. 5. Has the smith the flour or the bread? 6. The smith has the gold, you have the bread, and I have the flour. 7. Have you the leather? 8. Yes, I have the leather, the brewer has the beer, and you have the glass. 9. Who has the gold and the glass? 10. The smith has the gold, and the brewer has the glass.

LESSON V.   Section V.

INTERROGATIVE CONJUGATION.

1. All German verbs are conjugated interrogatively, in the present and imperfect, by placing the subject *last*, as in the case of the English verb *to be*; as,

Ist der Mann hier?	Is the man here?
War der Mann hier?	Was the man here?
Haben Sie das Buch?	Have you the book?
Sehen Sie das Buch?	Do you see the book (see you the book!)

2. PRESENT SINGULAR OF loben.

Affirmatively.   *Interrogatively.*

ich lobe,	I praise;	lobe ich?	do I praise? (praise I?)
Sie loben,	you praise;	loben Sie?	do you praise? (praise you?)
er lobt,	he praises;	lobt er?	does he praise? (praises he?)

3. PRESENT SINGULAR OF kaufen, schneiden AND trinken.

ich kaufe, I buy;	ich schneide, I cut;	ich trinke, I drink;
Sie kaufen, you buy;	Sie schneiden, you cut;	Sie trinken, you drink;
er kauft, he buys;	er schneidet, he cuts;	er trinkt, he drinks.

4. PRESENT SINGULAR OF hören, sagen AND verstehen.

ich höre, I hear;	ich sage, I say;	ich versteh'e, I understand;
Sie hören, you hear;	Sie sagen, you say;	Sie versteh'en, you understand;
er hört, he hears;	er sagt, he says,	er versteht', he understands.

Eisen, *n.* iron. Entweder, either. Essig, *m.* vinegar. — Kaffee, *m.* coffee. Koch, *m.* cook. — Noch, nor. — Oel, *n.* oil. — Pfeffer, *m.* pepper. — Salz, *n.* salt. Senf, *m.* mustard. — Thee, *m.* tea. — Wasser, *n.* water. Weder, neither. — Zucker, *m.* sugar.

Exercise 6.　　　Aufgabe 6.

1. Wer kauft das Eisen, und was kauft der Sattler? 2. Der Schmied kauft das Eisen, und der Sattler kauft das Leder. 3. Trinken Sie Bier oder Wein? 4. Ich trinke weder Bier noch Wein, ich trinke Wasser. 5. Was kauft der Brauer? 6. Er kauft entweder Kaffee oder Thee. 7. Was kauft der Koch? 8. Er kauft Oel, Essig, Senf, Pfeffer, Salz und Zucker. 9. Wer schneidet das Brod, und was schneidet der Sattler? 10. Der Koch schneidet das Brod, und der Sattler schneidet das Leder. 11. Hören Sie, was der Schmied sagt? 12. Ja, ich höre und verstehe, was Sie sagen und was er sagt. 13. Was kauft der Glaser, und wer kauft das Eisen?

Exercise 7.　　　Aufgabe 7.

1. Does the smith drink coffee or tea? 2. He drinks neither coffee nor tea. 3. Do you buy bread or flour? 4. I buy bread and the glazier buys flour. 5. What does the smith buy? 6. He buys the gold and the iron. 7. Either the brewer or the saddler cuts the leather. 8. I buy sugar and the cook buys vinegar, oil and mustard. 10. What does the saddler buy? 11. He buys leather and glass, and I buy iron. 12. Do you hear and understand what I say? 13. I hear and understand what you say, you hear and understand what I say, and what the brewer says

LESSON VI.　　　Lection VI.

Cases.

1. There are four cases, namely: the
NOMINATIVE, which answers to the English *nominative*; the
GENITIVE, which answers to the English *possessive*; the
DATIVE, which has no corresponding case in English, and the
ACCUSATIVE, which answers to the English *objective*.

2. The genitive may either precede or follow the governing noun: the latter arrangement being the more common; as,

Er hat das Buch des Schülers.	He has the book of the scholar.
(Er hat des Schülers Buch).	He has the scholar's book.
Das Dach des Hauses ist steil.	The roof of the house is steep.

3. The dative without a preposition generally answers to our objective governed by *to* or *for*; as,

Ich gebe dem Kinde das Glas.	I give (*to*) the child the glass.
Er macht dem Manne einen Hut.	He makes (*for*) the man a hat.

4. DECLENSION OF DEFINITE ARTICLE MASC. AND NEUT.
SINGULAR.

	Masculine.		Neuter.	
Nominative,	der,	the;	das,	the;
Genitive,	des,	of the;	des,	of the;
Dative,	dem,	to or for the;	dem,	to or for the;
Accusative,	den,	the;	das,	the.

5. The article agrees with its noun in gender, number and case.

6. German nouns have two forms of declension, called the *old* and the *new*. In the old declension the genitive, like our possessive, is formed by suffixing s (or es) to the nominative.

7. Nouns ending in el, en, er, chen and lein form the genitive by adding s, while the dative and accusative are like the nominative, as: *nom.* der Sattler; *gen.* des Sattler-s; *dat.* dem Sattler; *acc.* den Sattler, &c.

8. Nouns not ending in el, en, er, chen, and lein, add es* for the genitive and e* for the dative: the accusative being like the nominative; as, *nom.* das Buch; *gen.* des Buch-es; *dat.* dem Buch-e; *acc.* das Buch, &c.

9. DECLENSION OF NOUNS ADDING S IN THE GENITIVE.

	Masculine.		Neuter.	
Nom.	der Bruder,	the brother;	das Eisen,	the iron;
Gen.	des Bruders,	the brother's;	des Eisens,	of the iron;
Dat.	dem Bruder,	to the brother;	dem Eisen,	to the iron;
Acc.	den Bruder,	the brother;	das† Eisen,†	the iron.

10. DECLENSION OF NOUNS ADDING ES TO THE GENITIVE.

	Masculine.		Neuter.	
Nom.	der Mann,	the man;	das Kind,	the child;
Gen.	des Mannes,	of the man;	des Kindes,	of the child;
Dat.	dem Manne,	to the man;	dem Kinde,	to the child;
Acc.	den Mann,	the man;	das† Kind,†	the child.

---

* Words of this class, also, often drop the e of the *gen.* and *dat.*; as, *gen.* des Buchs; *dat.* dem Buch. This is especially true of words of more than one syllable, when the last is not under the full accent; as, des Kaufmanns; dem Kaufmann, instead of des Kaufmannes, dem Kaufmanne, &c.

† As in Greek and Latin, neuter words have the same form in the accusative as in the nominative.

11. PRESENT SINGULAR OF geben, schicken, AND versprechen.

ich gebe, I give;   ich schicke, I send;   ich versprech'e, I promise;
Sie geben, you give;   Sie schicken, you send;   Sie versprech'en, you promise;
er gibt (L. 33.6) he gives. er schickt, he sends.   er verspricht', he promises.

Bäcker, *m.* baker. Bauer, *m.* peasant. Bruder, *m.* brother. Buch, *n.* book, — Es, *n.* it. — Gehö'ren, *conj. like* hören, to belong. Geld, *n.* money. Hut, *m.* hat. — Kind, *n.* child. Korn, *n.* grain. — Mann, *m.* man. Müller, *m.* miller. — Ring, *m.* ring. — Schüler, *m.* scholar. Sohn, *m.* son. Stock, *m.* cane. — Vater, *m.* father. Verkau'fen, *conj. like* kaufen, L. 5. 3, to sell.

EXERCISE 8.   Aufgabe 8.

1. Schicken Sie dem Schmiede das Eisen? 2. Nein, ich schicke dem Glaser das Glas. 3. Schicken Sie dem Brauer das Korn des Bauers? 4. Nein, der Bauer schickt es dem Müller, der Müller schickt dem Bäcker das Mehl, und der Bäcker verkauft dem Koche das Brod. 5. Gehört der Hut dem Vater oder dem Sohn? 6. Der Hut gehört dem Sohne, und der Stock gehört dem Vater. 7. Geben Sie dem Manne das Geld? 8. Ich gebe es dem Manne, und er gibt es dem Kinde. 9. Was schickt der Bauer dem Brauer? 10. Wer verkauft dem Koche das Brod? 11. Gehört das Eisen dem Schmiede oder dem Glaser? 12. Wer gibt dem Bruder des Schülers den Ring, das Buch und den Stock? 13. Was versprechen Sie dem Bäcker, und was verspricht der Bäcker dem Kinde? 14. Versprechen Sie dem Schüler den Ring? 15. Nein, ich verspreche dem Manne das Geld.

EXERCISE 9.   Aufgabe 9.

1. Does the book belong to the brother of the baker? 2. No, it belongs to the peasant's son. 3. Do you promise the child the money? 4. No, I promise it to the man. 5. Who sends the miller the grain? 6. The father of the scholar sells the miller the grain. 7. What does the man sell to the scholar? 8. He sells the scholar the book, the cane and the hat. 9. What does the baker send to the cook? 10. Does the cook give the baker the money? 11. Who sends the saddler the iron? 12. Who sends the baker the flour? 13. The child's father gives the brother the ring. 14. The iron belongs to the smith. 15. The cook sends the miller the grain, and the miller sells it to the brewer.

LESSON VII. Section VII.

THE DATIVE WITH PREPOSITIONS.

1. The relation of the dative to words which precede it, is often expressed by prepositions*; as,

Er kommt aus dem Hause.	He comes out of the house.
Ich gehe nach dem Walde.	I am going to the forest.
Der Bruder geht mit dem Kinde zu dem Lehrer.	The brother goes with the child to the teacher.
Der Knecht kommt von dem Markte.	The servant is coming from the market.

CONJUGATION OF VERBS.

2. For the three forms of the present and imperfect, found in English, the German has but one; as,

ich gehe,	I go;	I do go;	I am going;
Sie gehen,	you go;	you do go;	you are going;
er geht,	he goes;	he does go;	he is going.

3. PRESENT SINGULAR OF spielen, kommen, AND schreiben.

ich spiele,	I play;	ich komme,	I come;	ich schreibe,	I write;
Sie spielen,	you play;	Sie kommen,	you come;	Sie schreiben,	you write;
er spielt,	he plays;	er kommt,	he comes;	er schreibt,	he writes.

Amtmann, *m.* magistrate. Apfel, *m.* apple. Aus, out of, from.— Bei, with (L. 55). Bleistift, *m.* pencil. Brief, *m.* letter.— Dorf, *n.* village. — Haus, *n.* house. Hund, *m.* dog. — Jäger, *m.* hunter.— Markt, *m.* market. — Messer, *n.* knife. Mit, with (L. 57). — Nach, to (see 1. note). — Von, from, of. — Wald, *m.* forest, woods. Wann, when. Wohnen, to live, reside. Zu, to.

EXERCISE 10. Aufgabe 10.

1. Kommt der Jäger aus dem Walde, aus dem Hause, oder von dem Markte? 2. Er geht entweder mit dem Bauer nach dem Dorfe, oder mit dem Kinde zu dem Amtmann. 3. Was schneidet der Schüler mit dem Messer? 4. Wer spielt mit dem Hunde? 5. Spielt das Kind mit dem Schmiede? 6. Wohnt der Jäger bei dem Müller, oder bei dem Bäcker? 7. Der Schüler schreibt den Brief mit dem Bleistift. 8. Schneidet das Kind den Apfel mit dem Messer des Bruders? 9. Nein, es schneidet das

---

* A preposition is required with the dative after verbs indicating direction *towards* an object; n a ch being employed before the name of a *place*, and zu before the name of a *person*; as, er geht nach dem Dorfe, und ich gehe zu dem Lehrer, he is going to the village, and I am going to the teacher.

Brod mit dem Messer des Vaters. 10. Gehen Sie zu dem Sattler, oder nach dem Dorfe? 11. Der Müller wohnt bei dem Bauer, und geht mit dem Schüler nach dem Dorfe zu dem Amtmann. 12. Wann gehen Sie nach dem Dorfe? Wann gehen Sie zu dem Amtmann, und was geben Sie dem Amtmann?

Exercise 11.   Aufgabe 11.

1. Who is coming out of the forest? 2. Is the hunter coming from the market, or is he going to the village? 3. Does the scholar live with the miller, or with the magistrate? 4. Who is going with the child to the glazier? 5. Is the man cutting the bread with the knife of the saddler? 6. Are you writing with the magistrate's (L. 6. 2) pencil? 7. Who is playing with the dog? 8. Who lives with the miller and who is going with the scholar to the peasant? 9. Who is going to the forest, and who is going to the miller? 10. When is the child going to the smith? 11. When does the hunter go to the forest? 12. When does the hunter come from the forest, and when do you go to the village? 13. The cook is coming from the market, and I am going to the magistrate.

LESSON VIII.   Section VIII

DEMONSTRATIVE PRONOUNS. Dieser and Jener.

1. Dieser refers to the nearer and jener to the more remote of two objects: when however an object not remote from the speaker is alluded to, and no comparison is made, dieser is often used, where "*that*" is employed in English; as,

Dieser Mann ist reich, und jener ist arm.	*This* man is rich, and *that* (one*) is poor.
Wer ist dieser Mann?	Who is *that* man?

2. DECLENSION OF dieser AND jener, SINGULAR.

Masc. Neut.	*Masc. Neut.*
N. dieser, dieses, this;	jener, jenes, that;
G. dieses, dieses, of this;	jenes, jenes, of that;
D. diesem, diesem, to or for this;	jenem, jenem, to or for that;
A. diesen, dieses, this;	jenen, jenes, that

3. Like dieser and jener are declined those indefinite numerals, and adjective pronouns, which like the definite article, have a distinct form for each gender: namely; aller, alles, all; einiger, einiges; etlicher, etliches, some; jeder, jedes, every; man-

---

* For "*one*" after a pronoun, or an adjective, no corresponding word is required in German.

PRESENT SING. OF sein, sitzen, AND liegen.

cher, manches, many a; solcher, solches, such; and welcher, welches, which.

4. PRESENT SINGULAR OF sein, sitzen, AND liegen.

ich bin, I am; ich sitze, I sit; ich liege, I lie;
Sie sind, you are; Sie sitzen, you sit; Sie liegen, you lie;
er ist, he is; er sitzt, he sits; er liegt, he lies.

Aller, all. An, at. Auf, on. — Baum, m. tree. — Bevor (see vor). — Fenster, n. window. — Garten, m. garden. Gross, great, large. Gut, good. — Hinter, behind. — In, in. — Jeder, see list 3. — Neben, beside. — Ofen, m. stove. — Papier, n. paper. — Reich, rich. — Stahl, m. steel. — Stehen, to stand, like verstehen, L. 5. 4. Stuhl, m. chair. — Tisch, m. table. Ueber, over, above. Unter, under, among. — Vor, prep. before, ehe. — Wahr, true. — Zimmer, n. room. Zwischen, between.

EXERCISE 12.   Aufgabe 12.

1. Welchen Hund hat dieser Mann? 2. Er hat den Hund des Jägers. 3. In welchem Hause ist der Glaser? 4. Er ist in dem Hause jenes Bauers. 5. Liegt das Buch auf diesem oder auf jenem Tische? 6. Es liegt auf jenem, und das Papier liegt unter diesem. 7. Ist jeder Mann reich? 8. Ist jedes Haus gross? 9. Dieses Kind wohnt in jenem Hause. 10. Dieser Mann sitzt auf dem Stuhle an dem Fenster. 11. Der Hund liegt zwischen dem Ofen und dem Tische. 12. Der Baum steht vor dem Hause, und der Garten liegt hinter dem Hause. 13. Er schreibt, ehe er spielt. 14. Der Sohn steht neben dem Vater. 15. Das Zimmer des Schülers ist über dem Zimmer des Amtmanns. 16. Haben Sie solches Eisen oder solchen Stahl? 17. Ich habe den Stahl des Sattlers. 18. Ist aller Stahl gut? 19. Was er sagt, ist wahr.

EXERCISE 13.   Aufgabe 13.

1. Has this hunter the dog of that peasant? 2. Which book has this man? 3. In which garden is the brother of this glazier? 4. Is all coffee good? 5. Which pencil and which paper have you? 6. On which chair is the book lying, and at which table is the man sitting? 7. Is the dog under that tree? 8. The tree stands between the house and the garden. 9. This room is over the room of the scholar. 10. Is every tree large? 11. Have you such tea, and such bread? 12. Has every smith such iron? 13. Is the peasant in this house? 14. In which room is the stove? 15. Which man is in that house? 16. In which house is the peasant? 17. Is the book lying before the scholar? 18. Are you going before he comes? 19. He says you have the paper: is it true?

LESSON IX. — Section IX.

INDEFINITE ARTICLE.

1. The indefinite article is less varied than the definite: having, for the nominative, masculine and neuter, but one form; as,

Masculine, ein Mann, a man; ein Tisch, a table.
Neuter, ein Pferd, a horse; ein Buch, a book.

POSSESSIVE PRONOUNS.

2. The possessive pronouns constitute a distinct class of words, agreeing, like the article, with the noun in gender, number and case, and answer to our *personal* pronoun in the possessive; as,

Wo ist mein Hut?	Where is my hat?
Er hat meinen Hut.	He has my hat.
Ich habe einen Hut von meinem Freunde.	I have a hat from my friend.

3. The indefinite article and the possessive pronouns (unlike the words in L. 8. 3.) take an additional syllable in forming the oblique cases. Except the accusative neuter. (See L. 6. 9. Note.)

4. DECLENSION OF INDEF. ART. AND POSS. PRON. SINGULAR.

	Masc.	Neut.		Masc.	Neut.	
Nom.	ein,	ein,	a;	unser,	unser,	our;
Gen.	eines,	eines,	of a;	unseres,	unseres,	of our;
Dat.	einem,	einem,	to or for a;	unserem,	unserem,	to or for our;
Acc.	einen,	ein,	a.	unseren,	unser,	our.

5. Like ein and unser, are declined dein, thy; euer, your; ihr, her, their; Ihr, your; mein, my; sein, his, its, and kein, no, not any.

Brett, *n.* board. — Denn, for. — Aber, but. — Dolch, *m.* dagger. — Feuer, *n.* fire. Freund, *m.* friend. — Hammer, *m.* hammer. Hobel, *m.* plane. Hof, *m.* court, yard. — Ihr, see list 5. — Kalt, cold. Kamm, *m.* comb. — Leuchter, *m.* candlestick. Licht, *n.* candle. — Meißel, *m.* chisel. — Pferd, *n.* horse. — Pflug, *m.* plow. Pult, desk. — Schwert, *n.* sword. Sehr, very, very much. Tischler, cabinetmaker, joiner. — Vetter, *m.* cousin. — Warm, warm. Waschtisch, *m.* washstand. Wetter, *n.* weather.

Exercise 14.   Aufgabe 14.

1. Hat Ihr Freund ein Schwert oder einen Dolch? 2. Mein Freund hat ein Buch, und sein Vetter hat einen Meißel. 3. Ist unser Freund in unserm Hause? 4. Nein, er ist in dem Zimmer seines Vetters, des Tischlers. 5. Wer hat das Licht meines Bruders? 6. Der Sohn meines Vetters hat das Licht und den Leuchter Ihres Bruders. 7. Hat das Kind den Hammer seines Vaters? 8. Nein, es hat keinen Hammer. 9. Der Tischler hat seinen Hobel und sein Brett; Sie haben Ihr Eisen und Ihren Hammer, und ich habe mein Pferd und meinen Pflug. 10. Ist Ihr Freund in Ihrem, in seinem, oder in meinem Hause? 11. Ihr Freund ist in Ihrem Hause; mein Freund hat mein Pferd in meinem Garten, und sein Kind spielt mit seinem Hunde in dem Hofe. 12. Liegt Ihr Buch auf Ihrem Tische, oder auf meinem Pulte? 13. Mein Buch liegt auf meinem Tische, und mein Bleistift auf Ihrem Pult. 14. Liegt mein Kamm auf meinem Pult? 15. Nein, Ihr Kamm liegt auf Ihrem Waschtische. 16. Ist es kalt in Ihrem Zimmer? 17. Nein, es ist sehr warm, denn ich habe ein Feuer in meinem Ofen, und das Wetter ist nicht sehr kalt.

Exercise 15.   Aufgabe 15.

1. Who has my horse and my dog? 2. Your brother has your dog, my father has your house, and the cabinetmaker has your table. 3. Has the child its brother's knife, or its father's pencil? 4. It has its father's pencil, its brother's book, and your cousin's plane and chisel. 5. Is the miller in his house, or in the house of his friend? 6. He is in the house of our friend the baker. 7. Has your friend's father my brother's horse? 8. No, he has no horse, but he has his candle and his candlestick. 9. Have you your friend's chisel, or his hammer? 10. I have his plow and his horse, and my cousin has his dog. 11. Have you a stove and a candle in your room? 12. Yes, I have your brother's stove, my candle, your candlestick, and my brother's ring. 13. Have you a horse or a dog? 14. No, I have neither a horse nor a dog. 15. Has your brother your desk? 16. No, he has no desk, but my desk is in my room in my friend's house. 17. It is cold in my room, for I have no fire in my stove; the room is very large, and the weather is very cold.

LESSON X.   Section X.

INTERROGATIVE PRONOUNS.

1. The interrogative pronouns are wer? who? welcher? which? or what? (declined like dieser, &c., L. 8), was* (indeclinable) what? and was für ein? what kind of a, or what?

---

* Weß (also wessen) sometimes occurs as the genitive of was.

INTERROGATIVE PRONOUNS. Jemand, Niemand.

2. DECLENSION OF wer AND was für ein.

		Masc.	Neut.
N.	wer? who?	was für ein?	was für ein?
G.	wessen? whose?	was für eines?	was für eines?
D.	wem? to, for whom?	was für einem?	was für einem?
A.	wen, whom?	was für einen?	was für ein?

3. Was is sometimes separated, by other words, from für ein; as,

Was ist dies für ein Haus? What kind of a house is this?

4. Welch (contraction of welcher), and was für ein, are also used in exclamation; as,

Welch (or was für) ein Riese! What a giant!

5. Was is sometimes used instead of warum? why? as,

„Was weint ihr Mädchen, warum klagt ihr Weiber?"   Why (what) weep ye maidens, why complain ye matrons?

6. Jemand answers to "anybody, somebody", and etwas to "anything, something." Niemand answers to "not anybody, nobody"; and nichts to "not anything, nothing"; as,

Jemand hat mein Buch.	Somebody has my book.
Hat Jemand mein Buch?	Has anybody my book?
Hat nicht Jemand mein Buch?	Has not somebody my book?
Hat er nicht etwas?	Has he not something?
Er hat nichts.	He has nothing (not anything).
Ich sehe Niemand.	I do not see anybody. (I see nobody).

7. Etwas is sometimes abbreviated to „was"; as,

Ich habe was Gutes. I have something good.

8. DECLENSION OF Jemand.

Nom.	Jemand,	anybody;
Gen.	Jemands or Jemandes,	anybody's or of anybody;
Dat.	Jemand or Jemandem,	to or for anybody;
Acc.	Jemand or Jemanden,	anybody.

Niemand is declined like Jemand; etwas and nichts are indeclinable.

9. Gar (or ganz und gar) *before* a negative answers to "at all" *after* a negative; as,

Ich habe gar nichts.	I have not anything at all.
Er hat gar kein Geld.	He has no money at all.
Es ist gar nicht kalt.	It is not at all cold

2

Aber, but, however. — Blech, n. tin. — Etwas, see 6. — Gar, see 9. — Jemand, see 6. — Jetzt, now. — Käse, m. cheese. Kein, not any, no. Koffer, m. trunk. Korb, m. basket. — Lesen, to read. Loben, to praise. — Maler, m. painter. — Nichts, not anything, nothing. Niemand, not anybody, nobody. — Schuh, m. shoe. So, so, as. — Traurig, sad. — Warum', why.

Exercise 16. Aufgabe 16.

1. Wer lobt den Schüler, und wen lobt der Schüler? 2. Jemand lobt den Schüler, aber der Schüler lobt Niemand. 3. Wessen Buch lesen Sie jetzt? 4. Ich habe gar kein Buch. 5. Haben Sie etwas in Ihrem Korbe? 6. Nein, ich habe etwas in meinem Koffer. 7. Wem geben Sie das Geld? 8. Ich gebe Niemand das Geld, aber ich gebe Jemand das Blech. 9. Jemand hat meinen Schuh, und ich habe Jemands Ueberschuh. 10. Was für Käse haben Sie auf Ihrem Tische? 11. Ich habe gar keinen Käse. 12. Wen loben Sie? 13. Ich lobe Niemand. 14. Haben Sie nichts in Ihrem Koffer? 15. Nein, gar nichts. 16. Was sagt Ihr Freund, der Maler? 17. Er sagt gar nichts. 18. Warum sind Sie so traurig? 19. Ich bin gar nicht traurig. 20. Mit was für einem Messer schneiden Sie Ihren Apfel? 21. Ich habe keinen Apfel und kein Messer. 22. Zu wem geht der Schüler? 23. Er geht zu Niemand.

Exercise 17. Aufgabe 17.

1. Whose pencil has your brother, the painter? 2. He has the pencil of his friend the scholar. 3. Has anybody your horse? 4. Yes, somebody has it. 5. Does anybody praise your brother? 6. Somebody praises my father, but nobody praises my brother. 7. What kind of paper has the scholar? 8. He has no paper at all. 9. To whom do you give your money? 10. I do not give it to anybody. 11. With what kind of a pencil do you write? 12. I write with the pencil of your cousin. 13. Have you anything in your hat? 14. No, I have not anything in my hat, but I have something in my trunk. 15. To whom is the child going? 16. It is not going to anybody. 17. Somebody has our horse and our plow. 18. What kind of a shoe is this? 19. It is the overshoe of our friend. 20. Who has my book? 21. Nobody has your book. 22. Has anybody anything in your room? 23. Yes, somebody has something in my room.

LESSON XI. Section XI.

FORMS OF THE ADJECTIVE.

1. Adjectives when used predicatively,* are uninflected; as,

| Der Stahl ist hart. | The steel is hard. |
| Das Eisen ist hart. | The iron is hard. |

---

* The terms attributive and predicative have, in Grammar, a strictly conventional sense, and should be distinctly understood. If we say, the deep river is here (der tief-e

2. When, however, adjectives are used attributively, they are subject to three modes of inflection, called the *old*, the *new*, and the *mixed* declensions.

3. Adjectives, when not preceded by one of the words in List L. 8. 3. or 9. 5, are inflected like Diefer, (L. 8. 3.) and are then of the

OLD DECLENSION.

Masculine.	*Neuter.*
Nom. gut-er,	gut-es, good;
Gen. gut-es, (en*)	gut-es, (* en) of good;
Dat. gut-em,	gut-em, to or for good;
Acc. gut-en,	gut-es, good.

4. The e of the terminations el, en, er, is generally dropped when, by inflection, another syllable is added; as,

| Er ist eitel. | He is vain. |
| Eitl-er Stolz (not eit-eler). | Vain pride. |

5. ENDING OF THE OLD DECLENSION IN THE NOMINATIVE.

Attributive.	*Predicative.*
Gut-er Stahl ist hart.	Good steel is hard.
Gut-es Eisen ist hart.	Good iron is hard.
Hart-er Stahl ist gut.	Hard steel is good.
Hart-es Eisen ist gut.	Hard iron is good.

6. Adjectives which qualify the neuter pronouns, etwas, was and nichts, are inflected according to the *old* declension, and are written with a capital initial; as,

Ich habe etwas Schönes.	I have *something* beautiful.
Er sagt nichts Schlechtes.	He says *nothing* bad.
Sie sprechen von etwas Neuem.	You speak of *something* new.
Was haben Sie Neues?	*What* have you new?

Alt, old. An'genehm, agreeable. Auch, too, also. — Blank, bright. Blau, blue. — Fein, fine. Füttern, to line. — Gelb, yellow. Gesetz, n. law. Grau, gray. Grob, coarse. Grün, green. — Immer, always, ever. — König, m. king. — Machen, to do, make. Mantel, m. cloak. — Neu, new. — Rock, m. coat. — Sammet, m. velvet.

Fluß ist hier), the adjective deep (tief-e), is attributive; for the quality depth is referred to, as a known and recognized attribute of the river. If we say, the river is deep here (der Fluß ist hier tief), the adjective is predicative; for we then merely affirm or predicate of the river, that it has the quality depth.

* The genitive of the *old* form is now seldom used; that of the *new* form being preferred Thus, gut-en Stahls; gut-en Eisens, &c., instead of gut-es Stahls; gut-es Eisens, &c.

Schlecht, bad. Schneider, *m.* tailor. Schuhmacher, *m.* shoemaker. Schwach, weak. Stark, strong. — Tuch, *n.* cloth. — Weich, soft.

Exercise 18.   Aufgabe 18.

1. Dieses Leder ist gelb, und jenes ist schwarz. 2. Ich habe gelbes Leder, und Sie haben schwarzes. 3. Ist der Wein des Bauers alt oder neu? 4. Ist alter Wein immer stark und neuer Wein immer schwach? 5. Haben Sie starken oder schwachen Wein? 6. Ich habe starken, alten Wein, und der Bauer hat neues Bier. 7. Ist das Eisen des Schmiedes gut oder schlecht? 8. Der Schmied hat gutes und auch schlechtes Eisen. 9. Der Schneider macht den Rock von feinem grauem Tuche. 10. Der Mann füttert den Mantel mit grobem blauem Sammet. 11. Der König schreibt das Gesetz mit blankem Stahl und schwarzem Eisen. 12. Der Schuhmacher macht den Schuh von grünem Leder. 13. Ist weiches Eisen gut? 14. Ja, und weicher Stahl ist schlecht. 15. Haben Sie guten Stahl oder schlechtes Eisen? 16. Der Wein ist alt und das Bier ist neu. 17. Er hat alten Wein und neues Bier? 18. Sehr warmes Wetter ist nicht angenehm. 19. Mein Rock ist von schwarzem Tuche. 20. Haben Sie gutes Wasser, guten Käse und gutes Brod?

Exercise 19.   Aufgabe 19.

1. Is your cloth black, green or blue? 2. I have black cloth and the tailor has blue cloth. 3. Has the shoemaker green, yellow or black leather? 4. The shoemaker has black leather, and the saddler has yellow leather. 5. Has the blacksmith good steel, or good iron? 6. He has good iron. 7. Do you line your coat with green or with blue velvet? 8. The tailor lines my coat with blue velvet. 9. Is your wine strong or weak? 10. I have neither strong wine nor strong beer. 11. New wine is not always weak, and old wine is not always strong. 12. Have you good bread and good coffee? 13. I have good bread, but my coffee is not very good. 14. Is very cold weather agreeable? 15. What kind of weather is agreeable? 16. Warm weather is agreeable. 17. Is good steel always hard, and is good iron always soft? 18. Why has the smith soft steel? 19. Why has the tailor old cloth? 20. Why does he line your coat with green velvet?

LESSON 12.   Section 12.

ADJECTIVES OF THE NEW DECLENSION.

1. An adjective when preceded by der, dieser, aller, einiger, etlicher, jeder, jener, mancher, solcher, welcher (relating to the noun that the adjective qualifies) is inflected according to the

NEW DECLENSION.

Masculine.	Neuter.
N der gut-e, the good;	das gut-e, the good;
G. des guten, of the good;	des guten, of the good;
D. dem guten, to, for the good;	dem guten, to, for the good;
A. den guten, the good;	das gut-e, the good.

2. ENDINGS OF THE NEW DECLENSION IN THE NOMINATIVE

Attributive. *Predicative.*

Aller hart-e Stahl ist nützlich.	All hard steel is useful.
Alles hart-e Eisen ist nützlich.	All hard iron is useful.
Der nützlich-e Stahl ist hart.	The useful steel is hard.
Das nützlich-e Eisen ist hart.	The useful iron is hard.
Dieser schön-e Vogel ist weiß.	This beautiful bird is white.
Dieses schön-e Papier ist weiß.	This beautiful paper is white.
Einiger sehr gut-e Wein.	Some (a little) very good wine.
Einiges nicht sehr fein-e Tuch.	Some not very fine cloth.
Jeder gut-e Mann ist ehrlich.	Every good man is honest.
Jedes gut-e Kind ist ehrlich.	Every good child is honest.
Jener ehrlich-e Mann ist gut.	That honest man is good.
Jenes ehrlich-e Kind ist gut.	That honest child is good.
Mancher* gut-e Mann ist arm.	Many a good man is poor.
Manches gut-e Kind ist arm.	Many a good child is poor.
Welcher schlecht-e Mann ist glücklich?	Which bad man is happy?
Welches schlecht-e Kind ist glücklich?	Which bad child is happy?

Arm, poor. — Bitter, bitter. — Dumm, stupid. — Fleißig, diligent, industrious. — Gerber, *m.* tanner. Glücklich, happy, fortunate. — Jung, young. — Klein, little. — Lehrer, *m.* teacher. Lehrling, *m.* apprentice. Lieben, to love. — Mancher, many a. Mensch, *m.* human being, man. — Scharf, sharp. Schön, beautiful, fine. Sehen, to see. Stolz, proud. — Träge, idle, indolent. — Unglücklich, unfortunate, unhappy. — Wagen, *m.* carriage, wagon. Wirklich, really. — Zufrieden, contented, satisfied.

EXERCISE 20.   Aufgabe 20.

1. Sehen Sie den großen Hund unter diesem großen Baum? 2. Ich sehe den großen Baum, aber nicht den Hund. 3. Wem gehört dieses schöne Haus und dieser schöne Wagen? 4. Das Haus gehört dem alten Jäger,

---

* Mancher, solcher and welcher sometimes drop the final syllable; the adjective that follows being inflected (see L. 11) according to the *old* declension; as, manch armer Mann (instead of mancher arme Mann); many a poor man. Manch gutes Kind (instead of manches gute Kind); many a good child. Welch schönes Wetter! (instead of welches schöne Wetter); what fine weather! Solch grobes Tuch (instead of solches grobe Tuch); such coarse cloth.

und der Wagen gehört dem unglücklichen Freunde dieses reichen Müllers. 5. Hat der fleißige Lehrling des guten Goldschmieds das scharfe Messer des alten Lehrers, oder das alte Buch des trägen Schülers? 6. Hat der junge Gerber das gelbe oder das schwarze Leder? 7. Er hat das schwarze; er hat auch das grüne Tuch des alten Schneiders. 8. Der Sattler hat das gelbe Leder und der Schuhmacher hat das schwarze. 9. Ist aller alte Wein stark, und alles neue Bier bitter? 10. Ist jeder reiche Mann wirklich zufrieden? 11. Mancher dumme Mensch ist stolz. 12. Ich sehe den großen, schönen Baum in dem kleinen Garten des armen Bauers. 13. Das kleine Kind liebt und lobt den alten Mann. 14. Dieser junge Mann hat den scharfen Meißel jenes fleißigen Tischlers. 15. Füttert der alte Schneider den neuen Mantel mit dem blauen Tuche? 16. Trinkt der arme Mann das kalte Wasser?

Exercise 21.   Aufgabe 21.

1. Have you the black cloth or the blue? 2. I have the black, and the young tailor has the blue, and also the green. 3. Has the old man the old horse and the old wagon? 4. This idle scholar has the good book of that industrious scholar. 5. Which young man has the new book of this little child? 6. To which poor man do you give the good money? Is the young peasant going with the old hunter to the village? 8. To whom does this old horse belong? 9. Does this old wagon belong to the old baker? 10. Which good leather has the good shoemaker, the blue, the green, or the black? 11. Many a good man is very poor. 12. Not every poor man is unhappy. 13. Which diligent scholar has the new book? 14. This very warm weather is not very agreeable. 15. Has the rich peasant the good dog of the good hunter? 16. The old tailor lines the old cloak with the old cloth.

LESSON XIII.   Section XIII.

ADJECTIVES OF THE MIXED DECLENSION.

1. An adjective when preceded by ein, mein, dein, sein, ihr, unser, euer, fein (relating to the noun that the adjective qualifies) is inflected according to the

MIXED DECLENSION.

Masculine.	*Neuter.*
N. mein gut-er, my good;	mein gut-es, my good;
G. meines guten, of my good;	meines guten, of my good;
D. meinem guten, to my good;	meinem guten, to my good;
A. meinen guten my good;	mein gutes, my good.

2. As already seen, the above words, ein, mein, &c. (unlike der, das, &c. L. 8. 3), do not indicate the gender of their

nouns; this, however, is effected by means of the adjective; the termination er, being masculine, and es, neuter; as,

Masculine, ein klein-er Mann; sein gut-er Bruder;
Neuter, ein klein-es Kind; sein gut-es Pferd.

3. ENDINGS OF THE MIXED DECLENSION IN THE NOMINATIVE.

Attributive.   Predicative.

Ein gut-er Mann ist ehrlich.	A good man is honest.
Ein gut-es Kind ist ehrlich.	A good child is honest.
Sein ehrlich-er Freund ist gut.	His honest friend is good.
Sein ehrlich-es Kind ist gut.	His honest child is good.
Mein schön-er Vogel ist weiß.	My fine bird is white.
Mein schön-es Papier ist weiß.	My fine paper is white.
Dein weiß-er Vogel ist schön.	Thy white bird is fine.
Dein weiß-es Papier ist schön.	Thy white paper is fine.
Ihr gut-er Bruder ist groß.	Her good brother is large.
Ihr gut-es Kind ist groß.	Her good child is large
Unser groß-er Baum ist schön.	Our large tree is fine.
Unser groß-es Haus ist schön.	Our great house is fine.
Euer alt-er Koffer ist grün.	Your old trunk is green
Euer alt-es Band ist grün.	Your old ribbon is green.
Kein wirklich gut-er Mann ist faul.	No really good man is lazy.
Kein gut-es Kind ist faul.	No good child is lazy.

4. CONNECTED VIEW OF THE THREE DECLENSIONS.

	OLD.	NEW.	MIXED.
		Masculine.	
N.	gut-er (Stahl);	der gut-e (Stahl);	mein gut-er (Stahl;)
G.	gut-es (or -en) (Stahls);	des gut-en (Stahls);	meines gut-en (Stahls;)
D.	gut-em (Stahl);	dem gut-en (Stahl);	meinem gut-en (Stahl);
A.	gut-en (Stahl);	den gut-en (Stahl);	meinen gut-en (Stahl).
		Neuter.	
N.	gut-es (Eisen);	das gut-e (Eisen);	mein gut-es (Eisen);
G.	gut-es (or -en) (Eisens);	des gut-en (Eisens);	meines gut-en (Eisens);
D.	gut-em (Eisen);	dem gut-en (Eisen);	meinem gut-en (Eisen);
A.	gut-es (Eisen);	das gut-e (Eisen);	mein gut-es (Eisen).

Berg, *m.* mountain.—Dach, *n.* roof. Dick, thick, large.—Faul, lazy, idle.—Gedul'dig, patient. Geschickt', skillful. Gewis'sen, *n.* conscience. Je, ever.—Kameel', *n.* camel. Keller, *m.* cellar. Kissen, *n.* pillow, cushion. Künstler, *m.* artist.—Nach'lässig, negligent. Nützlich, useful.—Sanft, soft, mild. Schatz, *m.* treasure. Schutz, *m.* defense, protection. Stamm, *m.* trunk, body. Steil, steep.—Thier, *n.* animal, beast. Tief, deep. Treu, faithful, true— Un'zufrieden, discontented, dissatisfied.—Vogel, *m.* bird.

Exercise 22.   Aufgabe 22.

1. Ist Ihr guter Freund, der geschickte Künstler, noch (L. 66.) ein junger Mann? 2. Ja, er ist noch jung, aber sein guter Freund, der Lehrer, ist ein sehr alter Mann. 3. Ist ein reicher Mann immer ein zufriedener und angenehmer Mann? 4. Nein, und ein armer Mann ist nicht immer ein unzufriedener Mann. 5. Hat Ihr kleiner Bruder einen schönen kleinen Vogel? 6. Nein, er hat ein schönes kleines Pferd. 7. Ihr neues Haus hat ein steiles Dach und einen tiefen Keller. 8. Ein gutes Gewissen ist ein sanftes Kissen. Ein treuer Freund ist ein starker Schutz und ein großer Schatz. 10. Ein steiler Berg steht hinter unserm neuen Hause. 11. Unser neues Haus steht vor einem steilen Berge. 12. Unser alter Apfelbaum hat einen dicken Stamm. 13. Ist das geduldige Kameel ein nützliches Thier? 14. Haben Sie kein gutes Bier und keinen guten Wein? 15. Ich habe gutes Bier, aber keinen guten Wein. 16. Ist ein guter Schüler je faul? 17. Nein, er ist weder faul, noch nachlässig. 18. Ich habe ein neues Buch und er hat ein altes. (L. 8. Note.)

Exercise 23.   Aufgabe 23.

1. Your good friend has your good iron and your good steel. 2. Is your old friend still in the small garden of our good cousin? 3. No, he is in our large garden with his old teacher. 4. Has our young cousin your new book and his old pencil? 5. No, he has your old book, his new pencil, our good stove and my green table. 6. A little yellow bird is sitting on the steep roof of your new house. 7. Is your old friend a skillful artist? 8. Yes, he is a skillful artist, and a very agreeable man. 9. The patient camel is a very strong and a very useful animal. 10. My young friend has my young horse. 11. Our old friend has our old horse in our old garden. 12. A rich man is not always a contented and a happy man. 13. Is a poor man always a discontented man? 14. Is a lazy man ever contented, or an industrious man ever discontented? 15. My lazy scholar is discontented. 16. Have you no good cheese? 17. I have good cheese, but no good bread. 18. You have my new book and I have his old one. (L. 8. Note.)

LESSON XIV.   Lection XIV.

SPEAKING AND WRITING GERMAN.

Guided by the instructions thus far given, the pupil may now profitably enter upon the practice of *speaking* and *writing*

SPEAKING AND WRITING GERMAN. 33

German. For this purpose, every sentence in the foregoing Lessons, may be regarded as a *Model:* the learner applying in every case the principles which the model sentence is designed to illustrate.* An ample stock of words, in addition to those already acquired by the learner, will be found page 190, and following. In this and in the English vocabulary, page 230, are contained all the words of the *subsequent* EXERCISES. Also, for the sake of more convenient reference, the words of the *preceding* exercises have been included in the same vocabularies.

Obs. As a want of familiarity with the various endings, especially those of the adjective, (they being the most difficult,) is a great hindrance to the right use of German, the pupil should give to the following exercise the utmost attention.

EXERCISE 24.   Aufgabe 24.

1. Tiefer glänzender Schnee liegt auf dem grünen Felde. 2. Das grüne Feld liegt unter tiefem Schnee. 3. Der tiefe Schnee liegt auf grünem Gras. 4. Grünes Gras liegt unter dem tiefen Schnee. 5. Kein tiefer Schnee liegt auf unserem grünen Felde. 6. Unser grünes Feld liegt unter keinem tiefen Schnee. 7. Hören Sie jenes reizende Lied? 8. Mein kleiner Bruder schenkt dem kleinen Kinde einen kleinen süßen Apfel. 9. Er liest (L. 33. 6) Ihr großes Buch mit großem Vergnügen. 10. Mein großes Pferd ist in meinem grünen Felde. 11. Das große Pferd meines alten Nachbars ist in dem großen grünen Felde des alten Bauers. 12. Der gute Freund des alten Schneiders geht mit dem alten Müller nach dem grünen Walde. 13. Mein guter Freund, der alte Schneider, deckt seinen alten Tisch mit rothem Tuche. 14. Ich habe gutes Leder von dem guten Gerber. Sie haben das gute Leder des guten Sattlers, und der gute Schuhmacher hat kein gutes Leder. 15. Das kalte Wetter deckt den breiten Fluß mit glattem Eis.

EXERCISE 25.   Aufgabe 25.

1. The green grass lies under the deep snow. 2. The deep snow lies upon the green grass. 3. Deep snow lies upon the green field of our old friend. 4. The deep snow lies upon the broad field. 5. The little scholar reads with great pleasure the large book of his good friend. 6. Green grass lies under deep snow. 7. The good book of my good friend lies on the good table. 8. Your old friend the old teacher, is with his old friend in the green field. 9. The large horse is in the little garden of our good neighbor. 10. My good dog goes with our good neighbor to the large green forest. 11. The cold weather covers the

---

* For further remarks, and illustrations of this plan, see "New Method", p. p. 62. 249 or "Fasquelle's French Course", p. p. 59. 267.

2*

river with smooth ice. 12. The glittering snow covers the green forest and the green field. 13. My old friend the old saddler covers my old trunk with old leather. 14. Has the good friend of the good smith good iron and good steel? 15. He has good iron and steel; he has also a good dog and a good horse.

LESSON XV.   Section XV.

Prepositions.

1. PREPOSITIONS GOVERNING THE DATIVE.

Aus, außer, bei, binnen, entgegen, gegenüber, gemäß, mit, nach, nächst, nebst, ob, sammt, seit, von, zu, and zuwider, govern the dative only.

2. PREPOSITIONS GOVERNING THE ACCUSATIVE.

Durch, für, gegen, ohne, sonder, um, and wider, govern the accusative only.

3. PREPOSITIONS GOVERNING THE DATIVE OR ACCUSATIVE.

An, auf, hinter, in, neben, über, unter, vor, and zwischen, govern the *dative*, when used with verbs of *rest*, or with those indicating motion *within* specified limits; and the *accusative*, when motion or tendency *towards* any place or object is indicated; as,

Er läuft in dem Garten.	He is running *in* the garden.
Er läuft in den Garten.	He is running *into* the garden.
Das Buch liegt auf dem Tische.	The book lies *on* the table.
Ich lege das Buch auf den Tisch.	I lay the book *upon* the table.
Er ist in dem Hause.	He is *in* the house.
Er geht in das Haus.	He goes *into* the house

4. Prepositions are frequently contracted with the definite article into one word; as,

Am (for an dem).	Er sitzt am Tische.	He sits at the table.
Ans (for an das).	Er geht ans Fenster.	He goes to the window.
Aufs (for auf das).	Er legt es aufs Brett.	He lays it on the board.
Beim (for bei dem).	Er ist beim Bruder.	He is with the brother.
Durchs („durch das).	Er geht durchs Feld.	He goes through the field.
Fürs (for für das).	Es ist fürs Kind.	It is for the child.
Hinterm („hinter dem).	Er steht hinterm Zaun.	He stands behind the fence.
Im (for in dem).	Er ist im Hause.	He is in the house.
Ins (for in das).	Er geht ins Haus.	He goes into the house.
Vom (for von dem).	Er kommt vom Markte.	He comes from the market.
Zum (for zu dem).	Er geht zum Freunde.	He goes to the friend.

Exercise 26.   Aufgabe 26.

1. Der alte Mann geht ins neue Haus und das kleine Kind geht in den kleinen Garten. 2. Mein alter Freund sitzt auf dem alten Stuhl an dem kleinen Fenster und legt das Buch auf den Tisch. 3. Das trockene Holz liegt hinterm Ofen und das kleine Kind geht hinter den Ofen. 4. Das weiße Papier liegt neben dem alten Buche unter dem runden Tische. 5. Der müde Schüler legt sein weißes Papier neben mein altes Buch unter das grüne Tuch. 6. Das neue Haus steht über dem tiefen Keller. 7. Das kleine muntere Pferd springt über den tiefen Graben. 8. Mein gutes Papier liegt auf dem Tische vor dem jungen Manne. 9. Er legt das gute Papier vor den jungen Mann zwischen das Buch und das Glas. 10. Das Papier liegt zwischen dem Buche und dem Glase. 11. Der alte Jäger geht um das kleine Feld und durch den großen Wald; er hat etwas Schönes für sein kleines Kind. 12. Ich habe nichts für den Jäger, denn er ist nicht mein Freund. 13. Was sagen Sie gegen den jungen Holländer? 14. Ich sage, er ist sehr unhöflich gegen (L. 56.) meinen Freund. 14. Wohnen Sie bei (L. 55. 2.) Ihrem Oheim? 15. Wann gehen Sie nach Hause? (L. 57. 3.) 16. Geht der Diener zu dem Schuhmacher oder zu dem Schneider? (L. 62. 2.) 17. Er geht zu seinem Vetter, und sein Bruder bleibt zu Hause. (L. 62. 3.)

Exercise 27.   Aufgabe 27.

1. Is the old friend of the old captain standing at the window, or is he going to (L. 53.) the window? 2. Is the scholar putting his wood on his stove? 3. No, for the wood is lying on the stove. 4. The little child is standing behind the large stove, and the faithful old dog is going behind the stove. 5 Is your brother in the house or is he going into the house? 6. The teacher lays his pencil beside his book: the child stands beside his friend. 7. Our room is over the room of our old uncle. 8. The old horse is standing under the tree and the young man is going under the tree. 9. The poor old beggar is standing before the house, and the rich young man is coming before the house. 10. My table is standing between the stove and the window. 11. The horse is going between the house and the garden. 12. Does the young man live at his cousin's? 13. Are you going to your brother's. 14. No, I remain at home. 15. Is your friend at home? 16. Yes, he is at home, and I am going home.

LESSON XVI.   Section XVI.

NEGATIVE CONJUGATION.

1. As in interrogative sentences (L. 5), so also in negative ones, German verbs are conjugated, in the present and imperfect, without an auxiliary; as,

Ich habe nicht.	I have not.
Er geht nicht.	He goes not. (He does not go.)
Er ist nicht hier.	He is not here.
Liebe nicht.	Love not. (Do not love.)

2. Nicht, when relating to a transitive verb commonly *follows* the object of that verb; but when that which is in one clause denied, is in another affirmed of a different object, the particle n i ch t, *precedes*; as,

Ich habe es nicht.	I have it not. (I have n't it).
Ich habe das Buch nicht.	I have not the book, (the book not).
Er lobt seinen Sohn nicht.	He does not praise his son.
Ich habe nicht das Buch, sondern den Bleistift.	I have not the book but the pencil.
Ich lese nicht das Buch, welches Sie lesen, sondern ein anderes.	I do not read the book that you read, but another.

3. Sondern occurs only after a *negation* and introduces the reverse of the negation; while

Aber may follow either a negation or an affirmation, and marks simply something additional; as,

Er ist nicht reich, sondern arm.	He is not rich but poor.
Er ist nicht reich, aber stolz.	He is not rich but proud.
Er ist reich, aber nicht stolz.	He is rich but not proud.

4. Nicht wahr? not true? (is it not true?) answers (like the French "n'est ce pas?") to our various interrogative phrases after an assertion; as,

Sie kennen ihn,		You know him, do you not?
Er ist Ihr Bruder,		He is your brother, is he not?
Er hat es gehabt,		He has had it, has n't he?
Sie wird gehen,	nicht wahr?	She will go, will she not?
Wir können hören,		We can hear, can we not?
Sie sind reich,		They are rich, are they not?
Sie sind nicht reich,		They are not rich, are they?

The interrogative, nicht wahr? sometimes precedes the assertion; as,

Nicht wahr? er ist sehr reich.   He is very rich, is he not?

NOUNS OF THE NEW DECLENSION.

5. Nouns of this declension ending in unaccented ar, e, el, or er, add n in all the oblique cases; as, *nom.* der Ungar, the Hungarian; *gen.* des Ungarn; *dat.* dem Ungarn; *acc.* den Ungarn.

Nouns of other terminations add en; as, *nom.* der Graf, the count, *gen.* des Grafen; *dat.* dem Grafen; *acc.* den Grafen.

NEW DECLENSION.

N. der Neffe,	the nephew;	der Soldat,	the soldier;
G. des Neffen,	of the nephew;	des Soldaten,	of the soldier;
D. dem Neffen,	to the nephew;	dem Soldaten,	to the soldier;
A. den Neffen,	the nephew;	den Soldaten,	the soldier.

Exercise 28.   Aufgabe 28.

1. Der Graf ist nicht der Freund, sondern der Feind des Prinzen. 2. Der Knabe lobt den Soldaten nicht. 3. Er lobt nicht den Soldaten, sondern den Matrosen. 4. Er lobt den Matrosen, aber nicht den Soldaten. 5. Der Grieche ist der Nachbar, aber nicht der Freund des Türken. 6. Der Böhme ist nicht nur der Nachbar des Baiern, sondern auch des Sachsen. 7. Der alte Soldat schreibt seinem Neffen, dem jungen Matrosen, einen Brief. 8. Der junge Matrose hat einen Brief von seinem Oheim, dem alten Soldaten. 9. Dieser reiche alte Russe hat einen Sclaven. 10. Der Sclave schlachtet den Ochsen seines Herrn. 11. Der Knabe spielt mit dem Affen und dem Bären. 12. Der Deutsche kauft den Wein des Franzosen, und der Franzose kauft das Tuch des Deutschen. 13. Dieser Knabe ist der Neffe des Grafen. 14. Das Wetter ist nicht warm, aber angenehm. 15. Das Wetter ist nicht warm, sondern kalt. 16. Dieses Buch ist nicht interessant, sondern langweilig; es ist nicht interessant, aber lehrreich. 17. Welchen Unterschied finden Sie zwischen „Nicht jedes interessante Buch ist lehrreich" und „Jedes interessante Buch ist nicht lehrreich?" 18. Dieser Mann ist ein Russe, nicht wahr? 19. Sie haben mein Buch, nicht wahr?

Exercise 29.   Aufgabe 29.

1. Why is the Bohemian the enemy of the Bavarian? 2. He is not the enemy but the friend of the Bavarian. 3. The Saxon is the neighbor but not the enemy of the Bohemian. 4. Not the German but the Hungarian is the enemy of the Russian. 5. The Frenchman praises the Hungarian and is the enemy of the Russian. 6. The boy has a letter from the nephew of the old soldier. 7. Has the Greek the sword of the Turk, or has the Turk the land of the Greek? 8. Who is slaughtering the ox of the sailor? 9. Has the nephew of the count a bear and an ape? 10. The weather is not cold but warm: it is warm but not pleasant. 11. The little boy has the hat of the sailor. 12. Not the soldier but the sailor has the little boy's book. 13. Is not every instructive book interesting? 14. This book is instructive, do you find it interesting, or tedious? 15. Is not every instructive book tedious? 16. He is going to the man, is he not? 17. You understand what I say, do you not? 18. Your cousin has a good horse, has he not?

LESSON XVII. Section XVII.

FEMININE GENDER.

1. In the feminine, the words contained in List. L. 8. 3, and 9. 5, all end in e: namely, alle, die, diese, einige, etliche, jede, jene, manche, solche, and welche: deine, eine, euere or eure, ihre, Ihre, meine, seine, unsere, and keine. These words have all the same form of inflection.

DECLENSION OF ARTICLES AND PRONOUNS. FEMININE

N. die, the;   diese, this;   eine, a;   meine, my;
G. der, of the;   dieser, of this;   einer, of a;   meiner, of my;
D. der, to the;   dieser, to this;   einer, to a;   meiner, to my;
A. die, the;   diese, this;   eine, a;   meine, my.

2. Feminine nouns, in the singular, are indeclinable.*

3. Appellations of females are formed from those of males, and titles of women from those of their husbands, by means of the suffix in (or inn); as,

der Freund, the friend;   die Freundin, the female friend;
der Lehrer, the teacher;   die Lehrerin, the preceptress;
der Engländer, the Englishman; die Engländerin, the Englishwoman;
der Gemahl, the consort (husband); die Gemahlin, the consort (wife);
der Schüler, the scholar;   die Schülerin, the female scholar;
der Löwe, the lion;   die Löwin, the lioness;
der Präsident', the president; die Präsidentin, the president's wife;
der Oberst, the colonel;   die Oberstin, the colonel's wife.

ADJECTIVES IN THE FEMININE GENDER.

4. When an adjective in the feminine is not preceded by one of the words in the above List (see 1.), it is inflected like diese, and is of the

OLD DECLENSION.

N. gut-e, good;   schön-e, beautiful;   (dies-e);
G. gut-er, of good;   schön-er, of beautiful;   (dies-er).
D gut-er, to, for good; schön-er, to, for beautiful; (dies-er).
A. gut-e, good;   schön-e, beautiful.   (dies-e).

---

* Nouns of this gender were formerly declined after the new declension. In certain phrases, as also in poetic language, these endings are still found in the dative, and occasionally in the genitive; as, Du sollst auf Erden für mich zeugen (Schiller); thou shalt witness for me upon earth. Seiner Frauen Schwester; his wife's sister

ADJECTIVES IN THE FEM. GENDER. NEW DECLENSION.

5. Feminine adjectives, when preceded by an article, or by a word of like declension (see 1.), are inflected according to the

NEW DECLENSION.

N. die gut-e,	the good;	meine gut-e,	my good;
G. der gut-en,	of the good;	meiner gut-en,	of my good;
D. der gut-en,	to, for the good;	meiner gut-en,	to, for my good;
A. die gut-e,	the good;	meine gut-e,	my good.

Exercise 30. Aufgabe 30.

1. Die Stimme der Nachtigall ist reizend. 2. Meine Freundin hört die Nachtigall mit großer Freude. 3. Schreiben Sie mit blauer oder mit schwarzer Tinte? 4. Ich schreibe mit Ihrer schwarzen Tinte. 5. Geduld ist eine Kunst und eine Tugend. 6. Eintracht gibt große Macht. 7. Die Liebe einer Mutter ist grenzenlos. 8. Die Sonne sagt mit süßer Stimme: „ich bin die Königin der Erde." 9. Hat Ihre Freundin diese blaue Tinte von einem Nachbar oder von einer Nachbarin? 10. Die Musik in dieser schönen, großen Kirche ist sehr gut. 11. Hat die kleine Tochter dieser schönen Dame die neue Kette meiner kleinen Schwester? 12. Meine kleine Cousine schenkt der Tante eine rothe Rose, und der Mutter eine weiße Lilie. 13. Die fleißige Biene sitzt auf der duftenden Blume. 14. Ihre Schwester hat Ihre neue Lampe in der Küche. 15. Zu wem gehen Sie, zu Ihrer Mutter oder zu Ihrer Tante? 16. Ich gehe mit meiner Schwester in die Stadt zu unserer Cousine. 17. Haben Sie eine neue Gabel und eine alte Tasse? 18. Nein, ich habe eine neue Feder und meine Schwester hat gute Tinte. 19. Ich habe günstige Nachricht von meiner Freundin, Frau W. (see L. 68).

Exercise 31. Aufgabe 31.

1. The sister of my friend has a beautiful rose. 2. The teacher has not much patience with the scholar. 3. Do you write with black ink? 4. I write with the black ink of my sister and the new pen of my cousin. 5. Whose new watch has your sister? 6. You have my sister's watch, have you also the new chain? 7. The industrious bee loves the fragrant rose. 8. The nightingale has a charming voice. 9. Whose love is boundless? 10. Who has my good lamp and my new pen? 11. Have you favorable news from your friend? 12. In which church is your mother? 13. My sister is writing our cousin a letter. 14. Does your aunt live in the city? 15. Does the bee love the lily? 16. The daughter of this old lady is my teacher. 17. The mother is in the kitchen, the daughter is in the church. 18. This music is not good. 19. This scholar is going to the teacher. 20. This lady is our neighbor. 21. My mother hears this news with great joy. 22. The rose is a beautiful flower. 23. I give my little sister a little rose. 24. The mother is going with the daughter into the new church.

LESSON XVIII. Section XVIII.

FORMATION OF DIMINUTIVES.

1. The terminations chen and lein suffixed to nouns give rise to a large class of words, called diminutives. These are always of the neuter gender, and generally take the Umlaut (L. 2. II. Note) if the radical vowel be capable of it;

der Hügel,	the hill;	das Hügelchen,	the hillock (little hill);
das Lamm,	the lamb;	das Lämmchen,	the lambkin (little lamb);
der Fluß,	the river;	das Flüßchen,	the rivulet (little river);
das Buch,	the book;	das Büchlein,	the little book;
die Frau,	the woman;	das Fräulein*,	the young woman.

2. The diminutives are often used as terms of endearment, or familiarity, and are likewise applied to objects where, in English, no idea of diminutiveness would be expressed; as,

Väterchen, (dear) father.   Mütterchen, (dear) mother.
Das Vöglein singt sein frohes Lied-   The little bird sings its joyful
chen.   (little) song.

FORMATION OF COMPOUND NOUNS.

3. In German, many compound nouns are formed, (often with change of termination of the former) where the English equivalents are connected by a hyphen, or where several separate words are used; as,

Schreibpapier	(from Schreib-en and Papier).	Writing-paper.
Preßfreiheit	(from Presse and Freiheit).	Freedom of the press
Lastthier	(from Last and Thier).	Beast of burden.
Wahrheitsliebe	(from Wahrheit and Liebe).	Love of truth.
Strohhut	(from Stroh and Hut).	Straw-hat.

4. The first word of the compound takes the accent, and the latter usually determines the gender; as,

Der Blumengarten.   The flower-garden.
Die Gartenblume.   The garden-flower.
Die Schildwache.   The sentinel.

Exceptions: der Abscheu; die Anmuth; die Demuth; die Großmuth; die Langmuth; die Sanftmuth; die Schwermuth; die Wehmuth; das Gegentheil; das Hintertheil; das Vordertheil.

5. The latter noun may be connected by a hyphen to one or more preceding words; as,

Der Stiefel- und Schuhmacher.   The boot and shoemaker.

---

* The words Fräulein and Mädchen, though regularly formed as diminutives, have lost their strict diminutive signification. The former signifies a young (unmarried) lady, and serves as a title of address, answering to the English word Miss; as, Fräulein N. ist hier, Miss N. is here. Mädchen corresponds to girl: Magd, from which Mädchen is derived being now chiefly employed in the signification of "servant".

GENDER OF NOUNS.   41

Exercise 32.   Aufgabe 32.

1. Das muntere Vögelchen sitzt auf dem Bäumchen und singt sein frohes Liedchen. 2. Das Knäbchen hat ein schönes Büchlein in seinem neuen Körbchen. 3. Das Lämmchen springt und spielt auf dem sonnigen Hügelchen. 4. Das Mädchen sucht ein schönes Blümchen für das kranke Brüderchen. 5. Das Knäbchen baut seinem Hündchen ein Häuschen. 6. Fräulein N. ist die Freundin meiner Schwester. 7. Dieses Mädchen ist sehr reich und sehr wohlthätig. 8. Das Kameel ist ein Lastthier, aber kein (L. 52. 11.) Zugthier. 9. Das Pferd ist ein Lastthier und auch ein Zugthier. 10. Der Ochs ist ein Zugthier und auch ein Schlachtthier; aber kein Lastthier. 11. Das Schwein ist nur ein Schlachtthier. 12. Der Hund ist ein Hausthier und der Wolf ist ein Raubthier. 13. Der Löwe ist ein großes und der Fuchs ist ein kleines Raubthier. 14. Die Eiche ist ein schöner, nützlicher Waldbaum, aber kein Obstbaum.

Exercise 33.   Aufgabe 33.

1. The little boy plays with his little dog. 2. Miss L. has the little book of the little girl. 3. The little brother of the girl is playing with the little lamb. 4. This young lady is very benevolent but not very rich. 5. Is the camel a draught-animal? 6. No, it is a beast of burden. 7. The dog is not a beast of prey and the wolf is not a domestic animal. 8. Is the ox a beast of burden? 9. No, he is a draught-animal. 10. Is the horse a draught-animal, or a beast of burden? 11. The horse is a beast of burden and also a draught-animal. 12. Is the oak a fruit tree or a forest tree? 13. The oak is a beautiful forest tree. 14. Is no forest tree a fruit tree? 15. The little dog plays with the little lamb. 16. The boy has a beautiful little tree in his garden.

LESSON XIX.   Section XIX.

GENDER OF NOUNS.

1. As already seen (L. 4. 2.), some words are regarded as differing in respect to gender from the objects which they represent. Other words, on the contrary, as is usual in English, mark the *real* gender of their objects. Hence arises what is termed the *grammatical*, and the *natural* gender.

2. In respect to appellations of persons, the grammatical is the same as the natural gender.

Exceptions: Das Weib, and diminutives (L. 18. 1.), as also some compound nouns (L. 18. 4.).

3. To the *masculine* gender belong

    a. Names of days, months, mountains, points of compass, seasons, and stones; as,

der Montag, Monday; der April, April; der Harz, the Harz;
der Nord, north; der Frühling, the spring; der Rubin, the ruby.

b. Nouns whose final letter is the same as the root of the verb from which they are derived; as,

der Bruch,	the fraction,	from	brechen,	to break;
der Fluß,	the river,	from	fließen,	to flow;
der Flug,	the flight,	from	fliegen,	to fly;
der Lauf,	the course,	from	laufen,	to run;
der Schuß,	the shot,	from	schießen,	to shoot;
der Trunk,	the draught,	from	trinken,	to drink;
der Wuchs,	the growth,	from	wachsen,	to grow.

4. To the *feminine* gender belong
   a. Nouns formed from the roots of verbs, by adding de, e, te, or t; as,

die Sprache,	the language,	from	sprechen,	to speak;
die Zierde,	the ornament,	from	zieren,	to adorn;
die Flucht,	the flight,	from	fliehen,	to flee;
die Gabe,	the gift,	from	geben,	to give;
die Schrift,	the writing,	from	schreiben,	to write;
die Geburt,	the birth,	from	gebären,	to bear;
die Falte,	the fold,	from	falten,	to fold.

b. Nouns ending in ei, heit, in (or inn), keit, schaft and ung; as,

die Heuchelei,	the hypocrisy;	die Kindheit,	the childhood;
die Heldin,	the heroine;	die Eitelkeit,	the vanity;
die Freundschaft,	the friendship;	die Uebung,	the exercise.

5. To the *neuter* gender belong
   a. Nouns beginning with the augment ge, those ending in chen, lein (L. 18.), niß, sal, sel, and thum, as also all words not properly nouns, but used as such; as,

das Schicksal, the fate, destiny; das Gedächtniß, the memory;
das Räthsel, the riddle; das Bißthum, the bishopric;
das Erhabene, the sublime (L.23.1.); das Lesen, L.35.3. the reading.

Exceptions: Masculine, Gebrauch, Gedanke, Gehalt, Genuß, Geruch, Gesang, Geschmack, Gestank, Gewinn, Irrthum, Reichthum, Wachsthum.
Feminine, Bedrängniß, Bekümmerniß, Besorgniß, Betrübniß, Bewandniß, Empfängniß, Ersparniß, Erlaubniß, Fäulniß, Finsterniß, Kenntniß, Wildniß. Trübsal is either feminine or neuter.

b. Names of countries and cities; as, Schweden, Berli'n, Hamburg, Sachsen, Dresden, &c.

Exceptions: those ending in ei are feminine, and a few others are masculine or feminine.

c. Names of metals; as,

das Gold, das Eisen, das Kupfer, das Blei, das Silber, &c.

Further exceptions to the above rules will best be learned by careful observation in reading.

GENDER OF NOUNS; EXERCISES, &C.   43

6. Some nouns have two genders and are employed in different significations; as,

der Band,	the volume;	das Band,	the ribbon;
der Bauer,	the peasant;	das Bauer,	the cage;
der Bund,	the alliance;	das Bund,	the bundle;
die Erkenntniß,	knowledge;	das Erkenntniß,	decision (judicial);
der Erbe,	the heir;	das Erbe,	the inheritance;
der Gehalt,	the contents;	das Gehalt,	the salary;
der Heide,	the pagan;	die Heide,	the heath;
der Kunde,	the customer;	die Kunde,	the news;
der Mensch,	man; human being;	das Mensch,	vile woman;
der Reis,	the rice;	das Reis,	the twig;
der Schild,	the shield;	das Schild,	the sign;
der See,	the lake;	die See,	the sea;
der Stift,	the peg;	das Stift,	foundation (charitable);
der Theil,	the part;	das Theil,	the share;
der Thor,	the fool;	das Thor,	the door;
der Verdienst,	the profits;	das Verdienst,	the merit.

7. Generic names of animals may be of either gender; as

der Luchs, the lynx;	die Ziege, the goat;	das Schaf, the sheep;
der Fisch, the fish;	die Auster, the oyster;	das Huhn, the fowl;
der Hase, the hare;	die Hyäne, the hyena;	das Pferd, the horse;
der Rabe, the raven;	die Taube, the dove;	das Thier, the animal.

EXERCISE 34.   Aufgabe 34.

1. Ich liebe den Frühling, den Sommer und den Herbst, aber nicht den Winter. 2. Der Smaragd ist grün, der Rubin ist roth. 3. Der Diamant ist sehr hart. 4. Die Eitelkeit ist oft eine Begleiterin der Faulheit. 5. Die Donau ist ein sehr langer Fluß. 6. Das weltberühmte Rom liegt an der Tiber. 7. Der Schwan ist ein großer, und die Ente ist ein kleiner Schwimmvogel. 8. Der Hase ist ein furchtsames, die Katze ein schlaues, und das Eichhörnchen ein munteres Thier. 9. Ein Sprichwort sagt: "Uebung macht den Meister". 10. Jeder gute Mensch haßt Heuchelei und Falschheit. 11. Das Kind hat den ersten Band dieses Werkes und auch das neue Band dieses Mädchens. 12. Der Elephant, das Kameel, der Tiger, der Löwe, die Hyäne, das Nashorn, das Flußpferd, das Krokodil, die Riesenschlange, der Strauß und der Paradiesvogel leben in einem heißen Lande. 13. Der Bär, der Wolf, der Fuchs, der Hase, das Kaninchen, das Rennthier, das Schaf, der Biber, die Gemse, die Gans und die Ente leben in einem kalten Lande. 14. Der Araber nennt das Kameel das Schiff der Wüste. 15. Der Schüler hat in seinem Zimmer einen Ofen, einen Tisch, einen Stuhl, eine Lampe, einen Koffer, einen Spiegel, ein Pult, ein Sopha, einen Teppich, eine Schaufel, eine Zange, eine Scheere, einen Bleistift, eine Feder, ein Tintenfaß und gutes Papier. 16. Der Koch kauft das Huhn, das Lamm, das Kalb, die Taube, den Aal, die Forelle und den Lachs. 17. Der Bauer verkauft die Gerste, den Hafer,

ben Kohl und den Weizen. 18. Wer kauft den Ring, den Stock, das Eisen, den Stahl und das Papier? 19. Hat der Knabe einen Adler, einen Habicht, eine Eule oder einen Raben? 20. Die Nachtigall singt in der Nacht. 21. Der Ahorn ist ein Waldbaum, was für ein Baum ist die Weide? 22. Was für ein Vogel ist die Lerche? 23. Das Kind hat einen Apfel, eine Birne, eine Mandel, eine Melone und eine Pfirsiche. 24. Der Grobschmied hat einen Amboß und der Maurer hat eine Kelle.

Exercise 35.   Aufgabe 35.

1. The summer is warm, the winter is cold. 2. The spring is pleasant, the autumn is unpleasant. 3. The glazier has a beautiful diamond. 4. The goldsmith has the gold, the silver, the emerald and the ruby. 5. Indolence is often the attendant of vanity. 6. The world-renowned Tiber is not a very large river. 7. The swan is white, the goose gray or white. 8. The squirrel lives in the woods, the hare in the field and the cat in the house. 9. No good man loves hypocrisy. 10. This girl has a new ribbon, and this boy has the first volume of your new work. 11. What large city lies on the Danube? 12. What does the Arab call the camel? 13. In what country do the rhinoceros, the hippopotamus, the tiger, the lion, the crocodile, the ostrich, the hyena and the elephant live? 14. Have you the bread, the cheese, the meat, the wheat and the barley? 15. No, I have the salt, the pepper, the mustard, the vinegar, the beer, the wine, the oil, the coffee, the tea, the sugar and the flour. 16. Has the man the glass, the gold, the iron, the steel, the leather, the paper, the pen, the pencil, the ink and the knife? 17. The old peasant has a large field, a large garden and a large house. 18. The miller buys the wheat and the rye, the brewer buys the barley, and the merchant buys the oats. 19. Have you the desk, the table, the sofa, the stove, the tongs, the shovel, and the chair of the cabinet-maker? 20. What kind of a bird is the eagle, and what kind of a beast is the wolf? 21. Are you writing with my pen or with your pencil? 22. Which fish does the girl buy, the trout, the salmon or the eel? 23. Which mechanic has an anvil and a hammer, and which has a chisel? 24. In what kind of a country do the duck, the swan, the goose, the beaver, the chamois, the rabbit, the reindeer, the bear, the wolf and the fox live? 25. Have you an apple, a peach or a pear for this little child? 26. Are you learning a foreign language?

LESSON XX.   Section XX.

MASCULINE, FEMININE AND NEUTER PLURAL

1. In the plural, the words contained in Lists L. 8. 3., and 9. 5., as also mehrere, several; have but one form for all genders: namely, alle, die, diese, einige, etliche, jede, jene, manche, solche, and welche; deine, euere or eure, ihre, Ihre, meine, seine, unsere and keine. These have all the same inflection.

DECL. OF ART. DEM. INTERROG. AND POSS. PRON. AND INDEF. NUM.

Nom. die;   diese;   welche;   meine;   alle;   keine;
Gen. der;   dieser;   welcher;   meiner;   aller;   keiner;
Dat. den;   diesen;   welchen;   meinen;   allen;   keinen;
Acc. die;   diese;   welche;   meine;   alle;   keine.

ADJECTIVES IN THE PLURAL.

2. In the plural, adjectives have but one form for all genders, and are inflected according to the *old* and *new* declensions.

3. When not preceded by one of the words in the above list (see 1.), the adjective is inflected like diese, and is of the

OLD DECLENSION.

Nom. gute, good;   alte, old;   (diese);
Gen. guter, of good;   alter, of old;   (dieser);
Dat. guten, to, for good; alten, to, for old; (diesen);
Acc. gute, good;   alte, old;   (diese).

4. Haben, sein AND loben, PRESENT PLURAL.

wir haben, we have;   wir sind, we are;   wir loben, we praise,
ihr* habt, you have; ihr seid, you are; ihr lobt, you praise;
sie* haben, they have; sie sind, they are; sie loben, they praise.

NOUNS OF THE OLD DECLENSION PLURAL.

5. *Masculine* and *neuter* nouns ending in e, el, en, er, chen and lein, have the same form in the plural as in the singular; as,

das Mittel, the means;   die Mittel, the means;
das Gebäude, the building; die Gebäude, the buildings;
der Morgen, the morning;   die Morgen, the mornings, &c.

Exceptions: the following *masculine* nouns take in the plural the Umlaut; Apfel, Hammel, Handel, Mangel, Mantel, Nabel, Nagel, Sattel, Schnabel, Vogel, Faden, Garten, Graben, Hafen, Ofen, Schaden, Acker, Bruder, Hammer, Schwager, Vater, (and the *neuter*) Kloster.

The feminine nouns Mutter and Tochter also take the Umlaut.

6. *Masculine* and *neuter* nouns of other terminations add e, and the masculine† assume the Umlaut, if capable of it; as,

---

*) For remarks on the use of ihr and sie, see L. 24. 11.

†) In this manner are declined also the following feminine nouns: Angst, Ausflucht, Art, Bank, Braut, Brust, Faust, Frucht, Gans, Gruft, Geschwulst, Hand, Haut, Kluft, Kraft, Kuh, Kunst, Laus, Luft, Lust, Macht, Magd, Maus, Nacht, Naht, Noth, Nuß, Sau, Schnur, Stadt, Wand, Welt, Wurst, Zunft, Zusammenkunft.

der Baum, the tree; die Bäume, the trees;
der Rock, the coat; die Röcke, the coats.

Exceptions: the following add **er** in the plural and take the Umlaut, if capable of it

a. *Neuter:* Aas, Amt, Bad, Bild, Blatt, Buch, Dach, Dorf, Ei, Fach, Faß, Feld, Geld, Gemüth, Geschlecht, Gespenst, Glas, Glied, Grab, Gras, Gut, Haupt, Haus, Hospita'l, Huhn, Kalb, Kamiso'l, Kind, Kleid, Korn, Kraut, Lamm, Lied, Loch, Maul, Nest, Parlament, Pfand, Rad, Regiment', Reis, Rind, Schloß, Schwert, Spita'l, Thal, Volk, Weib; and

b. *Masculine:* Bösewicht, Dorn, Geist, Gott, Leib, Mann,* Ort, Rand, Vormund, Wald, Wurm;

The following *masculines* do not assume the Umlaut;

c. Aal, Aar, Abend, Amboß, Anwalt, Arm, Docht, Dolch, Dorsch, Eidam, Gemahl', Grad, Habicht, Halm, Hauch, Herzog, Huf, Hund, Kapaun, Kobold, Kork, Kranich, Laut, Leichnam, Luchs, Molch, Monat, Mond, Mord, Pfad, Pfropf, Puls, Punkt, Salm, Schaft, Schuh, Staar, Stoff, Tag, Trunkenbold, Vielfraß, Unhold, Wiedehopf.

7. Some nouns have two (and one word, Band, has three) forms in the plural; as,

Band, Bänder, *n.* ribbons; Bande, *m.* bonds; Bände, *m.* volumes;
Bank, *f.* Bänke, benches; Banken, banks;
Bogen, *m.* Bogen, sheets of paper; Bögen, bows, arches;
Mond, *m.* Monde, planets; Monden, months;
Ort, *m.* Orte, places; Oerter, places, villages, &c.
Schild, Schilde, *m.* shields; Schilder, *n.* sign-boards;

8. The nom., gen. and acc. are alike, and the dat. adds n.

Exercise 36.   Aufgabe 36.

1. Sehen Sie schöne Bäume auf jenen Hügeln? 2. Ich sehe weder Hügel noch Bäume. 3. Geben Sie den Schneidern die Ringe der Schmiede? 4. Der Bauer hat einen Wagen, zwei Pflüge, drei Pferde, zwölf Schweine und neunzig (L. 51.) Schafe. 5. Die Söhne der Lehrer haben die Messer der Jäger. 6. Die Tischler haben gute Hobel und scharfe Meißel. 7. Liegen Ihre Bleistifte auf den Tischen der Schüler? 8. Nein, die Schüler legen die Bleistifte auf die Stühle. 9. Die Waschtische und Pulte in diesen Zimmern gehören den Tischlern. 10. Jene Koffer und Körbe gehören den Brauern. 11. Was lernen faule unaufmerksame Schüler? 12. Was für Bäume haben dicke Stämme? 13. Diese Früchte sind nicht reif. 14. Die Nüsse auf diesen Bäumen sind bitter. 15. Diese Gänse sind grau und jene sind weiß. 16. Die Mütter haben harte, und die Töchter weiche Hände. 17. Ich habe mehrere Aerte. 18. Diese Bänke sind zu hoch. 19. Meine Freunde wohnen in großen Städten. 20. Sind diese Männer Kaufleute oder Zimmerleute? 21. Unsere Leiber sind sterblich und unsere Geister unsterblich. 22. Die Dörfer sind nicht in den Wäldern. 23. Sind die Lämmer auf den Feldern? 24. Diese Männer

---

* In the plural of many compound words, Mann takes the plural Leute; as, Kaufleute, merchants; Zimmerleute, carpenters.

sind keine Bösewichter. 25. Diese Kinder sind drei Jahre alt. 26. Die Hunde sind treue Thiere. 27. Diese Schuhe sind von grobem Leder. 28. Ein Jahr hat zwölf Monate oder drei hundert fünf und sechzig Tage und ein Tag hat vier und zwanzig Stunden. 29. Diese Wagner haben schöne Wagen. 30. Diese Würmer kommen aus der Erde. 31. Die römischen Geschichtschreiber sprechen viel von den Göttern und Göttinnen. 32. Die Bäume in den Wäldern von Deutschland sind nicht sehr groß. 33. Pferde haben runde Hufe. 34. Adler, Staare und Wiedehopfe sind Vögel.

Exercise 37.   Aufgabe 37.

1. The trees on these hills are very small. 2. These smiths have the coats of those tailors. 3. The goldsmiths have beautiful rings. 4. These four pencils belong to those two scholars. 5. Have the brewers the plows of the smiths? 6. Have the cabinet-makers your tables or your wash-stands? 7. Have you fine horses? 8. No, but I have fine sheep. 9. Whose friends are skillful artists? 10. The benches in these rooms are not very high. 11. Have the sons of the teachers large trunks? 12. They have no trunks at all, they have large baskets. 13. Have the millers planes and chisels? 14. What kind of plows have the smiths? 15. Are these geese very old? 16. Who has large hands? 17. To whom do these axes belong? 18. Who lives in large cities? 19. This man has cows and sheep but he has no geese. 20. What kind of scholars learn nothing? 21. Do you learn much? 22. Do the lambs live in the forests? 23. Have these men good books? 24. No, they have good pencils. 25. These dogs are four years old. 26. These worms live in the earth. 27. Have these men good shoes? 28. They have the wagons of the wagon-makers. 29. A month has thirty days and a year twelve months. 30. These men have strong arms and heavy daggers. 31. Which men speak of their gods? 32. These forests are large but the trees are small. 33. Eagles are large, and starlings are small birds.

LESSON XXI.   Section XXI.

ADJECTIVES OF THE NEW DECLENSION PLURAL.

1. Adjectives when preceded by a word in List L. 20. 1 * and in all cases of the plural in en, and are of the

NEW DECLENSION.

Nom. die reif-en, the ripe;   meine reif-en, my ripe;
Gen. der reif-en, of the ripe;   meiner reif-en, of my ripe;
Dat. den reif-en, to the ripe;   meinen reif-en, to my ripe;
Acc. die reif-en, the ripe;   meine reif-en, my ripe.

*) By many writers the *nom.* and *acc. plu* of adjectives preceded by alle, einige, etliche, manche, mehre, solche, welche, are inflected according to the *old*, and the other cases according to the *new* declension; as, alle gute Menschen; er hat einige gute Freunde: thus forming in the plural a *mixed* declension.

NOUNS OF THE NEW DECLENSION.

2. Nouns of the New Declension have all cases of the plural like the oblique cases of the singular (L. 16. 1).

3. In the plural, most feminine nouns (L. 20. Note), are inflected according to the New Declension. Those ending with the suffix in, double the n in the plural; as, Königin, queen; Königinnen, queens.

INFLECTION OF NOUNS AFTER THE NEW DECLENSION PLURAL

Nom. Knabe-n;	Nabel-n;	Bär-en;	Freundin-nen;
Gen. Knabe-n;	Nabel-n;	Bär-en;	Freundin-nen;
Dat. Knabe-n;	Nabel-n;	Bär-en;	Freundin-nen;
Acc. Knabe-n;	Nabel-n;	Bär-en;	Freundin-nen.

4. The following masculine nouns are inflected according to the *new* Declension, and also take ѕ after the en of the genitive singular: Fels, Friede, Funke, Gedanke, Glaube, Haufe, Name, Same, Schade, Buchstabe, Wille. Thus, *nom.* Fels, *gen.* Felsens, *dat.* dem Felsen, &c., *plur. nom.* die Felsen, *gen.* der Felsen, &c.

These nouns, however, often end in the nominative singular in en, and are then regularly inflected according to the *Old* Declension; as, *Nom.* der Felsen, *gen.* des Felsens, &c.

Der Schmerz forms the genitive, and das Herz the genitive and dative singular, in the same way, and follow the *new* declension in the plural.

5. The following masculine nouns are inflected, in the singular, according to the *old*, and in the plural according to the *new* declension: Ahn, Bauer, Dorn, Flitter, Forst, Gau, Gevatter, Lorbeer, Mast, Nachbar, Pfau, See, Sporn, Stachel, Strahl, Strauß, Vetter, Unterthan, Zierrath; also the neuter nouns, Auge, Bett, Ende, Hemd, Ohr.

Bett and Hemd have also the forms, Bette and Hemder.

Foreign masculine nouns ending in unaccented or, and a few others, are also inflected in the singular according to the *old*, and in the plural according to the *new* declension; as, *nom.* der Professor, *gen.* des Professors, &c.; *nom. plu.* die Professoren, &c.

Some add ien in the plural; as, das Adverb; *plu.* die Adverbien, &c.

DECLENSION OF PROPER NOUNS.

6. Proper names of *persons* generally take ѕ in the genitive; as,

EXERCISES OF NOUNS AFTER THE NEW DECLENSION. 49

Nom. Heinrich, Henry;   Gen. Heinrich's, Henry's;
Nom. Gertrud, Gertrude;   Gen. Gertrud's, Gertrude's.

7. *Feminine* nouns ending in e, follow the *new* declension (L. 16. 5), and add also s in the genitive; as,

Nom. Charlotte, Charlotte;   Gen. Charlottens, Charlotte's.

8. *Masculine* nouns ending in a letter where euphony will not admit of an additional s, add ens; as,

Nom. Leibnitz, Leibnitz;   Gen. Leibnitzens, Leibnitz's.

9. *Foreign* proper names* which do not admit of the addition of s, generally indicate the case by means of the definite article; as,

N. Demosthenes, Demosthenes; G. des Demosthenes, of Demosthenes.

Exercise 38.   Aufgabe 38.

1. Die stolzen Fürsten und Grafen unterdrücken die armen Bauern. 2. Die armen Soldaten haben die magern Ochsen unserer guten Nachbarn. 3. Die fleißigen Knaben gehen in die guten Schulen und die fleißigen Bienen suchen die duftenden Blumen. 4. Die tapferen Ungarn hassen die übermüthigen Russen. 5. Die neuen Kanzeln in diesen großen Kirchen sind sehr schön. 6. Die jungen Freundinnen meiner guten Schwestern haben meine reifen Birnen. 7. Die armen Nachbarinnen unserer guten Freundinnen haben reife Pflaumen. 8. Die streitsüchtigen Franzosen sind die Nachbarn der friedlichen Deutschen. 9. Die Löwen und Bären sind Raubthiere. 10. Die Griechen sind keine guten Freunde der stolzen Türken. 11. Matrosen und Soldaten führen ein unsicheres und anstrengendes Leben. 12. Die Schriften der alten Griechen sind sehr schön. 13. Meine kleinen Brüder lesen die Reden des weltberühmten Cicero.

Exercise 39.   Aufgabe 39.

1. Are the young counts the neighbors of the old princes? 2. Have your young friends the ripe pears and the beautiful flowers of our good neighbors? 3. Are the valiant Hungarians the good neighbors of the peaceful Germans? 4. Are the soldiers and sailors Russians, Frenchmen or Danes? 5. The soldiers are Russians and the sailors are Greeks. 6. The good sailors on this ship are Danes; the Danes are good sailors. 7. The large old churches of the Germans are very beautiful. 8. The good boys have the beautiful flowers. 9. Our poor neighbors have our ripe plums and pears. 10. The large pulpits in our new churches are not beautiful. 11. We read the beautiful writings and speeches of the ancient Greeks. 12. The giants of the old times were great heroes. 13. My young friends are reading old legends.

---

* Those that may take s, sometimes omit it, and are preceded by the article; as Cicero, instead of Cicero's.

10. CONNECTED VIEW OF THE ARTICLE DEMONST. DECLENSIONS, SIN-

Singular.

Masc.	Fem.	Neut.	Masc.	Fem.	Neut.	Masc	Fem	Neut
N. der,	die,	das;	dieſer,	dieſe,	dieſes;	mein,	meine,	mein;
G. des,	der,	des;	dieſes,	dieſer,	dieſes;	meines,	meiner,	meines;
D. dem,	der,	dem;	dieſem,	dieſer,	dieſem;	meinem,	meiner,	meinem;
A. den,	die,	das;	dieſen,	dieſe,	dieſes;	meinen,	meine,	mein.

OLD DECLENSION OF THE ADJECTIVE AND NOUN.

Masc.	Fem.	Neut.	Masc.	Masc.	Neut.	Neut.
N. guter,	gute,	gutes;	Vater;	Mann;	Dach;	Mittel;
G. gutes (en),	guter,	gutes, (en);	Vaters;	Mannes;	Daches;	Mittels;
D. gutem,	guter,	gutem;	Vater;	Manne;	Dache;	Mittel;
A. guten,	gute,	gutes;	Vater;	Mann;	Dach;	Mittel.

NEW DECLENSION OF THE ADJECTIVE AND NOUN.

Masc.	Fem.	Neut.	Masc.	Masc.
N. der gute,	die gute,	das gute;	Herr;	Graf;
G. des guten,	der guten,	des guten;	Herrn;	Grafen;
D. dem guten,	der guten,	dem guten;	Herrn;	Grafen;
A. den guten,	die gute,	das gute;	Herrn;	Grafen.

MIXED DECLENSION OF THE ADJECTIVE.

Masc.	Fem.	Neut.
N. mein guter,	meine gute,	mein gutes;
G. meines guten,	meiner guten,	meines guten;
D. meinem guten,	meiner guten,	meinem guten;
A. meinen guten,	meine gute,	mein gutes.

EXAMPLES OF THE VARIOUS DECLENSIONS IN THE SINGULAR.

Good steel. The color of good steel. With good steel. The good smith has good steel. Old iron. The color of old iron. With old iron. The little child has old iron.

All good steel and all good iron. The price of the good steel and the good iron. With that good steel and this good iron. That good smith has the good steel and the good iron.

My good steel and your good iron. The price of my good steel and your good iron. With his young horse and my old wagon. My good friend has your old horse and my new wagon. The nephew of the soldier is going with the sailor. Why do you praise the sailor's nephew? The "nephew of his uncle" is a great tyrant, but is he a great man? The emperor, the king and the duke have the peasant's money. The proud prince is the wicked oppressor of his suffering people.

AND POSSESSIVE PRONOUN, ADJECTIVE AND NOUN, IN ALL
GULAR AND PLURAL.

Plural.

All Genders.

die;	diese;	meine;	—;	—;	—;	—;	—;	—;
der;	dieser;	meiner;	—;	—;	—;	—;	—;	—;
den;	diesen;	meinen;	—;	—;	—;	—;	—;	—;
die;	diese;	meine;	—;	—;	—;	—;	—;	—.

OLD DECLENSION OF THE ADJECTIVE AND NOUN.

All Gend.	*Masc.*	*Masc.*	*Fem.*	*Fem.*	*Neut.*	*Neut.*
gute;	Väter;	Männer;	Hände;	Mütter;	Dächer;	Mittel;
guter;	Väter;	Männer;	Hände;	Mütter;	Dächer;	Mittel;
guten;	Vätern;	Männern:	Händen;	Müttern;	Dächern;	Mitteln,
gute;	Väter;	Männer;	Hände;	Mütter;	Dächer;	Mittel.

NEW DECLENSION OF THE ADJECTIVE AND NOUN.

All Genders.		*Masc.*	*Fem.*	*Fem.*	*Neut.*
die guten;	meine guten;	Grafen;	Federn;	Tafeln;	Herzen;
der guten;	meiner guten;	Grafen;	Federn;	Tafeln;	Herzen;
den guten;	meinen guten;	Grafen;	Federn;	Tafeln;	Herzen;
die guten;	meine guten;	Grafen;	Federn;	Tafeln;	Herzen.

EXAMPLES OF THE VARIOUS DECLENSIONS IN THE PLURAL.

Industrious mechanics have hard hands. The arms of the industrious laborers are strong. Wicked princes write unjust laws with the sharp swords of bad and ignorant men. He writes with new pens, I with old ones. Do good princes oppress their poor subjects? Who are good princes? Are all princes, emperors, kings and dukes oppressors? Good men are never oppressors of the poor, the weak or the ignorant. Good citizens are also good soldiers in all just wars. This beautiful green field and those fine houses belong to the old enemies of our poor neighbors. These old men are the fathers and uncles of our young friends. The daughters of these old ladies are our good friends. The scholars of your sisters are my cousins. The new benches, chairs and tables in these schools are not good. These little girls are very diligent and attentive scholars. Idle men are neither great men nor good men; my young friends, do you forget it? Do you see those little birds on the steep roofs of those large houses behind the tall trees? All really good men are industrious men. Really good men are never indolent men. Are all good soldiers also good citizens? The soldiers have the fat oxen of the poor peasants. We are a fortunate people, for we have neither emperors, kings, dukes nor noblemen in our country

LESSON XXII. Section XXII.
COMPARISON OF ADJECTIVES.

1. The *comparative* is formed by suffixing r* or er; and the *superlative*, by suffixing st or est*, to the positive; as,

Positive.	Comparative.	Superlative.
mild, mild;	milder, milder;	mildest, mildest;
weise, wise;	weiser, wiser;	weisest, wisest;
schön, beautiful;	schöner, more beautiful;	schönst, most beautiful,
laut, loud;	lauter, louder;	lautest, loudest.

2. When the positive is a monosyllable, the root vowels a, o, u, generally assume the Umlaut; as,

alt, old;	älter, older;	ältest, oldest;
grob, coarse;	gröber, coarser;	gröbst, coarsest;
klug, prudent;	klüger, more prudent;	klügst, most prudent.

Exceptions: bunt, falb, fahl, fade, hohl, hold, kahl, karg, knapp, lahm, lass, matt, morsch, platt, plump, rasch, roh, rund, sacht, satt, schlaff, schlank, schroff, starr, stolz, straff, stumm, stumpf, toll, voll, wahr, zahm.

With regard to the following adjectives usage varies; some authors writing them with, others without the Umlaut: bang, barsch, blank, blass, bloss, brav, dumpf, falsch, flach, froh, fromm, gesund, glatt, klar, lose, nackt, nass, zart.

3. The following are irregular:

gross, large;	grösser, larger;	grösst, largest;
gut, good;	besser, better;	best, best;
hoch, high;	höher, higher;	höchst, highest;
nahe, near;	näher, nearer;	nächst, nearest;
viel, much, many;	mehr,† more;	meist (or mehrst), most.

4. The uninflected form of the comparative is used only predicatively; as,

Er ist reich, aber ich bin noch reicher. He is rich but I am still richer.

5. When the superlative is used predicatively, it usually stands in the dative after am (see L. 15. 4.); as,

Er ist am reichsten. He is the richest. Literally; he is at the richest.

6. When used attributively the comparative and superlative are subject to the same rules of declension as the positive; as,

---

* When the positive ends in e, the *comparative* adds only r; as, müde, weary; müder, more weary. When the positive ends in d, t, ß, sch, t, or z, the *superlative* adds est; as, mild, milder; mildest, mildest.

† Mehr is of ten rendered "longer"; as, er ist nicht mehr hier; he is no longer (not more) here; ich habe kein Geld mehr, I have no longer any money, (ich habe nicht mehr Geld; I have no more money).

EXERCISES ON THE COMPARISON OF ADJECTIVES.

Ein besserer Hut.	A better hat.
Der bessere Wein.	The better wine.
Mein theuerster Freund.	My dearest friend.
Der theuerste Freund.	The dearest friend.

7. The superlative is often suffixed to the genitive plural of all; as,

Dieser Hut ist der allerschönste.   This hat is the finest of all.

8. When two qualities of the same object are compared, the word mehr before the unchanged form of the positive is employed; as,

Er ist mehr tapfer als klug.   He is more brave than prudent.

9. Je — desto (sometimes desto — je), or je — je, with the comparative of adjectives, answers to "the—the", in the like construction in English; as,

Je größer desto besser.   The larger the better.
Je mehr je munterer.   The more the merrier.

10. After desto, the position of the verb and its subject is reversed; as,

Je fleißiger er ist, desto schneller lernt   The more diligent he is, the
er (instead of er lernt).   faster he learns (learns he).

Exercise 40. Aufgabe 40.

1. Ist die Eiche ein nützlicherer Baum als die Tanne? 2. Ist nicht das (L. 46.) Eisen ein nützlicheres Metall als das Gold? 3. Stahl ist härter als Eisen, welches ist das härteste Metall? 4. Welches ist das härteste Holz? 5. Welches das weichste? 6. Welches ist das glücklichste Land? 7. Welches das unglücklichste? 8. Welche Nation hat die schönste Sprache und welche die häßlichste? 9. Welche die leichteste und welche die schwerste? 10. Wo ist die Luft am kältesten und wo am wärmsten? 11. Welcher ist der größte und welcher der kleinste Vogel? 12. Wer ist freigebiger als die schwedische Nachtigall? 13. Wer ist ein größerer Geist als der jetzige Staatssecretär der Vereinigten Staaten? 14. Welches Land hat die schnellsten und besten Schiffe und Dampfboote? 15. Welche ist die beste Aufgabe in diesem Buche? 16. Wohnt Ihr Freund nicht mehr hier? 17. Je mehr ich verdiene, desto mehr gebe ich den Armen. 18. Welche ist die angenehmste Jahreszeit?

Exercise 41. Aufgabe 41.

1. Which is the largest animal, and which is the most useful? 2. Which is the most patient? 3. Is the hardest metal also the most useful? 4. In what country do we find the largest trees? 5. Is the winter a more pleasant season of the year than the autumn? 6. Why is the summer more pleasant than the spring? 7 In what country are the camel and the elephant more useful than the horse? 8. Do you find this language more difficult than that? 9. Why is the oak more useful than the pine? 10. Which is the richest nation in the world? 11. Is the lily more beautiful than

the pink? 12. Which is the largest of the United States, and which is the richest? 13. Are the richest men also the most generous? 14. Have you a better knife than this? 15. Is this a better hat than that? 16. Why is the most industrious man the happiest? 17. Why are we less happy than our neighbors?

LESSON XXIII. Section XXIII.

ADJECTIVES USED SUBSTANTIVELY AND ADVERBIALLY.

1. The adjective is used substantively, and is then written with a capital initial: —

  a. to express a quality taken in the abstract; as,

Vom Erhabenen zum Lächerlichen ist nur ein Schritt.	From the sublime to the ridiculous is but a step.
Es ist ihm ein Leichtes.	It is an easy thing for him.
Es ist für das allgemeine Beste.	It is for the general good (best).
Wissen Sie das Nähere von der Sache?	Do you know the particulars (nearer details) of the affair?

  b. when it refers to persons; as,

Der Gute ist glücklich, der Böse ist elend.	The good (man) is happy, the bad (man) is miserable.
Die Guten sind glücklich, die Bösen sind elend.	The good are happy, the bad are miserable.
Liebe deinen Nächsten wie dich selbst.	Love thy neighbor as thyself.
„Nicht fürchtet der Schwache, der Friedliche mehr, des Mächtigen Beute zu werden."	The feeble (man), the peaceful (man) is no longer afraid of becoming the prey of the strong.
Dieser Deutsche ist ein Gelehrter.	This German is a learned (man).
Dieser Gelehrte ist ein Deutscher.	This learned (man) is a German.
Jene Schöne ist sehr stolz.	That fair one is very proud.
Guten Morgen, mein Kleiner.	Good morning, my little fellow.
Er bemerkt wie die Grollenden (L. 27. *Obs.*) flüstern.	He perceives how the grumblers (grumbling ones) whisper.

2. The adjective sometimes rejects the inflectional endings in the nominative and accusative neuter; as,

  Kalt (for kaltes) Wasser. Alt (for altes) Eisen. Sein unwürdig (for unwürdiges) Vaterland.

3. When several adjectives qualify the same noun, the inflectional endings of all but the last, are sometimes dropped, and the omission marked by a hyphen; as,

Die schwarz-roth-goldene Fahne.	The black red golden banner.

4. The last syllable of compound, or derivative adjectives, is in like manner sometimes omitted; as,

Niemand war so freuden- und schlaflos wie er.	No one was as joyless and sleepless as he.

5. When several adjectives precede a noun in the dative masculine or neuter, the first one frequently takes the *old*, and the others the *new* declension; as,

Nach langem verderblichen Streit. Instead of, Nach langem verderblichem Streit. After long destructive strife.

6. Adjectives in all degrees of comparison (in the form in which they occur as predicate) are employed adverbially; as,

Sie schreiben schlecht, er schreibt schlechter, und ich schreibe am schlechtesten. — You write badly, he writes worse, and I write the worst.

Ich habe ein ganz neues Haus. — I have an entirely new house.

7. The superlative preceded by aufs or zum, is also used adverbially; as,

Er beleidigte ihn aufs Grausamste. He insulted him most cruelly.

8. The adjectives eitel and lauter, are sometimes placed without inflection before nouns, in the signification of "all", "nothing but"; as,

Wir stolzen Menschenkinder sind eitel arme Sünder. — We proud sons of men are nothing but poor sinners.

Sie ist lauter Leben. — She is all life.

9. Adjectives are formed from names of material by suffixing to nouns n, en or ern; and if capable of it, the radical vowel often assumes the Umlaut; as,

ledern, leathern, from Leder; golden, golden, from Gold.
stählern, steel, from Stahl; hölzern, wooden, from Holz.

10. A clause or sentence is sometimes used adjectively; as,

Die nie zu vergessende Schlacht bei Leipzig. — The never to-be-forgotten battle near (by) Leipsic.

Ein Satz ist ein in Worten ausgedrückter Gedanke. — A sentence is a thought expressed in words.
Literally, an in-words-expressed thought.

11. An Adjective preceded by the article, is sometimes placed *after* the noun which it qualifies; as,

Du sollst diesen Krieg, den fürchterlichen, enden. — Thou shalt end this dreadful war (this war, the dreadful).

12. Adjectives derived from the names of countries or nations do not begin with a capital letter except when used substantively; as,

Das deutsche Heer. — The German army.
Die französische Sprache. — The French language.
Ein preußischer Soldat. — A Prussian soldier.
Er wohnt im Bremischen. — He lives in (the territory of) Bremen.

Der kölnische Dom. — The Cathedral of Cologne

13. Adjectives are also formed from names of persons by the suffix isch, and generally written with a capital initial; as,

Die Kantische Philosophie.	The Kantian philosophy.
Das Tilly'sche Heer.	Tilly's army (the Tillian army).
Die Lutherische Kirche.	The Lutheran Church.

14. Instead of the adjective in isch, derived from names of places, the substantive form in er (undeclined) is generally used; as,

Die Leipziger Zeitung.	The Leipsic Gazette.
Der Magdeburger Dom.	The Cathedral of Magdeburg.
Wir sahen den Magdeburger Dom.	We saw the Cathedral of Magdeburg.

Exercise 42.   Aufgabe 42.

1. Mancher Reiche ist unzufrieden und folglich unglücklich; und mancher Arme ist zufrieden und glücklich. 2. Ein Unzufriedener, oder eine Unzufriedene ist nicht glücklich. 3. Der Nachlässige erfüllt nicht seine Pflichten, er ist daher nicht zufrieden und folglich nicht glücklich. 4. Der Neidische ist immer unzufrieden. 5. Ich beneide nicht die Reichen, aber ich bedauere die Armen. 6. Der Geizige führt ein elendes Leben. 7. Der Blinde ist unglücklicher und hülfloser als der Taube oder der Lahme. 8. Nicht jeder Gelehrte ist ein Weiser und nicht jeder Weise ist ein Gelehrter. 9. Das Praktische und Nützliche ist besser als das Schöne. 10. Diese schönen Kinder singen schön. 11. Der Bediente dieses jungen Deutschen ist der Vetter eines alten Gesandten. 12. Niemand ist elender und thörichter als der Neidische. 13. Der Fleißige lernt schnell, der Faule langsam. 14. Der Mensch verlangt erst das Neue, suchet das Nützliche dann mit unermüdlichem Fleiße. 15. Ein Reicher ist oft unglücklicher als ein Armer. 16. Ich habe einen ledernen Schuh, einen goldenen Ring und ein bleiernes Tintenfaß.

Exercise 43.   Aufgabe 43.

1. A miser is always an envious man, and therefore an unhappy one. 2. Many a learned man is not a wise one. 3. We pity the poor, but we do not envy the rich. 4. The practical is better than the agreeable and the beautiful. 5. He learns faster than we. 6. She is contented, and he is discontented, for she is industrious, and he is idle. 7. He learns slowly for he does not study industriously. 8. The idle man leads a miserable life for he is always discontented and consequently unhappy. 9. Who is more foolish and more miserable than the miser? 10. Do you write more letters than your brother? 11. The lame man pities the deaf one. 12. The blind man is still more unfortunate than the deaf one. 13. The industrious man is not often discontented. 14. Who learns slowly, and who learns rapidly? 15. I have a gold ring, a steel chain and a wooden table.

PERSONAL PRONOUNS AND THE REFLEXIVE PRONOUN ſich. 57

LESSON XXIV. Section XXIV.

PERSONAL PRONOUNS AND THE REFLEXIVE PRONOUN ſich.

1. The genitive of the German personal pronouns, unlike the *possessive* in English (see L. 9. 2), does not express the relation of property or possession, but simply answers to our objective with (and sometimes without) a preposition; as,

Gedenke meiner (*gen.*). Think of me, or remember me (*obj.*).
Es ſind euer ſechs und ihrer nur vier. (L. 49. 7.) There are six of you (of you six) and only four of them.

DECLENSION OF THE PERSONAL PRONOUNS.

SINGULAR.

N. ich, I; du, thou; (Sie, you);
G. meiner*, of me; deiner*, of thee; (Ihrer, of you);
D. mir, to me; dir, to, for thee; (Ihnen, to, for you);
A. mich, me; dich, thee; (Sie, you).

PLURAL.

N. wir, we; ihr, you; (Sie, you);
G. unſer, of us; euer, of you; (Ihrer, of you);
D. uns, to, for us; euch, to, for you; (Ihnen, to, for you);
A. uns, us; euch, you; (Sie, you).

SINGULAR.

Masculine. *Feminine.* *Neuter.*
N. er, he; ſie, she; es, it;
G. ſeiner*, of him; ihrer, of her; ſeiner, of it;
D. ihm, to him; ihr, to, for her; ihm, to, for it;
A. ihn, him; ſie, her; es, it.

PLURAL OF ALL GENDERS.

N. ſie, they; ſie, they; ſie, they;
G. ihrer, of them; ihrer, of them; ihrer, of them;
D. ihnen, to them; ihnen, to, for them; ihnen, to, for them,
A. ſie, them; ſie, them; ſie, them.

2. The pronouns of the first and second persons are often used reflexively, and then answer to our compound personal pronouns; as,

Ich lobe mich. I praise myself.
Du lobſt dich. Thou praisest thyself.
Wir loben uns. We praise ourselves.

---
* Instead of meiner, deiner, ſeiner, the forms mein, dein, ſein are sometimes used.

3. The reflexive pronoun ſich (French se) has but one form for both numbers and all genders, and is only used in the dative and accusative cases; as,

Der Mann lobt ſich.	The man praises himself.
Er gibt ſich viel Mühe.	He gives himself much trouble.
Die Frau lobt ſich.	The woman praises herself.
Das Kind lobt ſich.	The child praises itself.
Die Schüler loben ſich.	The scholars praise themselves.

4. Sich is frequently employed where in English the objective of the personal pronoun is used; as,

Er hat kein Geld bei ſich.	He has no money with him.
Sie haben Freunde bei ſich.	They have friends with them.

5. These pronouns are often used in a reciprocal signification, instead of, or placed before the proper reciprocal einander; as,

Die Hunde beißen ſich; or, die Hunde beißen ſich einander.	The dogs are biting each other, (or, the dogs are biting one another).
Die Schüler loben ſich; or, die Schüler loben ſich einander.	The scholars praise each other, (or, the scholars praise one another).
Warum haßt ihr euch? or, warum haßt ihr euch einander?	Why do you hate each other? (or, why do you hate one another?)

6. The pronoun of the second person singular is employed in addressing the Supreme Being; in proverbial phrases, and in the serious and sublime styles of composition; as,

Dir, mein Gott, Dir ergeb' ich mich!	To Thee, my God, to Thee I resign myself!
Vor allen Dingen wache über dich, daß du nie die innere Zuverſicht zu dir ſelber verlierſt!	Above all things, watch over thyself, that thou never lose the inward confidence to thyself!

7. The pronoun of the second person singular is also used in addressing relatives, intimate friends and children; as also when speaking to servants and other dependents; as,

Was lernſt du in der Schule?	What do you learn at school?
Johann, haſt du deine Arbeit gethan?	John, have you done your work?

8. The *plural* of the *second* person was formerly regarded as the most polite and respectful form of address, whether to one person or more, and this is still the case among the peasantry in some parts of Germany. At present, however, it is applied to the same class of persons in the plural, that

Du is in the singular: it is likewise used in addressing religious assemblies. Ihr, addressed to a single individual, implies his inferiority of rank or position; as,

Das glaubt ihr wirklich? sagte der König.	Do you really believe that? said the king.

9. The former use of the second person plural (see 8.) is still retained in the syllable Ew. (contraction of Ewer, an obsolete orthography of euer) which is now construed only with titles, and is followed by a plural verb; as,

Ew. Majestät sind viel witziger als ich.	Your Majesty is (are) much wittier than I.

10. In addressing an inferior, the pronoun of the *third* person singular is sometimes used; as,

Was wünscht Er?	What do you (does he) wish?
Wo wohnt Sie?	Where do you (does she) live?

11. In ordinary intercourse the form of address to one person or more, is with the pronoun of the third person plural, so that, when spoken, the context only can decide whether the second or the third person is meant. In writing, however, these pronouns when referring to the second person, are always written with a capital initial; as,

Haben Sie Ihre Bücher?	Have you your books?
Haben sie ihre Bücher?	Have they their books?
Hat sie ihre Bücher?	Has she her books?
Haben Ihre Freunde Ihre Federn?	Have your friends your pens?
Nein, Ihre Freunde haben sie.	No, your friends have them.

Obs. As the incorrect use of Du, ihr, and er in address, would be regarded as rude, it is better for learners in addressing strangers, always to employ the personal pronoun Sie, and the possessive Ihr.

12. Pronouns referring to neuter appellations of persons, generally follow the natural, instead of the grammatical, gender; as,

Das Söhnchen dieser Dame ist krank; ich fürchte er (or es) wird sterben.	The little son of this lady is sick; I fear he will die.

13. Pronouns representing inanimate objects, must be of the same gender as the nouns to which they refer: hence a pronoun of one gender must often be translated by one of another; as,

Der Hut ist schön, aber er ist zu klein. — The hat is handsome but *it* is too small.
Die Mütze ist schön, aber sie ist zu klein. — The cap is handsome but *it* is too small.

14. In referring to animals, and things, an adverb (formed from an adverb and a preposition) is often employed instead of a preposition and a pronoun; as,

Du hast einen schönen Beutel; hast Du Geld darin? (L. 38. 6.) — You have a fine purse, have you money in it? (therein?)

15. The neuter pronoun *es*, employed as a grammatical subject, may represent nouns of all genders, whether singular or plural. But the verb, in such case, agrees in number with the *noun*, and not, as in English, with the pronoun; as,

Es sind unsere Freunde, welche wir sehen. — It is (are) our friends whom we see.
Wissen Sie, wer es ist? — Do you know who it is?

16. When the logical subject itself is a personal pronoun, *es* comes after the verb; that is, the order of the words is exactly the reverse of the English; as,

Ich bin es.	It is I.	Er ist es.	It is he.
Sind Sie es?	Is it you?	Seid Ihr es?	Is it you?
Wir sind es.	It is we.	Sie sind es.	It is you.

17. Es often stands as the grammatical subject before active verbs, and is used in a variety of phrases where the corresponding English word is omitted: it also frequently answers to *one*, *so*, or *there*; as,

Es heult der Sturm, es braust das Meer. — The storm howls, the sea roars.
Es brachte der Wind den Schall grad von Süden her. — The wind brought the sound directly from the south.
Ich weiß es, daß er kommt. — I know (it) that he is coming.
Es ist Niemand hier. — There is nobody here.
Er ist reich, oder scheint es zu sein. — He is rich, or seems to be so.
Er ist Kaufmann, aber ich bin es nicht. — He is (a) merchant, but I am not one.
Es sind zwei Pferde im Garten. — There are two horses in the garden.

Exercise 44.   Aufgabe 44.

1. Wer lobt den Enkel? 2. Der Großvater lobt ihn. 3. Wer lobt die Großmutter? 4. Die Enkelin lobt sie. 5. Hat der Maurer den Ball? 6. Nein, der Böttcher hat ihn. 7. Hat das Mädchen die Brustnadel? 8. Nein, die Tante hat sie. 9. Hat die Putzmacherin Ihren neuen Hut? 10. Nein, der Hutmacher hat ihn. 11. Was hat die Schwester Ihres

Freundes? 12. Sie hat die Feder ihres Bruders. 13. Was haben die Schwestern Ihrer Freunde? 14. Sie haben die Federn Ihrer Brüder. 15. Loben Sie Ihre Freunde? 16. Nein, ich lobe sie nicht. 17. Loben Sie mich? 18. Nein, ich lobe Sie nicht. 19. Loben Sie Ihre Brüder? 20. Nein, ich lobe sie nicht. 21. Geben Sie uns Geld? 22. Nein, ich gebe Ihnen Brod. 23. Geben Sie Ihren Freunden Brod? 24. Nein, ich gebe ihnen Geld. 25. Was sagest du mir? 26. Ich sage dir nichts. 27. Was schenken Sie Ihrer Mutter? 28. Ich schenke ihr einen seidenen Geldbeutel. 29. Schenken Sie Ihrem Bruder etwas? 30. Nein, ich schenke ihm nichts. 31. Ich gehe mit meiner Schwester zu ihrer Freundin. 32. Er hat einen Ofen in seinem Zimmer, aber es ist kein Feuer darin. 33. Es ist ein großer Unterschied zwischen Lügen und Liegen. 34. Sie haben hübsche Bücher und lesen ziemlich gut darin. 35. Jener Schüler lobt sich, aber dieser lobt sich nicht. 36. Wirklich verdienstvolle Leute loben sich nicht.

Exercise 45.   Aufgabe 45.

1. Have you my pen? 2. No, the mason has it. 3. Who has my new black hat? 4. The old hatter has it. 5. Do you give the breastpin to your mother? 6. No, my sister gives it to her. 7. Does your old neighbor praise his friends? 8. No, he does not praise them, they praise him. 9. Do you praise your sister? 10. No, I do not praise her. 11. Do you praise your friends? 12. No, I do not praise them. 13. Has your brother your pens? 14. No, my sister has them. 15. What do you give me? 16. I give you nothing. 17. Do you give your friends anything? 18. Yes, I give them money. 19. Has the mason his ball? 20. No, his grandfather has it. 21. Has the milliner your silk hats? 22. No, her friend has them. 23. What do you say to the man? 24. I do not say anything to him. 25. Do you go with your friend to your father? 26. No, I go with him to his father. 27. Do you go with your friend to your mother? 28. No, I go with her to her mother. 29. She goes with me to her. 30. There is no bread on the table. 31. There are no good pens in my desk. 32. These children have pretty books, do they read in them? 33. We have pretty cold weather. 34. Industrious scholars do not praise themselves. 35. These proud boys praise themselves, but their father does not praise them. 36. We are going with you to your teacher.

LESSON XXV.   Section XXV.

ABSOLUTE POSSESSIVE PRONOUNS.

1. When the possessive pronouns relate, attributively, to a noun understood, and are not followed by an adjective, they are called absolute possessive pronouns. They are of two forms: mein-er, e, es, inflected like an adjective of the *old* declension; and der, die, das mein-ige or der, die, das mein-e, inflected like an adjective of the *new* declension.

ABSOLUTE POSSESSIVE PRONOUNS.

	Masculine.	Feminine.	Neuter.	
OLD DECLENSION.				
Nom	meiner;	meine;	meines;	mine;
Gen.	meines;	meiner;	meines;	of mine;
Dat.	meinem;	meiner;	meinem;	to, or for mine;
Acc.	meinen;	meine;	meines;	mine.
NEW DECLENSION.				
Nom.	der meinige;	die meinige;	das meinige;	mine;
Gen.	des meinigen;	der meinigen;	des meinigen;	of mine;
Dat.	dem meinigen;	der meinigen;	dem meinigen;	to, for mine;
Acc.	den meinigen;	die meinige;	das meinige;	mine.
Nom.	der meine;	die meine;	das meine;	mine;
Gen.	des meinen;	der meinen;	des meinen;	of mine;
Dat.	dem meinen;	der meinen;	dem meinen,	to, for mine;
Acc.	den meinen;	die meine;	das meine;	mine.

All genders in the plural.

	OLD.	NEW.	NEW.	
Nom.	meine;	die meinigen,	or die meinen;	mine;
Gen.	meiner;	der meinigen,	or der meinen;	of mine;
Dat.	meinen;	den meinigen,	or den meinen;	to, for mine
Acc.	meine;	die meinigen,	or die meinen;	mine.

EXAMPLES OF THE ABSOLUTE POSSESSIVE PRONOUNS.

Form of the old declension.	*Forms of the new declension.*	
Mein Hut ist schwarz und seiner ist weiß.	Mein Hut ist schwarz und der seine or der seinige ist weiß.	My hat is black and his is white.
Sein Hut ist schwarz und meiner ist weiß.	Sein Hut ist schwarz und der meine or der meinige ist weiß.	His hat is black and mine is white.
Mein Buch ist neu und seines ist alt.	Mein Buch ist neu und das seine or das seinige ist alt.	My book is new and his is old.
Sein Buch ist neu und meines ist alt.	Sein Buch ist neu und das meine or das meinige ist alt.	His book is new and mine is old.
Er geht zu meinem Freund und nicht zu deinem.	Er geht zu meinem Freund und nicht zu dem deinen or dem deinigen.	He is going to my friend and not to yours.

2. These pronouns are likewise substantively employed to denote property or obligation; as,

| Die Liebe sucht nicht das Ihre. | Charity seeks not her own. |
| Ich habe das Meinige gethan, thue das Deinige. | I have done mine (my duty), do thine. |

a. In like manner they refer, in the plural, to one's family or relatives: — likewise, when the application is obvious, to dependents, as servants, soldiers, &c. ; as,

Er verläßt die Seinigen nicht.	He forsakes not his own.
Er fiel mit den Seinen in der Schlacht.	He fell with his (soldiers) in the battle.

3. Kein and the numeral ein, when not followed by an adjective or a noun, are inflected like an adjective of the *old* declension (except that, in the neuter, they often end in s instead of es); as,

Er hat ein Buch, du hast eins (or eines), und ich habe keins (or keines).	He has a book, you have one, and I have none.
Er hat zwei Bücher und sie hat nur eins.	He has two books and she has only one.

b. Ein when preceded by the definite article is inflected like an adjective of the *new* declension ; as,

Der eine ist zu groß und der andere ist zu klein.	The one is too large and the other is too small.

4. The indeclinable forms meinesgleichen, deinesgleichen, &c., may refer to nouns of all genders and both numbers ; as,

Ist er denn meinesgleichen?	Is he my equal then?
Sie waren früher deinesgleichen.	They were formerly your equals.

Exercise 46. Aufgabe 46.

1. Ich habe meinen Pinsel und den Ihrigen, sein Buch und das meinige. 2. Welches Taschentuch haben Sie, das meinige oder das seinige? 3. Ich habe das seinige und auch das Ihrige. 4. Zu welchem Arzt gehst du, zu dem meinigen oder zu dem deinigen? 5. Ich gehe zu dem deinigen. 6. Er hat zwei Wörterbücher, Sie haben eins und ich habe keins. 7. Welches Sandfaß hat Ihr Freund, meines oder seines? 8. Er hat seines und ich habe Ihres. 9. Sein Vormund ist reich und meiner ist arm. 10. Mein Schlüssel ist groß und der seinige ist klein. 11. Das Weltmeer ist zwischen mir und den Meinigen. 12. Alle Menschen lieben die Ihrigen und verlangen das Ihrige. 13. Ich habe Ihre Zeitung und Sie haben die meinige. 14. Unsere Bücher liegen auf dem Tische, und die Ihrigen auf dem Pulte. 15. Welche Pferde haben Sie, die Ihren oder die meinen? 16. Ich habe die Ihren und die meinen. 17. Alle Menschen haben ihre Fehler und Eigenheiten, ich habe die meinigen, du hast die deinigen und er hat die seinigen. 18. Jedermann schätzt das Seine.

Exercise 47. Aufgabe 47.

1. Have you my carriage or yours? 2. I have yours. 3. Has the scholar your book or his? 4. He has his and mine. 5. Are our books in his room or in yours? 6. They are in mine, and his pens are in yours. 7. Do you go with my friend or with yours? 8. We go with yours. 9. Is his sister or mine in the garden?

10. Yours is in the garden, and his is going into the garden. 11. Have you my pen or yours? 12. I have neither yours nor mine, I have his. 13. Have you our books or yours? 14. We have yours and ours. 15. Our house is new and yours is old. 16. His pen is good and hers is bad. 17. Are your friends in your house or in ours? 18. They are in ours. 19. We have our friend's horses and he has ours. 20. Your paper is white and ours is blue.

LESSON XXVI.   Section XXVI.
USE OF THE TENSES.

1. The *present* is often used in relation to the *past*, when the period referred to is still unfinished; as,

Ich lese schon eine Stunde.   I (have) read already an hour.
Wie lange sind Sie in Dresden?   How long are you (have you been) in Dresden?

2. The *present* for the *future* is more usual in German than in English; as,

Morgen gehe ich nach Leipzig.   To-morrow I (shall) go to Leipsic.
Ich gebe Ihnen einen Gulden für das Buch.   I give (will give) you a florin for the book.

3. The *imperfect* corresponds mainly to the same tense in English; as,

Friedrich der Zweite war ein großer Krieger.   Frederic the second was a great warrior.
Sie arbeitete, während ich spielte.   She worked while I was playing

4. In compound tenses and principal sentences, the infinitive or participle comes *last*; as,

Ich habe ein Buch gehabt.   I have had a book.
Ich werde den Mann loben.   I shall praise the man.
Er hat nicht Zeit das Buch zu lesen.   He has not time to read the book.
Er wird es gehabt haben.   He will have had it.

5. The *perfect*, unlike the same tense in English, may be used with an adverb referring to *past*, as well as to present time; as,

Ich habe es gestern gehabt.   I (have) had it yesterday.

6. The *futures* are used as in English, and also to indicate a probability; in which case the *first* future is to be rendered by the *present*, and the *second* future, by the *imperfect*, or *perfect*, in connection with an appropriate adverb; as,

Er wird Ihr Bruder sein.   He is probably your brother.
Sie werden es gehört haben.   They have probably heard it.

7. Often, in German, a verb is repeated, or entirely omitted, where in English an auxiliary is employed; as,

CONJUGATION OF haben.

Er denkt wie ich (or, wie ich denke). He thinks as I do (or, as I think).
Sie kennen ihn, ich nicht. You know him, I (do) not.
Ich habe es gehört, er nicht (or, er hat es nicht gehört). I have heard it, he (has) not. He has not heard it.

8. CONJUGATION OF haben.

INFINITIVE

Present.
haben, to have

Perfect.
gehabt haben, to have had.

PARTICIPLES.

Present.
habend, having.

Perfect.
gehabt, had.

INDICATIVE.

Singular. *Plural.*

PRESENT.

ich habe, I have;
du hast, thou hast;
er hat, he has;

wir haben, we have,
ihr habt, you have;
sie haben, they have.

IMPERFECT.

ich hatte, I had;
du hattest, thou hadst;
er hatte, he had;

wir hatten, we had;
ihr hattet, you had;
sie hatten, they had.

PERFECT.

ich habe ⎫   I have   ⎫   wir haben ⎫   we have   ⎫
du hast ⎬ gehabt, thou hast   ⎬ had;   ihr habet ⎬ gehabt, you have ⎬ had.
er hat   ⎭   he has   ⎭   sie haben ⎭   they have ⎭

PLUPERFECT.

ich hatte   ⎫   I had   ⎫   wir hatten ⎫   we had   ⎫
du hattest ⎬ gehabt, thou hadst ⎬ had;   ihr hattet ⎬ gehabt, you had ⎬ had.
er hatte   ⎭   he had   ⎭   sie hatten ⎭   they had ⎭

FIRST FUTURE.

ich werde ⎫   I shall   ⎫   wir werden ⎫   we shall ⎫
du wirst ⎬ haben,   thou wilt   ⎬ have;   ihr werdet ⎬ haben,   you will ⎬ have.
er wird   ⎭   he will   ⎭   sie werden ⎭   they will ⎭

SECOND FUTURE.

ich werde ⎫   I shall   ⎫   wir werden ⎫   we shall ⎫
du wirst ⎬ gehabt haben, thou wilt ⎬ have had; ihr werdet ⎬ gehabt haben, you will ⎬ have had.
er wird   ⎭   he will   ⎭   sie werden ⎭   they will ⎭

IMPERATIVE

habe (du), have (thou).   habet or habt (ihr) have (ye, or you).

9. IDIOMS WITH haben.

Er hat gern ein warmes Zimmer.	He likes a warm room.
Habe alle Menschen lieb.	Love all men.
Ich habe nichts dagegen.	I have no objection.
Es hat nichts zu sagen.	It is no matter (worth speaking of).
Er hat Langeweile.	He feels ennui ("bored").
Er hat keinen Verdacht auf Sie.	He does not suspect you.
Ich habe ihn in Verdacht gestohlen zu haben.	I suspect him of having (to have) stolen.
Er hat kein Geld nöthig.	He is not in want of money.
Ich werde Acht auf ihn haben.	I will attend to (take care of) him.
Was hast du?	What ails you?
Du hast gut lachen.	You may well laugh.
Habe ich recht oder unrecht?	Am I right, or wrong?

EXERCISE 48.   Aufgabe 48.

1. Der strenge alte Lehrer des reichen Jünglings hatte in seiner Jugend einen guten Lehrer gehabt. 2. Kein Feldherr hat je eine bessere Armee gehabt als der französische Kaiser. 3. Die Engländer hatten lange einen sehr ausgebreiteten Handel gehabt und hatten daher eine bessere Flotte als die Franzosen. 4. Wird dieses jetzt so glückliche Land je einen König oder einen Kaiser haben? 5. Die Freunde der (L. 46.) Wahrheit und Gerechtigkeit in Europa werden ihre schlimmste Zeit noch nicht (L. 66.b.) gehabt haben. 6. Sie werden seinen Brief gehabt haben, ehe er kommt; denn er wird nicht vor acht Uhr kommen. 7. Haben Sie vorgestern Besuch gehabt? 8. Nein, ich habe keinen gehabt, und werde auch keinen haben; denn ich habe keine Freunde in dieser Gegend. 9. Ein Verwandter Ihres Freundes macht meinem Bruder einen Besuch. 10. Wie lange wohnen Sie in diesem Hause? 11. Wir wohnen schon länger als zehn Jahre darin.

EXERCISE 49.   Aufgabe 49.

1. No army has ever had a better general than Napoleon. 2. What nation has had a more extensive commerce than England? 3. Have the French ever had a better fleet than they now have? 4. Kings and emperors do not always (L. 39. 8.) love truth and justice. 5. That country is very unfortunate, for it has a bad king. 6. The friends of (L. 46.) truth in this country have probably had their worst time. 7. How long have you had this wagon? 8. Did you have company yesterday? 9. We had company day before yesterday, but we have had none to-day. 10. Have you relations in this city? 11. No, I have no relations in this country. 12. This relation of my friend is making us a visit. 13. Who has ever had, or ever will have better friends than we? 14. How long have you been in this city?

LESSON XXVII.   Section XXVII.

Regular Verbs or Verbs of the New Conjugation.

PRESENT INFINITIVE.

1. The present infinitive ends in en; as,
lob-en, to praise; lieb-en, to love; bet-en, to pray; ſtudir-en, to study; verkauf-en, to sell; bettel-n,* to beg.

Root.

2. The root is that part of the verb which precedes the en of the infinitive, and to which the various terminational endings are suffixed. Thus, the roots of the above verbs are, lob-, lieb-, bet-, ſtudir-, verkauf-, &c.

PRESENT PARTICIPLE.

3. The present participle is formed by suffixing end to the root; as,
lob-end, praising; lieb-end, loving; bet-end, praying; ſtudir-end, studying; verkauf-end, selling; bettel-nd,* begging.

PERFECT PARTICIPLE.

4. The perfect participle is formed by *suf*fixing t or et, and (in verbs that have the accent on the first syllable), *pre*fixing the augment ge to the root; as,
ge-lob-t, praised; ge-lieb-t, loved; ge-bet-et, prayed; ſtudir-t, studied; verkauf-t, sold; ge-bettel-t, begged.

Obs. The participles are subject to the same rules of declension and comparison (except that they do not take the Umlaut) as the adjective; as,

Ein liebender Vater.	A loving father.
Der geliebte Vater.	The beloved father.
Die reiſenden Maler.	The traveling painters.
Die Weinende.	The weeping one.
Der Trauernde.	The mourner.
Das rührendſte Schauſpiel.	The most touching spectacle.

PRESENT TENSE.

5. The first person singular adds e, the second eſt or ſt,† and the third et or t† to the root; as,

---

*) When the root ends in el, or er, the e of the termination is dropped; as, bettel-n, zitter-n, instead of bettel-en, zitter-en, &c. The e of the root is also often dropped in the first person singular of the present; as, ich bett-le, instead of ich bett-ele, &c.

†) In the indicative, the shorter forms (ſt and t) are usually preferred where euphony will admit; as, lobſt, lobt, rather than lobeſt, lobet, &c.

CONJUGATION OF THE REGULAR VERB.

1st. Person Singular.	2d. Person Singular.	3d. Person Singular
ich lob-e, I praise;	du lob-ſt, thou praisest;	er lob-t, he praises;
ich bet-e, I pray;	du bet-eſt, thou prayest;	er bet-et, he prays;
ich ſtudir-e, I study;	du ſtudir-ſt, thou studiest;	er ſtudir-t, he studies;
ich ſchneid-e, I cut;	du ſchneid-eſt, thou cuttest;	er ſchneid-et, he cuts.

The first and third person plural add en, and the second et or t to the root; as,

1st. Person Plural.	3d. Person Plural.	2d. Person Plural.
wir lob-en, we praise;	ſie lob-en, they praise;	ihr lob-et, or lob-t,* you praise;
wir bet-en, we pray;	ſie bet-en, they pray;	ihr bet-et, you pray;
wir leid-en, we suffer;	ſie leid-en, they suffer;	ihr leid-et, you suffer;

IMPERFECT TENSE.

6. The first and third persons singular add te, and the second person, teſt (if the root end in d, or t, ete and eteſt are added); as,

ich lob-te, I praised; er lob-te, he praised; du lob-teſt, thou praisedst,
ich ſchick-te, I sent; er ſchick-te, he sent; du ſchick-teſt, thou sentest;
ich bet-ete, I prayed; er bet-ete, he prayed; du bet-eteſt, thou prayedst;

The first and third persons plural add ten, and the second tet (if the root end in d, or t, eten and etet are added); as,

wir lob ten, we praised; ſie lob-ten, they praised; ihr lob-tet, you praised;
wir ſchick-ten, we sent; ſie ſchick-ten, they sent; ihr ſchick-tet, you sent·
wir bet-eten, we prayed; ſie bet-eten, they prayed; ihr bet-etet, you prayed

PERFECT AND PLUPERFECT TENSES.

7. The perfect and pluperfect are formed by combining the perfect participle with the present and the imperfect of haben (or ſein); as,

ich habe gelobt;	I have praised;
ich hatte gelobt;	I had praised;
wir hatten gehört;	we had heard;
ſie haben gelernt;	they have learned.

FIRST AND SECOND FUTURE TENSES.

8. The first and second futures are formed by combining the present and perfect infinitive with the present of the auxiliary werden; as,

ich werde loben;	I shall praise;
ich werde gelobt haben;	I shall have praised;
ſie wird ſchicken;	she will send;
ſie werden ſpielen;	they will play.

---

*) See second note on page 67.

9 CONJUGATION OF THE REGULAR VERB lieben.

INFINITIVE.

Present.
lieben, to love.

Perfect.
geliebt haben, to have loved.

PARTICIPLES.

Present.
liebend, loving.

Perfect.
geliebt, loved.

INDICATIVE.

Singular.   *Plural.*

PRESENT TENSE.

ich liebe, I love;   wir lieben, we love;
du liebst, thou lovest;   ihr liebet, you love;
er liebt, he loves;   sie lieben, they love.

IMPERFECT TENSE.

ich liebte, I loved;   wir liebten, we loved;
du liebtest, thou lovedst;   ihr liebtet, you loved;
er liebte, he loved;   sie liebten, they loved.

PERFECT TENSE.

ich habe } geliebt, I have } loved;   wir haben } geliebt, we have } loved
du hast } thou hast }   ihr habt } you have }
er hat } he has }   sie haben } they have }

PLUPERFECT TENSE.

ich hatte } geliebt, I had } loved;   wir hatten } geliebt, we had } loved
du hattest } thou hadst }   ihr hattet } you had }
er hatte } he had }   sie hatten } they had }

FIRST FUTURE TENSE.

ich werde } lieben, I shall } love;   wir werden } lieben, we shall } love.
du wirst } thou wilt }   ihr werdet } you will }
er wird } he will }   sie werden } they will }

SECOND FUTURE TENSE.

ich werde } geliebt ha-, I shall } have loved;   wir werden } geliebt ha-, we shall } have loved.
du wirst } ben, thou wilt }   ihr werdet } ben, you will }
er wird } he will }   sie werden } they will }

IMPERATIVE.

liebe (du) love (thou).   liebet or liebt (ihr), love (ye or you)

Exercise 50.   Aufgabe 50.

1. Was haben Sie heute in Bremen gekauft? 2. Ich habe heute gar nichts gekauft, aber ich kaufte gestern ein Paar (L. 47. 3.) Handschuhe, zwei Paar Schuhe und ein Dutzend Taschentücher. 3. Der Müller hat gestern hundert Faß Mehl verkauft. 4. Der Buchhändler hat mir gestern

- zwei Buch Schreibpapier (L. 18. 3.) und drei Buch Briefpapier geschickt. 5. Die Eltern werden ihre fleißigen Kinder loben und belohnen. 6. Unsere Freunde werden morgen oder übermorgen zu uns kommen. 7. Die Reformation machte den Niederländern das spanische Joch unerträglich, und weckte bei ihnen das Verlangen und den Muth es zu zerbrechen. 8. Von wem hast du diese Nachricht gehört, und warum glaubst du sie nicht? 9. Für wen haben Sie das Pferd und den Wagen bestellt? 10. Werden Sie morgen nach der Stadt oder zu Ihrem Freunde gehen? 11. Ich werde nicht zu ihm gehen, denn er wird nicht zu Hause sein, er wird morgen einen langen Spaziergang machen. 12. Hat er früher in der Stadt (L. 47. 1.) Hannover gewohnt? 13. Er hat in dem Königreich, aber nicht in der Stadt Hannover gewohnt. 14. Sie folgten uns, bis wir Euch begegneten. 15. Die Stadt Paris liegt an der Seine, und Wien an der Donau.

Exercise 51.   Aufgabe 51.

1. Have you ever lived in the city of Bremen? 2. Why have you not studied your lesson to-day? 3. I have studied it but have not yet learned it, for it is a very difficult one. 4. Our cousins have engaged a horse and a wagon and will come to us to-morrow. 5. How many quires of paper, and how many dozen pens shall you buy? 6. I shall buy no paper and no pens, but I shall buy a pair of shoes, two pairs of gloves and ten pounds of coffee. 7. Your brother has probably heard this news. 8. Our parents took a long walk this morning and we shall take one this evening. 9. When shall you go to Paris, and when will you come to my cousins? 10. Is the city of Bremen larger than the city of Hanover? 11. Did not your friends formerly live in Vienna? 12. Shall you be at home to-morrow evening? 13. The shoemaker has made me two pairs of shoes, and is making my brother a pair of boots. 14. We have bought a horse and sold our oxen.

LESSON XXVIII.   Section XXVIII.

1. The pronoun welcher, is used as a relative and answers to who, which, that.

DECLENSION OF THE RELATIVE welcher.

	Singular.			Plural.	
	MASC.	FEM.	NEUT.	ALL GENDERS.	
N.	welcher,	welche,	welches,	welche,	who, which, that;
G.	welches, dessen,	welcher, deren,	welches, dessen,	welcher, deren	whose, of whom, of which, &c.;
D.	welchem,	welcher,	welchem,	welchen,	to, for whom, which, &c.
A.	welchen,	welche,	welches,	welche,	whom, which, that.

2. The forms dessen, deren, of the genitive, are generally used, except when the pronoun is followed by the noun to which it belongs; as,

Der Mann, dessen (not welches) Buch ich habe, ist krank. — The man whose book I have is sick.
Cicero, welches großen Redners Schriften ich kenne. — Cicero, which great orator's writings I am acquainted with.
Die Leute, deren (not welcher) Geld Sie haben, sind reich. — The people whose money you have are rich.

3. In relative sentences the verb is placed last; as,

Der Mann, welchen ich lobe, ist arm. — The man whom I praise is poor.
Der Mann, welcher mich lobt, ist fleißig. — The man who praises me (who me praises) is industrious.
Ich lobe den Mann, welcher fleißig ist. — I praise the man who is industrious (who industrious is).

4. In compound tenses the main verb immediately precedes the auxiliary; as,

Der Mann, welchen ich gelobt habe, ist Ihr Freund. — The man whom I have praised, is your friend.

Examples.

Principal Sentence.	Relative Sentence.
Dieses ist das Buch,	welches ich gehabt habe.
Ist er der Mann,	welcher so reich ist?
Haben Sie gehört,	was er gesagt hat?
Hat er den Mann gelobt,	welchen ich gelobt habe?
Nicht alle sind zufrieden,	welche reich sind.

5. The relative sentence is frequently introduced between the parts of the principal one; (compare L. 26. 4.); as,

Subject of the Principal Sentence.	Relative Sentence.	Predicate of the Principal Sentence.
Nicht Alle,	welche reich sind,	sind zufrieden.
Der alte Mann,	welchen Sie gelobt haben,	hat Sie gelobt.
Der junge Soldat,	welcher ihn gelobt hat,	hat auch mich gelobt.
Alles,	was er gesagt hat,	ist verständlich.

6. Many other conjunctive words require the same collocation (L. 39.); as,

Er hat mehr Geld gehabt,	als ich gehabt habe.
Sie ist böse,	weil er das Buch gehabt hat.
Wir warteten,	bis wir es gehört hatten.
Sie werden kommen,	wenn sie nicht krank sind.
Wir sind zufrieden,	obgleich wir arm sind.
Er wohnt noch,	wo er gewohnt hat.

7. The pronoun der, die, das, is often used as a relative; **as,**

Ich lobe den Mann, d e r mich lobt. I praise the man *that* praises me.
Der Mann, d e n ich lobe, lobt mich. The man *that* I praise, praises me

RELATIVE PRONOUNS.

In this signification, its form is the same as that of the article, except in the genitive singular, and in the genitive and dative plural.

DECLENSION OF der, die, das, AS RELATIVE PRONOUN.

Singular. *Plural.*

	MASC.	FEM.	NEUT.	ALL GENDERS.
N.	der,	die,	das,	die, who, that, which;
G.	dessen,	deren,	dessen,	deren, whose;
D.	dem,	der,	dem,	denen, to, for whom, that, which;
A.	den,	die,	das,	die, whom, that, which.

8. The indeclinable so, is sometimes used as a relative; as,

Die Heiligen, so auf Erden sind.   The saints that are on earth.

9. Wer may be used with the force of an antecedent and relative; or may be followed by the pronoun der in a subsequent clause; as,

Wer meinen Beutel stiehlt, stiehlt Tand.
Who steals my purse steals trash.

Wen der Herr lieb hat, den züchtiget er.
Whom the Lord loveth (him or that one), he chasteneth.

10. Was is used with the force of antecedent and relative: it also stands as a simple relative after an antecedent that does not refer definitely to a previously expressed noun; as,

Ich sage Ihnen, was ich hörte; or I tell you what I heard.
Ich sage Ihnen das, was ich hörte. I tell you that which I heard.
Verstehen Sie Alles, was ich sage? Do you understand all that I say?

11. Welcher is sometimes used in the signification of "some"*, or "any"*, as a substitute for a previously expressed noun; as,

Ich habe Brod, hast du auch welches?
I have some* bread, have you some too?

Schicken Sie mir etwas Wein, wenn Sie welchen haben.
Send me some wine, if you have any (or some).

12. In referring to animals, and things, an adverb (formed from an adverb and a preposition) is used instead of a pronoun and a preposition (L. 38. 6.), as,

Das Messer, womit ich schneide.   The knife with which (wherewith) I cut.

Weißt Du, wovon er spricht?   Do you know, what he is speaking of?

Literally; do you know whereof he speaks?

---

*) "Some", or "any". before nouns, is translated into German, only when it signifies *a little* or *a few*, in which use it is rendered by etwas, or einiger. See L. 52. 6. 7.

13. In relative sentences the copula is not unfrequently omitted; as,

Der Mann, den ich gesehen, ist sehr arm.	The man whom I have seen is very poor.
Seine Macht war größer, als sie erwartet, größer, als sie gewünscht hatten.	His power was greater than they had expected, greater than they had wished.

14. When the relative pronoun refers to the first or second person, the personal pronoun is repeated after the relative; as,

Ich, der ich Dich so geliebt habe.	I who have so loved thee.
Wir, die wir so arm sind.	We who are so poor.
Du, der Du so glücklich bist.	Thou who art so fortunate.

15. The relative is sometimes placed before the word to which it refers; and is sometimes entirely omitted; as,

Die keinen Führer hatten, denen war sie Führer, instead of,	Who had no guide, to them she was (a) guide.
Sie war denen Führer, die keinen Führer hatten.	She was (a) guide to those who had no guide.
Die so denken, kennen ihn nicht.	(Those) that think thus do not know him.

Exercise 52.   Aufgabe 52.

1. Nehmen Sie heute die schönen Pferde, welche ich gestern gehabt habe? 2. Nein, ich habe den Wagen gekauft, den Sie vorgestern hatten. 3. Ist der Mann, welcher Ihren Wagen hat, Ihr Bruder? 4. Nein, er ist der Bruder des Mannes, in dessen Hause sie wohnen. 5. Die Knaben, deren Bälle Sie haben, sind die Kinder der Frau, deren Geld wir haben. 6. Der Vater liebt den Knaben, den die Mutter lobt. 7. Das Haus, das ich gekauft habe, ist sehr schön. 8. Der Freund, mit welchem ich in die Kirche gehe, ist ein Ausländer. 9. Wer Geld hat, hat gewöhnlich auch Freunde, aber wer keins hat, hat oft keine. 10. Der kleine Vogel, den sie dort auf dem Dache sehen, ist ein Sperling. 11. Der Knabe, welcher nicht fleißig ist, ist kein guter Schüler. 12. Der Hund, den ich jetzt habe, ist gut, aber der andere, den ich hatte, ist nicht gut. 13. Verstehen Ihre Schüler Alles, was Sie ihnen sagen? 14. Sie verstehen, was ich spreche, aber nicht, was ich lese. 15. Die Schuhe, die mir der Schuhmacher gemacht hat, sind zu eng. 16. Der Gerber, dessen Leder der Sattler hat, ist ein reicher Mann. 17. Der Unzufriedene bei den Gaben Gottes ist wie (L. 67. 5.) ein Mensch, der bei einem Gastmahl hungert. 18. Eines Andern Segen ist dem Neidischen ein Degen, der ihn verwundet; eines Andern Schatz ist dem Neidischen eine Katz', so ihn kratzet; eines Andern Kunst ist dem Neidischen ein Dunst, so ihm (L. 50. 7.) die Augen peiniget.

Exercise 53.   Aufgabe 53.

1. The dog that I bought yesterday is very large. 2. The men whose books I have are your friends. 3. The man of whom you are speaking is a brother of the shoemaker who made your shoes

4. The stove that you have in your room belongs to my friend
5. My friend whose stove you have in your room is a very rich man. 6. Does he understand all that you say to him? 7. He understands all that I say but not what you say. 8. The books that you see on that table, belong to the boy who has your pen. 9. The men whom you see in the garden are my neighbors. 10. The man in whose house we live is a tanner. 11. This child is the son of an old lady who is in that church. 12. The woman whose son made our table is in the house. 13. The mother praises the child that loves the father. 14. The foreigner with whom I am going into the garden is a Frenchman. 15. The books that your sister has bought are not new. 16. A boy who is industrious is a good scholar. 17. A man who is lazy is generally poor. 18. You who are so industrious will learn much. 19. I do not understand what you say.

LESSON XXIX.   Section XXIX.

DETERMINATIVE PRONOUNS.

1. Der, die, dasjenige; der, die, dasselbe (declined like der die, das meinige, &c., L. 25.), and solcher, refer to something specified in a succeeding clause; as,

Derjenige, welcher nachläßig ist, lernt nicht schnell.	He (the one) who is negligent does not learn rapidly.
Wir loben diejenigen, die wir lieben.	We praise those whom we love.
Er liest dasselbe Buch, das ich lese.	He reads the same book that I read.
Du hast heute denselben Bleistift, den ich gestern hatte.	You have the same pencil to-day that I had yesterday.
Wir lesen nur solche Bücher, welche lehrreich sind.	We read only such books as (which) are instructive.

2. For derjenige, der may be substitued, in which use its genitive plural is derer instead of deren; as,

Hart ist das Schicksal derer (derjenigen), die sich nicht ernähren können; sie fallen gewöhnlich denen zur Last, die man Reiche nennt.	Hard is the fate of those who cannot support themselves: they generally fall (become) a burden to those who are called the rich.
Der, den du meinst, hat den Preis nicht gewonnen.	The one that you mean, has not won the prize.
Ich bin nicht von denen, die mit Worten tapfer sind.	I am not of those who are valiant with words.

3. In referring to animals, or things, or when the genitive is used partitively; as also to avoid repetition or ambiguity; derselbe is often substituted for a personal pronoun; as,

Er hat mein Messer und schneidet seinen Apfel mit demselben (or damit L. 24. 14.)	He has my knife and is cutting his apple with it (with the same).
Er schneidet seinen Apfel, und gibt mir einen Theil desselben.	He cuts his apple and gives me a part of it (of the same).
Er lobt den Knaben, weil derselbe seine Mutter ehrt.	He praises the boy because he (the same) honors his mother.
Er liebt seinen Bruder, aber nicht die Kinder desselben.	He loves his brother but not his (brother's) children.

4. Solcher is sometimes used instead of a demonstrative or personal pronoun; as,

Als er solches hörte u. s. w.	As he heard this (such), &c.
Die Schnelligkeit mit der er solches ausführte, u. s. w.	The rapidity with which he executed it (such), &c.

5. The adverb eben is often used (intensively) before derselbe and der; as,

Er ist eben derselbe.	He is the very same.

6. The indeclinable selbst (or selber) is often used after a noun or pronoun, and answers to self or selves; as,

Der Mann selbst sagte es.	The man said it himself.
Ich selbst sah den Mann.	I saw the man myself.
Ich sah den Mann selbst.	I saw the man himself.
Wir selbst haben es.	We have it ourselves.
Die Schüler loben sich selbst.	The scholars praise themselves.

7. Selbst is also often an adverb equivalent to *"even"*; as,

Selbst der Knabe hatte es gethan.	Even the boy had done it.

Exercise 54.   Aufgabe 54.

1. Wir loben diejenigen, die wir lieben, und hassen zuweilen diejenigen, die wir noch nicht (L. 66. b.) kennen. 2. Ich habe zwei sehr schöne Pferde gekauft, haben Sie dieselben gesehen? (hast du sie gesehen?) 3. „Du selbst bist dein Teufel oder Engel". 4. Er hat die Fehler eines großen Mannes, ohne die Verdienste desselben. 5. Der Ruhm dessen, der lügt, dauert nicht lange. 6. Ich sehe das Fenster des Hauses, aber nicht die Thüre desselben. 7. Loben Sie die Schüler, weil dieselben fleißig sind? 8. Ich habe die Federn Ihrer Freunde, aber nicht die Messer derselben. 9. Der Oheim liebt seinen Neffen, aber derselbe ist undankbar. 10. Ich schicke diesen Ring demselben Manne, der ihn mir geschickt hat. 11. Sie haben Bücher genug, warum lesen sie dieselben nicht? 12. Haben Sie heute denselben Wagen, den Sie gestern gehabt haben? 13. Nein, ich habe denjenigen, den Sie vorgestern gehabt haben. 14. Der brave Mann denkt an sich selbst zuletzt. 15. Wir lieben nicht Alle, die wir loben. 16. Wir kennen sie, aber wir wissen nicht, wo sie wohnen. 17. Ich lese nur solche Bücher, die nützlich sind. 18. Nur diejenigen, welche fleißig sind, sind zufrieden. 19. Dasjenige ist gut, was nützlich ist. 20. Der Mann, der Ihren Tisch macht, ist derselbe, der *en meinigen gemacht hat.

Exercise 55.   Aufgabe 55.

1. Shall you buy those horses that I had yesterday if they are good? 2. No, I shall buy those that I had the day before yesterday. 3. The boots that the man made are too small and those that the boy made are too large? 4. It is not always those who have much money that are happy. 5. Not all those who are poor are discontented. 6. The hat that I now have is good, the one that I had yesterday is bad. 7. He who is proud is foolish. 8. Do you live in the same house in which I lived? 9. No, I live in the one in which your friend lived. 10. Even those who hated him praised him. 11. The king himself praised the gallant soldier. 12. This is the very same man to whom I sent the ring. 13. I who speak and you who hear will soon be with him for whom we weep. 14. These books are not the ones that I have bought. 15. Do you understand all that you read in this book? 16. We buy only such hats as are good. 17. Those who do not make themselves useful are discontented, and those who are discontented are not happy. 18. All those who are oppressed hate their oppressors. 19. This book is the very same one that I had day before yesterday. 20. That which is neither useful nor agreeable is not good.

LESSON XXX.   Section XXX.

DEMONSTRATIVE PRONOUN der, die, das.

1. Besides the various uses of der, die, das already noted (L. 4. 28. & 29.), it is used as a demonstrative, answering to *that*, and is frequently best rendered by a *personal* pronoun; as,

Der da und ich, wir sind aus Eger.	That (man) yonder and I (we) are from Eger.
Der schadet nicht mehr, ich habe ihn erschlagen.	He (that one) will do no more harm, I have slain him.
Er liebt seinen Bruder, aber nicht dessen Kinder.	He loves his brother, but not his (that's) children.
Du hast meinen Ball und den des Knaben, meine Feder und die des Lehrers, mein Buch und das des Schülers, meine Tische und die der Kinder.	You have my ball and the boy's (that of the boy), my pen and the teacher's (that, &c.), my book and the scholar's (that, &c.), my tables and the children's (those, &c.)

DECLENSION OF THE DEMONST. PRONOUN der, die, das.

	Singular.			Plural.
	MASC.	FEM.	NEUT.	ALL GENDERS.
N.	der,	die,	das, that;	die, those;
G.	dessen	deren	dessen, of that;	deren, of those;
D.	dem,	der,	dem, to, for that;	denen, to, for **those**;
A.	den,	die,	das, that;	die, those.

2. Das, and dieses (dieses being often contracted to dies) as also welches in connection with the verb sein, like es (L. 24.) may refer to nouns of all genders and in both numbers; as,

Wer ist das?	Who is that?
Dies sind Franzosen und das sind Italiener.	These are Frenchmen and those are Italians.
Sind das Ihre Freunde?	Are those your friends?
Welches sind die längsten Nächte?	Which are the longest nights?

3. The indeclinable pronoun man (like the French *on*) indicates persons in a general and indefinite manner and is variously rendered "one", "they" &c.: or, the active form of its verb is translated by our passive; as,

Man sagt, diese Leute haben viel Geld.	They say (or it is said) these people have much money.
Man weiß wo er ist.	It is known where he is.

   a. Man is used in the nominative only; when, therefore, an oblique case is required some other word must be employed; as,

Er will einen (not man) nie hören.	He will never listen to one.
Man sollte alle, sogar seine Feinde, lieben.	One should love all, even one's enemies.
Man sollte sich oft baden.	One should bathe one's-self often.

   b. A personal pronoun is never used as a substitute for „man"; as,

Was man heute thun kann, sollte man (not er) nicht auf morgen verschieben.	What one can do to-day, he (or one) should not postpone till to-morrow.
Man weiß nicht, was man (not er) zu thun hat.	One does not know what one (or he) has to do.

Exercise 56.   Aufgabe 56.

1. Welchen Tisch haben Sie, den des Zimmermanns oder den seines Bruders? 2. Ich habe den des Zimmermanns, der seines Bruders ist auch in meinem Zimmer. 3. Haben Sie die Feder Ihres Freundes oder die Ihrer Freundin? 4. Ich habe weder die meines Freundes noch die meiner Freundin. 5. Haben diese Schüler die Bücher des Knaben oder die des Mannes? 6. Werden Sie in den Häusern der Bauern oder in denen der Kaufleute wohnen? 7. Man findet mehr Unkraut auf den Feldern und Wiesen der Amerikaner als auf denen der Deutschen. 8. Man glaubt, sie werden morgen kommen. 9. Man sagt, daß diese Leute ihre Häuser verkauft haben. 10. Das, was man uns gestern von dem Kriege sagte, ist nicht wahr. 11. Was für Bücher sind das auf ihrem Tische? 12. Das sind französische und dies sind ungarische. 13. Ist es denn wirklich wahr, daß die Schiffe der Amerikaner schneller segeln als die der Europäer? 14. Die Häuser unserer Freunde sind größer als die der Ihrigen

EXERCISE 57.   Aufgabe 57.

1. You have the books of your friend, and I have those of mine. 2. We have your horse and your brother's, our wagon and our father's, your apples and those of your friends. 3. Do you write with our pens or with those of the children? 4. Are your gloves larger than your cousin's? 5. I have been told that you have bought a new carriage, is it true? 6. I have bought two, the captain's and teacher's. 7. These are my books and those are my brother's. 8. That is what I have been told, but I do not believe it. 9. Are the ships of the English better than those of the Dutch? 10. It is said that the Americans have better ships than the English, do you believe that it is true? 11. Is it believed that these people will sell their house? 12. Have you the books of our friends or those of yours? 13. We have those of ours. 14. What is said of these Hungarian books?

LESSON XXXI.   Section XXXI.
AUXILIARIES OF MODE.

1. Können indicates:

a. A possibility dependent on the capabilities of the subject; as,

Der Vogel kann fliegen.	The bird can fly.
Sie können es leicht thun.	You can easily do it.

b. A logical possibility; as,

Man kann es schon gethan haben.	It may have been done already.
Ich gehe nicht, es könnte regnen.	I am not going, it might rain.
Er kann Unrecht haben.	He may be wrong.

Obs. **Können** is often used transitively in the sense of "to understand, to know by heart"; as,

Er kann viele hübsche Lieder.	He knows many pretty songs.
Sie kann englisch und französisch.	She understands English and French.

IDIOMS WITH können.

Ich kann nicht umhin zu lachen.	I can not help laughing.
Ich kann nichts dafür, daß ich arm bin.	I can not help being poor.
Was kannst du denn dafür?	How can you help it?

2. Dürfen indicates:

a. A possibility dependent on the will of another; as,

Der Bauer darf nicht fischen.	The peasant is not allowed (by law) to fish.
Wer des Herrn Joch nicht trägt, darf sich mit seinem Kreuz nicht schmücken.	He who wears not the Lord's yoke must not adorn himself with his cross.

b. In the conditional mode, dürfen often indicates a logical possibility; as,

Es dürfte jetzt zu spät sein.	It might (may) now be too late.
Die Nachwelt dürfte Bedenken tragen dieses Urtheil zu unterschreiben.	Posterity might hesitate to subscribe to (approve) this verdict.

c. The infinitive of dürfen, preceded by zu, is often omitted in translating; as,

Er bat um Erlaubniß, sie besuchen zu dürfen.	He asked (for) permission to (be at liberty to) visit them.

3. Mögen indicates:

a. A possibility dependent on the will of the speaker or the subject, and is frequently used transitively; as,

Du magst den Brief lesen.	You may read the letter.
Ich mag nicht hier bleiben.	I do not wish to remain here.
Ich mag den Wein nicht.	I do not like (wish for) the wine.
Sie mögen uns nicht sehen.	They do not wish to see us.

b. A logical possibility as a concession on the part of the speaker; as,

Er mag ein treuer Freund sein.	He may be a true friend.
Sie mögen es gethan haben.	They may have done it

Obs. Mögen had formerly, and in some parts of Germany still has, the same signification as können; as,
Graben mag ich nicht. Lucas (Luke) 16. 3.

4. Sollen indicates:

a. A necessity dependent on the will of another, or on moral obligation; as,

Diese Furcht soll endigen; ihr Haupt soll fallen; ich will Friede haben.	This fear shall end; her head shall fall; I will have peace.
Ich soll in die Stadt gehen.	I am to go to the city.
Kinder sollen lernen.	Children should (shall) learn.

b. A logical necessity founded on the assertion of others, in which use sollen is usually rendered by "it is said", "is *or* are said to", "it is reported", or by phrases of similar import; as,

Sie sollen sehr reich sein.	They are said to be (or, it is said they are) very rich.
Herzog Johann soll irren im Gebirge.	Duke John is reported to be wandering in the mountains.

c. Sollen, with the verb to which it belongs, often answers in relative sentences, to an infinitive preceded by "*to*"; as,

Er weiß nicht was er thun soll.	He does not know what to do.
Zeige mir wie ich es machen soll.	Show me how to do it.

AUXILIARIES OF MODE.

5. **Wollen** indicates:

    a. A necessity dependent on the will of the subject; as,

Es soll so sein, ich will es so haben.	It shall be so, I will have it so.
Sie wollen nicht gehen.	They will not (do not wish to) go.
Ich wollte es ihm erklären, aber er wollte mich nicht hören.	I was going to explain it to him, but he would not hear me.

    b. A logical necessity dependent on the assertion of the subject; as,

Er will dich gesehen haben.	He insists (will have it) that he has seen you.
Er will, Sie haben Unrecht.	He insists that you are wrong.
Sie sollen in der Stadt sein, die Leute wollen sie gesehen haben.	They are said to be in the city; the people will have it that they have seen them.

6. **Müssen** is the equivalent of "must"; as,

Wir müssen Alle sterben.	We must all die.
Der Senne muß scheiden, der Sommer ist hin.	The shepherd must depart, the summer is past.

7. **Lassen** signifies "to let", "to permit", "to command", as also "to get or have" (in such phrases as to get or have a thing made or done, in which use it is construed with the infinitive active, with passive signification. L. 35. 6.); as,

Ich lasse ihn kommen.	I let him (or cause him to) come.
Er will sie nicht gehen lassen.	He will not let them go.

8. These verbs all have a complete conjugation. In their translation, therefore, wherever the corresponding English verb is defective, the deficiency must be supplied by using some equivalent word or phrase; as,

Ich mußte gestern gehen.	I was obliged to go yesterday.
Ich habe nicht gewollt, aber ich habe gemußt.	I have not wished to, but I have been obliged to.
Er wird gehen können.	He will be able to go.
Sie werden spielen wollen.	They will wish to play.
Es ist besser arbeiten zu wollen, als arbeiten zu müssen.	It is better to be willing to work, than to be obliged to work.

9. The perfect and pluperfect of these auxiliaries, as also **hören**, **sehen** and **fühlen** when used with other verbs, are formed, not with the past participle, but with the infinitive; as,

Ich habe nicht gehen können.	I have not been able to go.
Sie hat es nicht thun mögen.	She has not wished to do it.
Er hat lesen müssen.	He has been obliged to read.
Wir haben gehen dürfen, aber nicht gehen wollen.	We have been at liberty to go, but have not wished to go.
Ich habe ihn singen hören.	I have heard him sing.

AUXILIARIES OF MODE.

10. When two infinitives are thus employed, the inversion usual in relative sentences, does not take place; as,

Der Mann, welcher hat gehen müssen (not gehen müssen hat).	The man who has been obliged to go.
Ich weiß es, daß er wird kommen können.	I know that he will be able to come.

11. The main verb is often omitted after these auxiliaries; as,

Ich kann nicht mehr.	I can (do) no more.
Was wollen diese Leute?	What will these people (do)?
Sie müssen gleich fort.	You must go away immediately.
Was soll der Hut?	What shall the hat (indicate)?
„Ihr träumt! was soll ich dort?"	Ye dream! what should I (do) there?
Ein Jüngling wollte zur Stadt hinauf.	A young man wished to go (or get) up to the city.

12. CONJUGATION OF THE MODE AUXILIARIES

PRESENT TENSE.

ich kann,	darf,	muß,	will,	mag,	soll,
du kannst,	darfst,	mußt,	willst,	magst,	sollst,
er kann,	darf,	muß,	will,	mag,	soll.

IMPERFECT TENSE.

| ich konnte, | durfte, | mußte, | wollte, | mochte, | sollte. |

13. The second and third persons singular, and all persons of the plural, are formed as in regular verbs.

EXERCISE 58.   Aufgabe 58.

1. Wer hungrig ist, will essen, und wer durstig ist, will trinken. 2. Diejenigen, welche nichts wissen, sollen etwas lernen. 3. Wer krank ist, soll wenig essen. 4. Wer gesund bleiben will, muß mäßig essen und trinken. 5. Wer gut schlafen will, muß am Tage fleißig arbeiten. 6. Wer nicht fleißig und aufmerksam sein will, kann nicht schnell lernen. 7. Wer einen Brief schreiben will, muß Papier, Tinte und Feder haben. 8. Die Freuden der Erde soll man wie Gewürze genießen und nicht wie tägliche Speisen. 9. Können Sie mir sagen wo der Arzt wohnt? 10. Ich will mit Ihnen zu ihm gehen. 11. Werden Sie morgen mit mir nach der Stadt gehen können? 12. Ich werde gehen können aber ich werde nicht gehen wollen, denn ich werde übermorgen gehen müssen. 13. Die deutsche Sprache soll sehr schwierig sein, deßhalb muß der Schüler die Regeln und die Beispiele aufmerksam lesen. 14. Wer diese Sprache lernen will, darf nicht faul oder nachläßig sein. 15. Mein Vater hat mich nie tanzen lassen, er hat nie tanzen wollen und seine Kinder haben nie tanzen dürfen. 16. Wir werden bald sprechen können, wenn wir nur fleißig sein wollen. 17. Was wollte der Kaufmann Ihnen verkaufen? 18. Ich konnte nichts bei ihm finden was ich kaufen wollte. 19. Ein guter Lehrer muß Geduld haben.

20. Die Kinder wollen Aepfel und Kirschen, aber sie können keine kaufen, denn sie haben kein Geld. 21. Kannst du mir jene große Kanne bringen? 22. Wir können nicht umhin zu lachen, obgleich wir wissen, daß es unrecht ist. 23. Ich kann nichts dafür, daß ich arm bin. 24. Kann Ihr Herr (L. 68.) Bruder auch deutsch?

Exercise 59.   Aufgabe 59.

1. I wished to go with my friend but I could not for I was obliged to remain at home. 2. He who wishes to be rich or learned must be industrious. 3. Those who will not study cannot learn. 4. I wished to buy good horses but could find none. 5. When shall you be able to write a letter to your friends? 6. I shall be able to write one to day, but I shall not wish to write one. 7. Will your friends be obliged to stay in the house this evening? 8. They will not wish to go out of the house. 9. We have been able to go but we have not wished to go. 10. Have you been obliged to remain here? 11. We have been at liberty to go but we have wished to remain. 12. I cannot read for I am unwell. 13. You must be industrious if you wish to be healthy and happy. 14. These men are said to be very rich. 15. What shall I do with this money? 16. You may give it to your poor friends. 17. May I read your new books? 18. You may read them if you can. 19. You may go to your friend if you wish. 20. I do not wish to go to-day but I shall wish to go to-morrow. 21. Those boys say they can not help laughing. 22. I shall probably be in the city to-morrow, what shall I buy for you? 23. I can not buy anything, for I have no money, and nobody will lend me any. 24. It is said these children understand German, Italian, French and Dutch.

LESSON XXXII.   Section XXXII.

CONJUGATION OF sein AND werden.

1. Sein, "to be" is used as an auxiliary in forming the perfect, pluperfect, and second future of many active and neuter verbs; and hence is frequently translated by "to have"; as,

Er ist gewesen.	He has been.	(*lit.* he is been). (L. 34.1.)
Er ist gegangen.	He has gone.	(„ he is gone).
Sie war geblieben.	She had remained.	(„ she was remained).
Wir sind geworden.	We have become.	(„ we are become).
Sie werden schon gegangen sein.	They will already have gone.	(„ they will already be gone.)
Ist er in den Fluß gefallen?	Has he fallen into the river?	(„ is he fallen into the river?)
Sind unsere Freunde noch nicht angekommen.	Have our friends not yet arrived?	(„ are our friends not yet arrived?)

2. CONJUGATION OF sein.

INFINITIVE.

Present.
sein, to be.

Perfect.
gewesen sein, to have been.

PARTICIPLES.

Present.
seiend, being

Perfect.
gewesen, been.

INDICATIVE.

Singular.   *Plural.*

PRESENT TENSE.

Singular	Plural
ich bin, I am;	wir sind, we are;
du bist, thou art;	ihr seid, you are;
er ist, he is;	sie sind, they are.

IMPERFECT TENSE.

ich war, I was;	wir waren, we were;
du warst, thou wast;	ihr waret, you were;
er war, he was;	sie waren, they were.

PERFECT TENSE.

ich bin	} gewesen,	I have	} been;	wir sind } gewesen,	we have } been
du bist		thou hast		ihr seid	you have
er ist		he has		sie sind	they have

PLUPERFECT TENSE.

ich war	} gewesen,	I had	} been;	wir waren } gewesen,	we had } been
du warst		thou hadst		ihr waret	you had
er war		he had		sie waren	they had

FIRST FUTURE TENSE.

ich werde	} sein,	I shall	} be;	wir werden } sein,	we shall } be.
du wirst		thou wilt		ihr werdet	you will
er wird		he will		sie werden	they will

SECOND FUTURE TENSE.

ich werde	} gewesen sein,	I shall	} have been;	wir werden } gewesen sein,	we shall } have been
du wirst		thou wilt		ihr werdet	you will
er wird		he will		sie werden	they will

IMPERATIVE.

sei (du), be (thou).   seid (ihr), be (you).

IDIOMS WITH sein.

An wem ist die Reihe zu lesen?	Whose turn is it to read?
Sie ist an mir.	It is mine.
Mir ist sehr kalt; ihm ist zu warm.	I am very cold; he is too warm.
Mir ist nicht wohl.	I do not feel well.

Was ist dir?	What ails you?
Ich weiß nicht wie mir ist.	I don't know what ails me.
Sei gutes Muthes.	Be of good cheer.
Mir ist nicht wohl zu Muthe.	I do not feel well (mentally).
Es ist ihm Ernst damit.	He is in earnest about it.
Es ist Schade, daß er seinem Gegner nicht gewachsen ist.	It is a pity that he is not equal to his antagonist.
Das Pferd ist mir nicht feil.	My horse is not for sale.
Wem sind diese Kleider?	To whom do these clothes belong?
Sie ist ihm einen Gulden schuldig.	She owes him a florin.
Bist du im Stande es zu thun?	Are you able to do it?
Ich bin es nicht im Stande.	I am not able to do it.
Wer ist Schuld daran, daß er noch nicht angekommen ist?	Whose fault is it that he has not yet arrived?
Du selbst bist Schuld daran.	It is your own fault.
Es ist ein solches Gesetz vorhanden.	There is such a law in existence.
Es ist ihm darum zu thun.	That is his object.
Wovon ist die Rede?	What is being spoken of?
Das ist mir recht.	I am satisfied with that.
Es ist ihnen lieb.	They are glad of it.
Ich bin dir herzlich gut.	I love you heartily.
Lassen Sie es gut sein.	That's enough of it, leave off.
Es ist mir so, als ob ich es gehört hätte.	It seems to me as though I had heard it.
Ich weiß wie du bist.	I know you (your ways).
Es sei nun, daß u. s. w.	Supposing now, that, &c.
Was sein soll, schickt sich wohl.	Whatever is to be, is proper.

3. **Werden** is used as the auxiliary in forming the futures of verbs; and in this use answers to our auxiliaries, *shall* and *will;* as an independent verb, it signifies, to become, "*get*", grow; as,

Das Wetter wird kalt.	The weather is becoming (getting) cold.
Wir werden alle alt.	We are all growing old.
Was ist aus ihm geworden?	What has become of him?
Ich bin es los geworden.	I have got rid of it.
Der Rabe wird sehr alt.	The raven becomes very old. (The raven lives to a very great age).

Werden is often followed by the dative with „zu", where we use the nominative after become; the subject of werden before the dative is often rendered by the objective; the dative by the nominative; and werden by "*to have*"; as,

Das Wasser wird zu Eis.	The water becomes ice.
„Meinen armen Unterthanen muß das Ihrige werden".	My poor subjects must have their property.

4. CONJUGATION OF werden.

INFINITIVE.

Present. werden, to become.
Perfect. geworden sein, to have become.

PARTICIPLES.

Present. werdend, becoming.
Perfect. geworden, become.

INDICATIVE.

Singular.   *Plural.*

PRESENT TENSE.

ich werde, I become;   wir werden, we become;
du wirst, thou becomest;   ihr werdet, you become;
er wird, he becomes;   sie werden, they become.

IMPERFECT TENSE.

ich wurde or ward, I became;   wir wurden, we became;
du wurdest or wardst, thou becamest;   ihr wurdet, you became;
er wurde or ward, he became;   sie wurden, they became.

PERFECT TENSE.

ich bin ⎫   I have ⎫   wir sind ⎫   we have ⎫
du bist ⎬ geworden, thou hast ⎬ become;   ihr seid ⎬ geworden, you have ⎬ become.
er ist ⎭   he has ⎭   sie sind ⎭   they have ⎭

PLUPERFECT TENSE.

ich war ⎫   I had ⎫   wir waren ⎫   we had ⎫
du warst ⎬ geworden, thou hadst ⎬ become;   ihr waret ⎬ geworden, you had ⎬ become.
er war ⎭   he had ⎭   sie waren ⎭   they had ⎭

FIRST FUTURE TENSE.

ich werde ⎫   I shall ⎫   wir werden ⎫   we shall ⎫
du wirst ⎬ werden, thou wilt ⎬ become;   ihr werdet ⎬ werden, you will ⎬ become.
er wird ⎭   he will ⎭   sie werden ⎭   they will ⎭

SECOND FUTURE TENSE.

ich werde ⎫   I shall ⎫   wir werden ⎫   we shall ⎫
du wirst ⎬ geworden sein, thou wilt ⎬ have become;   ihr werdet ⎬ geworden sein, you will ⎬ have become.
er wird ⎭   he will ⎭   sie werden ⎭   they will ⎭

IMPERATIVE.

werde (du), become (thou).   werdet (ihr), become (you).

Exercise 60.   Aufgabe 60.

1. Dieser Mann, der jetzt so arm und elend ist, ist ein sehr reicher Handwerker gewesen. 2. Sind Sie je auf jenem hohen Berge gewesen? 3. Der Kaiser Joseph der Zweite war der Sohn der Kaiserin Maria Theresia; er war der Liebling seines Volkes, aber nicht seines Hofes. 4. Wer war der geschickteste Reiter in dem Heere des französischen Kaisers? 5. Wann sind Sie in Hamburg gewesen? 6. Wie lange sind Sie in diesem Lande? 7. Sind Sie nie unzufrieden und traurig gewesen? 8. Wann werden wir reich sein? 9. Wir werden alt und älter und sind eher am Ziele unseres Lebens, als uns angenehm ist. 10. Was wird aus dir werden, wenn du nicht fleißiger wirst? 11. Ich werde fleißiger werden, sobald als (L. 63. 2.) ich gesund werde. 12. Der ist nicht gut, der nicht sucht, immer besser zu werden. 13. Frankreich wurde im Jahr eintausend acht hundert und acht und vierzig eine Republik. 14. Es wird ein heißer Tag werden, sagte ein alter Krieger wenige Stunden vor der Schlacht zu seinem Kameraden. 15. Das Pferd wurde ganz wild und unbändig. 16. Der Kranke seufzt auf seinem Lager: „will es denn nie Tag werden?" und der Taglöhner unter dem Drucke seiner Arbeit: „wird es denn nicht bald Nacht werden?" 17. „Sohn, da hast du meinen Speer! meinem Arm wird er zu schwer". 18. Die Reihe ist an Ihnen, warum lesen Sie nicht?

Exercise 61.   Aufgabe 61.

1. When were you at your brother's? 2. Have those people ever been at your house? 3. Had they been in Berlin before they were in Vienna? 4. He will be in Magdeburg before you will be in Brunswick. 5. The emperor of Austria was the king of Hungary. 6. How long have you been in this city? 7. They have been rich, but have become very poor. 8. What has become of your friend? 9. The weather is becoming very cold. 10. You can become learned if you will be industrious. 11. The young sailor has become healthy again. 12. The weather is becoming warm and the days are becoming long. 13. The scholars in this school have been very idle, but they are now becoming more industrious. 14. I was obliged to wait so long that I became very tired. 15. The son gets rid of his money faster than his father earned it. 16. How much do I owe you? 17. Whose turn is it to read? 18. It is your fault if you do not know.

LESSON XXXIII.   Section XXXIII.

IRREGULAR VERBS, OR VERBS OF THE OLD CONJUGATION.

1. Irregular verbs are such as do not form their imperfect tense and past participle according to the rules in L. 27.

2. The infinitive of these, as of the regular verbs, ends in en. The imperfect changes the root vowel; and the past participle frequently differs from the infinitive only by the augment ge; as,

Infinitive.	Imperfect.	Past Participle.
kommen, to come;	ich kam, I came;	gekommen, come.
fallen, to fall;	ich fiel, I fell;	gefallen, fallen.
geben, to give;	ich gab, I gave;	gegeben, given.
sehen, to see;	ich sah, I saw;	gesehen, seen.
laufen, to run;	ich lief, I ran;	gelaufen, run.

3. In some, the root vowel is found to be different in each of the three parts; as,

gehen	to go;	ich ging,	I went;	gegangen,	gone.
sprechen,	to speak;	ich sprach,	I spoke;	gesprochen,	spoken.
singen,	to sing;	ich sang,	I sang;	gesungen,	sung.
springen,	to spring;	ich sprang,	I sprang;	gesprungen,	sprung.

4. In others, the root vowel of the imperfect tense and the second participle is the same; as,

klimmen, to climb;	ich klomm, I climbed;	geklommen, climbed.
riechen, to smell;	ich roch, I smelled;	gerochen, smelled.
treiben, to drive;	ich trieb, I drove;	getrieben, driven.
schwellen, to swell;	ich schwoll, I swelled;	geschwollen, swelled or swollen.

5. Some change the radical vowel, and also add the terminations common to regular verbs; as,

bringen, to carry;	ich brachte, I carried;	gebracht, carried.
denken, to think;	ich dachte, I thought;	gedacht, thought.
senden, to send;	ich sandte, I sent;	gesandt, sent.
wissen, to know;	ich wußte, I knew;	gewußt, known.

6. The present tense forms the different persons like the regular verbs, except in the second and third persons singular of about sixty verbs, where the root vowel is changed, or if capable of it, assumes the Umlaut; as,

ich gebe, I give;	ich falle, I fall;	ich lese, I read;
du gibst, or giebst, thou givest;	du fällst, thou fallest;	du liesest, thou readest;
er gibt, or giebt, he gives;	er fällt, he falls;	er liest, he reads.

7. In the imperfect, the second and third persons are regularly formed from the first; as,

gehen.

ich ging, I went;	wir gingen, we went,
du gingst, thou wentst;	ihr ginget, you went;
er ging, he went;	sie gingen, they went.

geben.

ich gab, I gave;	wir gaben, we gave;
du gabst, thou gavest;	ihr gabet, you gave;
er gab, he gave;	sie gaben, they gave.

8. For complete alphabetical List of Irregular verbs see page 178.

Exercise 62.   Aufgabe 62.

1. Wer bäckt das Brod? 2. Der Soldat birgt sich, weil du das befiehlst. 3. Er bläst das Waldhorn. 4. Der Bauer bricht den Hanf und drischt den Weizen. 5. Die Seele empfängt Eindrücke von Außen. 6. Das Gute empfiehlt sich selbst. 7. Der Mann fährt auf dem Wagen. 8. Der Schnee fällt. 9. Der Knabe fängt die Vögel. 10. Der Soldat ficht. 11. Er flicht sich einen Hut. 12. Der Ochs frißt das Gras und säuft Wasser. 13. Das Kind ißt Brod und trinkt Milch. 14. Er gibt mir das Buch, welches mir am besten gefällt (L. 50. 2). 15. Der Dachs gräbt sich ein Loch. 16. Er hält das Pferd. 17. Der Hut hängt an dem Nagel. 18. Er läuft und läßt die andern auch laufen. 19. Sie liest ihr Buch. 20. Sie mißt (or misset) das Tuch. 21. Er nimmt mein Buch. 22. Warum schilt er? 23. Der Hund schläft, und der Knabe schlägt die Trommel. 24. Der Schnee schmilzt, die Knospe schwillt. 25. Was siehst du? wie spricht er? 26. Die Biene sticht, der Dieb stiehlt, der Kranke stirbt. 27. Er trägt schöne Kleider; er trifft immer das Ziel. 28. „Er tritt meine Religion in den Staub". 29. Das Bier verdirbt. 30. Er vergißt, was sie spricht. 31. Das Gras wächst. 32. Sie weiß nicht, was sie will. 33. Er wirft einen Stein. 34. Ich weiß, was er mir verspricht.

Exercise 63.   Aufgabe 63.

1. I do not know who is throwing the stones. 2. Does she speak German? 3. He does not forget what he reads. 4. The stream swells when the snow melts. 5. The thief steals the shoes that he wears. 6. The bee stings and dies. 7. The soldier is beating the drum. 8. The bird sleeps on the tree. 9. She scolds because he takes her book. 10. The carpenter is measuring the room. 11. The boy runs and lets the dog run too. 12. Who is holding my horse? 13. Where is the cloak hanging? 14. The man that is braiding hats gives us a book which pleases us. 15. Who is digging this hole? 16. Why does the soldier fight? 17. What is this boy eating? 18. What animal eats grass? 19. What does the horse drink? 20. The tree is falling. 21. Who is catching the birds? 22. How does the soul receive impressions? 23. Who thrashes the wheat and breaks the hemp? 24. Why dost thou conceal thyself? 25. What does he command? 26. Who is riding on your wagon? 27. My friend recommends me to you.

Exercise 64.   Aufgabe 64.

1. Der Hund biß den Dieb. 2. Der Ast brach. 3. Der Kaufmann betrog seinen Kunden. 4. Er empfahl mich einem Manne, der mich sehr freundlich empfing. 5. Ich blieb den ganzen Tag. 6. Sie ergriffen seine Hände. 7. Sie erschracken, als er erschien, und die furchtbare Stimme erscholl. 8. Er fiel in den Fluß und ertrank. 9. Sie aßen die Aepfel, die sie stahlen. 10. Wir fuhren auf der Eisenbahn. 11. Sie fingen die Vögel, welche aus den Nestern flogen. 12. Die Soldaten fochten nicht

tapfer, sondern flohen. 13. Deine Brüder fraß das Schwert, wo das Blut in Strömen floß. 14. Er gebot uns zu gehen, aber weil es uns hier gefiel, so (L. 39. 2.) blieben wir. 15. Er gab mir das Geld und ging. 16. Er genaß langsam. 17. Wir genossen gestern sehr wenig. 18. Er gewann mehr als ich verlor. 19. Er goß den Wein in das Glas. 20. Sie glichen ihren Freunden (L. 50. 2). 21. Sie gruben einen tiefen Graben. 22. Er hob seinen Stock und hieb nach mir. 23. Er hieß sie kommen, aber sie kamen nicht. 24. Er half uns, obgleich er uns nicht kannte. 25. Wir lasen das Buch, das er uns lieh. 26. Die Schildkröte kroch, der Hase lief. 27. Sie lagen auf ihren Betten und litten. 28. Die Bösewichter logen, sie nahmen meinen Wagen und nannten ihn ihr Eigenthum. 29. Er pries seine Waare und rieth uns sie zu kaufen. 30. Er saß und schrieb den ganzen Tag. 31. Das Kind stand und schrie. 32. Der Schnee schmolz, der Strom schwoll. 33. Sie tranken und sangen; einer schwamm und der andere sank. 34. Sie schlugen ihn, während er schlief. 35. Er rief mich und schalt, weil ich sein Pferd ritt. 36. Sie schien traurig. 37. Er schritt heraus und schloß die Thüre. 38. Er stieg auf den Berg. 39. Sie standen, bis sie starben. 40. Er stritt mit ihnen und trieb sie aus dem Felde. 41. Sie traten in das Haus und verschwanden. 42. Er vergaß, was er versprach. 43. Er traf das Ziel. 44. Es wuchs schnell. 45. Er wusch den Salat. 46. Er wußte, daß ich den Speer warf. 47. Er zog sein Schwert und zwang sie zu gehen.

EXERCISE 65. Aufgabe 65.

1. The branches broke and the boys fell. 2. The dogs bit the boys that stole the apples. 3. The man to whom you recommended me, cheated me. 4. We did not remain long, for they did not receive us kindly. 5. The boy was frightened and seized my hand. 6. We called him but he did not appear. 7. Do you ride on the wagon? 8. The soldiers ate bread and drank wine, and their horses ate hay and drank water. 9. Our soldiers fought gallantly, and those of our enemy fled. 10. The birds flew out of the cage but the boys caught them again. 10. Tears flowed from his eyes. 11. It did not please us there, and we did not remain long. 12. They commanded us to go to the city, but we did not go, for they gave us no money. 13. Did your friends recover? 14. We won less than our friends lost. 15. They poured the wine into the glasses. 16. They saw the horse and raised their hands. 17. Why were they digging that ditch? 18. I knew him because he resembled his brother who came to us while we were reading the books which you lent us. 19. He struck at them because they drank so much and sang so loud. 20. We crept before we walked. 21. The boys whistled and the dogs ran. 22. We took the books that lay on the table. 23. Did you call him a villain? 24. We knew that they lied. 25. We sat around the table and wrote and they stood around the stove. 26. He rode the horse and drove the oxen. 27. They praised their horse and advised us to buy it. 28. Why did they seem so sad? 29. He scolded me because I slept so long 30. They threw their spears and drew their swords. 31. Did

you forget what he promised you? 32. Did they hit the mark? 33. Who washed the gloves? 34. Did the trees grow rapidly? 35. Did they lock the door? 36. Why did they quarrel with us? 37. The stream swelled because the snow melted.

Exercise 66.   Aufgabe 66.

1. Der Hund hat den Dieb gebissen. 2. Er hat uns betrogen. 3. Er hat mir etwas gebracht. 4. Er hatte an uns gedacht. 5. Hast du den Weizen gedroschen? 6. Er hat uns freundlich empfangen, aber Niemand hat uns ihm empfohlen. 7. Ich habe nie ein solches Gefühl empfunden. 8. Man hat die Verbrecher ergriffen. 9. Er hat den Apfel gegessen; hat er den Vogel gefangen? 10. Ich habe sie gefunden; sie haben gefochten. 11. Der Hund hat das Fleisch gefressen. 12. Er hat mir nichts gegeben. 13. Es hat uns nicht gefallen. 14. Wir haben nichts genossen. 15. Was hat er gewonnen? 16. Wer hat den Wein in das Glas gegossen? 17. Wer hat dieses Loch gegraben? 18. Er hat das Pferd gehalten. 19. Er hat uns geholfen. 20. Er hat uns gekannt. 21. Sie hat mir ein Buch geliehen, und ich habe es gelesen. 22. Die Federn haben auf dem Tische gelegen. 23. Er hat nicht gelogen. 24. Der Müller hat das Getreide gemessen und gemahlen. 25. Nie habe ich diese Gefahren gemieden. 26. Er hat uns Diebe genannt, weil wir seine Bücher genommen haben. 27. Warum hat er gepfiffen? 28. Sie haben ihre Waaren gepriesen. 29. Er hat sich (L. 50. 7.) die Augen gerieben. 30. Er hat sie gerufen. 31. Warum hast du uns gescholten? 32. Er hatte das Schaf geschoren. 33. Er hat den Bären geschossen und geschunden. 34. Sie hatten zu lange geschlafen. 35. Hast du die Messer geschliffen? 36. Wir haben die Thüren geschlossen. 37. Hat er das Brod geschnitten? 38. Ich hatte geschrieben und sie haben geschrieen. 39. Sie hat es geschworen. 40. Wir haben ihn gesehen. 41. Hat er das Lied schön gesungen? 42. Er hat eine Stunde gesessen. 43. Er hat das Holz gespalten. 44. Haben sie die Wolle gesponnen? 45. Was sie gesprochen hat, hat ihn gestochen. 46. Der Mann, der da gestanden hatte, hat mein Pferd gestohlen. 47. Sie haben lange genug gestritten, was hat er gethan? 48. Warum hat er diesen Hut getragen? 49. Er hat das Ziel getroffen. 50. Hast du alle Wein getrunken? 51. Ich habe vergessen. 52. Was hat er verloren? 53. Es hat ihn verdrossen. 54. Hat er uns verziehen? 55. Er hat das Tuch gewoben und gewaschen; hat er einen Stein geworfen? 56. Er hatte einen Kranz für sie gewunden. 57. Hatte er nichts von der Sache gewußt? 58. Sie hatten ihre Schwerter gezogen. 59. Sie haben uns gezwungen hier zu bleiben.

Exercise 67.   Aufgabe 67.

1 He has beaten the dog that has bitten him. 2. I have often thought of him. 3. Have you recommended this book to us? 4. Have you threshed the wheat? 5. They have always received us kindly. 6. Have you ever experienced such a feeling? 7. The boys have eaten the bread and drank the beer. 8. The dogs have eaten the meat and drank the water. 9. They have caught their horses. 10. What have you found? 11. Why have the soldiers fought? 12 I have shot a large bird. 13. Have you seen the

books that I have read? 14. Into which glass have you poured the wine? 15. Why have they dug this hole? 16. Who has held my horse? 17. Have they helped us? 18. Have my books lain on your table? 19. Has anybody lied? 20. Who has ground the wheat? 21. Have you measured the cloth? 22. Has he avoided the danger? 23. Have they called him a villain? 24. Who has taken my pen? 25. He has called me but he has not scolded me. 26. Who has sharpened your knife? 27. Have you locked the doors? 28. Who has cut the bread? 29. Had you written him a letter? 30. Have you ever sung this song? 31. Have you sat longer than they have stood? 32. I have spun the wool and he has split the wood. 33. The bees have stung the horse. 34. Has anybody stolen anything? 35. He had not spoken at all. 36. Why have they quarreled? 37. Who has worn the hat? 38. What have you lost? 39. Who has thrown the stones? 40. Why have they drawn their swords? 41. Have you washed the cloth that he has woven? 42. It vexes him that he has lost his money. 43. Have you forgotten what you have promised me? 44. Why have you slept so long? 45. Has any one compelled you to go? 46. Who has whistled? 47. Have you praised the goods? 48. Have you ever known such a man? 49. He has written, and they have spoken.

LESSON XXXIV.   section XXXIV.
USE OF THE AUXILIARIES haben AND sein.

1. Haben is used as the auxiliary of all transitive, reflexive (L. 43.) and impersonal (L. 44.) verbs, as also of the verbs of mode (L. 31); and of all objective verbs that govern the genitive (L. 49.) and dative (L. 50.). Except begegnen, folgen and weichen (see 2.).

2. Intransitive verbs indicating direction from or towards a place or an object, or a change from one condition to another, as also bleiben, begegnen, folgen and weichen, require the auxiliary sein, which in this use, should of course be rendered by "to have"; as,

Sind sie schon gegangen?	Have (are) they already gone?
Der arme Knabe ist gefallen.	The poor boy has (is) fallen.
Ist er denn noch nicht gekommen?	Has (is) he then not yet come?
Der Vogel ist weg geflogen.	The bird has (is) flown away.
Sie sind in das Feld gezogen.	They have marched into the field.
Er ist nach Amerika gereist.	He has (is) gone (traveled) to America.
Er wird in's Haus gegangen sein.	He will have (be) gone into the house.
Er war nach der Stadt geeilt.	He had (was) hastened to the city.
Sie sind auf das Land geritten.	They have ridden into the country.

3. When the following verbs do not express direction *from* or *towards* a place they require the auxiliary haben; namely eilen, fließen, sinken, jagen, klettern, kriechen, landen, saufen, quellen, reisen, reiten, rennen, segeln, schiffen, schwimmen, springen, stoßen, treiben, wandern; as,

Warum hast du so geeilt?	Why have you hastened so?
Hast du nicht heute geritten?	Have you not ridden to-day?
Sie haben nicht viel gereist.	They have not traveled much.

Some neuter verbs; as, liegen, sitzen, stehen, are sometimes used with the auxiliary sein; as,

Höher war seine Macht nie gestanden.	His power never had stood higher.

Exercise 68.   Aufgabe 68.

1. Er ist entschlafen. 2. Er ist uns entronnen. 3. Wie lange ist er geblieben? 4. Sie sind nach der Stadt gefahren. 5. Der Mann ist gefallen. 6. Der Vogel ist geflogen. 7. Das Wasser ist über das Feld geflossen. 8. Der Plan ist gelungen. 9. Der Knabe ist genesen. 10. Was ist geschehen? 11. Es ist aus der Erde gekrochen. 12. Der Hund ist nach dem Wald gelaufen. 13. Das Unternehmen ist mißlungen. 14. Das Wasser ist aus dem Felsen geflossen. 15. Er ist nach der Stadt geritten. 16. Er war in das Haus geschlichen. 17. Er war über den Graben gesprungen. 18. Sie waren aus dem Schloß getreten. 19. Der letzte Ton war verschollen. 20. Der Baum ist sehr schnell gewachsen. 21. Das Haus wird gefallen sein. 22. Sie werden gekommen sein. 23. Er war auf den Mast geklettert. 24. Der Knabe ist über den Fluß geschwommen. 25. Einer war uns gefolgt, und der Andere war uns begegnet. 26. Der Schnee ist geschmolzen und die Flüsse sind geschwollen. 27. Das Obst ist schnell gereift. 28. Die Soldaten sind in das Feld gezogen. 29. Er war nach der Stadt geeilt.

Exercise 69.   Aufgabe 69.

1. Have you remained long enough? Who has gone to the city? 3. Do you know what has happened? 4. The boy has sprung across the ditch. 5. Our plan has not succeeded. 6. The children had hastened into the house. 7. Has the snow melted? 8. The hunters had climbed upon the trees. 9. Our soldiers had fled and the enemy had come into our country. 10. He has ridden (on horseback) to the forest, and she has ridden (in a carriage) to the city. 11. The patient has recovered. 12. Has he fallen asleep? 13. How have they escaped us? 14. Our friend has fallen out of the wagon. 15. The young birds have flown out of the nest. 16. The worms have crawled out of the earth. 17. The horse has run out of the stable. 18. The apples had ripened. 19. The water will have flowed into the house. 20 Why have you followed us? 21. Have you met your friends? 22. He may already have gone.

LESSON XXXV.   Section XXXV.

INFINITIVE.

1. When the infinitive is preceded by an auxiliary or by any one of the following words, the particle zu is omitted;

heißen,* to bid;   helfen, to help;   lehren, to teach;
lernen, to learn;   hören, to hear;   sehen, to see;
fühlen, to feel;   machen, to make; as,

Er lernt singen, und lehrt mich spielen.	He learns to sing, and teaches me to play.
Sie hießen uns gehen.	They told us to go.

2. After the following verbs the infinitive is best translated by our present participle:

fahren, to ride (in a vehicle);   führen, to conduct;   finden, to find;
reiten, to ride (on horseback);   bleiben, to remain;   haben, to have;
gehen, to walk;   heißen;*   sein, to be; as,

Er blieb stehen und ich ging fischen.	He continued standing (to stand) and I went a fishing (to fish).
Einer fährt spazieren, und der Andere reitet spazieren.†	One rides (goes riding) in a carriage and the other on horseback.
Sie hatte eine Wanduhr im Hause stehen.	She had a clock standing in the house.
Es ist theuer leben in England.	It is expensive living in England.
Heißt* das arbeiten?	Do you call that working?
Ist er schlafen gegangen?	Has he gone (in order) to sleep? i. e. to bed?

3. The infinitive (usually preceded by the article, or a pronoun) is used as a neuter noun and is rendered by our present participle used substantively; as,

Das Lügen ist ein Laster.	Lying is a vice.
Fort mit deinem Prahlen.	Away with your boasting.
„Du Schwert an meiner Linken! was soll dein heitres Blinken?"	Thou sword upon my left, what means thy cheerful gleaming?

---

*) „Heißen" when intransitive is rendered by the passive of "to call", "to name"; or by the substantive "name", with the verb "to be"; as, er heißt Karl, ne is "called", (or "named", or his "name is") Charles. Wie heißt das auf Deutsch? or, wie heißt das im Deutschen? What is that "called" in German?

†) Spazieren is used chiefly with gehen, fahren, reiten, and führen, and denotes that the action performed is for exercise, or pleasure; as,

Er reitet sehr oft, aber er reitet nie spazieren.	He rides very often, but he never rides for pleasure.
Ich gehe alle Tage spazieren.	I go walking (take a walk) every day.
Wir machten einen Spaziergang.	We took (made) a walk.

USE OF THE INFINITIVE.

Er ist des Wartens müde. — He is tired of (the) waiting.
Er denkt nur an Essen und Trinken. — He thinks only of eating and drinking.

4. The infinitive (generally without zu) often stands as the subject, or object of a verb; as,

Sterben ist nichts, doch leben und nicht sehen, das ist ein Unglück. — To die is nothing, but to live and not see that is a misfortune.
Handeln ist leicht, denken schwer. — To act is easy, to think difficult.

5. The infinitive with zu follows the particles anstatt and ohne; as,

Er spielt, anstatt zu lesen. — He plays instead of reading (to read).
Sie sind krank, ohne es zu wissen. — They are sick without knowing it.
Du hinderst mich, zu schreiben. — You keep me from writing.

6. The infinitive active is often used in a passive sense; as,

Dieses Haus ist zu vermiethen, und jenes ist zu verkaufen. — This house is to let, and that one is to be sold (to sell).
Es ist keine Zeit zu verlieren. — There is no time to be lost (to lose).
Wo ist dieses Buch zu haben? — Where is this book to be had?
Er läßt einen Hut machen. — He is getting a hat made.
Man ließ ihn bestrafen. — They caused him to be punished

7. Um before the infinitive signifies *"in order"*, but is frequently omitted in translating; as,

Er ist nach Deutschland gereist, um die Sprache zu lernen. — He has gone to Germany (in order) to learn the language.
Er war zu schwach, um die Arbeit zu vollenden. — He was too weak to finish the work.

8. Wissen often stands in the sense of "to know how", "to be able", before an infinitive; as,

Er weiß sich zu helfen. — He knows how to help himself.

Exercise 70.   Aufgabe 70.

1. Heißen Sie ihn gehen oder bleiben? 2. Einer lehrt mich französisch sprechen, und der andere lernt es lesen. 3. Die Nachtigall wird sich bald hören lassen. 4. Diese Matrosen werden morgen oder übermorgen fischen gehen. 5. Der alte Bauer hat viel guten alten Wein im Keller liegen. 6. Befehlen ist leicht, gehorchen schwer. 7. Ich liebe das Lesen, aber ich hasse das Schreiben. 8. Wir sind eures Prahlens und Schwatzens herzlich müde. 9. Welche Ursache hat sie traurig zu sein? 10. Ich habe weder Zeit noch Lust sein Singen zu hören. 11. Jeder gute Schüler weiß wann die Reihe an ihm ist zu lesen. 12. Ein so albernes Märchen ist nicht zu glauben. 13. Sie lassen ihren Bedienten ihr Zimmer fegen. 14. Der Richter ließ den Verbrecher ins Gefängniß werfen. 14. Lebe um zu lernen, und lerne um zu leben. 15. Er weiß zu leben und sich das Leben angenehm

zu machen. 16. Die Kinder sind spaziren gefahren, und di Schüler sind spaziren geritten. 17. Er ist fischen gegangen, anstatt zu st ren. 18. Sie sind in die Schule gegangen um Englisch zu lernen.

Exercise 71.   Aufgabe 71

1. Who taught you to speak German? 2. I le·rned to speak it in Germany. 3. This stupid boy remained sitting the whole evening. 4. The man had a small table standing beside his bed. 5. We shall not have time to see our friends this evening. 6. My mother taught me to sing and my brother teaches me to play. 7. When shall you go a fishing, to-morrow, or day after to-morrow? 8. Why have our friends been to the city without visiting us? 9. They went to their cousins instead of coming to us. 10. I am tired of his singing. 11. They have books enough but not time to read them. 12. These horses are to be sold. 13. This man has something to say to your friend. 14. The captain is getting a new coat made. 15. The general caused the soldier to be thrown into prison. 16. This man's conduct is not to be praised. 17. This silly story is not to be believed. 18. Is it not your turn to read? 19 We must go immediately, there is no time to lose.

LESSON XXXVI.   Section XXXVI.

PARTICIPLES AND IMPERATIVE.

1. The present participle governs the same case as the verb from which it is derived, and always follows its object; as,

Die Honig sammelnde Biene.   The honey-gathering bee.
Dein dich liebender Bruder.   Thy (thee) loving brother.

2. The present participle is used predicatively only when it rejects its participial character and is used simply as an adjective; as,

Die Hitze war drückend.   The heat was oppressive.
Das Lied ist reizend.   The song is charming.

3. After the verb kommen, the second participle is used in some phrases, where in English the first is employed; as,

Heulend kommt der Sturm geflogen.   Howling the storm comes flying (flown).

4. The word gehen, in some phrases with the second participle of verlieren, is not translated; as,

Der Wein wird verloren gehen.   The wine will be (lit. "go") lost.
Das Geld ist verloren gegangen.   The money is (gone) lost.

5. The past participle is sometimes used as the imperative; as,

Nicht so laut gesprochen.	Do not speak so loud.
Fleißig gearbeitet.	Labor diligently.

6. There is a third future participle formed only from transitive verbs by adding b to the infinitive preceded by zu: it always has a passive signification and implies necessity or obligation; as,

Er ist ein zu lobender Mann.	He is a man who should be praised.
Die zu fürchtende Gefahr.	The to-be-feared danger.
Das zu bauende Haus.	The house (which is) to be built.

IMPERATIVE.

7. When the *second* person of the imperative is used, the subject is generally omitted; when, however, the *third* is used, the subject is expressed; as,

Karl, bringe mir dein Buch.	Charles, bring me your book.
Kinder, geht in das Haus.	Children, go into the house.
Karl, bringen Sie mir Ihr Buch.	Charles, bring me your book.
Schicke er das Pferd morgen.	Send the horse to-morrow.
So sei es, sagte er.	So be it (so let it be), said he.

8. The present indicative, and the auxiliary sollen are sometimes used with the force of the imperative; as,

Du machst immer Anstalt und bist niemals fertig.	Be constantly making preparations and never be ready.
Ihr schweigt, bis man euch anruft.	Keep silence till you are called upon.
Du selbst sollst es thun.	Do it yourself.
Der Johann soll kommen.	Let John come (cause John to come).

9. „Dadurch, daß" before a finite verb often answers to "by" before a present participle; as,

Man schadet euch dadurch, daß man euch zu sehr lobt.	You are injured *by* being praised too much.

Literally, you are thereby injured, that you are too much praised.

Exercise 72.   Aufgabe 72.

1. Der brausende Wind treibt das schwankende Schiff durch die schäumenden Wellen. 2. Dort kommt ein Mann in voller Hast gelaufen. 3. Der alte Mann schrieb mit zitternder Hand. 4. Er reitet geschwind, und hält in dem Arm das seufzende Kind. 5. So sei es, spricht Albrecht mit donnerndem Laut. 6. Weinend rief der zu bemitleidende alte Mann: „Mein Sohn ist ein zu bestrafender Verbrecher". 7. Der lächelnde Frühling erweckt die schlafenden Blumen. 8. Die brennende Sonne schmilzt den glänzenden Schnee. 9. Ihr Bruder ist ein zu beneidender Mensch. 10. Der kühne Taucher wirft sich in die brausende Fluth. 11. Bringe mir meinen Mantel und meine Handschuhe. 12. Schicken Sie Ihren Bedienten zu

mir. 13. „Und keuchend lag ich, wie ein Sterbender, zertreten unter ihrer Hufe Schlag." 14. „Du übernimmst die spanischen Regimenter, machst immer Anstalt und bist niemals fertig, und treiben sie dich, gegen mich zu ziehn, so (L. 39. 2.) sagst du ja, und bleibst gefesselt stehn."

Exercise 73.   Aufgabe 73

1. The falling snow covers the fallen tree. 2. The horse comes running, the bird comes flying. 3. Give the trembling old man a coat. 4. My friend is a very learned man. 5. I hear the singing birds and the bleating sheep. 6. The smiling spring brings us beautiful flowers. 7. So be it, said the king, smiling. 8. He has the weeping child in his arm. 9. The burning sun drives the lowing cattle into the forest. 10. The foaming wave flies over the trembling ship. 11. The snow melts before the burning sun. 12. A standing tree is more beautiful than a fallen one. 13. The hoping husbandman sees with joy the swelling buds. 14. Do not sing so loud. 15. Who is the most learned man in Europe? 16. These travelers call themselves traveling artists. 17. He governs them by treating them kindly.

LESSON XXXVII.   Section XXXVII.

COMPOUND VERBS. SEPARABLE.

1. The particles ab, an, auf, aus, bei, da or dar, ein, empor, fort, gegen, heim, her, hin, in, mit, nach, nieder, vor, weg, zu, zurück (and their compounds, L. 38.), are often compounded with verbs; and as they may stand apart from the verb, they are called separable particles.*

2. In compound tenses, formed from the infinitive and an auxiliary, and in subordinate sentences, the particle is placed before the verb; as,

Er wird bald ankommen.	He will soon arrive.
Wir müssen ausgehen.	We must go out.
Kann er den Stein aufheben?	Can he lift up the stone?
Du darfst heim gehen.	You are at liberty to go home.
Sie sollten ihn nicht aufhalten.	You should not detain him.
Er mag nicht einschlafen.	He does not wish to go to sleep.
Sie sind es, der mich aufhält.	It is you who detain me.
Er ist böse, weil Sie ausgehen.	He is angry because you go out.
Sie ist traurig, weil er die Blume abbrach.	She is sad because he broke off the flower.
Ich war hier, ehe er aufstand.	I was here before he got up.

---

*) In like manner are used with verbs several nouns (sometimes written with a capital and sometimes with a small initial) and adjectives; as, das Concert wird Statt finden (or stattfinden); the concert will take place: er wird ihm Trotz bieten (or trotzbieten); he will bid him defiance· er wird ihn todtschlagen; he will kill him (strike him dead).

3. **Zu** of the infinitive* (when used), and the augment ge of the past participle,* are placed between the particle and the verb; as,

Es ist Zeit auszugehen (not zu ausgehen). It is time to go out.
Es ist Unrecht ihn aufzuhalten (not zu aufhalten). It is wrong to detain him.
Er hat mich aufgehalten (not ge=aufhalten). He has detained me.
Sie sind ausgegangen (not ge=ausgangen). They have gone out.

4. In principal sentences and simple tenses the particle is placed at the end of the sentence; as,

Die Gäste kommen eben an. The guests are just arriving.
Warum gehen Sie aus? Why are you going out?
Er brach die Blume ab. He broke off the flower.
Hielt er den Boten auf? Did he detain the messenger?

5. When one of these particles is prefixed to a verb not accented on the first syllable, zu of the infinitive follows the prefix, and the augment ge is rejected; as,

Er ist zu stolz es an=zu=erkennen. He is too proud to acknowledge it.
Er hat es an=erkannt. He has acknowledged it.

6. These compounds generally take a signification different from, but often kindred to the components used separately; as,

Ich stehe meinem Freunde bei. I assist (stand by) my friend.
Ich stehe bei meinem Freunde. I stand by (near) my friend.
Er stellte sich mir vor. He introduced himself to me.
Er stellte sich vor mich. He placed himself before me.

Exercise 74.   Aufgabe 74.

1. Nehmen Sie Ihre Bücher weg? 2. Nein, denn ich habe sie schon weggenommen. 3. Gehen Ihre Freunde heute aus? 4. Nein, sie sind schon ausgegangen. 5. Schreibt der Knabe den Brief ab? 6. Nein, er hat ihn schon gestern abgeschrieben. 7. Der fleißige Bauer hat seine Feld=früchte eingesammelt, ausgedroschen und aufgespeichert. 8. Um welche Zeit geht die Sonne auf? 9. Sie ist schon aufgegangen. 10. Der Mond steigt hinter dem Gebirge auf und erfüllt die Erde mit seinem sanften Lichte. 11. Die tadelnde Wahrheit des ächten Freundes ist das Messer des Wundarztes, das ein eiterndes Geschwür aufschneidet; es schaffet Schmerzen, aber zum Heil des Leidenden. 12. Der Vogel ist weggeflogen und das Pferd ist weggelaufen. 13. Ich habe meine Handschuhe ange=zogen, und jetzt ziehe ich meine Ueberschuhe an. 14. Die müden Reiter sind von ihren abgematteten Pferden abgestiegen. 15. Sie sprechen die deutschen Wörter sehr gut aus. 16. Als wir anfingen, deutsch zu lernen, konnten wir die Wörter nicht leicht aussprechen.

---

*) Verbs derived from compound nouns, or adjectives, follow the conjugation of simple verbs, i. e. take the augment, and zu of the infinitive, before the entire word; as, er hat gefrühstückt; he has breakfasted: es ist schwer zu haushaben; it is difficult to manage es hat gewetterleuchtet; it has lightened.

USE AND FORMATION OF ADVERBS. 99

Exercise 75. Aufgabe 75

1. Who has taken away my gloves? 2. Your brother took them away yesterday. 3. At what time do you go out this evening? 4. I shall not go out this evening, I went out this morning. 5. When will your friends go away? 6. They have already gone away. 7. Can you pronounce these words well? 8. I can pronounce them but not very well. 9. Have you already begun to read German? 10. No, but I shall begin to-morrow, my friend began yesterday. 11. Does he pronounce well? 12. Yes, he pronounces very well. 13. Why don't you take away your table? 14. I have not time to take it away. 15. I am copying letters for my friend who went away yesterday.

LESSON XXXVIII. Section XXXVIII.

ADVERBS.

.1. Da, dort, hier, and wo, are used with verbs of rest, and with those that indicate action within specified limits; as,

Da ist der Kahn, und dort der See.	Here is the boat, and there the lake.
Hier liegt das Papier, wo ist die Tinte?	Here lies the paper, where is the ink?

2. Da, dort, hier, and wo, when combined with hin (thither) and her (hither), are used when motion or tendency toward a place is signified; as,

Er ist da und ich gehe dahin.	He is there and I am going there (thither).
Bleibe hier, er wird bald hierher kommen.	Remain here, he will soon come here (hither).
Wo ist er, und wohin geht er?	Where is he, and where (whither) is he going?

3. Hin and her* are frequently separated from wo, and placed at the end of the sentence; as,

Wo gehen Sie hin (wohin gehen Sie)? Where (whither) are you going?
Wo kommt er her (woher kommt er)? Where is he coming from?

4. Hin and her when compounded with other words, still retain their distinctive meanings (hin indicating direction *from* and her direction *towards*, the speaker or subject). As, however, we have no words precisely answering to these particles, the force of hin and her in compounds, is often lost in translating; as,

---

*) Hin and her are sometimes used with verbs of rest; hin, in the signification of "past", "gone", and her, denoting proximity, as, der Sommer ist hin; the summer is past: sie standen um ihn her; they stood round about him.

Direction from the speaker.   *Direction towards the speaker.*
Er sprang hinaus. He sprang out.   Er sprang heraus. He sprang out.
Er stieg hinauf. He ascended.   Er stieg herauf. He ascended.
Er steigt hinab. He descends.   Er steigt herab. He descends.
Er ging hinunter. He went down.   Er kam herunter. He came down.
Er ruderte zu ih­ He rowed across   Er ruderte zu uns He rowed across
  nen hinüber.   to them.   herüber.   to us.
Die Kinder liefen hin und her.   The children ran to and fro.

5. These compounds after the dative preceded by a preposition; or after the accusative, are usually translated by a preposition before the objective; as,

Er flog zum Fenster hinaus.   He flew out of the window.
Sie kamen die Treppe herunter.   They came down the stairs.

6. With da, hier, and wo, many prepositions are combined, and the compound thus formed is often substituted for the dative and accusative of pronouns (L. 24, 14. 28, 12.); as,

Ich habe ihr Buch und lese darin.   I have your book and am reading in it.
Sind Sie damit zufrieden?   Are you satisfied with it?
Wissen Sie wovon er spricht?   Do you know what he is speaking of?
Er nahm meinen Tisch und legte seine Bücher darauf.   He took my table and laid his books on it (thereon).

7. Adverbs are formed by the union of nouns with nouns; nouns with pronouns; nouns with adjectives; nouns with prepositions; and prepositions with prepositions; as,

schaarenweise, hordewise (in hordes); meinerseits, for my part; glücklicherweise (or glücklicher Weise), fortunately; stromauf, up stream; bergab, down hill; überaus, exceedingly.

Adverbs are formed from various parts of speech by means of the suffixes lich, lings, wärts, s; as,

täglich, daily; blindlings, blindly; himmelwärts, heavenwards; flugs, suddenly; rechts, right (to the right); links, left (to the left); morgens, in the morning; abends, in the evening; anders, otherwise.

EXERCISE 76.   Aufgabe 76.

1. Wo ist Ihr Bruder? 2. Er ist in Wien, sein Freund ist auch da. 3. Reisen Sie auch dahin? 4. Entweder reise ich dahin oder er kommt hierher. 5. Wo gehen unsere Freunde hin? 6. Sie gehen nach dem Dorfe; sollen wir auch dahin gehen? 7. Wir wollen heute hier bleiben und morgen dahin gehen. 8. Wollen Sie den Berg hinauf gehen? 9. Wo kommt ihr her und wo geht ihr hin? 10. Wir kommen aus Schwaben und gehen nach Preußen. 11. „Der Mann muß (L. 31. 11.) hinaus (gehen) in's feindliche Leben". 12. Wohl ihm, er ist hingegangen, wo kein Schnee mehr ist. 13. Der Taucher taucht in das Meer

hinab, um Perlen heraufzuholen. 14. Bei großen Stürmen sind die Schiffe oft in Gefahr, denn die Wellen schlagen mit Gewalt heran, das Schiff schwankt hinüber und herüber. 15. Des Morgens schreibt er und des Abends liest er. 16. Hinab, hinauf geht unser Lauf.

Exercise 77.   Aufgabe 77.

1. Where are you going? 2. I am going to the village, will you go there too? 3. I will go there but not to-day. 4. The boy sprang down into the water. 5. Our friends are in Vienna and we shall also go there. 6. Are your cousins coming here this week? 7. No, for they are already here. 8. We went up the Rhine from Coblenz to Mayence. 9. The carpenter fell down from the roof. 10. The horse ran down the mountain. 11. The boys went up the hill. 12. We must go to the forest, will you go there with us? 13. No, we must remain where we are. 14. I will go up if you will come down.

LESSON XXXIX.   Section XXXIX.

COLLOCATION OF WORDS.

1. When a subordinate sentence is introduced by one of the following words, the same order obtains as in relative sentences (L. 28. 3.); namely, als, bevor, bis, da, dafern, damit, daß, dieweil, ehe, falls, je, indem, insofern, nachdem, ob and its compounds, seitdem, ungeachtet, während, wann, warum, weil, wann, wie, and wo; as,

Wir wissen, warum er es gethan hat, und wo er hingegangen ist.	We know why he has done it, and where he has gone.
Er wartete, bis er sie gesehen hatte.	He waited till he had seen them.
Sobald er das hörte.	As soon as he heard that.

2. Da, weil, wenn* and wie are followed by the correlative so, at the head of a succeeding clause; as,

Da er nicht zu mir kommen will, so gehe ich zu ihm.	As he will not come to me (so) I go to him.
Wenn er nicht krank ist, so kommt er.	If he is not sick (so) he will come.

3. When obgleich, obwohl or obschon introduces a subordinate sentence followed by a principal one, the latter is introduced by so — doch; as,

Obgleich die Luft unsichtbar ist, so ist sie doch ein Körper.	Although the air is invisible, it is nevertheless a substance.

---

*) Wenn is often omitted, and the verb placed before its subject; as, Bist du reich, so unterstütze die Armen, bist du gelehrt, so unterrichte die Unwissenden. Art thou rich, (so) assist the poor, art thou learned, (so) instruct the ignorant.

Sometimes other words are placed between ob, and the word with which it is compounded; as,

Ob er gleich (or obgleich er) mein Although he is my friend.
Freund ist.

4. Aber, allein, denn, entweder, oder, nämlich, sondern and und do not change the natural order of the sentence; as,

Sie ist nicht schön, aber sie ist lie She is not beautiful, but she is
benswürdig. amiable.
Er ist fleißig; allein er lernt wenig. He is industrious, still he learns (but) little.

5. When a sentence begins with another word than its subject (except as above specified) the subject usually follows its verb; as,

Nie habe ich sie gemieden und schwer Never have I avoided them and
lich werde ich ihnen ganz entgehen. hardly shall I entirely escape them.
Denn ihn habe ich beleidigt. For him have I (I have) offended.
Diesen Mann kenne ich, jenen aber This man I know (know I), that
habe ich nie gesehen. one however I have (have I) never seen.
Zu lange schon hast du geschlum Too long already hast thou (thou
mert. hast) slumbered.
Länger kann ich nicht warten. Longer I can not (can I not) wait.
Nur mit dem Leben werden unsere Only with life will our sufferings
Leiden aufhören. (our sufferings will) cease.
Daß diese Sprache viel schwieriger That this language is much more
als die englische ist, haben Sie difficult than the English, you
wohl schon eingesehen. have probably already seen.
Da* liegt Ihr Buch. There lies your book (there your books lies).

6. Sometimes a causal conjunction in a leading clause is best omitted in translating; as,

Er ist deßhalb unzufrieden, weil sein He is (therefore) discontented
Freund nicht hier ist. because his friend is not here.

7. Adverbs (except genug) precede the adjectives and adverbs which they qualify; as,

Es ist schon ziemlich kalt. It is already pretty cold.
Der Hut ist groß genug. The hat is large enough.

---

* As the same word may be an adverb or a conjunction, it may require the construction of the relative sentence, or the inversion of subject and verb; as, da kommt Ihr Freund, there comes your friend: da ihr Freund kommt, so will ich warten, as (or since) your friend is coming, I will wait: damit bin ich zufrieden, with that (therewith) I am satisfied: damit ich nicht zu gehen brauche, geht er selbst, in order that I may not need to go, he goes himself.

8. Adverbs follow the verbs that they qualify (in compound tenses the first auxiliary); those of time preceding those of place ; as,

Er war gestern hier.	He was here yesterday.
Sie kommen oft zu uns.	They often come to our house.
Er wird morgen hier sein.	He will be here to-morrow.
Ich sehe ihn oft, aber er sieht mich nie.	I see him often but he never sees me.
Er wird diesen Abend nach der Stadt fahren.	He will drive to the city this afternoon.

9. Adverbs of time precede the object (except when it is a personal pronoun); while those of manner referring exclusively to the verb, commonly follow the object; as,

Er machte gestern seine Arbeit sehr schlecht.	He did his work yesterday very badly.
Er hat gestern seine Arbeit sehr schlecht gemacht.	He has done his work (yesterday) very badly. (See L. 26.5).
Er hat sie heute besser gemacht.	He has done it better to-day.
Er hat mir gestern diese Mittheilung schriftlich gemacht.	He made this communication to me yesterday in writing.

Exercise 78.   Aufgabe 78.

1. Endlich zeigten die Bürger ihre Waffen, und fingen an sich zu vertheidigen. 2. Ich hatte ihn gesehen, ehe seine Freunde angekommen waren. 3. Warten Sie, bis ich den Brief gelesen habe. 4. Wir wissen, daß er übermorgen kommen wird. 5. Je mehr Gott dir gegeben hat, desto mehr sollst du den Armen geben. 6. Je nachdem man gehandelt hat, wird man glücklich oder elend sein. 7. Ich weiß nicht, ob er da ist. 8. Seitdem sein Vater hier ist, ist er viel zufriedener. 9. Wir wissen, wie er das gethan hat, und wo er hingegangen ist. 10. Aus Dämpfen und Dünsten entstehen Nebel und Regen. 11. Sie wissen nicht, warum ich das gesagt habe. 12. Alle seine Kräfte wollte er sammeln und sie mit dem Feinde verbinden. 13. Unser Schiff nennt er einen Nachen. 14. Sie sind krank, deßhalb können sie nicht ausgehen. 15. Sie können nicht ausgehen, weil sie krank sind. 16. Weil sie krank sind, so können sie nicht ausgehen. 17. Sie sind krank und können deßhalb nicht ausgehen. 18. Er kann deßhalb nicht ausgehen, weil er krank ist. 19. Ueber uns sehen wir den Himmel und unzählige Sterne.

Exercise 79.   Aufgabe 79.

1. He has written more books than he has bought. 2. They saw me before I saw them. 3. We will wait here till you can go with us. 4. You know that I have not seen him. 5. The longer a man lives, the shorter time has he yet to live. 6. According as one is idle or industrious, will one be unhappy or contented. 7. I do not know whether he will come or not. 8. I have seen him since I have been here. 9. Do you know how long he remained in the city?

10. No, I know that he has been there, but I do not know how long he remained. 11. We know him but we do not know where he lives. 12. This boy is sad because his father is sick. 13. Because he has not much money he is discontented. 14. Although he is rich he is nevertheless discontented. 15. I am tired and can, therefore, write no longer. (L. 66.).

LESSON XL.   Section XL.

COMPOUND VERBS. INSEPARABLE.

1. The unaccented particles be, emp, ent, er, ge, ver, zer, when prefixed to verbs, reject the augment in the past participle, and take zu of the infinitive before them; as,

Er hat sein Haus verkauft.	He has sold his house.
Er hat ein Haus zu verkaufen.	He has a house to sell.
Wer hat dieses Verbrechen begangen?	Who has committed this crime?
Er befahl ihnen, (L. 50. 2.) ihre Häuser zu beleuchten.	He commanded them to illuminate their houses
Ich habe versucht, es ihm zu erklären, aber ich glaube nicht, daß er mich verstanden hat.	I have tried to explain it to him but I do not believe that he has understood me.
Ach, ich habe euren Jammer nur vergrößert.	Alas! I have only increased your grief.
Wie hat man euch empfangen?	How were you received?
Das hat mir nie gehört.	That has never belonged to me.
Du hast den Spiegel zerbrochen.	You have broken the looking-glass.

2. Durch, hinter, über, um, unter, voll, wider, and wieder, when accented, are separable, and when unaccented, inseparable; as,

Er wiederhol'te, was er gehört hatte.	He repeated what he had heard.
Er holte das Buch wieder.	He brought the book again.
Das Wasser ist durchgelaufen.	The water has run through.
Das Gerücht durchlief die Stadt.	The report spread through the city.
Er hat uns übergesetzt.	He has conveyed (ferried) us over.
Er hat ein Trauerspiel aus dem Deutschen übersetzt.	He has translated a tragedy from the German.

3. The particle miß, in some words, takes the accent, and, in the infinitive and past participle, is treated like other separable particles; as,

Es hat miß'getönt; es scheint mißzutönen.	It has sounded wrong: it seems to sound wrong (to mis sound).

4. In some verbs the augment is used before the prefix miß (but is oftener wholly rejected); as,

Er hat ihn gemiß'handelt (or miß= He has maltreated (abused)
handelt.) him.

Exercise 80. Aufgabe 80.

1. Ich hoffe morgen einen Brief zu erhalten. 2. Der arme Mann hat sein Geld erhalten. 3. Ich habe das Wort vergessen und das Papier verloren. 4. Die Deutschen haben viele nützliche Künste erfunden. 5. Meine Schüler haben sich gut betragen. 6. Man hat mir dieses Buch empfohlen. 7. Ich habe einen Brief von einem meiner Freunde erhalten, worin er seine Reise beschrieben hat. 8. Einer erwartet Geld von seinem Vater, und der Andere verdient sein Geld. 9. Wir mußten den alten Mann in das Meer begraben. 10. Der Bauer hat seinen Weizen verkauft. 11. Ihr Bruder hat mich mißverstanden, ich habe ihm nichts versprochen. 12. Er hat seinen Spiegel zerbrochen. 13. Unsere Freunde haben uns besucht, sie versuchten deutsch zu sprechen, aber wir konnten sie nicht verstehen. 14. Das tapfere Heer hat den Feind vertrieben. 15. Er hat seine Pflicht erfüllt und seine Freunde haben ihn belohnt. 16. Was für ein Verbrechen haben diese Leute begangen? 17. Sie haben einen Mann beraubt und ermordet. 18. Ich habe das noch nicht erhalten, was du mir versprochen hast. 19. Der Knabe hat seine Knöpfe polirt, anstatt sein Buch zu studiren.

Exercise 81. Aufgabe 81.

1. Have you received your money? 2. No, but I expect it to-morrow. 3. Have you studied this book much? 4. I have not had much time to study it. 5. Have you understood all that you have studied? 6. I have understood it but I have forgotten a part of it. 7. I earn the money that I receive. 8. Somebody has broken my knife. 9. We tried to speak German but they could not understand us. 10. I can recommend this book to you, I have studied it myself. 11. The poor man was obliged to sell his bed. 12. This man has committed no crime. 13. The thief has buried the murdered man in the forest. 14. He has robbed his friend. 15. Have you sold anything to-day? 16. Yes, I have sold my horse. 17. What have you promised me? 18. I have not promised you anything. 19. Either you have forgotten, or I have misunderstood you. 20. Do your duty and I will reward you.

LESSON XLI. Section XLI.

SUBJUNCTIVE.

1. The subjunctive is used:

   a. In subordinate sentences to indicate a wish or a result; in which use it answers to our potential; as,

EXAMPLES OF THE SUBJUNCTIVE AND THE INDICATIVE.

Er eilt, damit er nicht zu spät an- — He hastens in order that he may
komme. — not arrive too late.
Ich rathe dir, daß du fleißiger werdest. — I advise you that you (should) become more diligent.
Er muß fleißig sein, damit er lerne. — He must be diligent in order that he (may) learn.
Ehre deinen Vater und deine Mutter, damit dir's (dir es) wohl gehe und du lange lebest auf Erden. — Honor thy father and thy mother that it (may) go well with thee and that thou (mayest) live long on earth.

    b. In quoting a statement or an opinion without vouching for its correctness, as also in indirect questions; in which use it is rendered by the indicative; as,

Ich hörte, daß er sein Geld verloren habe. — I heard that he has lost his money.

Here I simply assert that I have heard the *report*, without knowing, or choosing to express an opinion as to its truth. But if, on the contrary, the indicative is used, the report is assumed to be true; as, ich hörte, daß er sein Geld verloren hat, (hat instead of habe).

    2. In this mode *our imperfect* and *pluperfect* are frequently translated by the *present* and *perfect*; as,

Er sagte, daß er kein Geld habe, (instead of hätte). — He said that he had (has) no money.
Man glaubte, er habe das Geld gestohlen. — It was thought he had (has) stolen the money.

EXAMPLES OF THE SUBJUNCTIVE AND THE INDICATIVE.

Subjunctive.	Indicative.	Indicative.	Indicative.
Ich hörte, daß er krank sei.	I heard, that he is sick.	Ich hörte, daß er krank ist.	I heard (and know) that he is sick.
Man sagt, er habe viel Geld.	They say he has much money.	Ich weiß, daß er viel Geld hat.	I know that he has much money.
Man glaubt, daß er kommen werde.	It is thought that he will come.	Man weiß, daß er kommen wird.	It is known that he will come.
Meinst du, daß ich dein Feind sei?	Thinkest thou that I am thy enemy?	Weißt du, daß ich dein Feind bin?	Knowest thou that I am thy enemy?

    3. The subjunctive is often used in the *third* person with the signification of the *imperative*; as,

Er nehme seine Entfernung. — He take (let him take) his distance.
Gesegnet sei, wer dich segnet. Gen. 27, 29. Dein Reich komme. Matt. 6, 10

The *first* person of the plural is sometimes thus used; as,
Gehen wir in den Garten.   Let us go into the garden.
(Thus, gehen wir &c., instead of, laßt uns in den Garten gehen).

4. SUBJUNCTIVE OF sein, haben AND werden.

PRESENT TENSE.

ich sei	ich habe	ich werde
du seiest (or seist)	du habest	du werdest
er sei	er habe	er werde
wir seien (or sein)	wir haben	wir werden
ihr seiet	ihr habet	ihr werdet
sie seien (or sein).	sie haben.	sie werden.

IMPERFECT TENSE.

ich wäre	ich hätte	ich würde
du wärest (or wärst)	du hättest	du würdest
er wäre	er hätte	er würde
wir wären	wir hätten	wir würden
ihr wäret (or wärt)	ihr hättet	ihr würdet
sie wären	sie hätten.	sie würden.

PERFECT TENSE.

ich sei		ich habe		ich sei	
du seist		du habest		du seist	
er sei	} gewesen.	er habe	} gehabt.	er sei	} geworden, or worden
wir seien		wir haben		wir seien	
ihr seiet		ihr habet		ihr seiet	
sie seien		sie haben		sie seien	

PLUPERFECT TENSE.

ich wäre		ich hätte		ich wäre	
du wärest		du hättest		du wärest	
er wäre	} gewesen.	er hätte	} gehabt.	er wäre	} geworden, (worden).
wir wären		wir hätten		wir wären	
ihr wäret		ihr hättet		ihr wäret	
sie wären		sie hätten		sie wären	

FIRST FUTURE TENSE.

ich werde		ich werde		ich werde	
du werdest		du werdest		du werdest	
er werde	} sein.	er werde	} haben.	er werde	} werden.
wir werden		wir werden		wir werden	
ihr werdet		ihr werdet		ihr werdet	
sie werden		sie werden		sie werden	

SECOND FUTURE TENSE.

ich werde		ich werde		ich werde	
du werdest		du werdest		du werdest	
er werde	} gewesen sein.	er werde	} gehabt haben.	er werde	} geworden (worden) sein.
wir werden		wir werden		wir werden	
ihr werdet		ihr werdet		ihr werdet	
sie werden		sie werden		sie werden	

SUBJUNCTIVE OF REGULAR VERBS.

5. In the present the third person is like the first; the second takes the longer forms (eſt and et, L. 27. 5.): the imperfect adds in the first and third persons singular, ete; and in the plural, eten; in the second singular, eteſt; and in the plural etet. Compare L. 27. 6. & 7. The other tenses are formed by combining the infinitive or past participle with subjunctive forms of haben, ſein and werden.

PRESENT AND IMPERFECT SUBJUNCTIVE OF loben.

Present.
ich lobe,   wir loben,
du lobeſt, ihr lobet,
er lobe,   ſie loben.

Imperfect.
ich lobete,   wir lobeten,
du lobeteſt, ihr lobetet,
er lobete,   ſie lobeten.

6. In the present and imperfect subjunctive of irregular verbs, the *first* and *third* persons are alike, and the *second* is regularly formed from the first. See List of Irregular Verbs, page 178.

EXERCISE 82.   Aufgabe 82.

1. Ich hörte, daß er hier gewesen, aber ich wußte nicht, ob es wahr sei. 2. Haben Sie auch gehört, ich sei vom Pferde gefallen? 3. Nein, ich hörte Sie seien aus dem Wagen gefallen. 4. Mein Bruder sagt, daß man Sie gelobt habe. 5. Die Franzosen behaupten, sie seien die Gebildetsten in der Welt. 6. Ihre Schwester glaubte, Sie seien in der Stadt gewesen; ich meinte aber, daß Sie im Walde gewesen seien. 7. Die Engländer sind der Meinung, sie seien die Herren des Meeres. 8. Dieser Reisende erzählt, daß er zweimal in Rom und dreimal in Venedig gewesen sei. 9. Er hofft, daß er in acht Tagen in Wien sein werde. 10. Ich glaube, daß viele Menschen hier auf Erden ihr Gutes gehabt haben werden. 11. Er sagte zwar, er sei krank, aber viele glauben, es sei Verstellung von ihm gewesen. 12. Ich hörte mit Bedauern, Sie hätten das Nervenfieber gehabt. 13. Er fragte mich, ob ich mein Buch gelesen hätte. 14. Er glaubt, er werde nie wieder glücklich sein. 15. Er hat mir versprochen, daß er morgen zu mir kommen werde. 16. Er meinte, ich möchte es lesen, aber ich könnte nicht. 17. Man bind' ihn an die Linde dort. 18. Er sagte, er müsse gehen.

EXERCISE 83.   Aufgabe 83.

1. I hope I shall see them to-morrow. 2. She insists upon it that they are here. 3. He made me believe that he was my friend. 4. We heard that you were unwell. 5. Why do you think that he is your enemy? 6. Because my friends told me that he hates me. 7. I have heard that my brother has lost his horse. 8. They say these people are very poor. 9. He says we were in his garden. 10. Did you hear that I had found my money? 11. I had not heard that you had lost your money. 12. This man says that he

has been in Vienna. 13. It is said that the ship has arrived. 14. These people think that we are very rich. 15. A good scholar studies diligently that he may learn rapidly. 16. He thought I could not write. 17. They said that they must have the money.

LESSON XLII. Section XLII.
CONDITIONAL.

1. The conditional mode is employed:
   a. Where a condition is supposed which is regarded as doubtful or impossible; as,

Ich könnte es thun, wenn ich Zeit hätte.	I could do it if I had time.
Er würde es thun, wenn er an Ihrer Stelle wäre.	He would do it if he were in your place.
Man könnte unabhängig sein, wenn man keine Bedürfnisse hätte.	One might be independent if one had no wants.

EXAMPLES OF THE CONDITIONAL AND THE INDICATIVE

Conditional.		Indicative.	
Ich könnte es thun, wenn ich Zeit hätte.	I could do it if I had time.	Ich hatte Zeit, aber ich konnte es nicht thun.	I had time, but I could not do it.
Er würde kommen, wenn er dürfte.	He would come if he were at liberty to.	Er konnte kommen, aber er wollte nicht.	He could come, but he would not.
Sie würde bleiben, wenn sie nicht gehen müßte.	She would remain if she were not obliged to go.	Sie wollte nicht bleiben, obgleich sie nicht gehen mußte.	She would not remain, although she was not obliged to go.
Er würde es gehört haben, wenn er da gewesen wäre.	He would have heard it if he had been there.	Er war da gewesen, aber er hatte es nicht gehört.	He had been there, but he had not heard it.

2. Instead of the first and second future, the forms of the imperfect and pluperfect subjunctive are often employed; the word wenn being omitted and the verb placed before its subject (L. 39. Note); as,

Ich hätte es gethan, wäre ich da gewesen: *instead of*,	I had done it, had I been there: *instead of*,
Ich würde es gethan haben, wenn ich da gewesen wäre.	I would have done it, if I had been there.
Er wäre da gewesen, hätte er Zeit gehabt: *instead of*,	He had been there, had he had time: *instead of*,
Er würde da gewesen sein, wenn er Zeit gehabt hätte.	He would have been there if he had had time.
Wüßte ich wo er ist, so ginge ich zu ihm: *instead of*,	[*Here, as seen, our idiom forbids a literal translation*];
Wenn ich wüßte wo er ist, so würde ich zu ihm gehen.	If I knew where he is, I would go to him.

CONDITIONAL.

3. Sometimes the condition is not expressed; as,

Hätte ich es nur gewußt! or,	Had I only known it! or,
Wenn ich es nur gewußt hätte!	If I had only known it!
Ich hätte es nicht geglaubt.	I would not have believed it.

4. The conditional is often employed:
    b. Interrogatively to express surprise at, or dissent from an assertion; as,

Wann hätte Friedland (i. e. the duke of Friedland) unsers Raths bedurft?	When has Friedland needed our advice? (i. e. he has never needed it.)
Du wärest so falsch gewesen?	You had been so false?
Gastfreundlich hätte England sie empfangen?	England has received her hospitably? (do you say?)

5. CONDITIONAL OF *sein haben* AND *werden*.

FIRST CONDITIONAL.

ich würde		ich würde		ich würde	
du würdest		du würdest		du würdest	
er würde	} sein.	er würde	} haben.	er würde	} werden.
wir würden		wir würden		wir würden	
ihr würdet		ihr würdet		ihr würdet	
sie würden		sie würden		sie würden	

SECOND CONDITIONAL.

ich würde		ich würde		ich würde	
du würdest		du würdest		du würdest	
er würde	} gewesen sein.	er würde	} gehabt haben.	er würde	} geworden (worden) sein.
wir würden		wir würden		wir würden	
ihr würdet		ihr würdet		ihr würdet	
sie würden		sie würden		sie würden	

EXERCISE 84.   Aufgabe 84.

1. Das Beste, was wir thun könnten, wäre, gleich abzureisen. 2. Wer hätte geglaubt, daß er uns verlassen würde? 3. Er hätte es gewiß nicht gethan, wenn wir ihn gütig behandelt hätten. 4. Kein vernünftiger Mensch würde so gehandelt haben. 5. Er könnte recht gut leben, wenn er nicht so verschwenderisch wäre. 6. Ich würde gleich zu ihm gehen, wenn ich nur wüßte, wo er ist. 7. Sie wäre gewiß von der Brücke hinab gefallen, wenn ihre Freundin sie nicht gehalten hätte. 8. Er würde elend sein, wenn er so leben müßte wie ich (L. 26. 7.). 9. Wenn ich das gewußt hätte, so wäre ich ganz anders verfahren. 10. Ich würde mit Ihnen gehen, wenn ich nicht so viel zu thun hätte. 11. Wenn ich das Buch gesehen hätte, so würde ich es gekauft haben. 12. Wir würden schon sprechen können, wenn wir fleißig studirt hätten. 13. Wenn sie Zeit hätten, würden sie uns gewiß begleiten. 14. Wenn ich englisch könnte, so würde ich gleich nach Amerika auswandern. 15. Ich glaube nicht, daß du lange dort bleiben würdest, wenn du auswandern solltest. 16. Ich würde das Holz kaufen, wenn es gut wäre.

REFLEXIVE VERBS.

Exercise 85. Aufgabe 85.

1. What would you do with this book if it were yours? 2. I would study and try to learn the language that it teaches. 3. What would you do if you were rich? 4. I would travel and study. 5. I should be satisfied if I could speak as well as you do. 6. If I had had a good teacher I should have learned much faster. 7. Would you sell this house if it were yours? 8. No, I would live in it. 9. I do not believe you could sell it. 10. If you had called, I should certainly have heard you. 11. You would have money enough if you were only industrious. 12. We could have bought the horses if we had had the money. 13. I would write you a German letter if I could. 14. We should have seen your friends if they had been at home. 15. They would come if they had not so much to do.

LESSON XLIII. Section XLIII.

REFLEXIVE VERBS.

1. The number of verbs that are used exclusively as reflexives, is much larger in German than in English; as,

Ich schäme mich.	I am ashamed.
Was hat sich ereignet?	What has happened?
Sie sehnt sich nach Ruhe.	She longs for quiet.
Das Heer ergab sich.	The army surrendered (itself).
Ich unterstehe mich, das zu thun.	I venture to do that.
Er ereifert sich.	He is becoming angry.
Er widersetzt sich dem Befehl.	He opposes (himself to) the command.
Sie haben sich an ihm vergriffen.	They have attacked (laid hands on) him.
Ich getraue mich nicht dahin.	I do not venture (trust myself) there.
Er erkundigte sich nach ihnen.	He inquired after them.
Wir können uns hiermit behelfen.	We can make shift with this.
Er hat sich erholt.	He has recovered.
Er besinnt sich.	He bethinks himself.
Sie haben sich gut aufgeführt.	They have behaved themselves well.
Er bestrebt sich, es zu thun.	He tries (exerts himself) to do it.

Many other verbs, though not exclusively reflexive, are often used as such; as,

Sie betragen sich gut.	They behave themselves well.
Was grämt ihr euch?	Why do you grieve?
Sie haben sich entschlossen.	They have resolved.
Man sollte sich in die Umstände schicken.	One should adapt one's-self to circumstances.

REFLEXIVE VERBS.

Er befindet sich wohl. — He is (finds himself) well.
Wie befinden Sie sich? — How do you do? (find yourself?).

2. Verbs are often used reflexively whose corresponding English ones are employed intransitively or passively; as,

Das Wetter hellt sich auf. — The weather is clearing (itself) up.

Die Soldaten sammeln sich um ihren Führer. — The soldiers assemble (themselves) around their leader.

Wir hielten uns in Berlin auf. — We stopped (ourselves) in Berlin.

Das Buch hat sich gefunden. — The book has been found.

Der Himmel bedeckt sich mit Wolken. — The sky is being covered (covering itself) with clouds.

Soll der Frevel sich vor unsern Augen vollenden? — Shall the outrage be accomplished (accomplish itself) before our eyes?

Der Grund läßt sich hören. — The reason is plausible (lets itself be heard).

Das läßt sich sehen. — That looks well (lets itself be seen).

Das lasse ich mir nicht zweimal sagen. — I don't wait to be told that twice (do not let it be said to me twice).

Exercise 86. Aufgabe 86.

1. Jeder gute Bürger unterwirft sich den gerechten Gesetzen seines Landes. 2. Das feindliche Heer hat sich endlich ergeben müssen. 3. Die Kraft, mit welcher die Muskeln sich zusammenziehen und ausdehnen, ist sehr groß. 4. Alle Dünste und Dämpfe, welche beständig von der Erde aufsteigen, sammeln sich in der Atmosphäre, und indem sie sich verbinden, entsteht daraus Regen, Schnee, Nebel, Wind und jede andere Veränderung der Luft. 5. Diejenigen, welche sich selbst loben, machen sich sehr oft lächerlich. 6. Die Söhne Karls des Großen mußten sich in den Waffen, im Reiten und im Schwimmen üben. 7. Der Gläubige zeigt sich im Ungemach wie ein Fels im Meere, wenn die Meereswogen um ihn toben. 8. Das blaue Gewölbe, welches wir Himmel nennen, ist ein unermeßlicher Raum, in welchem die Erde, die Sonne, der Mond und unzählige Sterne sich bewegen. 9. Das Heer lagerte sich um die Stadt und forderte dieselbe auf, sich zu übergeben. 10. Die Bürger glaubten, sie könnten sich vertheidigen, und weigerten sich, sich dem stolzen Feinde zu unterwerfen. 11. „Im Osten erhob sich der Mond und schwamm wie ein leichter Nachen im Wiederscheine des Abendroths." 12. Er weigert sich, mit uns zu gehen, und ich freue mich, daß er nicht gehen will.

Exercise 87. Aufgabe 87.

1. My friend has determined to go to France. 2. They are ashamed that they have been so idle and inattentive. 3. The clouds are gathering, I think it will soon rain. 4. The boy refuses to go with us because he wishes to visit one of his friends who is

sick. 5. They defended themselves bravely but were finally obliged to surrender. 6. We should oppose all unjust laws 7. I am glad that we can go, and that we have so fine weather 8. This occurred while you were stopping in Berlin. 9. One should not deliberate too long. 10. Everybody should endeavor to do his duty. 11. The army encamped on a large field not far from the city, and summoned the citizens to surrender. 12. We should not praise ourselves. 13. I am glad you have visited my friend; how does he do? 14. He is very well, but his brother and his cousin are not very well. 15. There have been three men here this afternoon who have inquired after you; one of them said he had determined to remain here until you should return, but he allowed himself to be persuaded to go with the others. 16. He who can easily adapt himself to circumstances, is to be called fortunate, even if he is poor and deserted. 17. The people have not been able to defend themselves, and have again submitted to their cruel oppressors.

LESSON XLIV.   Section XLIV.

IMPERSONAL VERBS.

1. Besides the verbs, es donnert, it thunders: es blitzt, it lightens: es regnet, it rains: es schneit, it snows, &c., which (as in English) are properly impersonal, many others are used impersonally; as,

Es freut mich.	I am glad (*lit.* it rejoices me).
Es thut mir sehr leid.	I am very sorry.
Es gelingt mir, meinen Freund zu überzeugen.	I succeed in convincing my friend.
Endlich glückte es ihm.	Finally he succeeded.
Es hungert und dürstet ihn.	He is hungry and thirsty.
Es friert uns.	We are cold.
Es heißt, er werde bald kommen.	It is said he will come soon.
Hier heißt es mit Recht, daß u.s.w.	Here it is justly said that, &c.
Das heißt, wenn sie es billigen.	That is (that is to say) if you approve it.

2. In the use of impersonal verbs the nominative es is sometimes omitted, and the accusative or dative placed before the verb; as,

Mich hungert, for, es hungert mich.	I am hungry, *lit.* it hungers me.
Mir schwindelt, for, es schwindelt mir.	I feel dizzy.
Es ekelt mich jeder Speise, or mir ekelt vor jeder Speise.	I loathe all food.
Dem Vater grauset's	The father is frightened.

Similar to this is the phrase mich dünkt, or mich däucht*, answering to "methinks".

3. Geben impersonally used, indicates existence in a general and indefinite manner, and is rendered by "to be"; the *object* of geben, being used as the *subject* of "to be"; as,

Es gibt keine Rosen ohne Dornen.   There are no roses without thorns.
Was gibt's (gibt es) Neues?   What is there new? (what news is there?)
Was gibt's?   What is the matter? (what is there?)

4. Fehlen, gebrechen and mangeln, are often used impersonally with two datives; the latter one being preceded by „an"; as,

Es fehlt ihm an Muth.   He is deficient in courage.
Es mangelt mir an Geld.   I am in want of (I lack) money.
Woran gebricht es Ihnen?   What are you in want of?

5. Some verbs are used impersonally and reflexively; as,

Es versteht sich (or es versteht sich von selbst), daß nicht alle reich sein können.   Of course (or, as a matter of course) not all can be rich.
Es gebürt sich nicht, so zu handeln.   It is not becoming thus to act.
Es schläft sich gut hier.   One can sleep well here.

Exercise 88.   Aufgabe 88.

1. Es ist ihm endlich gelungen, seinen Freund zu überzeugen. 2. Sein Plan ist gelungen, und doch ist er unzufrieden. 3. Es fragt sich, ob wir morgen gehen können? 4. Es gehört sich, den Sonntag zu heiligen. 5. Es schickt sich, ältere Leute zu achten. 6. Es ereignet sich selten, daß gute, verständige Leute sich entzweien. 7. Es thut dem Knaben sehr leid, daß er so nachläßig gewesen ist. 8. Es würde mich sehr freuen, ihn wiederzusehen. 9. Dürstet Sie? 10. Nein, aber mich hungert und friert. 11. Es versteht sich, daß er heute nicht kommen wird; denn die Wege sind zu schlecht. 12. Es trägt sich zuweilen zu, daß anhaltender Regen die ganze Ernte verdirbt. 13. Auf der Insel Malta gibt es keine Schlangen; in Sardinia gibt es keine Wölfe; in Deutschland gibt es keine Krokodile; auf Island gibt es nichts Giftiges, aber in der ganzen Welt ist kein Ort, wo es keinen Neid gibt.

Exercise 89.   Aufgabe 89.

1. I would be very glad to accompany you home but I am afraid it will rain, do you not see how it lightens, and hear how it thunders? 2. I think it will snow to-morrow, it is questionable whether our friends will be able to come as they have promised. 3. The peasants have finally succeeded in selling their horses. 4. I am very sorry not to have seen them, but it was so cold while they were

---

* With däucht, dünkt, the dative (instead of accusative) is often used; as, mir däucht or dünkt, or es däucht or dünkt mir.

in the city that I could not go out. 5. It sometimes happens that lazy people are very rich, but never that they are wise, learned, useful or happy. 6. This man is not hungry, but he is very cold. 7. Of course you will visit us as soon as you can, will you not? 8. It is not proper to do that. 9. Is there a better beverage in the world than cold water? 10. They say they are very sorry that they did not succeed in convincing us that we were wrong. 11. A man who is deficient in courage is not a (L. 52. 11.) good soldier. 12. What is the matter, why are all those people running into the house?

LESSON XLV.   Section XLV.

PASSIVE VERBS.

1. The passive is formed by connecting the auxiliary werden, with the past participle of the main verb; as,

Das Pferd wird beschlagen.	The horse is being shod.
Das Haus wird gebaut.	The house is being built (or is building).
Die Bücher werden verkauft.	The books are being sold (or are selling).

Obs. The past participle in connection with the verb „sein", denotes that an action is completed; as,

Das Pferd ist beschlagen.	The horse is shod.
Das Haus ist gebaut.	The house is built (finished).
Die Bücher sind verkauft.	The books are sold.
Sie werden gelobt werden.	You will be praised.

2. When the past participle of werden is used as an auxiliary, it rejects the augment ge, and is translated by *been*, while sein is translated by *"to have"* (L. 32. 34.); as,

Er ist gelobt worden.	He has been praised.
Die Bücher waren verkauft worden.	The books had been sold.
Die Bücher werden verkauft worden sein.	The books will have been sold.

3. Passive verbs are often used impersonally to denote an action or event in progress; as,

Es wird gesungen.	There is singing (going on, or being done).
Es wurde bis spät in die Nacht gefochten.	The fighting was continued (it was fought) till late in the night.
Es wurde ihm von allen Seiten zu Hülfe geeilt.	From all sides it was run to his assistance.—*Milton.*
Dort wird alle Tage getanzt und gespielt.	There, there is dancing and playing every day.

4. PARADIGM OF
Geliebt werden,

	INDICATIVE.				SUBJUNCTIVE.		
	PRESENT TENSE.				**PRESENT TENSE.**		
SING. 1 2 3 PLUR. 1 2 3	ich werde du wirst er wird wir werden ihr werdet sie werden	geliebt,	I am thou art he is we are you are they are	loved.	ich werde du werdest er werde wir werden ihr werdet sie werden	geliebt,	I may thou mayst he may we may you may they may	be loved.
	IMPERFECT TENSE.				**IMPERFECT TENSE.**		
SING. 1 2 3 PLUR. 1 2 3	ich wurde du wurdest er wurde wir wurden ihr wurdet sie wurden	geliebt,	I was thou wast he was we were you were they were	loved.	ich würde du würdest er würde wir würden ihr würdet sie würden	geliebt,	I might thou mightst he might we might you might they might	be loved.
	PERFECT TENSE.				**PERFECT TENSE.**		
SING. 1 2 3 PLUR. 1 2 3	ich bin du bist er ist wir sind ihr seid sie sind	geliebt worden,	I have thou hast he has we have you have they have	been loved.	ich sei du seiest er sei wir seien ihr seiet sie seien	geliebt worden,	I may thou mayst he may we may you may they may	have been loved.
	PLUPERFECT TENSE.				**PLUPERFECT TENSE.**		
SING. 1 2 3 PLUR. 1 2 3	ich war du warst er war wir waren ihr waret sie waren	geliebt worden,	I had thou hadst he had we had you had they had	been loved.	ich wäre du wärest er wäre wir wären ihr wäret sie wären	geliebt worden,	I might thou mightst he might we might you might they might	have been loved.
	FIRST FUTURE TENSE.				**FIRST FUTURE TENSE.**		
SING. 1 2 3 PLUR. 1 2 3	ich werde du wirst er wird wir werden ihr werdet sie werden	geliebt werden,	I shall thou wilt he will we shall you will they will	be loved.	ich werde du werdest er werde wir werden ihr werdet sie werden	geliebt werden,	(if) I shall „ thou wilt „ he will „ we shall „ you will „ they will	be loved.
	SECOND FUTURE TENSE.				**SECOND FUTURE TENSE.**		
SING. 1 2 3 PLUR. 1 2 3	ich werde du wirst er wird wir werden ihr werdet sie werden	geliebt worden sein,	I shall thou wilt he will we shall you will hey will	have been loved.	ich werde du werdest er werde wir werden ihr werdet sie werden	geliebt worden sein,	(if) I shall „ thou wilt „ he will „ we shall „ you will „ they will	have been loved.

Geliebt werden, TO BE LOVED.

A PASSIVE VERB.
to be loved.

CONDITIONAL.	IMPERAT.	INFINITIVE.	PARTIC.
PRESENT TENSE.	PRESENT TENSE. werde du, werde er, werden wir, werdet ihr, werden sie } geliebt, be thou loved, &c.	PRESENT TENSE. geliebt werden, to be loved.	PRESENT.
IMPERFECT TENSE.	IMPERF. TENSE.	IMPERF. TENSE.	IMPERFECT.
PERFECT TENSE.	PERFECT TENSE.	PERFECT TENSE. geliebt worden sein, to have been loved.	PERFECT. geliebt, loved.
PLUPERFECT TENSE.	PLUPERF. TENSE.	PLUPERF. TENSE.	PLUPERF
FIRST FUTURE. ich würde, du würdest, er würde, wir würden, ihr würdet, sie würden } geliebt werden, I should be loved, &c.	FIRST FUTURE.	FIRST FUTURE. werden geliebt werden, to be about to be loved.	1st. FUTURE.
SECOND FUTURE. ich würde, du würdest, er würde, wir würden, ihr würdet, sie würden } geliebt worden sein, I should have been loved, &c.	SECOND FUTURE.	SECOND FUTURE.	2d. FUTURE.

SYNTAX OF THE DEFINITE ARTICLE.

Exercise 90.   Aufgabe 90.

1. Der Fleißige wird geachtet und gelobt, und der Faule wird verachtet und getadelt. 2. Die steilsten Felsen werden von den Gemsenjägern erklettert. 3. Der günstige Augenblick wird von dem Klugen ergriffen. 4. Es wurde mehr gespielt als gearbeitet. 5. Der Streit wurde auf beiden Seiten mit großer Erbitterung geführt. 6. Das Werk ist endlich vollendet worden und wird bald erscheinen. 7. Endlich ist es ausgefunden worden, wer der Dieb ist. 8. Es wird bereinst ein ernstes Gericht gehalten werden, nachdem alle Völker werden versammelt worden sein. 9. Der Nachbar glaubt, daß der Vater von seinem Kinde getäuscht werde. 10. Die Geschichte meldet, daß Troja von den griechischen Fürsten zerstört worden sei. 11. Der Arme klagt, daß er gewaltsam fortgeschleppt worden sei. 12. Der betrübte Vater glaubt, sein Sohn werde von dem erbitterten Feinde erschossen worden sein. 13. Die Freundin behauptete, daß das Unglück durch die Schuld des Nachbars herbeigeführt worden wäre. 14. Prometheus war von Jupiter an einen Felsen geschmiedet worden. 15. Das Haus wird von einem sehr geschickten Mann gebaut.

Exercise 91.   Aufgabe 91.

1. Do you know why you have been blamed by your friends? 2. I was blamed by them because the letter that has been promised by me had not been written before they arrived here. 3. I hope the enemy will be defeated and driven out of the country. 4. My letter will have been read before yours will have been written. 5. We are not often hated by those who are loved by us. 6. The bad will be punished and the good will be rewarded. 7. Good men are often slandered while they live, and praised and honored after they are dead. 8. The ring of the rich young traveler has been found by one of his servants. 9. These beautiful baskets are said (L. 31. 4. b.) to have been made by the blind man to whom the flute was sent yesterday. 10. Those indolent boys deserve to be punished. 11. There has been more done to-day than yesterday. 12. We are often deceived by those who praise us, for we are often praised by flatterers. 13. The hunter says he has been bitten by a bear that had been shot by one of his companions. 14. Has it not yet been made out by whom the money was stolen? 15. Do you know by whom these letters were written? 16. These people think they have been deceived by us.

LESSON XLVI.   Section XLVI.

SYNTAX OF THE DEFINITE ARTICLE.

1. The definite article is often used in German, where in translating it is omitted:

    a. Before nouns (in the plural as well as singular) taken in a general sense, as,

Die Rose heißt die Königin der Blumen.	The rose is called the queen of (the) flowers.
Das Pferd ist ein nützliches Thier.	The horse is a useful animal.
Die Pferde sind nützliche Thiere.	(The) horses are useful animals.
Die Freiheit ist des Menschen höchstes Gut.	(The) freedom is (the) man's highest good.
„Der Himmel hilft, die Hölle muß uns weichen!"	(The) Heaven helps, (the) hell must yield!

    b. Before the names of lakes, mountains, days, months, seasons, ranks, bodies or systems of doctrine, the superlative of adjectives, masculine or feminine names of countries, as also before the words Hof, Kirche, Markt, Mühle, Schule, and Stadt; as,

Der Vesuv ist ein Vulkan'.	(The) Vesuvius is a volcano.
Der Sonntag in Europa ist sehr verschieden von dem Sonntag in Amerika.	(The) Sunday in Europe is very different from (the) Sunday in America.
Der Mai ist schöner als der März.	(The) May is pleasanter than (the) March.
Die meisten Eltern schicken ihre Kinder in die Schule und in die Kirche.	(The) most parents send their children to (the) school and to (the) church.
Sind Sie je in der Schweiz gewesen?	Have you ever been in (the) Switzerland?

    c. Before nouns specifying time, or quantity, where in English the indefinite article is used; as,

Ich sehe ihn zweimal des Jahrs.	I see him twice a (the) year.
Es kostet fünf Groschen das Pfund.	It costs five groshens a (the) pound.

    d. In many expressions which mark a change in the condition of a person or thing, and in English require the nominative, or objective *after* a verb, the dative with zum (or zur) is employed; as,

Man machte ihn zum Hauptmann.	He was made a captain.
Es ist zum Sprichwort geworden.	It has become a proverb.

    e. Before the proper names of persons when preceded by an adjective; before the names of relatives or intimate friends; when the name of an author is put for his works, and in the oblique cases of such as do not by inflectional endings, indicate the case; as,

Die schöne Helena.	The beautiful Helen.
Der arme Heinrich.	(The) poor Henry.
Sage dem Johann, er soll kommen.	Tell John, to come *(he shall come)*.
Die Verbannung des Aristides.	The banishment of Aristides.
Sie lesen jetzt den Herder.	They are now reading Herder

f. The definite article (when the sense is not thereby obscured) may be used instead of a possessive pronoun; as,

Er hat den Hut noch auf dem Kopfe.	He still has his hat on his head.
Was hast du in der Hand?	What have you in your (the) hand?

When used with beide, halb, so, solcher, wie, and zu, the article comes first; as,

Die beiden Diener blieben einen halben Tag.	Both the servants remained half a (a half) day.
Ein wie alter Mann ist er?	How old a man is he?

2. The definite article is omitted before names of the cardinal points, when motion from or towards them is expressed, as also in a variety of phrases where it is employed in English; as,

Im Herbst ziehen die Vögel von Norden nach Süden.	In autumn the birds migrate from *the* north to *the* south.
Ueberbringer dieses ist ein Freund von mir.	*The* bearer of this is a friend of mine.
Das ist nicht Mode (Sitte) bei uns.	That is not *the* fashion (custom) with us (in our country).

3. In legal reports, the usage of the two languages is similar; as,

Kläger behauptet, daß u. s. w.	Complainant maintains that, &c.

4. The indefinite article is often omitted before nouns used as the predicate of sein, or werden; as,

Er wurde erst Soldat, nachher König.	He became first (a) soldier, afterwards (a) king.

5. The indeclinable dergleichen (such, such like), may relate to nouns of all genders and both numbers, and in any case; as,

Dergleichen Wein ist theuer.	Such wine is dear.
Trinken Sie je dergleichen?	Do you ever drink the like?

Exercise 92.   Aufgabe 92.

1. Die Armuth ist oft der verdiente Lohn der Faulheit. 2. Die Hoffnung ist der treueste Tröster der Menschen. 3. Im Juli ist das Wetter sehr heiß. 4. Der Vater ist am Hof, die Mutter in der Kirche, der Sohn auf der Universität, der Knecht auf dem Markt und das Kind in der Schule. 5. Sage dem Johann, er soll von jetzt an viermal die Woche auf den Markt gehen. 6. Erst segelten wir nach Osten und dann nach Süden. 7. In Deutschland ist es Sitte, daß man den Hut abnimmt, wenn man Freunden begegnet. 8. Ein solcher Mann würde ein solches Verbrechen gewiß nicht begehen. 9. Er ist ein zu alter Mann Soldat zu werden. 10. Können Sie noch eine halbe Stunde warten? 11. Wie! nennst du ein so elendes Geschöpf deinesgleichen? (L. 25. 4.) 12. Der Freie liebt gewöhnlich den Frieden

PROPER AND COMMON NAMES. 121

Exercise 93.   Aufgabe 93.

1. Indolence is an unpardonable vice. 2. To so miserable a life as this, I would prefer death. 3. This is too large a stove for so small a room. 4. The eloquence and patriotism of Demosthenes saved his country. 5. March is a very windy unpleasant month, the Germans sometimes call it Frühlingsmonat, because it is the first month of spring. 6. Why do you wear such a hat? 7. We go to town three times a year. 8. This cloth cost six florins an ell. 9. In France it is the custom for people to take off their hats when a funeral procession passes by. 10. I will wait half a day longer if you will go with me. 12. How long an exercise have you written to-day? 13. The servant has gone to market to buy beef, eggs, potatoes and the like.

LESSON XLVII.   Section XLVII.

PROPER AND COMMON NAMES.

1. The proper and common names of places and countries, as also of months, are placed in apposition; as,

Die Stadt Berlin ist in dem Königreich Preußen.   The city (of) Berlin is in the Kingdom (of) Prussia.
Der Monat Mai ist schön.   The month (of) May is fine.

2. The date (without a preposition intervening) precedes the name of the month; as,

Vom fünften Mai bis zum vier und zwanzigsten August.   From the fifth (of) May till the twenty-fourth (of) August.

3. Nouns denoting weight, measure and quantity, stand in the same case as those they limit and (feminines excepted) are not declined; as,

Drei Paar (see 5.) Handschuhe.   Three pairs (of) gloves.
Zwei Pfund Kaffee.   Two pounds (of) coffee.
Er hat acht Stück Vieh.   He has eight head (of) cattle.
Drei Ellen Tuch.   Three ells (of) cloth.

Obs. When the latter noun, however, is qualified by some other word, it is put in the genitive; as,

Drei Pfund dieses Kaffees.   Three pounds of this coffee.
Zwei Buch des besten Papiers.   Two quires of the best paper.

4. Like nouns of weight, &c., (see 3.) is used the word Art (kind or sort); as,

Er hat eine neue Art Papier.   He has a new kind (of) paper.
Er spricht von einer besonderen Art Hunde.   He is speaking of a particular kind (of) dogs.

5. Ein Paar (*literally* a pair) often answers to "a few" and is used undeclined, before nouns in any case; as,

Er hat ein Paar Freunde bei sich.   He has a *few* friends with him
Er kommt in ein Paar Tagen.   He is coming in a *few* days.

6. **Mann**, referring to organized bodies of men, retains the singular form; as,

Ein Regiment von tausend Mann.   A regiment of a thousand men.

EXERCISE 94.   Aufgabe 94.

1. Am ersten Mai wird die Armee in die Stadt ziehen. 2. Der alte Viehhändler hat hundert Stück Vieh gekauft. 3. Er trinkt jeden Morgen zwei Glas Wasser. 4. Wollen Sie mir ein Stück Brod geben? 5. Ich will Ihnen zwei Stück Fleisch geben. 6. Wir fuhren am fünf und zwanzigsten Januar von der Stadt New-York ab, und kamen am achtzehnten Februar in der Stadt Bremen an. 7. Der Monat Mai ist viel angenehmer als der Monat April. 8. Die Stadt Berlin ist die Hauptstadt des Königreichs Preußen. 9. Das ist eine Art Frucht, die ich nie gesehen habe. 10. Er hat zwei Paar Handschuhe und sechs Ellen Tuch gekauft. 11. Der Dom in der Stadt Magdeburg ist sehr schön. 12. Das Königreich Sachsen ist sehr klein. 13. Er hat noch ein wenig Geld, denn ein guter Freund hat ihm neulich ein Paar Thaler geschickt.

EXERCISE 95.   Aufgabe 95.

1. Here is a little piece of paper for you. 2. Our friends live in the city of Vienna. 3. The shoemaker has sent you a pair of shoes. 4. I have bought three barrels of flour and a hundred pounds of coffee. 5. The kingdom of Prussia is larger than the kingdoms of Saxony and Bavaria. 6. We were in the city of Dresden in the month of June. 7. The city of Hamburg is rich and very beautiful. 8. This man says he has a new kind of paper. 9. Will you give me a glass of water? 10. Will you not take a glass of wine? 11. I have already drank a glass of wine. 12. We remained only a few days and did not see much. 13. On the sixteenth of August we were in the city of Cologne.

LESSON XLVIII.   Section XLVIII.

PREPOSITIONS AND ADJECTIVES WITH THE GENITIVE.

1. The following prepositions are construed with the genitive; viz, anstatt *or* statt, instead; außerhalb, outside, without; diesseit(s), on this side; halb, halben *or* halber, on account (of); innerhalb, inside, within; jenseit(s), on that (the other) side, beyond; kraft, by virtue of; längs, along; laut, according to; oberhalb, above; trotz, in spite of; um — willen, for the sake of; ungeachtet, notwithstanding; unterhalb, below; unfern, unweit, near, not far from; vermittelst, mittelst, by means of; vermöge, by dint of; während, during; wegen, on account of; zufolge, according to.

2. Trotz and längs may be used with the dative; as,

Längs dem Wege (or des Weges).   Along the road (the way).
Trotz meinem Suchen (or meines   In spite of my search (seeking).
Suchens).

3. Zufolge, when preceding its noun, requires the genitive; when following it, the dative; as,

Zufolge des Berichts, or dem Be=   According to the report.
richt zufolge.

4. Halb, halber or halben, always follows its noun; ungeachtet and wegen may precede or follow it; as,

Alters halber.   On account of age.
Man schätzt ihn wegen seines Fleißes   He is esteemed on account of
und liebt ihn seiner Tugend wegen.   his industry, and loved on
                                       account of his virtue.

5. In um—willen the genitive always stands between um and willen; as,

Um des Freundes willen.   For the friend's sake.

6. Halben, wegen and willen, are often compounded with the genitive case of pronouns, in which use t is substituted for the final r; and sometimes with the relative pronoun, in which t is added to the genitive; as,

Meinetwegen;   (for my sake)   instead of meinerwegen.
Ihretwillen;   (for your sake)   instead of Ihrerwillen.
Um dessen:willen;   (for whose sake)   instead of um dessenwillen.

7. Anstatt (compounded of an and Statt) may be divided · Statt taking its original character as a noun; as,

An seines Bruders Statt, or anstatt   In his brother's stead, or instead
seines Bruders.   of his brother.

8. The following adjectives are construed with and usually follow the genitive:

bedürftig, in want; benöthigt, necessitated, in want; bewußt, conscious, aware; eingedenk, mindful; fähig, capable; froh, glad; gewärtig, in expectation, waiting; gewiß, certain, sure; kundig, having a knowledge, skilled; ledig, free, single; leer, void, empty; mächtig, powerful, (master of); schuldig,* guilty; theilhaft (ig), participant, sharing; überdrüßig, tired, disgusted; verdächtig, suspected, suspicious; verlustig, deprived (of); würdig, worthy, gewahr, aware; gewohnt, accustomed to; los, free, rid; müde, tired, weary; satt, satiated; voll, full; werth, worthy, worth.

---

* „Schuldig sein," with the accusative answers to "to owe", "to be indebted"; as, er ist mir zehn Gulden schuldig, he owes me ten florins.

Des deutschen Winters ungewohnt.	Unaccustomed to the German winter.
Die Erde ist voll der Güte des Herrn.	The earth is full of the goodness of the Lord. Ps. 33, 5.
Sie wurden der inneren Kraft sich bewußt.	They became conscious of their inherent strength.

9. The last seven adjectives of the above list are more commonly used with the accusative; as,

Ich bin diesen Anblick gewohnt.	I am accustomed to this sight.
Es ist einen Gulden werth.	It is worth* a florin.
Ein Korb voll Aepfel.	A basket full of apples.

In this use voll often takes the ending er; as,

Voller Gnade und Wahrheit.	Full of grace and truth.

10. Gewiß, leer and voll are often followed by von, fähig by zu, and froh by über; as,

Er ist zu Allem fähig.	He is capable of anything.
Voll von Feinden ist die Welt.	Full of foes is the world.
Dein Herz sei nicht froh über sein Unglück.	Let not thy heart be glad when he stumbleth (*lit.* over his misfortune).

Exercise 96. Aufgabe 96.

1. Wenn das Pferd seiner Stärke bewußt wäre, könnte Niemand es bändigen. 2. Ich bin viel Geld schuldig, aber ich bin keines Verbrechens schuldig. 3. Er würde diese Arbeit, deren er ganz ungewohnt ist, nicht thun, wenn er nicht des Geldes benöthigt wäre. 4. Ist dein Bruder deiner Hülfe bedürftig, so frage nicht, ob er derselben würdig ist. 5. Mancher Mensch verbringt sein Leben uneingedenk seiner ewigen Bestimmung. 6. Die meisten Verluste sind eines Ersatzes fähig. 7. Kein Geiziger kann seines Lebens froh werden. 8. Er ist seiner Uebereilung gewahr geworden. 9. Ich bin des Lebens und Herrschens müde. 10. Der tapfere Tell ist frei und seines Armes mächtig. 11. Innerhalb der Stadt wüthete die Pest, und außerhalb derselben der Feind. 12. Er hat meinen Hut anstatt des seinigen genommen. 13. Während meines Aufenthalts in D. wurde ich des Stadtlebens ganz überdrüssig. 14. Kraft seines Amtes verhaftete er alle, die er des Verraths verdächtig hielt. 15. Um seines Vaters Willen bleibt er in dieser Stelle, obgleich er einer bessern würdig ist. 16. „Der König und die Kaiserin, des langen Haders müde, erweichten ihren harten Sinn und machten endlich Friede". 17. Dieser Tag war es, um dessentwillen er Krone und Leben dem untreuen Glücke anvertraute.

Exercise 97. Aufgabe 97.

1. We live on the other side of the river not far from the bridge. 2. On account of the cold weather we remained at home. 3. He has

---

* In referring to the amount of one's wealth, "*worth*" is rendered by „reich'; as er ist zehn tausend Gulden reich, he is worth ten thousand florins

taken your hat instead of his cap. 4. Those people are destitute of money and in want of help. 5. They are not tired of walking but they are not acquainted with the road. 6. This is a labor to which I am entirely unaccustomed, and I do it only because I am in want of money. 7. Men often become guilty of a crime because they owe much money. 8. I am sure of his innocence for I know that he is not capable of such an action. 9. He who is always mindful of his destiny does not become tired of his life. 10. Our friends live on this side of the river below the bridge 11. During our stay in Berlin my friend became master of the language. 12. For his friend's sake he remains here although he is tired of city life. 13. He is conscious of his strength, sure of his aim, and certain of his cause. 14. By means of good books and great industry one can learn rapidly.

LESSON XLIX. §ection XLIX

VERBS GOVERNING THE GENITIVE.

1. The following verbs govern the genitive; namely, achten, entrathen, ermangeln, gedenken, gewahren, harren, lachen, spotten, walten, warten, bedürfen, begehren, brauchen, entbehren, erwähnen, genießen, pflegen, schonen, verfehlen, vergessen, wahren, wahrnehmen.

The last twelve more frequently govern the accusative: achten, harren and warten are followed by auf; and lachen, spotten and walten, by über with the accusative; as,

Ich brauche nicht des Helmes, or | I do not need (am not in want
den Helm. | of) the helmet.
Sie spotten meiner (or über mich). | You mock (deride) me.
Wir harren deines Winkes (or, auf | We wait thy beck.
deinen Wink).

2. Verbs governing the genitive, when used passively, take the impersonal form; as,

Es wird meiner (or meiner wird | I am mocked.
L. 44. 2) gespottet.
Deiner wird (or es wird deiner) | You are thought of.
gedacht.

3. The following reflexives. also, require the genitive after the accusative (or dative) which they govern; anmaßen, annehmen, bedienen, befleißen or befleißigen, begeben, bemächtigen, bemeistern, bescheiden, besinnen, entäußern, entblöden, entbrechen, enthalten, entschlagen, entsinnen, erbarmen, erfrechen, erinnern, erkühnen, erwehren, freuen, getrösten, rühmen, schämen, überhe-

ben, unterfangen, unterwinden, vermessen, versehen, wehren, weigern, wundern: enthalten is often followed by von, erbarmen, freuen, schämen and wundern, by über; and besinnen and freuen, by auf; as,

Ich schäme mich der Rolle die ich spielte.	I shame me of the part I played. (*W. Scott*).
Bedien' dich schnell deiner Macht.	Avail yourself quickly of your power.
Er erinnert* sich der Briefe.	He remembers the letters.
Er wunderte sich nicht wenig über mein Schwadroniren.	He wondered not a little at my swaggering.

4. The verbs, es gelüstet (or lüstet), es jammert, es reuet, es lohnt sich, also take a genitive after the accusative; as,

Es jammert mich des Kindes.	I pity the child (am grieved on account of it).
Du lässest dich des Uebels reuen.	Thou repentest thee of the evil.
Es lohnt sich der Mühe nicht.	It is not worth the trouble.

Es gelüstet is sometimes followed by nach; as,

Mich (L. 44. 2.) gelüstet nicht nach dem theuern Lohn.	I do not covet the dear (rich) reward.

5. The transitive verbs anklagen, belehren, berauben, beschuldigen, entheben, entledigen, mahnen, überheben, vertrösten, würdigen, zeihen, entbinden, entblößen, entladen, entkleiden, entlassen, entsetzen, entwöhnen, lossprechen, überführen, überzeugen, versichern, govern the genitive of a thing, and the accusative of a person; as,

Natur lässt sich des Schleiers nicht berauben.	Nature permits not herself to be robbed of the veil.
Sie klagen ihn des Diebstahls an.	They accuse him of (the) theft.
Er wird des Diebstahls angeklagt.	He is accused of theft.
Er hat sich seines Feindes entladen.	He has rid himself of his enemy.

6. The last eleven are frequently followed by von; mahnen, by an; and vertrösten by auf; as,

Ich fühle mich von aller Noth entladen.	I feel relieved from all distress.
Warum an seiner Herkunft Schmach so rauh ihn mahnen?	Why remind him so rudely of the disgrace of his origin?

7. Often the genitive of a pronoun under the government of a numeral, does not require translation; as,

---

* In referring to a thing learned, the word behalten, "*to keep*", "*to retain*" answers to our "remember"; as, ich kann die Wörter nicht behalten, I can not remember the words.

Er hat vier Freunde, und ich habe ihrer nur drei.	He has four friends, and I have only three.
Ich habe nur fünf Pferde, und er hat deren neun.	I have only five horses, and he has nine (of them).
Er hat viel Wein, und ich habe dessen nur wenig.	He has a great deal of wine, and I have but little (of it).
Wir haben so der guten Freunde wenig.	We have so, few good friends (of the good friends few).

8. The genitive is often used adverbially; as,

Eines Tages wandelte er u.s.w.	One day he was walking, &c.
Des Morgens liest er.	In the morning he reads.

Exercise 98. Aufgabe 98.

Es (L. 24. 17.) schont der Krieg auch (L. 63. 5.) nicht des Kindleins in der Wiege. 2. Der Kranke vergaß seiner Schmerzen, der Trauernde seines Kummers, die Armuth ihrer Sorgen. 3. Mancher Mensch pflegt so sorgfältig seines Körpers, daß er seiner Seele kaum gedenkt. 4. Ihr fürchtet der Sphäre zu verfehlen, die Eures Geistes würdig ist. 5. Genieße des Lebens — aber gedenke auch des Todes. 6. Die Freuden der Erde bedürfen der Würze des herben Wechsels zu ihrer Erhaltung und Veredlung. 7. Wer des Unglücklichen nicht schont, sondern desselben spotten kann, der verdient, daß man auch seiner im Unglück vergesse. 8. Ihres Freundes wartet noch ein schwerer Kampf. 9. Des Königs wurde heute gar nicht erwähnt.

Exercise 99. Aufgabe 99.

1. He often thinks of thee but them he has forgotten. 2. Among others he mentioned his cousin. 3. Do not forget the poor, while you are enjoying so many pleasures. 4. He who ridicules the poor shows a bad heart. 5. Never forget the sufferings and sacrifices of those who achieved the freedom which you now enjoy. 6. Your friend does not need your assistance. 7. We should forget our sorrows and remember our joys. 8. Threaten as thou wilt, I laugh at thy threats. 9. The matter was mentioned in my presence. 10. He has taken care of his sick friend.

Exercise 100. Aufgabe 100.

1. Sie erinnern sich wohl (L. 67.6.) noch des jungen Mannes, der im vorigen Jahre des Raubes angeklagt war. 2. Er war beschuldigt einen reichen Viehhändler auf der Landstraße seines Geldes beraubt zu haben. 3. Man konnte ihn jedoch dieses Verbrechens nicht überführen. 4. Er hatte sich bereits aller Hoffnung einer Freisprechung begeben und sich des Gedankens entschlagen, als unschuldig erklärt zu werden. 5. Der Richter jedoch enthob ihn aller Sorge. 6. Nachdem er den Angeklagten aufgefordert hatte, gutes Muthes zu sein und sich alles Kummers zu entschlagen, erklärte er: Ich bin der vollen Meinung, daß man diesen jungen Mann nicht des Raubes bezüchtigen kann. 7. Denn nicht Jeder, der sich des Bettelns schämt und aller Mittel entblößt ist, wird ein Räuber. 8. Ich will seines guten Betragens geschweigen, denn er hat sich immer eines

orbentlichen Lebens beflissen. 9. Ich erinnere euch aber der Thaten im letzten Kriege, deren er sich mit Recht rühmen kann. 10. Freuet euch seiner Freisprechung und würdiget ihn eurer Freundschaft. 11. Spottet seiner nicht, weil er im Kerker war, sondern erbarmet euch vielmehr seiner und gedenket seiner Leiden. 12. Jeder, der seiner lacht, schäme sich seines eigenen Betragens. 13. Alle Anwesenden freuten sich dieser Rede, und man entledigte augenblicklich den Angeschuldigten seiner Fesseln. 14. Ich kann mich dieser Leute erinnern, aber ich kann ihre Namen nicht behalten. 15. Er freute sich des klugen Raths und ging hinaus und begab sich an die Arbeit.

EXERCISE 101.   Aufgabe 101.

1. The old soldier boasts of the deeds that he has performed. 2. Do you remember the promise that you gave me? 3. I do not remember that I gave you any promise. 4. Can you remember all the long words that you have found in this book? 5. Have you accused any one of this crime? 6. Who has robbed the traveler of his money? 7. He has been convinced of his error, but convicted of no crime. 8. The tyrant avails himself of his power. 9. An honest man would be ashamed of such an action. 10. The enemy has obtained possession (possessed himself) of the city. 11. Do you remember the old gentleman with whom we traveled from Brunswick to Bremen? 12. Yes, I still remember him. 13. It is difficult for those who have a bad memory to remember the rules of a language. 14. Are you of the opinion that he is guilty of this crime?

LESSON L.   Section L.

USE AND GOVERNMENT OF THE DATIVE.

1. Verbs of giving, taking away, and the like, govern the dative and accusative; as,

Er hat es mir genommen und es dir gegeben.	He has taken it *from* me, and given it *to* you.
Was hat er Ihnen gemacht?	What has he made *for* you?
Wir schrieben ihr einen Brief.	We wrote (*to*) her a letter.
Sie schickte uns das Geld.	She sent (*to*) us the money.

2. Many verbs govern the dative, while the corresponding ones, in English, govern the objective; as,

Er hilft mir (not mich) und ich danke ihm (not ihn).	He helps me, and I thank him.
Seine Mütze paßt ihm, aber sie steht ihm nicht gut.	His cap fits him, but it does not become him.
Er will mir nicht verzeihen, daß ich ihm widersprochen habe.	He will not pardon me that I have contradicted him.

Was fehlt dem Manne? — What ails the man?
Das gefällt ihr* nicht. — That does not please her.

3. The dative is used with such expressions as, leid, kund, weh thun, Hohn sprechen, Wort halten, zu Theil werden, &c.; as also with the impersonal verbs, ahnet, däucht, dünkt, ekelt, grauet, schwindelt, and träumt; as,

Dir hat von diesen Thaten bloß geträumt. — You have only dreamed of these deeds.
Mir grauet, weiter fortzufahren. — I dread to continue (go farther).
Des Lebens ungemischte Freude ward keinem Sterblichen zu Theil. — Life's unmixed joys were (became) the lot of no mortal.
Mir wird so wohl, mir wird so weh. — I feel so well, I feel so ill.
Es thut mir im Herzen weh. — It pains me to the heart.

4. When verbs governing the dative, are used passively, they take the impersonal form; as,

Ihm wird geholfen und mir wird gedankt. — He is helped and I am thanked.
Ihnen wurde widerstanden. — They were resisted (it was resisted to them).

Similar to this is the phrase, dem sei wie ihm wolle, instead of das sei wie es wolle; be that as it may (will).

5. Some verbs govern either the dative or accusative according to their signification; as,

Ich rief ihm, aber er hörte mich nicht. — I called to him, but he did not hear me.
Ich rief ihn in das Zimmer. — I called him into the room.
Er hat sein Geld bekommen. — He has got (obtained) his money.
Diese Speise bekommt mir nicht. — This food does not agree with me.

6. The dative often *precedes* the adjectives by which it is governed; as,

Der Komet ist uns nicht sichtbar. — The comet is not visible to us.
Die Sache ist ihm unbegreiflich. — The affair is incomprehensible to him.
Was ihn euch verhaßt macht, macht ihn mir werth. — What makes him hateful to you, makes him estimable to me.

---

* Gefallen, with its dative, is often the equivalent of the English verb "*to like*"; as, dieses Tuch gefällt mir, I like this cloth; literally, this cloth suits, or pleases me. Gefallen lassen = "to submit to"; as, sie lassen sich alles gefallen; they submit to everything (they let everything please them).
   The adverb gern (comparative lieber), fain, gladly, with an appropriate verb, often answers to "*to like*", *to be fond of*"; as, er raucht gern; he likes to smoke (is fond of smoking): gehen Sie gern ins Theater? do you like to go (are you fond of going) to the theater? ich habe ihn gern; I like him: er möchte lieber gehen als bleiben; he would rather go than stay.

Ergeben dem Freunde, or dem Freun- | Devoted to the friend, *or* to the
be ergeben. | friend devoted.

7. The dative is often employed instead of a possessive pronoun, or the genitive of a noun; as,

Euch wohnt ein Engel an der Seite. | An angel dwells at your side.
(wohnt an eurer Seite).
Dem König wird der linke Arm zer- | The king's left arm is shattered.
schmettert (des Königs linker Arm).
Keinem Manne kann ich Gattin sein. | I can be no man's wife (I can be wife to no man).

8. The dative is sometimes idiomatically employed, where remote reference only is had to the speaker, or to the person addressed; in which use it is seldom regarded in translating; as,

Es sind Euch gar trotzige Kamera- | They are right insolent fellows
den. | (for you).
Gehe mir nicht aufs Eis. | (Pray) don't go on the ice.

9. When the dative and accusative are under the government of the same verb, the accusative, except when it is a personal pronoun, comes *last;* as,

Ich gebe ihm das Buch. | I give him the book.
Ich gebe es ihm. | I give it to him.
Er schickt ihr die Feder. | He sends her the pen.
Er schickt sie ihr. | He sends it to her.

10. The dative with bei, von, zu, answers in various phrases, to our possessive, preceded by *at, from, of,* and *to;* as,

Er wohnt bei dem Schneider. | He lives at the tailor's.
Gehst du zu deinem Vetter? | Are you going to your cousin's?
Sie kommen eben von ihrem Freund. | They are just coming from their friend's.
Ist er ein Verwandter von Ihnen? | Is he a relative of yours?

For prepositions governing the dative*, and the dative or accusative †, see L. 15.

Exercise 102.   Aufgabe 102.

1. Ich danke Ihnen, daß Sie mir geholfen haben. 2. Er würde mir gewiß schaden, wenn er mir beikommen könnte. 3. Dieser Hut paßt mir, aber er steht mir nicht gut. 4. Was fehlt Ihnen und Ihrem Freunde? 5. Es fehlt mir nichts; ob ihm etwas fehlen mag, weiß ich nicht. 6. Der

---

* „Schreib mit, nach, nächst, nebst, sammt, bei, seit, von, zu, zuwider, entgegen, außer, aus, stets mit dem Dativ nieder!"

† „An, auf, hinter, neben, in, | Wenn man fragen kann: wohin?
über, unter, vor und zwischen | Bei dem Dativ stehn sie so,
Stehn bei dem Accusativ, | Daß man nur kann fragen: wo?"

Knabe hat sich in den Finger geschnitten. 7. Ganz Oesterreich lag dem edelmüthigen Ungarn zu Füßen. 8. Diesem eigensinnigen Menschen ist gar nicht zu helfen. 9. Es thut mir leid, daß er sich weh gethan hat. 10. Dem König, welcher sich über diese Feindseligkeit beklagte, wurde geantwortet, „der Kaiser habe der Soldaten zu viel: er müsse seinen guten Freunden damit helfen." 11. Endlich gelang es dem Minister, dem König über sein wahres Interesse die Augen zu öffnen. 12. Wenn in alten Zeiten ein Mächtiger dem andern feind war, so sagte er demselben ab. 13. Aus allen Orten, die ihm angehörten, sammelte dieser mächtige Herr die Männer, die ihm anhingen. 14. Nachdem sie seinem Vorhaben beigestimmt hatten, verpflichteten sie sich, ihm beizustehen, und dem Kriege beizuwohnen. 15. Solch ein mächtiger Herr war Heinrich der Löwe, Herzog von Baiern, welchem große Länder zugehörten und Tausende von Kriegern gehorchten. 16. Doch die Krone eines Kaisers schwebte ihm immer vor Augen. 17. Der Herzogshut genügte ihm nicht. 18. Er traute seiner eigenen Kraft und trotzte dem Kaiser. 19. Der Kaiser forderte ihn auf, sich seinen Befehlen zu fügen, und drohte ihm mit der Acht. 20. Doch dem Herzoge, der einem Löwen glich, galt weder Vernunft, noch guter Rath. 21. Ihm gefiel nur seine eigene Meinung, und er dachte der Kraft, die ihm gebrach. 22. Er widerstrebte dem Verlangen, dem Kaiser eine Ehre zu erweisen, die demselben gebührte. 23. Der Kaiser, der dem Herzoge schon seit langer Zeit übel wollte und ihm, wegen seines Stolzes zürnte, kam ihm zuvor, und überzog ihn mit Krieg. 24. Der Kriegszug mißlang dem Kaiser nicht. 25. Der Herzog konnte der feindlichen Macht nicht widerstehen und erlag dem Kaiser in der Schlacht. 26. Er mußte nach England fliehen und nur seine Familie und einige Freunde folgten ihm. 27. Hier entsagte er jeder Hoffnung und fluchte dem Stolze, als der Ursache seines Elends.

Exercise 103.   Aufgabe 103.

1. I will assist him because he has assisted me. 2. Threaten me as thou wilt, I defy thee and thy power. 3. His enemies cannot injure him for they cannot get at him. 4. So great an honor is due to no man. 5. This hat fits me but it does not please me. 6. Those who flatter you are not true friends. 7. He struggled against the demand but could not resist his powerful enemy. 8. It is not my duty to obey such men as these. 9. Your advice is of no value to him, for he cannot renounce his evil company. 10. Have you met your friends to-day? 11. These children resemble their parents. 12. Do you know what ails these people? 13. I will not contradict you, though I think you are wrong. 14. Nearly all his adherents remained true to him and followed him into exile. 15. I have written them several letters, but they have not yet answered me. 16. The prince says, the land, the sea, the rivers, and even the men belong to him. 17. My horse has got away from me and I have not yet been able to find him.

Exercise 104.   Aufgabe 104.

1. Ein gutes Kind ist seinen Eltern gehorsam und dankbar. 2 Das Rauchen ist denen sehr unangenehm die es nicht gewohnt sind. 3. Mir

ist es lieb, daß ich dir in dieser Sache nützlich sein kann. 4. Das Wetter war uns gestern sehr günstig, aber heute ist es ganz das Gegentheil. 5. Gut zu werden ist dem Lasterhaften schwer, denn er bleibt gewöhnlich seinen Neigungen treu. 6. Dem Königreich Spanien ist Frankreich überlegen. 7. Was ihn euch widrig macht, macht ihn mir werth. 8. Ihr seid dieser Königin nicht unterthan. 9. Vieles, was uns nicht gefährlich ist, ist uns doch sehr lästig. 10. Im Range ist er seinem Bruder gleich, im Charakter seinem Vater ähnlich. 11. Nichts ist mir so verhaßt, als Falschheit und Heuchelei. 12. Du bist des Leibes ledig, Gott sei der Seele gnädig. 13. Dieses Buch ist mir lieb; wer es stiehlt, der ist ein Dieb. 14. Es ist mir unvergeßlich, wie sehr ich dir verbunden bin. 15. Den Soldaten war das Lob ihres verehrten Feldherrn sehr schmeichelhaft. 16. Dieser Aufenthalt ist ihm fast unerträglich geworden. 17. Tadel und Lob sind dem Gemüthe des Menschen, was Sturm und Sonnenschein dem Wachsthum sind. 18. Die Ehre sollte dem Menschen theuerer als das Leben sein.

Exercise 105.   Aufgabe 105.

1. These things may be useful and agreeable to you, but they are very unpleasant to me, and injurious to my friends. 2. Every good man is grateful to his benefactors. 3. This weather is very unfavorable for us. 4. It is very unpleasant to me that I am obliged to remain here so long. 5. Every good citizen is obedient to the just laws of his country. 6. Will this happy country ever be subject to a king? 7. What is more hateful to a good man than hypocrisy? 8. I am much obliged to you that you have been useful to my friends in this matter. 9. The soldiers were with blind obedience devoted to their leader. 10. This house is very similar to the one in which you live. 11. No country in the world is superior to ours. 12. The few friends that this man has are very dear to him. 13. Many things are burdensome which are not dangerous to us. 14. Those are to be called good, who remain true to their principles. 15. The praise of a good man is very flattering to us. 16. He is gracious to those who are obedient to him.

LESSON LI.   Section LI.

NUMERALS.

1. The declension of ein has already been given (L. 9. 4. & 25. 3). Zwei and drei when not accompanied by any word that makes their case evident, are inflected in the genitive and dative like adjectives of the *old* declension; as,

Die Aussage zweier Zeugen.   The assertion of two witnesses
Ich habe es Dreien (drei Personen) I have told it to three (three
   erzählt.   persons).

Instead of zwei, zween and zwo sometimes occur: in some

compounds the form zwie appears; as, Zwielicht, twilight; Zwietracht, discord.

2. From vier to zwölf, inclusive (except sieben) the cardinal numbers, when not followed by a noun nor referring to one previously expressed, take en in the dative, and e in the other cases; as,

Ich habe es Fünfen (fünf Personen) gesagt.	I have told it to five (five persons).
Er fährt mit Sechsen (or sechs Pferden).	He drives six (six horses).

3. When the cardinal numbers are used substantively, they are feminine: (except hundert and tausend, which are neuter); as,

Warum nennt ihr die Fünfe eine heilige Zahl?	Why call ye (the) five a sacred number?
Es waren ihrer Hunderte.	There were hundreds of them.

4. When hundert and tausend are followed by a noun, the article is omitted; as,

Er hat hundert Pferde und tausend Schafe.	He has (a) hundred horses and (a) thousand sheep.

5. From the cardinal numbers and the syllable tel (or stel) are formed the fractional numbers (except halb, half); as,

Ein Drittel, a third;   Vier Fünftel, four-fifths;
Neun Zehntel, nine-tenths; Neunzehn Zwanzigstel, nineteen-twentieths.

6. Halb, (as also ganz) before the neuter names of countries, is not declined; otherwise it is regularly inflected as an adjective; as,

Halb Frankreich ist in Feindes Hand.	Half France is in (the) enemy's hand.
Ganz Deutschland lag ihm zu Füßen.	All Germany lay at his feet.
Er hat einen halben Apfel.	He has half an apple.
Er hat sein ganzes Vermögen verloren.	He has lost his whole (entire) fortune.

7. In connecting halves with whole numbers, the word halb is suffixed to the ordinals; as,

Drittehalb, *third a half;* that is, two wholes and a half $= 2\frac{1}{2}$.
Viertehalb, *fourth a half;* that is, three wholes and a half $= 3\frac{1}{2}$, &c.

Instead of zweitehalb, the form anderthalb, *one* and *a half,* is commonly used.

8. Another class of nouns is formed from the *cardinal* numbers, by the addition of er, and ling; as,

Ein Zwilling, a twin; ein Achtziger, an octogenarian (a man eighty years old); ein Dreier, a coin of the value of three Pfennige. The former is often applied to wine; as, drei und zwanziger; wine of the vintage of 1823.

9. Fach or fältig suffixed to cardinal numbers answers to "fold" in the same position; as,

Die Einfältigen behütet der Herr.	The Lord preserveth the simple Ps. 116. 6.
So ich Jemand betrogen habe, das gebe ich vierfältig wieder.	If I have taken anything from any man by false accusation, I restore *him* fourfold.
Die Sache ist ganz einfach.	The thing is perfectly simple.

Einfältig is often used in the sense of "silly" (ignorantly simple); as,

Sein Betragen war höchst einfältig. His behavior was extremely simple.

10. Einmal, zweimal, anwers to, once, twice: compounded with other cardinal numbers, Mal, answers to "times", in the same position; as,

Ich habe ihn viermal gesehen und zweimal gesprochen. I have seen him four times, and spoken to him twice.

Mal, when separated from the numeral, is regularly declined as a noun; as,

Ich habe ihn nur ein einziges Mal gesehen. I have seen him only once (one single time).

11. „Ens" suffixed to the ordinals answers to "ly" in the same position; as,

Drittens, thirdly; neuntens, ninthly, &c.

12. Lei (an obsolete noun, meaning kind or sort) compounded with numerals, is variously translated; as,

Er weiß allerlei (or allerhand) hübsche Geschichtchen.	He knows all sorts of pretty stories.
Sie haben einen Strauß aus vielerlei Blumen.	They have a bouquet of many kinds of flowers.
Es ist mir einerlei, was er denkt.	It is all one (a matter of indifference) to me what he thinks

13. The interrogative ordinal, der, die, das wievielste, (from wie viel, how much, how many) is usually rendered "what" or "which"; as,

Der wievielste ist heute?	What day of the month is to-day?
Den wievielsten haben wir heute?	What date have we to-day?
Das wievielste Mal ist dieses das vierte oder das fünfte?	Which time is this, the fourth or the fifth?

14. CARDINAL AND ORDINAL NUMBERS.

Cardinals.		*Ordinals.*
Eins (ein, eine, ein)	1.	der erste, the first.
zwei	2.	„ zweite, the second.
drei	3.	„ dritte, (not dreite), the third.
vier	4.	„ vierte, the fourth.
fünf	5.	„ fünfte, the fifth.
sechs	6.	„ sechste, the sixth.
sieben	7.	„ siebente, the seventh.
acht	8.	„ achte, (not achtte), the eighth.
neun	9.	„ neunte, the ninth.
zehn	10.	„ zehnte, the tenth.
elf	11.	„ elfte, the eleventh.
zwölf	12.	„ zwölfte, the twelfth.
dreizehn	13.	„ dreizehnte, the thirteenth.
vierzehn	14.	„ vierzehnte, the fourteenth.
fünfzehn	15.	„ fünfzehnte, the fifteenth.
sechzehn	16.	„ sechszehnte, the sixteenth.
siebenzehn or siebzehn	17.	„ siebenzehnte or siebzehnte, 17th.
achtzehn	18.	„ achtzehnte, 18th.
neunzehn	19.	„ neunzehnte, 19th.
zwanzig	20.	„ zwanzigste, 20th.
ein und zwanzig	21.	„ ein und zwanzigste, 21st.
zwei und zwanzig, &c.	22.	„ zwei und zwanzigste, 22d., &c.
dreißig	30.	„ dreißigste, 30th.
ein und dreißig	31.	„ ein und dreißigste, 31st.
zwei und dreißig, &c.	32.	„ zwei und dreißigste, 32d., &c.
vierzig	40.	„ vierzigste, 40th.
fünfzig	50.	„ fünfzigste, 50th.
sechzig (not sechszig)	60.	„ sechzigste, 60th.
siebenzig or siebzig	70.	„ siebenzigste or siebzigste, 70th.
achtzig	80.	„ achtzigste, 80th.
neunzig	90.	„ neunzigste, 90th.
hundert	100.	„ hundertste, 100th.
hundert und eins	101.	„ hundert und erste, 101st.
hundert und zwei	102.	„ hundert und zweite, 102d.
hundert und drei, &c.	103.	„ hundert und dritte, 103d., &c.
zwei hundert	200.	„ zweihundertste, 200th.
dreihundert	300.	„ dreihundertste, 300th.
tausend	1000.	„ tausendste, 1000th.
zwei tausend	2000.	„ zweitausendste, 2000th.
drei tausend	3000.	„ dreitausendste, 3000th.
zehn tausend	10,000.	„ zehntausendste, 10,000th.
hundert tausend	100,000.	„ hunderttausendste, 100,000th.

Exercise 106.   Aufgabe 106.

1. Es sind tausend Menschen auf diesem Schiffe. 2. Hunderte von Schweden, Norwegern und Dänen, und Tausende von Deutschen wandern nach Amerika aus. 3. Ich gebe nicht mehr als anderthalb Thaler für dieses Buch. 4. Sieben Achtel seines ganzen Heeres bestand aus Söldnern. 5. Sind Sie nicht schon dreimal hier gewesen? 6. Nein, dies ist das erste Mal, daß ich hier bin. 7. Der wievielste ist heute? 8. Wir haben heute den zwanzigsten, nicht wahr? (L. 16. 4.) 9. Man sagt, dieser Gärtner habe allerlei schöne Blumen zu verkaufen. 10. Es ist mir ganz einerlei, was er sagt, oder denkt, oder wie er handelt. 11. Einmal des Jahres gehe ich nach Wien, und zweimal nach Berlin. 12. Kannst du mir den Unterschied sagen zwischen zwiefach und doppelt? 13. Erstens hat er Vermögen, zweitens besitzt er große Talente, drittens hat er einen hohen Rang.

Exercise 107.   Aufgabe 107.

1. Thousands of the citizens of the United States are Englishmen, Frenchmen, Germans and other Europeans. 2. What day of the month is to-day? 3. What day of the month have we to-day, the ninth or the tenth? 4. It is all the same to me whether such a man loves or hates, praises or blames me. 5. I have heard that twenty times. 6. He gave them three and a half florins for their book. 7. This is the first time that you have visited us. 8. That old peasant says he has a hundred horses and a thousand sheep. 9. All Europe trembled before its irresistible conqueror. 10. I have to-day for the first time been in the palace of a king. 11. In the third battle, a third of the whole army fell.

LESSON LII.   Section LII.

Aller, Ander, Einander, Beide, Alle, Einiger, Etlicher, Etwas, So etwas, Irgend, Jeder, Jeglicher, Solcher, Keiner, Kein, Viel.

1. **Aller**, when followed by a pronoun, often drops the final syllable; as,

Ich habe all mein Geld und all meine Freunde verloren.   I have lost all my money and all my friends.

   a. The neuter singular is often used in the sense of "*everything*", "*everybody*"; as,

Kein Mensch kann Alles lernen.   No man can learn everything.
Alles, was leben kann, lobe den Herrn.   Let all that can praise, praise the Lord.

   b. **Aller**, as applied to divisions of time, is used in the plural only and answers to, "*every*": "*all*", in such phrases as, *all day*, &c., being expressed by ganz; as,

Aller, Ander, Einander, Beide, &c. 137

Ich sehe ihn alle Tage.	I see him every day.
Er kommt alle zwei Stunden.	He comes every two hours.
Sie blieb den ganzen Tag.	She staid all (the whole) day.

c. Alle, in connection with beide, is, of course, omitted in translating; as,

| Ich habe alle beide gesehen. | I have seen (all) both. |

d. Alle is sometimes equivalent to, "all gone"; as,

| Sein Geld ist alle. | His money is all gone. |

2. Ander is often used to signify "*next*", but never like *other*, as in the phrase "the other day", to denote indefinite past time; as,

| Morgen geht er nach Berlin, und den andern Tag nach Leipzig. | To-morrow he goes to Berlin and the next day to Leipsic. |

3. When the English word "other" implies something additional, it is translated by the adverb noch; as,

Wollen Sie noch einen Mantel haben?	Will you have another cloak? (besides this?)
Wollen Sie einen andern Mantel haben?	Will you have another cloak? (instead of this?)
Hast du nichts Anderes gehört?	Have you heard nothing else?
Das ist etwas Anderes.	That is another thing.
Er geht, wenn er anders Zeit hat.	He will go, that is, if he has time.
Ich muß mich anderswo erkundigen.	I must inquire elsewhere.

4. Einander (L. 24. 5) is often compounded with prepositions, and used as a (separable) prefix to verbs; as,

Auseinandertreiben; to disperse. (drive from each other).
Auseinandergehen; to disperse, disunite, part.
Durcheinanderwerfen; to mix, scatter confusedly.

5. Beide (both, two), may refer to objects taken separately; as,

| Welches von den beiden Büchern hat er? | Which of the two books has he? |

In referring to two things, different in kind, the form of the neuter singular, beides, is often employed; as,

| Ich hatte einen Bleistift und eine Feder, aber ich habe beides verloren. | I had a pencil and a pen, but I have lost both. |
| Sie irren sich, denn beides liegt auf dem Tisch. | You mistake (your-self) for both are (each is) lying on the table. |

6. **Einiger** and **etlicher** signify, in the singular, "*a little*", "*some*", and in the plural, "*a few*", "*some*";* as,

Einige behaupten das Gegentheil.	Some maintain the contrary.
Einige Zeit darauf kam er.	A little time afterwards he came

7. **Etwas** is often used before nouns and adjectives in the sense of "*a little*" "*somewhat*"; as,

Schicken Sie ihm etwas Wein.	Send him a little wine.
Das Wetter ist etwas kälter.	The weather is somewhat colder.

So etwas signifies "*such a thing*"; **etwas anderes**, "*another thing*" "*something else*".

8. **Irgend** marks great indefiniteness, and is generally rendered "*any*", "*whatever*", "*some other*"; as,

Kennen Sie irgend einen Menschen, der es thun kann?	Do you know any man (whatever) that can do it?
Wenn es irgend möglich ist.	If it is in any way possible.

9. **Jeder** and **jeglicher** are sometimes preceded by the indefinite article (which, of course, is omitted in translating), and are inflected, as is also, **solcher** in like position, according to the *mixed* declension; as,

Der Tod eines jeden Menschen ist gewiß.	The death of every man is certain.
Das Beispiel eines solchen Mannes war entscheidend.	The example of such a man was decisive.

10. **Keiner, keine, keines**, with **beiden**, answers to the pronoun "*neither*"; as,

Ich glaubte, er habe mein Buch und das Ihrige; aber er sagte, er habe keines von beiden.	I thought he had my book and yours, but he said he had neither (of them).

11. **Kein** is often employed where, in English, the indefinite article, or the word "any", with a negative is used; as,

Er ist kein Franzose, nicht wahr?	He is not a Frenchman, is he?
Er hat mir keinen Brief geschrieben.	He has not written me a letter.
Er hat keine Freunde mehr. (L. 22. N.)	He has no longer any friends.

12. **Kein** and **ein**, like the possessive pronouns, are frequently followed by „eigen" (*own*); as,

---

* Some and any before a noun, except in the signification of "*a few*", or "*a little*", are not generally translated in German.; as, have you some good pens? haben Sie gute Federn? I have some new books; ich habe neue Bücher.

Er wohnte früher in seinem eigenen Hause, jetzt aber hat er kein eignes Haus.	He formerly lived in his own house; but now he has no house of his own (no own house).
Haſt du ein eignes Pferd?	Have you a horse of your own? (an own horse?)

13. **Viel** and **wenig**, when referring to a quantity, or to a number taken collectively, are not generally inflected, except when preceded by the definite article, or an adjective pronoun; as,

Er hat viel Geld und viel Freunde.	He has much money and many friends.
Doch viel iſt mir bewußt.	But much is known to me.
Da war wenig Ehre zu erwerben.	There was little honor to be gained there.
Er hat fein vieles Geld und ſeine vielen Freunde verloren.	He has lost his much (large amount of) money, and his many friends.
Viel Menſchen trinken mehr als wenig Menſchen.	Many men drink more than a few men.

14. **Viel** and **wenig** are also declined, when they refer to a number taken as *individuals*; also, when referring *substantively* to persons; and, often, when preceded in the singular by prepositions; as,

Viele Menſchen trinken keinen Wein.	Many men drink no wine.
Wenige Menſchen ſind ganz zufrieden.	Few men are perfectly contented.
Viele ſind berufen, aber Wenige ſind auserwählt.	Many are called, but few are chosen.

15. When declined in the singular, except as above specified, **viel** and **wenig** have the signification *many*, or *few kinds*; as,

Er trinkt viel Wein, aber nicht vielen Wein.	He drinks much wine, but not many kinds of wine.
Lerne viel, aber nicht Vieles auf einmal.	Learn much, but not many things at once.

16. The superlative of **viel** (**meiſt**) is often preceded by the definite article, or a possessive pronoun; as,

Die meiſten Menſchen beurtheilen Andere ſtrenger als ſich ſelbſt.	(The) most men judge others more severely than themselves.
Unſere meiſten Leiden ſind die Folge unſerer eigenen Fehler.	The most of our sufferings are the consequence of our own errors.

EXERCISE 108.   Aufgabe 108.

1. Er heißt alles Feinde und Empörer, was nicht mit ihm ist. 2. Verstehst du Alles, was ich dir sage? 3. Wir alle wollen mit dir gehen. 4. Er setzte uns den allerbesten Wein vor. 5. Bringe mir noch Aepfel und eine andere Flasche Wein. 6. Wollen Sie Bücher kaufen? 7. Ich habe schon welche gekauft, aber ich will noch einige kaufen. 8. Beides ereignete sich und die schlimmen Folgen von Beidem stellten sich ein. 9. Das Wetter ist schon etwas (or ein wenig) kälter geworden. 9. Wer hätte so etwas geglaubt? 10. Kennst du irgend Jemand, der so etwas thun würde? 11. Ein Jeder von seinen Freunden hat ihn verlassen. 12. Er hat viel Wein getrunken und viel Geld dafür ausgegeben. 13. Das viele Geld, das er erbte, hat er ausgegeben für den vielen Wein, den er getrunken hat. 14. Lerne nicht auf einmal Vieles, sondern viel. 15. Jeden Tag, den Sie zu uns kommen wollen, wollen wir alle mit Ihnen spaziren gehen. (L. 35. Note).

EXERCISE 109.   Aufgabe 109.

1. This overcoat is too small, take it away and bring me another. 2. The weather is so cold that I must have two overcoats, bring me another one. 3. As soon as my money was all gone I had no longer any friends. 4. Which of these carriages shall you buy? 5. I shall not buy either of them, for neither of them pleases me. 6. If you will wait another day we will all go with you. 7. Do you wish to buy anything more? 8. I have a little money and he has a great deal. 9. Many of my acquaintances reside in this city. 10. The few friends that he has are more powerful than his many enemies. 11. Who has more enemies and fewer friends, more trouble and less pleasure than the miser? 12. I understand all that you say and can read all the letters that you have written. 13. I would like to buy a few pears, and a few more apples. 14. To-morrow I shall go to Mannheim, and the next day to Mayence. 15. Every book that I have is in this room. 16. Do you wish to buy some more horses? 17. The weather is becoming somewhat warmer.

LESSON LIII.   Section LIII.

An, EXAMPLES OF ITS USE.

Der Mann sitzt an dem Tische.	The man is sitting *at* the table.
Der Hund liegt an der Kette.	The dog lies *at* (is fastened by) the chain.
Er lehnte sich an die Wand.	He leaned (himself) *against* the wall.
Sie ist an fünfzig Jahre alt.	She is *about* (*towards*) fifty years old.
Sie werden irre an dir.	They are becoming perplexed *about* you.

Mir liegt gar nichts an der Sache.	I care nothing at all *about* the matter.
Man kennt den Vogel an den Federn.	One knows the bird *by* the feathers.
Er liegt am Fieber darnieder, und leidet sehr an Kopfweh.	He is lying sick *of* a fever, and suffers very much *from* headache.
Ich will es an seiner Statt thun.	I will do it *in* his stead.
Arm an Freuden, reich an Hoffnung.	Poor *in* joys, rich *in* hope.
So viel an mir ist, will ich ihm helfen.	As far as *in* me lies, I will help him.
Es ist nichts als Haut und Knochen an ihm.	There is nothing *of* him but skin and bones.
Sie wohnen in Frankfurt am Main.	They live in Frankfort *on* the Maine.
Sie schreibt an ihren Bruder.	She is writing *to* her brother.
Er ist an den Bettelstab gekommen.	He has become a beggar (come *to* the beggar's staff).
Die Sache ist an den Tag gekommen.	The affair has come *to* light.
Die Schuld liegt nur an ihm.	The fault is (lies) only *with* him.
Er hat Ekel an Allem, was er sieht.	He is disgusted *with* (*at*) all that he sees.
Er ist oben an und ich bin unten an.	He is *at* the head, and I am *at* the foot.
Sie wohnen neben an.	They live next door, (in the next house).
Er hat seine Waare an den Mann gebracht.	He has found a customer.
Wir wollen ihm an die Hand gehen.	We will assist him.
An der Sache ist nichts.	The affair is of no consequence, *or*, it is unfounded.
An wem ist die Reihe?	Whose turn is it?
Die Reihe zu lesen ist an mir.	It is my turn to read.
Die Reihe kommt morgen an dich.	Your turn comes (it comes your turn) to-morrow.

EXERCISE 110.   Aufgabe 110.

1. Der Knabe saß an dem Tische und schrieb einen Brief an seinen Vetter, der in Frankfurt an der Oder wohnt. 2. „Arm am Beutel, krank am Herzen." 3. Ich erkannte ihn an der Stimme. 4. Er hat es an meiner Statt gethan. 5. Ich habe schon ein halbes Jahr an diesem Buche gearbeitet, und es fehlte mir an Geduld, länger daran zu arbeiten. 6. „Da hing der Becher an spitzen Korallen." 7. Die Sache an und für sich betrachtet scheint nicht verwerflich zu sein. 8. Er erinnerte mich an mein Versprechen. 9. Ist die Reihe an mir? 10. Wer nicht weiß, wann die Reihe an ihm ist zu lesen, ist ein nachläßiger Schüler. 11. Die Reihe bei dem Kranken zu wachen, wird morgen Abend an dich kommen. 13. Der Hut hängt an dem Nagel; der Regenschirm steht an der Wand. 14. Von jetzt an werde ich fleißig studiren. 15. Ich dachte gar nicht daran, sonst

würde ich ihm geschrieben haben. 16. Er setzte sich an den Tisch und fing an, einen Brief an den Hauptmann zu schreiben.

Exercise 111.   Aufgabe 111.

1. Frankfort on the Maine is a larger city than Frankfort on the Oder. 2. Why do you not read? it is your turn, is it not? 3. No, it is my brother's, I always read as soon as my turn comes. 4. He seated himself at a desk which stood against the wall, and began to copy a letter which had been written to him. 5. The young soldier wished to suffer in his father's stead. 6. My friend recognized me by my voice. 7. He is rich in joys, although he is poor in purse. 8. More people suffer from headache than from toothache. 9. Thousands of people die every year of consumption. 10. There hangs your hat on the bough of a tree. 11. Has it come to light who committed this deed? 12. I shall take no part in this affair. 13. I would have done it if I had thought of it. 14. From this time on I shall be more careful.

LESSON LIV.   Section LIV.

Auf, and Aus. EXAMPLES OF THEIR USE.

1. Die Kinder sind auf dem Markte, und der Diener ist auf der Post.	The children are *at* market, and the servant is *at* the post-office.
Warum sind Sie böse auf den Mann?	Why are you angry *at* the man?
Er kleidet sich auf französische Art.	He dresses (himself) *after* the French fashion.
Es kostete auf hundert Gulden.	It cost *about* a hundred florins.
Können Sie auf uns warten?	Can you wait *for* us?
Er ist auf dem Rathhause oder auf dem Schloße.	He is *in* the city-hall (council-house), or *in* the castle.
Auf diese Weise werden wir wenig ausrichten können.	*In* this way we shall be able to accomplish but little.
Wie heißt das auf Deutsch?	What is that called *in* German?
Er wohnt schon ein Jahr im Lande und ist noch nicht auf dem Lande gewesen.	He has already lived a year in the (this) country, and has not yet been *in* the country (out of the city).
Der Bauer ist schon auf dem Felde.	The peasant is already *in* the field.
Diese Leute sind stolz auf ihr Geld.	These people are proud *of* their money.
Ich halte nicht viel auf solche Leute.	I do not think much *of* such people.
Sie gehen schon auf den Berg.	They are already going *on* the mountain.
Es kommt darauf an, wie man es anfängt.	It depends *on* how one attempts it.
Er hat es auf Abschlag bezahlt.	He has paid it *on* account.

EXERCISES ON THE USE OF **Auf** AND **Aus**.   143

Sie setzten es auf meine Rechnung.	They charged it *to* my account.
Warum ist die Thüre auf?	Why is the door *open*?
Geht er auf den Markt oder auf die Post?	Is he going *to* market, or *to* the post-office?
Sie geht auf die Hochzeit, und er geht auf den Ball.	She is going *to* the wedding, and he is going *to* the ball.
Auf daß die Welt es bald vergesse.	In order that the world may soon forget it.
Man geht leichter Berg ab als Berg auf.	One goes down hill easier than *up* hill.
Es ist neun Uhr, und er ist noch nicht auf.	It is nine o'clock, and he is not *up* yet.
Wieviel auf der Uhr ist es?*	What time (what o'clock) is it?
Es ist drei auf der Uhr.*	It is three o' (of the) clock.
Haben Sie Verdacht auf ihn?	Do you suspect him?
2. Ich weiß es aus Erfahrung.	I know it *by* experience.
Ich mache mir nichts aus der Sache.	I care nothing *about* the matter
Aus diesem Grunde gehe ich nicht.	*For* this reason I do not go.
Diese Leute sind aus Berlin.	These people are *from* Berlin.
Er schrieb uns von Leipzig aus.	He wrote to us *from* Leipsic.
Was ist aus ihm geworden?	What has become *of* him?
Aus den Augen, aus dem Sinne.	*Out* of sight, *out* of mind.
Es ist aus mit ihm.	It is *out* (all over) with him.
Er that es aus freien Stücken.	He did it *of* his own accord.
Er schrie aus vollem Halse.	He cried *with* all his might.
Aus Freunden werden oft Feinde.	Friends often become enemies.
Er weiß weder aus noch ein.	He is entirely at a loss what to do.
Sie haben sich aus dem Staube gemacht.	They have run away; "they are among the missing".
Sie war außer sich.	She was beside herself.

Exercise 112.   Aufgabe 112.

1. Ich setzte mich auf eine Bank und wartete auf die Boten, die ich auf den Markt, die Post und das Rathhaus geschickt hatte. 2. Wer auf sein Geld stolz ist, hat gewöhnlich sonst nichts, worauf er stolz sein könnte. 3. Er ist böse auf uns, weil wir sagten, daß wir nicht viel auf ihn halten. 4. Wir werden auf diese Weise gar nichts ausrichten können. 5. „Ich bestehe darauf, daß sich der Lord entferne." 6. Wissen Sie, wie dieses auf Deutsch heißt? 7. Das dürfen Sie nicht auf meine Rechnung setzen. 8. Ich glaube nicht, daß ich lange leben würde, wenn ich auf dem Lande leben müßte. 9. Nicht Jeder, der in dem Lande wohnt, wohnt auch auf

---

* These forms are usually abbreviated by omission of the article and preposition; as, wieviel Uhr ist es? what time is it? es ist drei Uhr, it is three o'clock.

Portions of an hour may be reckoned from a past hour, or (followed by auf), from a future one: as, es ist ein Viertel nach drei, or es ist ein Viertel auf vier; it is a quarter after three, or a quarter on (or towards) four: Es fehlt ein Viertel an (or bis) acht, or es sind drei viertel auf acht; it lacks a quarter of eight; or it is three quarters on (or towards eight). After halb, auf is omitted; as, es ist halb acht, it is half past seven.

dem Lande. 10. Sie kamen um halb drei an, und blieben bis drei Viertel auf zehn. 11. Die Sonne ist aufgegangen, und er ist noch nicht aufgestanden. 12. Warum hast du Verdacht auf diesen alten Mann? 13. Hast du deine Thüre aufgemacht? 14. Was wird aus dir werden, wenn du nicht fleißiger wirst? 15. Aus diesem Grunde habe ich mich entschlossen, mein Vaterland zu verlassen. 16. Das gelbe Fieber ist aus Amerika zu uns gekommen. 17. Man sollte nicht nur die Sätze, sondern auch die einzelnen Wörter auswendig lernen. 18. Dieser Juwelenhändler ist ein Jude aus Frankfurt an der Oder. 19. Wie oft gehen Sie auf das Land?

Exercise 113.   Aufgabe 113.

1. I do not think much of a man who is proud of his wealth. 2. He still insists upon it that he saw us last evening at the wedding. 3. I have never in my life been at a ball. 4. Why are those men angry at you? 5. Do you believe you will be able to accomplish anything in this way? 6. It is only a quarter past four, and the peasant is already in the field. 7. We have sent our servants to market and are waiting for them. 8. Do you live in the country? 9 No, but I often go to the country. 10. Do you know what that is called in French? 11. It is not late, the sun is not up yet. 12. All this you can charge to my account. 13. Whom do you suspect? 14. I do not suspect anybody. 15. These people are from England, and those, from America. 16. For this reason I shall not go out to-day. 17. They have done it out of fear. 18. He was completely beside himself. 19. There will be nobody here but my brothers. 20. Have you learned all those words by heart? 21. Do you know what has become of that man who was here yesterday? 22. How do you say in German, "out of sight, out of mind?"

LESSON LV.   Section LV.

Bei, Durch, Für.—EXAMPLES OF THEIR USE.

1. Sie sagten, sie hätten kein Geld bei sich.	They said they had no money *about* (with) them.
Es waren bei neun Tausend.	There were *about* nine thousand.
Er faßte ihn bei der Hand.	He grasped him *by* the hand.
Sie bleibt bei ihrer Aussage.	She abides *by* her assertion.
Er war nicht bei Sinnen.	He was not *in* his senses.
Er war in der Schlacht bei Prag.	He was in the battle *of* (at) Prague.
Bei dem Haus ist ein Garten.	*Near* (by) the house is a garden.
Wir werden bei ihm einsprechen.	We shall call *on* him.
Es wurde bei Lebensstrafe verboten.	It was forbidden *on* (under) pain of death.
Das ist nicht Sitte bei uns.	That is not (the) custom *among* (with) us.
Er wachte mit mir bei dem Kranken.	He watched with me *with* the sick (man).

EXERCISES ON THE USE OF Bei, Durch, Für. 145

2. Bei, with the dative, often answers to *at* before the possessive; as,

Der Stiefel ist beim Schuhmacher.	The boot is *at* the shoemaker's.
Das Mädchen ist bei ihrer Tante.	The girl is *at* her aunt's.
Die Kinder wohnen bei dem Schmiede.	The children live *at* the smith's.

Bei is used in the same manner with pronouns; as,

Er ist auf Besuch bei seinem Oheim, aber er wohnt nicht bei ihm.	He is on a visit *at* his uncle's, but he does not live *with* him (*at* his house).
Bei wem wohnen Sie?	With whom (*at* whose house) do you live?
Er ist jetzt bei uns.	He is now *at* our house.
3. Sie beschämen mich durch diese Ehre.	You confuse (embarrass) me *by* this honor.
Er schwamm durch den Strom.	He swam *across* the stream.
Sie drangen mitten durch die Armee.	They penetrated *through* the midst of the army.
Durch Geld, pflegt man zu sagen, kann man Alles ausrichten.	*With* money, one is accustomed to say (it is accustomed to be said), anything can be done.
Das Pferd ging mit mir durch.	The horse ran *away* with me.
Es soll durchaus nicht so sein.	It shall *by no means* be so.
Es ist durchaus unentbehrlich.	It is *absolutely* indispensable.
4. Sie arbeiten Tag für Tag.	They labor day *by* (after) day.
Ich, für meinen Theil, liebe so etwas nicht.	I, *for* my part, do not like such things.
Er hat es für sein Leben gern.	He is extravagantly fond of it.
Sie hat für einen Gulden Thee gekauft.	She has bought a florin's worth of tea.
Er hält es für seine Pflicht.	He considers it his duty.
Er hielt nicht dafür, den Bund zu schließen.	He was not in favor of concluding the treaty.
Das Mühlrad von der Flut gerafft, umwälzt sich für und für.	The water wheel seized by the flood revolves *unceasingly*.

EXERCISE 114.   Aufgabe 114.

1. Gustav Adolph gewann mit seinem Leben die Schlacht bei Lützen. 2. Die königlichen Schlösser bei Potsdam sind sehr schöne Gebäude. 3. Der liebende Vater seines Volkes, wie der König sich nennt, schickt seine Kinder bei Tausenden zur Schlachtbank. 4. Diese Gräuelthat ist bei hellem Sonnenschein geschehen. 5. Bei aller seiner Klugheit läßt er sich zur Thorheit verleiten. 6. Er geberdet sich, als ob er nicht bei Sinnen wäre. 7. Ich kann Ihnen nicht sagen, wieviel Uhr es ist, denn ich habe keine Uhr bei mir. 8. Wer ist jener Mann, der jetzt bei Ihnen ist? 9. Er ist ein alter Mann, bei dem ich in Leipzig wohnte. 10. Vieles, was bei uns für Höflichkeit gilt, gilt bei den Chinesen für Grobheit. 11. Ich sage und bleibe dabei, daß ich ihn bei unserm Nachbar gesehen habe. 12. Du bist unsere Zuflucht

für und für. Psalms 90. 1. 13. Ich bin den ganzen Monat durch im Hause geblieben. 14. Durch seine Faulheit hat er sich in Elend gestürzt 15. Er hat das Geld gestohlen und ist durchgegangen. 16. Der Koch hat für zwei Gulden Kaffee gekauft. 17. Er hält es für seine Pflicht, bei seinem Freunde zu bleiben.

Exercise 115.   Aufgabe 115.

1. Does your friend live at your house or at your uncle's? 2. This man is very rich, but he never has any money with him. 3. The battle of Leipsic freed Germany from French rule. 4. What ails the man? he acts as though he were not in his senses. 5. Oelper is a small village near Brunswick. 6. He took me by the hand and called me by name. 7. By my honor said he, I have never been at their house. 8. Is this the custom in your country? 9. The sun shines by day, and the moon by night. 10. With all our prudence we are often deceived. 11. Are the strangers still at your house? 12. Did your horse run away with you? 13. Do you consider it your duty to work for your friend? 14. Why do you consider that man your enemy? 15. He has offended them by his rude behavior. 16. I wish to buy three florins' worth of sugar

LESSON LVI.   Section LVI.

Gegen, Gegenüber, Entgegen, In. — EXAMPLES OF THEIR USE.

1.
Er sagt, er habe eine Arznei gegen das gelbe Fieber.	He says he has a remedy *against* (for) the yellow fever.
Gegen den Strom kann man nicht gut schwimmen.	*Against* the stream one can not swim well.
Dein Schmerz ist nichts gegen den meinigen.	Your pain is nothing, *in comparison with* mine.
Der gefangene König wurde gegen drei Generale ausgewechselt.	The captive king was exchanged *for* three generals.
Sie waren sehr höflich gegen uns.	They were very polite *to* us.
Sie ist gegen zehn Jahre alt.	She is *towards* (about) ten years old.
Er hob seine Augen gen Himmel.	He raised his eyes *towards* Heaven.

2. **Gegenüber** usually follows its object, but is sometimes resolved into its component parts, and takes the dative between them; as,

| Die Kirche steht dem Schloße gegenüber, (or gegen dem Schloße über). | The church stands *opposite* to the castle. |

3. **Entgegen** usually denotes motion or direction *towards* an object; as

Sie kamen uns entgegen. — They came *towards* (to meet) us.
Sie ziehen dem Feinde entgegen. — They march *against* (to meet) the enemy.

Die Früchte reifen uns entgegen. — The fruits are ripening *to meet* us, (*i. e.* our wants).

4. Sie waren im Begriff abzureisen. — They were *about* to start (on the point of starting).

Er ist in der Schule, und sie ist in der Kirche. — He is *at* school and she is *at* church.
Sie haben in Voraus bezahlt. — They have paid *in* advance.
In diesem Lande wohnen viele reiche Leute auf (L. 54. 1.) dem Lande. — *In* this country a great many rich people live *in* the country.
Das ist mir nie in den Sinn gekommen. — That never came *into* my mind.
Er hat sie im Stich gelassen. — He has left them *in* the lurch.
Er ist ins Gedränge gekommen. — He has got *into* difficulty.
Gehen sie ins Theater, ins Concert, oder in die Oper? — Are you going *to* the theater, to the concert, or *to* the opera?
Das Kind sprang in die Höhe, und klatschte in die Hände. — The child sprang *up* and clapped its hands.
Er hat sie in Schutz gegen uns genommen. — He has protected them (taken them in protection) *against* us.
Er redete in Einem fort. — He spoke incessantly (*in* one strain).

Du bist in der letzten Zeit nicht mehr so offen gegen mich wie früher. — You are, of late, not so frank *towards* me as formerly.
Wir werden in den ersten Tagen abreisen. — We shall depart *within* a few days.
Warum hast du ihn in Verdacht? — Why do you suspect him?
Dieser Geck sagt, jenes Frauenzimmer habe sich in ihn verliebt. — This coxcomb says, that lady has fallen in love with him.
Er drang in den König sich zu erklären. — He besought the king to explain (declare) himself.
Es thut mir leid, Ihre Hülfe in Anspruch nehmen zu müssen. — I am sorry to be obliged to claim your assistance.

Exercise 116. — Aufgabe 116.

1. Als die Kinder uns sahen, eilten sie uns entgegen. 2. Sie warfen sich dem anrückenden Feinde entgegen, und jagten ihn bald in die Flucht. 3. „Dann kannst du ohne Furcht und Grau'n dem Tod entgegengehen." 4. Dieser Schüler ist ein gegen Jedermann höflicher Knabe. 5. Er ist zwar nicht sehr groß, aber gegen dich ist er ein Riese. 6. Wenn du dich entschlossen hast, gegen deinen König zu fechten, so habe ich nichts dagegen zu sagen. 7. Gegen diese Krankheit gibt es keine Arznei. 8. Als wir aus der kleinen Kapelle kamen, die dem Schloße gegenüber steht, flog uns eine Staubwolke entgegen. 9. Alles Böse, welches Philipp der Zweite gegen die Königin von England beschloß, war Rache, die er dafür nahm, daß sie seine protestantischen Unterthanen in Schutz gegen ihn genommen hatte. 10. Ich bin in der letzten Zeit so sehr beschäftigt gewesen, daß ich weder ins

Concert noch in die Oper habe gehen können. 11. Ist „ich habe ihn in Verdacht", gleichbedeutend mit: „ich habe Verdacht auf ihn?"

EXERCISE 117.   Aufgabe 117.

1. Those soldiers whom we saw at the concert were very polite to us, but very rude to the strangers. 2. He who fights against his fatherland is a traitor, but there are kings and emperors in Europe against whom a citizen may fight without being a traitor. 3. Why do you not go to school? 4. I have been at school, but it *is* out. 5. I was on the point of going to the opera as it began to rain. 6. Why do you suspect him of having committed this crime? 7. The hotel in which we stopped stands opposite the church. 8. As soon as we saw them we went to meet them. 9. For this disease there is no remedy. 10. This man has for the last few days been very rude to his friends, and seems deaf to all their exhortations to become otherwise. 11. If you wish to go with your friends to the concert or the opera I have no objection to it.

LESSON LVII.   Section LVII.

Mit, Nach. — EXAMPLES OF THEIR USE.

1. Ich gehe mit ihm, wir gehen mit der ersten Gelegenheit.
   I am going *with* him; we go *by* the first opportunity.

Einer seiner Mitschüler ging mit.
   One of his fellow scholars went along (with him).

Er will es mit ihm aufnehmen.
   He will try it with him (does not fear him).

Das geht nicht zu mit rechten Dingen.
   There is witchcraft (something supernatural) about it.

Sie macht alle Moden mit.
   She follows all the fashions.

Mit nichten.
   By no means. Not so.

Es steht nicht gut mit ihnen.
   It goes badly with them.

Man sagt, und mit Recht, daß u.s.w.
   It is said, and justly, that, &c.

Mitunter ist er ein wenig grob.
   Besides (moreover) he is a little rude.

2. Er ist der erste nach mir.
   He is the first *after* me.

Sie schickten nach dem Arzte.
   They sent *after* (for) the physician.

Alle schossen nach demselben Vogel.
   All shot *at* the same bird.

Das Schiff ist nach Danzig bestimmt.
   The ship is bound *for* Danzig.

Er zeichnet nach der Natur.
   He draws *from* nature.

Ich spiele nicht nach Noten.
   I do not play *by* note.

Es ist nach seinem Plan.
   It is *after* (according to) his plan.

Dieses ist nach meinem Geschmack.
   This is *according to* my taste.

Sie sind nach Amerika gereist.
   They have gone *to* America.

Wir segelten nach Osten.
   We sailed *towards* the east.

Das Fleisch schmeckt nach Zwiebeln.
   The meat tastes *of* onions.

Nach und nach verschwand es.
   By degrees (little by little) it disappeared.

Nach frequently *follows* its object; as,

Der Beschreibung nach muß es sehr schön sein.	According to the description, it must be very beautiful.
Ich kenne ihn nur dem Namen nach.	I know him only *by* name.
Meiner Meinung nach hat er recht.	*In* (according to) my opinion he is right.

3. Nach Hause (or Haus), after verbs of motion, answers to "*home*" in like position; as,

Sie gehen jetzt nach Hause.	They are now going home.

Exercise 118.   Aufgabe 118.

1. Nach dem Falle Carthagos ging das römische Reich seiner Auflösung immer mehr entgegen. 2. Mein Freund gedenkt in den ersten Tagen eine Reise nach Ostindien anzutreten. 3. Es mag sein, daß der Rock ganz nach der neuesten Mode ist, aber er ist durchaus nicht nach meinem Geschmack. 4. Es war heute Morgen ein Herr hier, der nach Ihnen fragte. 5. Habe ich denn Unrecht, daß ich nach meiner eigenen Ueberzeugung handle? 6. Sobald es im Frühling anfängt warm zu werden, fliegen die wilden Gänse nach Norden. 7. Ich schickte nach dem Arzte, aber der Bote kam wieder nach Hause zurück, ohne ihn gefunden zu haben. 8. Spielen Sie nicht nach Noten? 9. Nachdem er seinen Brief gelesen hatte, eilte er nach der Stadt. 10. Dieses Wasser schmeckt nach Eisen.

Exercise 119.   Aufgabe 119.

1. Shall you go home this afternoon? 2. No, I shall go to the city, and my friend will go to the village. 3. Is this cloak according to your taste or shall I show you another? 4. Have you sent for a physician? 5. I shall go home after I have visited my friends. 6. We were at your house this morning and asked for you and were told that you had gone to the woods. 7. A few minutes after six o'clock the servant came home without having found the physician for which we had sent. 8. According to your description the country to which you are going must be almost a paradise. 9. It has gradually decreased until it has become very small. 10. Why did the old sailor strike at you with his crutch? 11 Those who judge a man by his exterior, often mistake.

LESSON LVIII.   Section LVIII.

Ob, Ohne, Seit. — EXAMPLES OF THEIR USE.

1. Ob (as a preposition) is mainly used in poetry, with the dative, sometimes with the genitive; as,

„Ob dem Altar' hing eine Mutter Gottes."	Over (or above) the altar hung a picture of the virgin.
Entrüstet sind' ich sie ob dem neuen Regiment'.	I find them provoked at the new government.
Ihr seid verwundert ob des seltsamen Geräths.	You are surprised at the strange (curious) implement.

2. As a conjunction, ob answers to *whether, if, though;* as,

Er sieht aus, als ob er krank wäre.	He looks as though he were sick.
Ich weiß nicht, ob er kommt oder nicht.	I do not know whether he is coming or not.
Ob er (L. 39. 3.) gleich reich ist, so ist er doch nicht geachtet.	Although he is rich, nevertheless he is not respected.

3.
Ohne Zweifel wird er kommen.	*Without* doubt he will come.
Ohne Sie wäre ich verloren gewesen.	*But for* you I should have been lost.
„Und regt ohn' Ende Die fleißigen Hände."	And ceaselessly moves The industrious hands.
Ich habe ohne dieß (or ohnedies) eine angenehme Nachricht erhalten.	I have besides this received (an) agreeable (piece of) news.
Es ist ohnehin schon kalt genug hier.	It is already cold enough here without that.

4.
Seit seines Vaters Tode wohnt er bei seinem Oheim.	Since his father's death he lives with his uncle.
Seit jenem Tage habe ich ihn nicht gesehen.	Since that day I have not seen him.
Er ist seit einem Jahre krank.	He (is) has been sick for a year.
Seit wann ist er hier?	How long (since when) has he been here?
Ich habe ihn seit einem Jahre nicht gesehen.	I have not seen him for (since) a year.

Seit is sometimes used adverbially; as,

Seit wir da waren.	Since we were there.

Generally, however, dem is suffixed to it; as,

Seitdem ich ihn sah u. s. w.	Since I saw him, &c.

Exercise 120.   Aufgabe 120.

1. „Wie ein Engelsbild ob einer Todtengruft läßt Oberon sich jetzt auf einem Wölkchen sehen." 2. Ich möchte wissen, ob er zurückkommen wird. 3. Warum sehen Sie mich so ängstlich an, als ob Sie mich bedauerten? 4. Ich fühle mich nicht unglücklich, obgleich ich so arm und verlassen bin. 5. Obgleich die Luft unsichtbar ist, so ist sie doch ein Körper. 6. Er hat es dennoch gethan, obgleich das Verbot dagegen war. 7. Ob ich schon wandere im finstern Thal, fürchte ich kein Unglück. Pf. 23, 4. 8. Seit der Abreise meiner Verwandten fühle ich mich sehr einsam, obgleich ich viele Freunde hier habe. 9. Seitdem er reich geworden ist, scheint er weniger zufrieden zu sein als während er arm war. 10. Er ist schon seit vier Wochen krank.

Exercise 121.   Aufgabe 121.

1. Do you know whether they have been here since our arrival? 2. Although they have been here since I arrived I have not seen them. 3. I have not seen them, although they have been here since my arrival. 4. Since they have become industrious they

are much more contented than while they were so idle. 5. I have lived for five years in this house. 6. These immigrants look as though they were very poor. 7. For three days past I have not felt well. 8. I recognized him although I had not seen him for more than five years. 9. It is all the same to me whether you go or stay.

LESSON LIX.   Section LIX.

Ueber.—EXAMPLES OF ITS USE.

Sein Zimmer ist über dem meinigen.	His room is *above* (over) mine.
Das geht über meinen Horizont (colloquial).	That is (goes) *above* (beyond) my comprehension.
Sie gingen über die Brücke.	They went *across* (over) the bridge.
Das geht über Menschen Vermögen.	That (goes) is *beyond* human power.
Wir reisten über Straßburg.	We went *by way of* Strasburg.
Ueber diesen Punkt hat er noch nicht entschieden.	*Concerning* (upon) this point he has not yet decided.
Heute über acht Tage reist er ab.	A week *from* to-day he departs.
Man hat ihn über der That ergriffen.	He has been caught *in* the act.
Sie sind über Land gegangen.	They have walked *into* the country.
Er klagt über seine Armuth.	He complains *of* his poverty.
„Er heb seine Augen auf über seine Jünger." (L 6. 20).	He lifted up his eyes *on* his disciples.
Sie blieben über Nacht auf der Straße.	They remained *over* night in the street.
Lasset die Sonne nicht über eurem Zorne untergehen.	Let not the sun go down *upon* your wrath.
Ueber dieser langweiligen Rede schlief er ein.	*Under* (during) this tedious speech he fell asleep.
Ich habe über diese Sache geschrieben.	I have written *upon* this subject.
Die Zufriedenheit geht über den Reichthum.	Contentment is better than (goes *beyond*) wealth.
Er hielt sich über uns auf.	He found fault *with* (ridiculed) us.
Gott ist überall gegenwärtig.	God is *everywhere* present.

Ueber sometimes follows its object; as,

Den Sommer über wohnt er auf dem Lande.	*During* the summer (the summer over) he lives in the country.

EXERCISE 122.   Aufgabe 122.

1. Als wir über die Brücke gingen, sahen wir gerade über uns einen Luftballon. 2. Der Faule stirbt über seinen Wünschen; denn seine Hände wollen nichts thun. 3. Werden Sie über Hamburg oder Bremen nach

England reisen? 4. Er ist gewiß nicht über zehn Jahre alt. 5. Der Gesandte hielt eine lange Rede über die Pflichten, die der Bürger seinem Vaterlande schuldig ist. 6. Sie war über diese Antwort ganz verlegen. 7. Es geht nichts über die Ruhe der Seele und das Bewußtsein, seine Schuldigkeit gethan zu haben. 8. Man hält nicht viel auf einen, der sich über jede Kleinigkeit aufhält. 9. Heute über vierzehn Tage werden wir über Berlin nach Frankfurt an der Oder abreisen. 10. Den Winter über wohnen wir in der Stadt. 11. Die Reisenden übernachteten in der Stadt.

Exercise 123.   Aufgabe 123.

1. Two weeks from to-day we start by way of Harburg for Hamburg. 2. Those who drink wine and beer; or those who smoke should never complain of their poverty. 3. We were over three months on the ship. 4. Have you ever meditated much on this question? 5. If you ridicule others, others will ridicale you. 6. One went over the bridge and the other swam across the river. 7. They are very angry at your conduct. 8. We staid over night in the city of Carlsruhe. 9. This kind of wine one finds everywhere. 10. That is entirely beyond my strength.

LESSON LX.   Section LX.

Um. — EXAMPLES OF ITS USE.

Sie gingen um die Stadt herum.	They went *around* the city.
Sie standen um ihn herum.	They stood round *about* him.
Was wissen Sie um die Sache?	What do you know *about* the affair?
Ich weiß nichts darum.	I know nothing *about it*.
Wir werden um zwei Uhr kommen.	Whe shall come *at* two o'clock.
Von Braunschweig nach Posen über Leipzig und Dresden zu reisen, ist viel (sehr) um.	To go from Brunswick to Posen by way of Leipsic and Dresden, is a great way *around*.
Es ist um zwei Fuß zu lang.	It is too long *by* two feet.
Der Baum ist umgefallen.	The tree has fallen *down*.
Sie laufen um die Wette.	They are running *for* a (the) wager.
Es thut mir wirklich leid um ihn.	I am really sorry *for* him.
Um Alles in der Welt thue es nicht.	*For* all (in) the world do it not.
Um meinetwillen braucht es nicht zu geschehen.	It needs not be done *for* my sake (on my account.)
Verdiene ich dieses um dich?	Do I deserve this *from* you?
Er fiel seinem Vater um den Hals.	He fell *upon* his father's neck.
Die Zeit ist schon um.	The time is already *up*.
Wie würde es alsdann um mein Versprechen stehen?	How would it then stand (be) *with* my promise?
Um so besser für uns.	*So much* the better for us.
Er ist zu unglücklich, um nicht bedauert zu werden.	He is too unfortunate not to be pitied.

EXAMPLES ON THE USE OF Unter, Von, Vor. 153

Um Vergebung. Ich bitte Sie um Verzeihung.	Your pardon! I beg your pardon.
Ich sehe ihn einen Tag um den andern.	I see him every other day.
Er spricht, wie es ihm ums Herz ist.	He speaks as he thinks (as it is about his heart).

Um often marks a loss or privation; as,

Das Schiff ging unter, und die ganze Mannschaft kam um (or ums Leben).	The ship went down, and the whole crew perished.
Die Thorheit bringt mehr Menschen um als die Arbeit.	Folly destroys more men than labor (does).

Exercise 124. Aufgabe 124.

1. Sie kamen ins Zimmer, wo wir um den Tisch saßen, und setzten sich um den Ofen. 2. Um deinetwillen nur hat er das gethan; verdient er also eine solche Behandlung um dich? (von dir?) 3. Um sechs Uhr geht die Sonne unter, um neun geht der Mond auf. 4. Vergangene Woche kam der Arzt alle Tage zu mir, jetzt aber kommt er einen Tag um den andern. 5. Er glaubte, man wollte ihn um sein Geld bringen, deßhalb rief er um Hülfe. 6. Er ist um fünf Jahre älter als sie. 7. Der Knabe fiel seinem Vater um den Hals und bat ihn um Verzeihung. 8. Was thut man nicht um Geld. 9. Tausende von den französischen Soldaten kamen auf dem Rückzug aus Rußland um. 10. Könige bringen oft einen Menschen um seine Freiheit, sogar um sein Leben, weil er so spricht, wie es ihm ums Herz ist. 11. Der Engel des Herrn lagert sich um die her, die ihn fürchten. 12. Umsonst näherte sich Tilly mit seiner Armee auf einen Kanonenschuß weit dem Lager des Königs, um ihm eine Schlacht anzubieten; Gustav, um die Hälfte schwächer als Tilly, vermied sie mit Weisheit; sein Lager war zu fest, um dem Feinde einen gewaltsamen Angriff zu erlauben.

Exercise 125. Aufgabe 125.

1. At what time will you come to me? 2. Shall we go around the field or through the woods? 3. He is older by five years than his cousin. 4. As we were sitting around the table we heard some one call for help. 5. You can see them only every other day. 6. We shall be obliged to start at three o'clock, for we must go a great way around. 7. For his sake they will remain here till this evening. 8. The time that we were to remain here is out. 9. If you can come at nine o'clock, so much the better. 10. In this battle more than three thousand men perished. 11. They deprived him of his money and his watch.

LESSON LXI. Section LXI.

Unter, Von, Vor. — EXAMPLES OF THEIR USE.

1. Ich rechne Sie unter meine Freunde.	I reckon you *among* my friends.
Unter andern geschah auch dieses.	*Among* other things, this too, happened

Er ist unter der Arbeit eingeschlafen.	He has fallen asleep *at* the work.
Er saß unter mir am Tisch.	He sat *below* me at the table.
Sie ist unter diesem Namen bekannt.	She is known *by* (under) this name.
Komm mir nie wieder unter die Augen.	Never come *before* my eyes again.
Das Buch ist unter der Presse.	The book is *in* (the) press.
Nur unter dieser Bedingung will er es thun.	Only *on* this condition will he do it.
Er ist unter die Soldaten gegangen.	He has become a soldier, (gone among the soldiers).
Der da wandelt mitten unter den sieben Leuchtern. Rev. 2. 1.	Who walketh *in the midst* of the seven golden candlesticks.
Es ist unmöglich, alle Köpfe unter einen Hut zu bringen.	It is impossible to make all men think alike.
Er hat es mir unter vier Augen gesagt.	He has told it to me in confidence (beneath four eyes).
Es liegt Alles unter einander.	Everything is lying in confusion.
2. Es wurde von einem Blinden geschrieben.	It was written *by* a blind man.
Sie leben von ihrer Arbeit und er von seinen Einkünften.	They live *by* (from) their labor and he *upon* his income.
Ist er ein Freund von Ihnen?	Is he a friend *of* yours?
Er that es von freien Stücken.	He did it voluntarily (of his own accord).
Es ging gut von Statten.	It went off (succeeded) well.
3. Wir schützten ihn vor ihnen.	We protected him *against* (from) them.
Das Schiff liegt vor Anker.	The ship lies *at* anchor.
Sie waren vor zwei Wochen hier.	They were here two weeks *ago*.
Sie weinten vor Freude.	They wept *for* joy.
So will ich mich nicht vor dir verbergen.	Then will I not hide myself *from* thee. (Job 13, 20.).
Er schoß den Bären vor den Kopf.	He shot the bear *in* the head.
Sie haben den Vortheil vor mir.	You have the advantage *of* me.
Er war fast außer sich vor Zorn.	He was almost beside himself *with* rage.
Es wird bald vor sich gehen.	It will soon take place.

Exercise 126. Aufgabe 126.

1. Wir saßen auf Bänken um einen Tisch unter dem Baume in dem Garten. 2. Ich glaube, das Beste, was du unter diesen Umständen thun könntest, wäre, unter die Soldaten zu gehen. 3. Ist denn keiner unter uns, der diese Schmach räche? 4. Ich kenne ihn nicht, wenigstens nicht unter diesem Namen. 5. Der Gast bat den Wirth um eine Unterredung unter vier Augen. 6. Das Buch ist schon unter der Presse, und wird in den ersten Tagen erscheinen. 7. Meine Haare sind unter Freuden grau gewor-

ben, sagte der dankbare Greis, als er unter dem Schatten der Bäume saß, die er als Jüngling gepflanzt hatte. 8. Mitten unter Verwundeten und Todten warf er sich nieder und betete. 9. Alle über achtzehn und unter vierzig mußten unter die Soldaten gehen. 10. Du hast einen großen Vortheil vor mir. 11. Diese Leute habe ich schon vor fünf Jahren in München kennen gelernt. 12. Der Kaiser kniete vor dem Herzog und bat ihn um Beistand. 13. „Herr", sagte der Bauer, „Ihr müßt schneller laufen, wenn Ihr vor dem großen Schweden-König ausreißt." 14. Tilly brannte vor Ungeduld, die Schmach seiner Niederlage durch einen glänzenden Sieg auszulöschen. 15. Man kommt von einem Ort, worauf, und aus einem Ort, worin man sich befindet.

Exercise 127.   Aufgabe 127.

1. Among the inhabitants of this village are some who are very rich. 2. The ship is already under sail. 3. On these terms, and on no others, I will assist you. 4. Do not forget that this is to remain a secret between us. 5. What did that man tell you with whom you were sitting under the tree? 6. What would you do under such circumstances? 7. It is beneath the dignity of any man thus to act. 8. The youngest is not under twenty, and the oldest is not over fifty years old. 9. That is much below the value of the book, I can not sell it under five florins. 10. Is the new history of Germany already in press? 11. The strangers sat below us at the table. 12. One year ago we were among our friends and our ship was lying at anchor in the harbor. 13. I shall see you again before your departure. 14. The soldiers almost perished from thirst and fatigue. 15. We were in Munich a few days ago.

LESSON LXII.   Section LXII.

Zu. — EXAMPLES OF ITS USE.

1. Er kommt immer zur rechten Zeit.	He always comes *at* the right time.
„Ich will dir zur Seite stehen."	I will aid thee, (stand *at* thy side).
Es steht Ihnen Alles, was ich habe, zu Diensten.	All that I have, is *at* your service.
Sie fielen zu Tausenden.	They fell *by* thousands.
Wie ist er zu diesem Gelde gekommen?	How did he come *by* this money?
Reisen Sie zu Wasser oder zu Lande?	Do you travel *by* water or *by* land?
Ich habe ihn heute zum ersten Male gesehen.	I have seen him to-day *for the* first time.
Er kauft Tuch zu einem Rocke.	He is buying cloth *for* a coat.
Zum Zweiten sollt ihr mir berechnen	*For* the second (secondly) you

und sagen, wie bald ich zu Rosse die Welt mag umjagen.	shall calculate and tell me how soon I can ride (chase) round the world *on* horseback.
Er reis't zu Fuße, ich zu Pferde.	He travels *on* foot, I *on* horseback.
Er zog ihn zur Verantwortung.	He called him *to* account.
Er stellte ihn zur Rede.	He demanded an explanation.
Wir haben Abraham zum Vater.	We have Abraham *to* our father.
Das gereicht ihm zur Ehre.	That redounds *to* his honor.
Ich rufe ihn zum Zeugen an.	I call him *to* witness.
Das kann zum Beweise dienen.	That may serve as (for) a proof.
Dir zu Gefallen will ich es thun.	For your sake (to please you) I will do it.
Ich möchte gehen, aber es ist zu kalt.	I would like to go, but it is *too* cold.
Du hast ihn zum Feinde gemacht.	You have made an enemy of him.
Man hat dich zum Besten.	They are making a laughing stock of you.
Er hat seine Gesundheit zu Grunde gerichtet.	He has destroyed his health.
Sie haben es endlich zu Stande gebracht.	They have finally brought it about.
Die Haare standen ihm zu Berge.	His hair stood on end.
Ich habe ihn nie zu Gesichte bekommen.	I have never got a sight of him.
Er konnte vor Lachen kaum zu Athem kommen.	He could scarcely catch (come to) breath for laughing.
Es kam ihm sehr zu Statten.	It was very fortunate for him.
Er will zur Ader lassen.	He wishes to be bled.
Er hält das Seine zu Rath.	He takes care of his own (what he has).
Wir logirten im Wirthshause zum Adler.	We stopped at the Eagle Hotel.
Ich konnte nicht zu Worte kommen.	I could not make myself heard.
Warum ist die Thüre zu?	Why is the door shut?
Er ging auf sie zu.	He went up to them.
Wir segelten nach Süden zu.	We sailed towards the south.
Das ist wirklich zum toll werden.	That is really enough to make one mad.
Er machte sich den Umstand zu Nutze.	He profited by the circumstance.
Das geht nicht mit rechten Dingen zu.	There is some witchcraft about it.

2. The *dative* with zu after verbs of motion (like bei with those of rest) often answers to our *possessive* preceded by "*to*"; as,

Er geht zu dem Schuhmacher.	He is going to the shoemaker's

Zu is used in the same manner with pronouns; as,

Er kommt oft zu uns.	He often comes to us (i. e. to our house).

3 Zu Hause, after verbs of rest, answers to *"at home"*;
Er blieb den ganzen Tag zu Hause.   He remained all day *at home*

Exercise 128.   Aufgabe 128.

1. Heute zum erstenmal in dieser Woche bist du zur rechten Zeit gekommen. 2. Ich reise lieber zu Wasser als zu Lande, und zu Pferde als zu Fuß. 3. Zur Zeit der Kreuzzüge herrschten ganz andere Sitten und Gebräuche als zu unserer Zeit. 4. Wie ist ein so armer Mann zu so vielem Gelde gekommen? 5. Wie viel Tuch brauche ich zu einem Mantel? 6. Als ich die Thüre zumachte, sprang der Dieb zum Fenster hinaus. 7. Dir gereicht es zur Ehre, ihm zur Schande. 8. Ich möchte gern zu meinen Freunden gehen, aber der Weg ist zu weit und das Wetter zu schlecht. 9. Sobald er mich sah, kam er auf mich zu. 10. Er ist noch nicht zu Hause, aber er wird bald nach Hause kommen. 11. Man geht zu einem Freunde, und bleibt bei einem Freunde; man geht nach Hause und bleibt zu Hause.

Exercise 129.   Aufgabe 129.

1. Shall you remain at home, or go to your friend's to-day? 2. I would rather travel on foot than on horseback. 3. He was your true friend and you have made a bitter enemy of him. 4. The boy threw the ball out of the window. 5. How came you by all this money? 6. The tailor who came to our house yesterday, has been buying cloth for a coat and a vest. 7. The Europeans emigrate by thousands to America and Australia. 8. I will come to your house to-morrow if I have not too much to do at home and the weather is not too cold. 9. To have acted thus, redounds to his honor. 10. I have, to-day, for the first time seen your friend who was in Paris at the time of the revolution. 11. The boy thinks he has already worked too long, and that it is time to go to bed.

LESSON LXIII.   Section LXIII.

Aber, Allein, Als, Also, Auch. — Examples of their use.

1. Er kann es thun, will er aber? — He can do it, will he *though*?
Der König aber verzieh ihm. — The king *however* pardoned him
Und aber schoß ein Strahl herab. — And *again* a ray shot down.
Bei der Sache ist ein aber. — There is a *but* (difficulty) in the matter.

2. Niemand als er kann es thun. — Nobody *but* him (than he) can do it.
Sie sind viel reicher als wir. — They are much richer *than* we.
Er bettelt lieber, als daß er arbeitet. — He begs rather *than* to work.
Ich erkenne keinen Menschen als meinen Herrn. — I acknowledge no human being *as* my master.
Sie ist eben so liebenswürdig als schön. — She is just as amiable *as* beautiful.

Als er das hörte stand er auf. | As (when) he heard that, he got up.
Er kommt so bald als er kann. | He comes as soon *as* he can.

3. After so, als is often omitted, and must be supplied in translating; as,

Er lief so schnell er konnte. | He ran as fast *as* he could.
So bald er mich sah, kam er auf mich zu. | As soon *as* he saw me, he came up to me.

4. Ich mußte also handeln. | I was obliged *so* to act.
Ich darf dich also erwarten? | I may expect you *then*?
Er hat es versprochen, also muß er es thun. | He has promised it, *hence* (therefore) he must do it.

5. Wenden Sie sich jedes Mal an mich, so oft es auch sein mag. | Apply to me every time, *however* often it may be.
Ist auch nichts dabei zu gewinnen, so will ich es doch thun. | *Even* if there is nothing to be gained by it, I will nevertheless do it.

Willst du auch gehen? | Will you go *too*?
Wirst du aber auch halten, was du versprochen hast? | But will you perform *too* (keep), what you have promised?
Er spielt nicht, auch singt er nicht. | He does not play, nor does he sing.
Ich auch nicht. | Nor I either.

Exercise 130.   Aufgabe 130.

1. Er hatte viele Freunde aber in der Noth, in der er sich jetzt befand, blieb ihm Niemand als ein alter Knecht getreu. 2. Lieber als daß er zum Verräther wurde, ließ er sich auf die grausamste Weise umbringen. 3. Er sagte, er werde so bald als möglich zurückkommen. 4. So lange Maximilian lebte, genossen sie einer vollkommenen Duldung auch in ihrer neuen Gestalt, unter seinem Nachfolger aber änderte sich die Scene. 5. Er selbst ist Schuld daran, kann also nicht klagen. 6. Er ist nicht allein ein großer, sondern auch ein guter Mann. 7. Wie also auch der Erfolg sein mochte, so stand es gleich schlimm um die Verbündeten. 8. Er will es nicht thun, und ich auch nicht. 9. Wer er auch sein mag, oder was er auch sagen mag, ich fürchte mich nicht vor ihm. 10. Der beklagt sich nicht seines Unverstandes und seiner Unwissenheit, wenn er nur sieht, daß sein Nachbar auch nicht viel kann.

Exercise 131.   Aufgabe 131.

He is a true friend but he is poor and has nothing but good advice to give you. 2. Shall you go to the city alone? 3. A man who is guilty of no crime should recognize no human being as his master. 4. As soon as we had read your books we sent them back to you. 5. Rather than to become a slave he died. 6. I regard him as a true friend whatever you may say of him. 7. Even if he is your enemy you can nevertheless say nothing against him. 8. If thou hast a true friend thou art not poor, however great thy poverty may be. 9. However bad he may be, he is still a man, and we as Christians must help him. 10. It is your wish, then, that they should remain here. 11. He who loves nothing but the beautiful becomes a spendthrift and he who loves nothing but the useful is in danger of becoming a miser.

LESSON LXIV.
Section LXIV.

Bald, Bis, Da, Daß. — EXAMPLES OF THEIR USE.

1. Sie werden bald hier sein. — They will *soon* be here.
Er ist bald zufrieden gestellt. — He is *easily* (soon) satisfied.
Ich wäre bald gefallen. — I *almost* fell (was on the point of falling).

Bald ist er froh, bald traurig. — *Sometimes* he is glad, *sometimes* sad.

2. Er wird bis übermorgen bleiben. — He will remain *till* day after to-morrow.
In acht bis zehn Tagen soll es fertig sein. — In (from) eight *to* ten days it shall be ready.
Ich begleitete ihn bis Berlin und blieb bis Ostern. — I accompanied him *as far as* Berlin, and remained *till* Easter.
Bis wohin sind sie gefahren? — How far (as far as to what place) did you ride?
(Wie weit sind Sie gefahren?) — (How far did you ride?)

a. Before nouns, bis is usually followed by a preposition, which is generally omitted in translating; as,

Bleibe bis zum Abend. — Remain till (to the) evening.
Er stieg bis auf die höchste Spitze des Berges. — He ascended up to (as far as) the highest point of the mountain.
Wir gingen bis nach Dresden. — We went as far as Dresden.
Sie verfolgten ihn bis über die Grenzen. — They followed him (as far as) across the borders.
Alle bis auf Sie sind zufrieden. — All except you are satisfied.
Er ist fast bis zum Wahnsinn entzückt. — He is delighted almost to delirium.

Wir werden keinen Frieden haben, eher, als bis wir werden den Feind geschlagen haben. — We shall have no peace (sooner than) till we shall have defeated the enemy.

3. Da noch alles lag in weiter Fern', da hattest du Entschluß und Muth; und jetzt, da der Erfolg gesichert ist, da fängst du an zu zagen. — *As* (*when*) all yet lay in the (far) distance (*then*) thou hadst determination and courage — and now, *that* the result is secured (*now*) thou beginnest to despair.

Da er krank ist, so geht er nicht. — *As* he is sick he does not go.
Und da saß er eines Morgens. — And *there* he sat one morning.
Wie! ist er schon da? — How! is he already *here*!

a. After a relative ba is frequently omitted in translating; as,

Der da ift, der da war, und der da
fein wird.
Which is, and which was, and which is to come.

4. Wir wiffen, daß er kommt.
We know that he is coming.

Wie lange ift es, daß Sie ihn gesehen haben.
How long (is it) since you have seen him?

Während daß er da blieb.
While (*that*) he remained there.

Exercise 132.   Aufgabe 132.

1. Guftav Adolph, an der Spitze einer fiegreichen Armee, hätte von Leipzig bis Prag, Wien und Preßburg wenig Widerftand gefunden. 2. Ueb' immer Treue und Redlichkeit bis an dein kühles Grab, und weiche keinen Finger breit von Gottes Wegen ab. 3. Die ganze Ebene von Lützen bis an den Floßgraben war mit Verwundeten, mit Sterbenden, mit Todten bedeckt. 4. Das Frohlocken war ohne Grenzen, die Freude an dem neuen König ging bis zur Anbetung. 5. Graf Tilly folgte dem linken Ufer des Weferftroms, und bemächtigte sich aller Päffe bis Minden. 6. Wallenftein kam eben aus Ungarn zurück, bis wohin er dem Grafen Mannsfeld gefolgt war, ohne aber seine Vereinigung mit Bethelm Gabern verhindern zu können. 7. Seine Erpreffungen waren bis zum Unerträglichen gegangen. 8. Da ich nicht auf dem Markte gewesen bin, so weiß ich nicht, ob er da war oder nicht. 9. Du sprichft mein Urtheil aus, da du mich tröfteft. 10. Da ihr die That gefchehen ließt, wart ihr nicht ihr felbft. 11. Denn wer da bittet, der empfängt; und wer da fuchet, der findet; und wer da anklopft, dem wird aufgethan. Matth. 7, 8. 12. Es follte kein Tag vergehen da man nicht etwas Nützliches thue. 13. Es mag fein, daß er bis zum zehnten Mai hier bleiben wird.

Exercise 133.   Aufgabe 133.

1. We were in the city yesterday, and as the weather was bad we remained there till this morning. 2. If you will remain here till I can answer the letter that I have just received I will go with you as far as Meissen. 3. In three to four weeks you will have read as far as the three hundredth page. 4. I shall not get up from this table until I shall have written two more letters. 5. The water was so deep where we rode through the river, that it came up to the saddles. 6. How far will you go with us, if we remain here till to-morrow? 7. We will go as far as your uncle's with you. 8. We had gone as far as the village, and as it began to rain we were obliged to remain till three o'clock. 9. All except him are perfectly satisfied. 10. Since you wish it, I will remain here till you return. 11. They only went as far as the bridge. 12. Thinking you had already seen our books we did not send you any.

LESSON LXV.   Lection LXV.

Dann, Denn, Doch, Eben, Ehe, Erst, Etwa, Gar, Immer, Ja, Je. — EXAMPLES OF THEIR USE.

1. Erst sorgt man für sich, dann für Andere.
First, one cares for one's self, and *then*, for others.

Er kommt dann und wann zu uns.
He comes, now and then, to our house.

2. Ich kann ihn nicht tadeln, denn ich weiß, daß er es gut meinte.
I can not blame him, fc: I know that he meant it well.

Was ist denn das?
Why? what is that?

Was hast du denn wieder vor?
Well! what are you at again?

Ich schätze ihn höher als Feldherr, denn als Staatsmann.
I esteem him more highly as a general, than as a statesman.

Er wird kommen, es sei denn, daß er krank ist.
He will come unless (be it then, — if he does not, — that) he is sick.

Er wird es nicht thun, es sei denn, daß Sie mit ihm sprechen.
He will not do it, unless you speak to him.

3. Ob er gleich wußte, daß ich allein sein wollte, so blieb er doch.
Although he knew I wished to be alone, he, nevertheless remained.

Ich bat ihn, zu gehen, doch er wollte nicht.
I besought him to go, but he would not.

Ich möchte doch wissen, wo er ist.
I should really like to know where he is.

Das ist doch komisch (seltsam).
That is curious (comical) though.

Doch ist er auch klein, so ist er nicht faul zu trotzigem, stolzem Befehle.
But though (even if) he is small, he is not idle in (giving) proud haughty commands.

Gehen Sie doch mit uns.
Do go with us.

O, daß ich doch bei euch wäre.
O, that I were only with you!

a. Doch is sometimes used as a gentle contradiction; as,

Sie haben mir nicht geschrieben.
You have not written to me.

Doch! or O doch!
O, yes, I have.

4. Sie singt eben so gut, wie er.
She sings just as well as he.

Er hat es so eben gethan.
He has just done it.

Eben so soll es Andern ergehen.
Even so shall it be done to others.

Eben darum eilte er so sehr.
For that very reason he hastened so.

5. Ich werde Sie sehen, ehe Sie abreisen.
I will see you before I depart.

Je eher je lieber.
The sooner the better (the rather).

Ich möchte eher sterben.
I would sooner (rather) die.

Er ist eher zu bedauern, als zu beneiden.	He is rather to be pitied than to be envied.
6. Erst wollte er es thun, dann besann er sich aber anders.	At first he was going to do it (but) then he decided otherwise.
Sie ist erst dreizehn Jahre alt.	She is only thirteen years old.
Wir werden erst morgen abreisen.	We shall not start till to-morrow.
Dann erst gebe ich es zurück.	Not till then will I return it.
7. Es sind etwa acht Wochen, daß ich da war.	It is about eight weeks since I was there.
Wenn etwa ein solcher vorhanden ist.	If (perchance) such a one is in existence.

8. **Gar** as an adjective, answers to "done", "finished"; as,

Das Brod ist gar.	The bread is done (thoroughly baked).
Das Leder ist gar.	The leather is thoroughly tanned.

b. As an adverb, gar, before the word nicht, answers to "*at all*"; and in other positions, to "*very*", "*ever*", "*extremely*", &c.; as,

Er ist gar nicht hier gewesen.	He has not been here at all.
Sie ist gar zu stolz.	She is entirely too proud.
Er spricht gar zuversichtlich.	He speaks very confidently.
Er ist nicht gar zu ordentlich.	He is not very (entirely too) regular.
Es ist schädlich, wenn nicht gar gefährlich.	It is injurious, if not even dangerous.
9. Er ist immer fröhlich.	He is always cheerful.
Er wird thun, was ich nur immer verlangen mag.	He will do whatever I may require.
Sie ist noch immer unzufrieden.	She is still (ever) discontented.
Sie werden immer stolzer.	They are getting prouder and prouder.
10. Denn der Tag ist nahe, ja des Herrn Tag ist nah.	For the day is near, even the day of the Lord is near.
Ich habe Sie ja lange nicht gesehen.	(Why!) I have not seen you for a long time.
Ach, guter Hans Bendix, das ist ja recht Schade.	Alas, good Hans Bendix, that is (indeed) really a pity.
Gehen Sie ja nicht.	Do not, by any means, go.
Bleiben Sie ja zu Hause.	Remain, by all means, at home.
11. Haben Sie ihn je gesehen?	Have you ever seen him?
Ich habe dich je und je geliebt.	I have always loved thee.
Sie gingen je zwei und zwei.	They went by two and two (two by two).

Du kannst es thun oder lassen, je nachdem es dir gut dünkt.	You can do it or leave it, according as it seems good to you.
Je länger hier, je später dort.	The longer here, the later there.

Exercise 134.   Aufgabe 134.

1. Wie wird die Feste denn sich nennen, die wir da bauen? 2. Ich wollte gern den Biedermann erretten; doch es ist rein unmöglich, ihr seht selbst. 3. Dem Nächsten muß man helfen; es kann uns Allen Gleiches ja begegnen. 4. So höre denn und acht' auf meine Rede! denn, was dich preßte, sieh, das wußt' ich längst. 5. Sie werden endlich doch von selbst ermüden, wenn sie die Lande ruhig bleiben sehn. 6. Du bist gebunden. — Ja, Unglücklicher, du bist's; doch nicht durch Wort und Schwur. 7. Denn bis an diese letzte Gränze selbst belebter Schöpfung, wo der starre Boden aufhört zu geben, raubt der Vögte Geiz. 8. Dem Kaiser selbst versagten wir Gehorsam, da er das Recht zu Gunst der Pfaffen bog. 9. Obgleich sie erst fünfzehn Jahre alt ist, so kann sie doch schon englisch, französisch und italienisch. 10. Er wird erst morgen kommen können. 11. Nichts waren jetzt alle seine vergangenen Siege, da ihm der einzige entging, der jenen allen erst die Krone aufsetzen sollte.

Exercise 135.   Aufgabe 135.

1. First, came the general, then the colonel. 2. We must wait for them, for we have promised to do it. 3. You are rich, and healthy, why then are you so discontented? 4. He is greater as a statesman than as a soldier. 5. They are very rich but yet they are not contented. 6. He is very poor, and yet he seems to be perfectly contented. 7. The longer we live the shorter time have we still to live, and according as our actions have been good or bad will our future life be happy or miserable. 8. Do not by any means trust those who flatter you. 9. Do let me go with you. 10. We shall not go until this afternoon. 11. If you should come to the city again do not by any means fail to visit us. 12. I must respect him, for he is a good man, but I am angry at him because he punished me.

LESSON LXVI.   Section LXVI.

Nicht, Noch, Nun, Schon, So.

1. Er thut oft, was er nicht soll.	He often does what he should not.
Er thut nicht oft, was er soll.	He does not often do what he should.
Er thut oft nicht, was er soll.	He often does not do what he should.
Ich kann nicht länger warten.	I can wait no (not) longer.
Wie unglücklich ist nicht der Mensch ohne Hoffnung!	How unfortunate is (not) the man without hope!

a. **Nicht** (as also **kein**) sometimes occurs with negative words and is not translated; as,

Habt ihr nichts Eigenes nicht?	Have you (not) nothing of your own?
Und nirgends kein Dank.	And nowhere (no) any gratitude.
Was hindert mich, daß ich es nicht thue?	What hinders me from (not) doing it?
2. Das ist noch besser als das andere.	That is still better than the other.
Ich kann weder lesen noch schreiben.	I can neither read nor write.
Ich kann ja nicht lesen, noch rechnen und schreiben.	(But) I can not read, nor cipher nor write.
Noch Stand, noch Alter ward geschont.	Nor rank nor age was spared.
Werden wir in Deutschland besiegt, so ist es alsdann noch Zeit euren Plan zu befolgen.	If we are conquered in Germany then there will yet be time to follow your plan.

b. Used with negative words, **noch** precedes them; as,

Ich habe ihn noch nicht gesehen.	I have not yet (yet not) seen him
Sind Sie noch nie da gewesen?	Have you never yet been there?

c. **Noch** often marks addition, increase or intensity (L. 52. 3.); as,

Nehmen Sie noch einen Mantel.	Take another cloak.
Er hat noch einmal so viel als ich.	He has twice as much as I have.
Singen Sie es noch einmal.	Sing it again.
Man sei noch so vorsichtig, man fehlet doch.	Let one be never so careful one errs notwithstanding.
3. Von nun an will ich fleißig sein.	From now on I will be diligent.
Nun! was fehlt schon wieder.	Well! what is the matter again already?
Welchen Entschluß nun sie faßten, so hatte er seinen Zweck erreicht.	Whatever resolution they adopted, he had accomplished his purpose.
4. Sie sind schon angekommen.	They have already arrived.
Er wird schon kommen.	He will certainly come (or come in time).
Damit bin ich schon zufrieden.	With that I am perfectly satisfied.
Das kann ich schon ausfinden.	That I can easily find out.
5. Warum sprechen Sie so schnell?	Why do you speak so fast?
Ich spreche nicht so schnell wie Sie.	I do not speak as fast as you do.
Er kommt, sobald er kann.	He is coming as soon as he can.
So ein Buch habe ich nie gesehen.	Such a book I have never seen.
So! ist er schon angekommen?	Indeed! has he already arrived?
Er hat so ganz unrecht nicht.	He is not altogether wrong.
Es geht ihm nur so so (colloquial).	He gets along only so so.

EXAMPLES ON THE USE OF Sonſt AND Und.

So ihr bleiben werdet an meiner Rede, ſo ſeid ihr meine rechten Jünger.	If ye continue in my word, then are ye my disciples indeed. John 8, 31.
Nicht ſo bald war der Plan entworfen, als er ſeinen Marſch antrat.	No sooner was the plan drawn up, than he set out upon his march.
Um ſo beſſer für uns.	So much the better for us.

EXERCISE 136.   Aufgabe 136.

1. Die Erbſtaaten Rudolphs, ſo anſehnlich ſie auch waren, befanden ſich in einer Lage, die den Regenten in die äußerſte Verlegenheit ſetzte. 2. So oft und in ſo drohender Sprache auch die Stände ihre Vorſtellungen erneuerten, er beharrte auf der erſten Erklärung. 3. Wollen Sie mir den Gefallen thun, das Lied noch einmal zu ſingen? 4. Ich habe ihn noch nicht geſehen, denn er iſt noch nie hier geweſen. 5. Er iſt noch einmal ſo alt als ich. 6. Den Verbrecher wird die verdiente Strafe ſchon ereilen. 7. So du Gerechtigkeit vom Himmel hoffeſt, ſo erzeig' ſie uns. 8. Bringen Sie mir noch einen Mantel; einer iſt nicht genug. 9. Bringe mir einen andern Mantel, dieſer iſt zu dünn. 10. Daß ein deutſcher Reichsfürſt ſo etwas von einem ſchwediſchen Edelmann begehrte, wird man nie vergeſſen. 11. Der Neidiſche iſt ſchon zufrieden mit ſeiner Armuth, wenn er nur ſieht, daß ſein Nächſter nicht reich wird.

EXERCISE 137.   Aufgabe 137.

1. Are your brother and your cousin still here? 2. Neither my brother nor my cousin is here, nor have they been here. 3. Have you not yet become acquainted with those officers? 4. Have you then never yet seen a better painting than this? 5. Who has ever heard such a thing? 6. Will you do us the favor to play that piece again? 7. This man is at least twice as old as the other one. 8. I will take another pair of gloves, these are too heavy. 9 The weather is so cold that I will take another cloak, I do not believe one will be enough. 10. He has not much courage, if he submits to such a thing as that.

LESSON LXVII.   Lection LXVII.

Sonſt, Und, Vielleicht, Wie, Wohl.

1. Was ſonſt haſt du gehört, und wen ſonſt geſehen?	What else have you heard, and whom else (have you) seen?
Ich habe ſonſt nichts gehört.	I have heard nothing else.
Hüte dich davor, ſonſt wirſt du ſchwer leiden.	Be on your guard against it, otherwise you will suffer severely.
Ich könnte wohl, wenn ich ſonſt wollte.	I could, perhaps, that is, if I would.
Sonſt war es ganz anders.	Formerly it was entirely otherwise.

2. Und wär's mein eigner Bruder, es kann nicht sein. — Even if it were my own brother, it can not be.

3. Er wird vielleicht noch kommen. — He will perhaps come yet.
Wollen Sie vielleicht mitgehen? — Will you (perhaps) go with us?

4. Wissen Sie vielleicht wie alt er ist? — Do you know how old he is?
Er spricht ganz wie er denkt. — He speaks just as he thinks.
Sie ist eben so fleißig wie er. — She is just as industrious as he.
Wie er gelebt hatte, so starb er. — As he had lived, so he died.

5. Wie is often followed by a subject with a verb understood where the English word corresponding to the subject, stands in the objective after "like"; as,

Er handelt wie ein Wahnsinniger. — He acts (as) like a maniac.
Es glänzt wie Gold. — It glitters like gold (as gold glitters).

Socrates blühte als Jüngling wie eine Rose, lehrte als Mann wie ein Engel, und starb als Greis wie ein Verbrecher. — Socrates bloomed as (a) youth, like a rose, (as a rose blooms), taught when he was a man, like an angel, and died when he was an old man like a criminal (as a criminal dies).

6. Wann wird er wohl kommen? — When will he probably come?
Wohl läßt der Pfeil sich aus dem Herzen ziehen. — The arrow may indeed be drawn out of the heart.
Das kann wohl wahr sein. — That may perhaps be true.
Können Sie mir wohl sagen, wo er wohnt? — Can you (perhaps) tell me where he lives?
Ja wohl! das kann ich. — Yes indeed, that I can.
Was konnte ich wohl sonst sagen? — What else then could I say?

Exercise 138. Aufgabe 138.

1. Dieses ist mein ganzer Reichthum, sonst habe ich gar nichts. 2. Ist nicht sonst Jemand bei Ihrem Herrn Oheim? 3. Sonst erfreute mich so etwas, jetzt aber ist es mir gleichgültig. 4. Haben Sie vielleicht ein Paar (L. 47.) Thaler, die Sie mir auf einige Tage leihen könnten? 5. Wie kann man aufrichtig sein, wenn man nicht spricht wie man denkt? 6. Wie der Anfang so das Ende, oder, wie man es anfängt, so treibt man es. 7. Dort lebt ein Gastfreund mir, der über diese Zeiten denkt wie ich. 8. Und so fliehen unsre Tage, wie die Quelle, rastlos hin! 9. Euch lüstet's wohl, wie Babington zu enden? 10. Es sind wohl hundert Jahre her, da lebte hier ein Mann, der durch geschäftigen Verkehr viel Hab' und Gut gewann.

Exercise 139. Aufgabe 139.

1. Have you anything else to say to me? 2. They were formerly much more contented than now. 3. You must come to me, otherwise I shall not visit you. 4. He who is proud of his birth, generally has nothing else of which he could be proud.

5. He talks like a wise man, but he acts like a fool. 6. When shall we probably see you again? 7. Perhaps we shall be here again next week. 8. His cousin is just as old and just as rich as he. 9. How do you know how old or how rich they are? 10. With you, but with nobody else, he speaks as he thinks.

LESSON LXVIII.   Section LXVIII.

1. The words Herr, Frau and Fräulein, placed before proper names, answer to Mr., Mrs., and Miss. In address, when the name is omitted, Herr and Fräulein, preceded by the possessive pronoun, answer in the singular to Sir, Miss, and in the plural to Gentlemen, Ladies. The form of address to married ladies, when the name is omitted, is, in the singular, Madam'; in the plural, Meine Damen.

2. These words are also placed before designations of relationship (when the reference is not to one's own relatives), and the first two, before titles; as, Ihr Herr Vater, your father; Ihre Frau Mutter, your mother; seine Frau Schwester, his (married) sister; seine Fräulein Schwester, his (unmarried) sister; die Herren Obersten, the colonels; die Frau Präsidentin, the president's wife.

Ich habe heute Herrn N., Frau N. und Fräulein N. gesehen.	I have to day seen Mr. N., Mrs. N. and Miss. N.
Guten Morgen, mein Herr, wie befindet sich Ihr Herr Vater?	Good morning Sir, how is your father?
Ihr Herr Gemahl und Ihre Fräulein Tochter sind bei Ihrem Herrn Oheim.	Your husband and your daughter are at your uncle's.
Guten Abend, mein Fräulein, wie befinden sich Ihre Frau Mutter und Ihre Fräulein Schwestern?	Good evening Miss, how are your mother and your sisters?
Der Herr Gesandte und seine Frau Gemahlin waren gestern Abend im Concerte.	The ambassador and his lady were at the Concert last evening.
Können Sie mir sagen, wo der Herr Secretär L. wohnt?	Can you tell me where Mr Secretary L. resides?
Ich habe Ihre Herren Brüder und Ihre Fräulein Schwestern gesehen.	I have seen your brothers and your sisters.
Guten Abend meine Herren, wie befinden Sie sich?	Good evening Gentlemen, how do you do?
Ist der Herr Professor zu Hause?	Is the professor at home?

DIALOGUES
WITH REFERENCE TO GRAMMATICAL FORMS.

Guten Morgen! Schon so früh auf?	Good morning! Are you up so early?
Wie geht es Ihnen? Wie befinden sie sich?	How are you? How do you do?
Ganz wohl, dem Himmel sei Dank!	Quite well, thank heaven!
Welch' köstliches Wetter!	What delightful weather!
Welch' ein herrlicher Tag.	What a fine day.
Des Morgens ist es etwas kühl.	In the morning it is rather cool.
Ich bin des Mittags immer zu Hause.	At noon I am always at home.
Des Abends geht sie gewöhnlich in Gesellschaft.	In the evening she usually goes to a party.
Er pflegte meinen Vater des Montags zu besuchen.	He used to visit my father on Mondays.
Ist er nach Hause zurückgekehrt?	Is he returned home?
Sie wohnt in unserm Hause.	She lives at our house.
Diese Häuser sollen verkauft werden.	These houses are to be sold.
In allen Häusern wurden Nachsuchungen angestellt.	Researches were made in every house.
Unsere Väter waren mäßiger als wir.	Our fathers were more temperate than we are.
Bitte, reichen Sie mir jenen Teller.	Hand me that plate, if you please.
Diese Teller sind rein.	These plates are clean.
Was hat die Magd mit den andern Tellern gemacht?	What has the maid done with the other plates?
Dies ist schönes Brod.	This is excellent bread.
Lassen Sie einige Brode holen.	Send for some loaves (rolls).
Es liegt auf dem Stuhle.	It is lying on the chair.
Sind die neuen Stühle schon bezahlt?	Are the new chairs paid for?
Jawohl, und die Tische ebenfalls.	Yes: and the tables likewise.
Wann gehen Sie zu Bette?	When do you go to bed?
Gewöhnlich um halb elf.	Usually at half past ten.
Ist das Bett schon gemacht?	Is the bed made?
Hier sind zwei Betten, welches wollen Sie?	Here are two beds, which will you have?
Meine Uhr ist abgelaufen.	My watch is run down.
Die Uhren gehen alle unrichtig.	All the clocks go wrong.
Geben Sie mir die Messer dort.	Give me the knives yonder.
Dieses Messer ist nicht zu gebrauchen.	This knife is useless.
Sie mißtrauen einander.	They distrust each other.
Wir haben es ihnen gesagt.	We told them so.
Sie hat uns gewarnt.	She warned us.

Ist dies Ihre Stube (Ihr Zimmer)?	Is this your room?
Sie (es) ist ziemlich geräumig.	It is pretty spacious.
Gefällt sie (es) Ihnen?	Do you like it?
Wem gehört diese (dieses)?	To whom does this one belong?
Unserer Cousine.	To our cousin.
Er hat sein Pferd verkauft.	He has sold his horse.
Mit dem meinigen bin ich nicht zufrieden.	I am not satisfied with mine.
Der (die, das) seinige wäre besser gewesen.	His would have been better.
Was haben Sie (sie) mit den Ihrigen (ihrigen) gemacht?	What have you (they) done with yours (theirs)?
Wessen Schreibfeder hat sie gebraucht?	Whose pen has she used?
Die meinige: Darum leihen Sie mir die Ihrige.	Mine. So lend me yours.
Die Eurigen (plur.) sind den seinigen vorzuziehen.	Yours are preferable to his.
Wo ist der (die, das) unsrige?	Where is ours?
Weiß sie, welchen Band wir genommen haben?	Does she know which volume we have taken?
Freilich weiß sie es.	To be sure she does.
Ich möchte denjenigen haben, welchen (den) er nicht braucht.	I should like to have the one he does not want.
Sehen Sie, welch' ein schönes Pferd.	Look, what a beautiful horse.
Welches meinen Sie, den Braunen oder den Schimmel?	Which do you mean, the brown one or the grey?
Dasjenige (das), welches gesattelt ist.	The one that is saddled
Derjenige, welcher ehrlich ist (wer ehrlich ist).	He that is honest.
Wer es auch sein möchte.	Whoever it might be.
Auf wen ist die Wahl gefallen?	Who has been chosen?
Auf wessen Befehl wurde er festgenommen?	At whose order was he arrested?
In Hinsicht dessen, was wir vorgebracht haben.	With respect to what we have urged.
Das, was er sagt, ist nicht ohne Grund.	What he says, is not without reason.
Dem, was er behauptete, setzte man Vieles entgegen.	To what he affirmed, much was opposed.
Kennen Sie jenen Mann dort?	Do you know that man yonder?
Diesem bin ich oft begegnet.	I have often met this one.
Jene Frau ist die Schwester meines Hauswirthes.	That woman is my landlord's sister.
Er hat deren zwei.	He has two (of them).
Jener Knabe ist sehr fleißig.	That boy is very diligent.
Auf jener Seite	On that side (page, hand).
Geben Sie mir diejenige, mit welcher Sie fertig sind.	Give me the one you have done with (have finished).

8

Hat er denjenigen (den) gekauft, welchen ich aussuchte?	Has he bought the one I chose?
Diejenige, welche man für die Klügste hält.	She who is thought to be the cleverest.
Mit benjenigen (denen) will ich nichts zu schaffen haben.	I will have nothing to do with those.
Das kann Ihnen Jedermann sagen.	Any one can tell you that.
Ich stehe zu jeder Zeit zu Ihren Diensten.	I am always at your service.
Jedes Mal, wenn er kommt.	Every time he comes.
Wie viele Male ist seine Erwartung getäuscht worden?	How many times has he been disappointed?
Eine andere Zeit wäre mir gelegener gewesen.	Some other time would have suited me better.
Schicken Sie mir die anderen Bücher.	Send me the other books.
Was will er mit den andern machen?	What will he do with the others?
Jeder Andere würde ihm geholfen haben.	Any other person would have aided him.
Das andere Pferd ist verkauft worden.	The other horse has been sold.
Seine anderen Freunde sind derselben Meinung.	His other friends are of the same opinion.
Es sind dieselben Leute.	They are the same people.
Ich bin demselben Manne begegnet.	I met the same man.
Es ist dasselbe.	It is the same thing.
Die Versammlung findet in demselben Saale statt.	The meeting takes place in the very same hall.
Er ging durch dieselbe Thür.	He went through the same door.
Er ist der Bruder dessen, der nach Amerika ging.	He is the brother of him that went to America.
Das Eigenthum Derer, die ihre Abgaben bezahlt hatten, wurde geschont.	The property of those who had paid their taxes, was spared.
Dergleichen Fälle gibt es viele.	There are many such instances.
Ein Ereigniß der Art kommt nur selten vor.	Such an event occurs but rarely.
Es gibt nur Einen Fall.	There is but one instance (case).
Vieles von dem, was er sagte.	Much of what he said.
Wie viel bin ich Ihnen schuldig?	How much do I owe you?
Man fragte nach der Meinung vieler Leute.	The opinions of many persons were consulted.
Mit wie vielen Pferden reis'te er ab?	With how many horses did he set out?
Seine vielen Rathgeber konnten sein Verderben nicht abwenden.	His numerous advisers could not avert his ruin.
Wie viele Male sagten Sie?	How many times did you say?
Manchmal.	Many a time.
Mancher hat sich getäuscht gesehen.	Many a one has been disappointed

Manche Blume blüht ungesehen.	Many a flower blooms unseen.
Man spricht von Frieden.	Peace is spoken of.
Man hat seitdem nichts von ihm gehört.	He has not been heard of since.
Man kann nicht zwei Herren dienen.	One cannot serve two masters.
Man weiß nicht, wem man trauen soll.	One does not know whom to trust.
Wenn man spricht, so lachen sie.	When one speaks, they laugh.
Was will man mehr?	What more can one expect?
Er hat etwas (einiges) Geld geerbt.	He has inherited some money.
Gestern berieth sie sich mit einigen Freunden.	Yesterday she consulted some friends.
Es war vor einiger Zeit.	It was some time ago.
Hätte ich nur einige Hoffnung ihn wiederzusehen.	Had I but some hopes of seeing him again.
Mit einigem Fleiß und einiger Beharrlichkeit wird es ihm gelingen.	With a little diligence and perseverance he will succeed.
Sie sagten irgend etwas.	They said something or other.
Versprich nie etwas, was du nicht erfüllen kannst.	Never promise what you are unable to perform.
Sie gab dem Bettler etwas Brod.	She gave the beggar some bread
Das wollte ich wohl, wenn ich etwas hätte.	I would, if I had any.
War irgend Jemand da?	Was any one there?
Beide Häuser wurden niedergebrannt.	Both houses were burnt down.
Wir Beide sind von einem Alter.	Both of use are of the same age.
Jene Beiden sind diesen Beiden vorzuziehen.	Those two are preferable to these two.
Seine beiden Brüder sind auf der Universität.	His two brothers are at the university.
Welcher von Beiden ist der verständigste?	Which of the two is the most sensible?
Eine von meinen beiden Schwestern wird uns rufen lassen.	One of my two sisters will have us called.
Was er auch sagen mochte, war umsonst.	Whatsoever he said, was in vain.
Welches Buch Sie auch meinen.	Whichever book you mean.
Ich bin mit Allem zufrieden.	I am satisfied with every thing.
Alle seine Aussichten sind vernichtet.	All his prospects are destroyed
Allen seinen Bestrebungen zum Trotze.	In spite of all his endeavors.
Aller Augen waren auf ihn gerichtet.	The eyes of all present were directed to him.
Er hat Alles, was er braucht.	He has all he needs.
Ich sehe ihn alle Tage.	I see him every day.
Sie möchte alle Woche, ja, alle Abende ins Schauspiel gehen.	She would like to go to the play every week, nay, every evening.
Wir alle wollen auf das Land gehen.	We are all of us going into the country

Man muß vor allen Dingen ein reines Gewissen zu bewahren suchen.	We must endeavor above all things to keep a clear conscience.
Mehrere Schiffe sind angekommen.	Several ships have arrived.
Gestern brachte ich den Abend mit mehreren Freunden zu.	Yesterday I passed the evening with several friends.
Niemand weiß was daraus geworden ist.	No one knows what became of it.
Es war Niemand gegenwärtig.	No one was present.
Hat keiner von den Männern den Muth gehabt, ihn zu ergreifen?	Had none of the men courage enough to seize him?
Es war gar keine Hoffnung dazu vorhanden.	There were no hopes at all of it.
Haben Sie Geld bei sich? Denn ich habe keins.	Have you any money about you? For I have none.
Er will Keinen (Niemand) gesprochen haben.	He says he has spoken with no one.
Sie gehen mit Niemand (Keinem) als mit ihren Verwandten um.	They associate with none but their relations.
Es gibt keinerlei Waaren, die dort nicht zu haben wären.	There are no goods of any kind, which are not to be had there.
Er hat Vielerlei mitgebracht.	He has brought a variety of things with him.
Ich habe mancherlei anzuschaffen.	I must procure several different articles.
Das ist mir einerlei, sage ich Ihnen.	That is all the same to me, I tell you.
Das ist ja zu wenig.	Why, that is too little.
Es ist nicht weniger als man gewöhnlich bezahlt.	It is not less than is usually paid.
Man muß sich mit Wenigem begnügen.	We ought to be content with a little.
Wenige Leute werden ihm Glauben schenken.	Few persons will credit him.
Wie wenig ließ ich mir von einem solchen Glücke träumen.	How little did I dream of such a happiness.
Sie kommt immer dann, wenn man sie am wenigsten erwartet.	She always comes when she is least expected.
Sein Nachbar ist wohlhabend; ich glaube es wenigstens.	His neighbor is opulent; at least I believe so.
Sie waren es, der mich darauf aufmerksam machte.	It was you that pointed it out to me.
Sie waren es, die uns zu hintergehen suchten.	It was they who strove to deceive us.
Es ist sehr zu hoffen, daß er sich nicht irrt.	It is much to be hoped that he is not mistaken.
Es stehen einige Bäume am Wege.	There are some trees standing by the road-side.
Es wurde viel getanzt.	There was much dancing.

Es gibt mehrere Arten.	There are several kinds.
Es finden sich nur wenige Leute dazu geneigt.	But few people are inclined to it.
Es ragt ein Thurm aus dem Walde empor.	A tower rises from the forest.
Er sagte es, aber ich glaube es kaum.	He said so, but I hardly believe it.
Ich will es, aber sie wollen es nicht.	I will, but they will not.
In so fern als es uns betrifft.	As far as regards us.
Es gibt nur einen Fall.	There is but one instance.
Was gibt es?	What's the matter?
Es waren viele Schiffe in den Hafen eingelaufen.	Many vessels had entered the harbor.
Sind Sie es?	Is it you?
Ich bin es.	It is I.
Zu bedauern war es, daß es so wenig zu thun gab.	It was to be regretted that there was so little to do.
Es fanden sich Viele zu rechter Zeit ein.	Many persons arrived in time.
Wie viel haben Sie dafür gegeben?	Ho much did you give for it?
Sie wurde unwillig darüber.	She grew angry about it.
Was hat Ihr Compagnon dabei gewonnen?	What has your partner gained in it?
Dadurch hoffe ich meinen Gegner zu besänftigen.	By this means I hope to pacify my opponent.
Ich habe nicht daran gedacht.	I did not think of it.
Dazu kommt noch, daß sie sein Mißfallen erregte.	Besides that, she excited his displeasure.
Davor behüte uns der Himmel!	Heaven defend us from it!
Als wir so sprachen, kam er dazu.	While we were talking, he joined us.
Es gab einige gute darunter.	There were some good ones amongst them.
Was verstehen Sie darunter?	What do you understand by it?
Sie wissen kaum, was sie damit machen sollen.	They hardly know what to do with it (them).
Damit zog er den Hut und ging fort.	With that he raised his hat and went away.
Sie that es selbst.	She did it herself.
Nehmen Sie sich in Acht, sonst werden Sie sich Schaden thun.	Take care or you will hurt yourself.
Sie irren sich sehr, wenn Sie glauben, daß ich mich vor ihnen fürchte.	They are much mistaken if they think I fear them.
Der Vogel befreite sich von der Schlinge.	The bird freed itself from the springe.
Sie haben sich von seiner Rechtschaffenheit überzeugt.	They have satisfied themselves of his probity.
Sein Bruder hat sich anwerben lassen.	His brother has enlisted.

Wenn ich mich nicht irre, so habe ich ihn irgendwo getroffen.	If I am not mistaken, I have met with him somewhere.
Sie hat sich verheirathet.	She has got married.
Wir haben uns entschlossen, seine Bedingungen anzunehmen.	We have determined to accept his terms.
Hast Du Dir die Sache überlegt?	Have you reflected on the matter?
Ich will mir ein paar Stiefel bestellen.	I intend to order myself a pair of boots.
Man täuscht sich sehr leicht.	We easily deceive ourselves.
Man kann sich von seiner Bestürzung keine Vorstellung machen.	His consternation is not to be imagined.
Ihr habt Euch vom Scheine täuschen lassen.	You have suffered yourselves to be deceived by appearances.
Der Bruder und die Schwester lieben einander zärtlich.	The brother and sister are very fond of each other.
Sie kamen einander zu Hülfe.	They came to each other's assistance.
Sie wagen es nicht, einander zu trauen.	They dare not trust one another.
Ist Jemand da?	Is any one there?
Ich sehe Niemand.	I see nobody.
Heute morgen ist Jemand vorgekommen.	Some one has called this morning.
Jedermann ist davon überzeugt.	Every body is convinced of it.
Das hätte Jedermann vorhersehen können.	Any one might have foreseen that.
Ein guter Name ist besser als Reichthümer.	A good name is better than riches.
Er erfreut sich eines großen Vermögens.	He enjoys a large fortune.
Du wohnst in einem angenehmen Stadttheile.	You live in a pleasant part of the town.
Sie hat sich einen grünen Schleier gekauft.	She has bought a green veil.
Ein artiges Kind macht seinen Eltern Freude.	A good child gladdens the heart of its parents.
Der Inhalt des ersten Bandes mißfällt mir.	I don't like the contents of the first volume.
Mit der ersten Gelegenheit.	With the first opportunity.
Er hat seinen treuen Hund verloren.	He has lost his faithful dog.
Die arme Waise ist sehr zu bemitleiden.	The poor orphan is greatly to be pitied.
Sie hat im vorigen Jahre geschrieben.	She wrote last year.
Er saß am Ofen und las.	He sat reading near the stove.
Sie reis'ten am vergangenen Freitag ab.	They set out on Friday last.
Ich lag schon zu Bette (im Bette).	I already lay in bed.
Es wäre am Besten wir gingen hin.	We had better go there.

Der Schütze stand dicht am Baume.	The marksman stood close to the tree.
Ist er im Hause?	Is he in the house?
Sie traten in das Haus.	They entered the house.
Er hat uns gestern zum letzten Male besucht.	Yesterday he visited us for the last time.
Zum großen Leidwesen seiner Mutter.	To the great regret of his mother.
Der Knabe geht früh zur Schule (in die Schule).	The boy goes early to school.
Unterm Monde ist nichts beständig.	There's nothing constant under the moon.
Morgen will sie zur (in die) Kirche gehen.	To-morrow she will go to church.
Die Soldaten standen unterm Gewehre.	The soldiers were under arms.
Ihr seid fast nie zu Hause.	You are scarcely ever at home.
Laßt uns nach Hause gehen.	Let us go home.
Mein Bruder steht beim ersten Regiment.	My brother is in the first regiment.
Wer würde so handeln, der nur irgend Ehrgefühl hat.	Who that has any feeling of honor would act thus?
Hat er Ihretwegen den Verweis bekommen?	Did he receive the rebuke on your account?
Nein, unsertwegen.	No, on our account.
Ihretwegen mag ich seinen Unwillen nicht erregen.	I am not going to incur his displeasure on their account.
Sie thaten es meinetwegen (um meinetwillen).	They did it for my sake.
Ich bin bereit ihretwillen Alles zu erdulden.	For her sake I am ready to suffer any thing.
Meinetwegen mögen sie es versuchen.	They may try it for all I care.
Ich bin Ihnen sehr verbunden.	I am much obliged to you.
Sage mir wo Du bist.	Tell me where you are.
Er ist mein bester Freund.	He is my best friend.
Sie ist bei ihren Verwandten.	She is with her relations.
Wir sind ganz anderer Ansicht.	We are of quite a different opinion.
Gut; Ihr seid also entschlossen?	Well, you are determined then?
Wo sind sie zu finden?	Where are they to be found?
Ich war zu Hause.	I was at home.
Du warst zu voreilig.	Thou wert too hasty.
Wer weiß, wo er war.	Who knows where he was.
Wir waren darüber ganz erfreut.	We were overjoyed at it.
Ihr waret auch eingeladen.	You were invited too.
Sie waren mit ihrem Loose unzufrieden.	They were dissatisfied with their lot.
Ich werde früh auf sein.	I shall be up early.
Du wirst sie gewiß auf ihres Onkels Stube finden.	Thou wilt certainly find her in her uncle's room.

Man weiß nicht, wann er hier sein wird.	It is not known when he will be here.
Wir werden erfreut sein, Sie zu sehen.	We shall be glad to see you.
Ihr werdet abwesend sein, wenn wir kommen.	You will be absent when we come.
Sie werden schon davon benachrichtigt sein.	They will be already informed of it.
Ich bin lange krank gewesen.	I have been long ill.
Du bist in Frankreich gewesen, wie ich höre.	Thou hast been in France, I am told.
Er ist eine Zeit lang damit beschäftigt gewesen.	He has been occupied with it for some time.
Wir sind auf dem Lande gewesen.	We have been in the country.
Ich hoffe, daß Ihr recht fleißig gewesen seid.	I hope you have been very diligent.
Sind sie nicht bei ihrem Vetter zum Besuch gewesen?	Have they not been visiting their cousin?
Ich war nur einige Tage dort gewesen.	I had been there but for a few days.
Wir waren auf Reisen gewesen, als wir die Nachricht erhielten.	We had been travelling, when we received the intelligence.
Wenn Sie wieder da sind, werde ich bei Ihrem Bruder gewesen sein.	By the time you return I shall have been at your brother's.
Seien Sie so gütig, mir zu sagen, an wen ich mich zu wenden habe.	Be so kind as to tell me whom to apply to.
Nun gut, er sei zur rechten Zeit hier.	Well then let him be here in the right time.
Sei doch nicht so unaufmerksam.	Don't be so inattentive.
Sie sagten, er sei krank.	They said he was ill.
Wenn ich wüßte, daß er noch nicht wieder genesen wäre.	If I knew he was not yet recovered.
Man vermuthet, daß er in acht Tagen hier sein werde.	It is supposed he will be here in a week's time.
Glaubt man, daß er oft dort gewesen sei?	Is he thought to have been there often?
Sie sagte mir geradezu, daß ich zu offenherzig gewesen wäre.	She told me plainly that I had been too candid.
Ich würde damit zufrieden sein.	I should be satisfied with it.
Würde ein Anderer so unbillig gewesen sein?	Would any one else have been so unreasonable?
Sie wäre zu glücklich gewesen.	She would have been too happy.
Er hat an sie geschrieben.	He has written to them.
Wir hatten sehr viele Mühe mit ihm.	We had a great deal of trouble with him.
Ich werde hoffentlich viel Vergnügen haben.	I shall have much pleasure, I hope.
Er wird schwere Pflichten haben.	He will have severe duties.
Wir werden wenig zu thun haben.	We shall have little to do

Fragen Sie, ob sie morgen Gesellschaft haben werden.	Enquire whether they will have company to-morrow.
Sie hat noch keinen Thee gehabt.	She has not had any tea yet.
Da sie keine Lust gehabt hatten, ins Schauspiel zu gehen.	As they had not had a mind to go to the play.
Jetzt wird er seinen Willen gehabt haben.	By this time he will have had his will.
Man behauptete (es wurde behauptet), daß ich ihn zum Nachfolger haben würde.	It was asserted, that I should have him for a successor.
Sie würden ihn gern zum Lehrer gehabt haben (sie hätten ihn gern zum Lehrer gehabt).	They would gladly have had him as a teacher.
Wir glaubten, er habe an seinen Wohlthäter geschrieben.	We thought he had written to his benefactor.
Jedermann meint, er habe Unrecht gehabt.	Every one thinks he was in the wrong.
Wären wir nicht gewesen, so hätten sie einen bösen Unfall gehabt.	But for us they would have met with a sad accident.
Ich hätte ihn gewarnt (ich würde ihn gewarnt haben), wäre es nöthig gewesen.	I would have warned him, had it been necessary.
Hätten sie sich doch nur Zeit genommen.	Had they but taken time.
Das Schiff wird morgen ankommen.	The ship will arrive to-morrow.
Die Ueberfahrt wird eine stürmische sein (or werden).	The passage will be a rough one.
Seine Schuldner wollen ihn nicht befriedigen.	His debtors will not satisfy him.
Man sagt, daß sie sich verheirathen wird.	They say, she is going to be married.
Der Verbrecher wollte nicht gestehen.	The criminal would not confess.
Ich werde mich bemühen, Ihr Vertrauen zu verdienen.	I shall endeavor to merit your confidence.
In acht Tagen werden wir die Güter empfangen.	We shall receive the goods in a week's time.
Das Haus wird jetzt gebaut.	The house is now building.
Die Flotte wurde damals ausgerüstet.	The fleet was fitting out at that time.
Die Landstraßen werden bald ausgebessert werden (sein).	The roads are soon to be repaired (will soon be).
Ist mein Brief richtig abgegeben worden?	Has my letter been properly delivered?
Noch niemals war Jemand so hintergangen worden.	Never had any one been so taken in.
Die Zeugen sollen aufgefordert worden sein, vor Gericht zu erscheinen.	The witnesses are said to have been summoned to appear before the court.

8*

8. ALPHABETICAL LIST OF IRREGULAR VERBS

Note that in the following list many *compound* forms are not set in its *simple* form.

INFINITIVE.	PRESENT INDICATIVE.	IMP. INDIC.
Backen a) to bake,	ich backe, du bäckst, er bäckt,	ich buk
Bedingen b), to bargain,	ich bedinge, ꝛc.	ich bedung
Bedürfen, to need,	ich bedarf, wir bedürfen, ꝛc.	ich bedurfte
Befehlen, to command,	ich befehle, du befiehlst, er befiehlt,	ich befahl
Befleißen (sich) c), to attend to,	ich befleiße, ꝛc.	ich befliß
Beginnen d), to begin,	ich beginne, ꝛc.	ich begann
Beißen, to bite,	ich beiße, du beißest, er beißt,	ich biß
Beklemmen e), to grieve,	ich beklemme, ꝛc.	ich beklemmte
Bergen, to conceal,	ich berge, du birgst, er birgt,	ich barg
Bersten, to burst,	ich berste, ꝛc.	ich borst or barst
Besinnen (sich), to think of,	ich besinne, ꝛc.	ich besann
Besitzen, to possess,	ich besitze, ꝛc.	ich besaß
Betrügen, to deceive,	ich betrüge, ꝛc.	ich betrog
Bewegen f), to induce, move,	ich bewege, ꝛc.	ich bewog
Biegen, to bend,	ich biege, ꝛc.	ich bog
Bieten g), to offer, to bid,	ich biete, ꝛc.	ich bot
Binden, to bind,	ich binde, ꝛc.	ich band
Bitten, to entreat, to beg,	ich bitte, ꝛc.	ich bat
Blasen, to blow,	ich blase, du bläsest, er bläst,	ich blies
Bleiben, to remain,	ich bleibe, ꝛc.	ich blieb
Bleichen h), to fade,	ich bleiche, ꝛc.	ich blich
Braten, to roast,	ich brate, du bratest or brätst, er bratet or brät.	ich briet
Brechen, to break,	ich breche, du brichst, er bricht,	ich brach
Brennen i), to burn,	ich brenne, ꝛc.	ich brannte
Bringen, to bring,	ich bringe, ꝛc.	ich brachte
Denken, to think,	ich denke, ꝛc.	ich dachte
Dingen k), to bargain,	ich dinge, ꝛc.	ich dung
Dreschen, to thresh,	ich dresche, du drischest, er drischt,	ich drasch or drosch
Dringen l), to press, to urge,	ich bringe, ꝛc.	ich drang
Dürfen, to be able,	ich darf, du darfst; wir dürfen, ꝛc.	ich durfte
Empfangen, to receive,	ich empfange, du empfängst, ꝛc.	ich empfing
Empfehlen, to recommend,	ich empfehle, du empfiehlst, ꝛc.	ich empfahl
Empfinden, to feel,	ich empfinde, ꝛc.	ich empfand
Entrinnen, to escape,	ich entrinne, ꝛc.	ich entrann
Entschlafen, to fall asleep.	ich entschlafe, ꝛc.	ich entschlief
Entsprechen, to answer,	ich entspreche, ꝛc.	ich entsprach
Erbleichen m), to turn pale,	ich erbleiche, ꝛc.	ich erblich
Erfrieren, to freeze,	ich erfriere, ꝛc.	ich erfror
Ergreifen, to seize, to catch,	ich ergreife, ꝛc.	ich ergriff
Erkiesen n), to select,	ich erkiese, ꝛc.	ich erkieste
Erkühren o), to choose,	ich erkühre (erküre), ꝛc.	ich erkohr, (erkor)
Erlöschen p), to extinguish,		
Ersaufen, to be drowned,	ich ersaufe, du ersäufest, er ersäuft	ich ersoff
Erschallen, to resound,	ich erschalle, ꝛc.	ich erscholl
Erscheinen, to appear,	ich erscheine, ꝛc.	ich erschien
Erschrecken q), to be frightened.	ich erschrecke, du erschrickst, ꝛc.	ich erschrak
Ertrinken, to be drowned,	ich ertrinke, ꝛc.	ich ertrank

OR VERBS OF THE OLD CONJUGATION.

down. In such case, the student has only to look for the verb

IMP. SUBJ.	IMPERATIVE.	PARTICIPLE.	REMARKS.
ich büke	backe	gebacken.	a) Regular when active; as, er backte Brod; das Brod buk.
ich bedünge	bedinge	bedungen.	b) Regular when it means, to add a condition, to modify. Bedingt, conditional, is regular.
ich bedürfte		bedurft.	
ich beföhle	befiehl	befohlen.	
ich befliffe	befleiß	befliffen.	
ich begänne	beginne	begonnen.	c) Befleißigen (sich), to apply one's self, is regular.
ich biffe	beiß or beiße	gebiffen.	
ich beklemmete	beklemme	beklommen.	d) In the Imperf. subj. begönne is also used.
ich börge	birg	geborgen.	
ich bärste	berste or birst	geborsten.	e) Beklemmt is not frequently used, and is employed, only in the sense of compressed.
ich besänne	besinne	besonnen.	
ich besäße	besitze	besessen.	
ich betröge	betrüge	betrogen.	
ich bewöge	bewege	bewogen.	f) Irregular when it means, to induce; regular when it means, to move a *body* or affect the *sensibilities*.
ich böge	biege	gebogen.	
ich böte	biete	geboten.	
ich bände	binde	gebunden.	
ich bäte	bitte	gebeten.	
ich bliefe	blafe	geblafen.	g) Beutst and beut, in the present, are poetical.
ich bliebe	bleibe or bleib	geblieben.	
ich bliche	bleiche	geblichen.	
ich briete	brate	gebraten.	h) Bleichen, to bleach in the sun, active, is regular.
ich bräche	brich	gebrochen.	
ich brennete	brenne	gebrannt.	i) Often regular when active: Ich brennte Holz, weil es beffer braunte als Torf.
ich brächte	bringe	gebracht.	
ich dächte	denke	gedacht.	
ich dünge	dinge	gedungen.	
ich bräsche or dröfche	drisch	gebroschen.	k) Dingte is sometimes used in the imperfect, in the sense of to hire.
ich dränge	bringe	gedrungen.	
ich dürfte	—	gedurft.	l) For brang, brung was formerly in use.
ich empfänge	empfange	empfangen.	
ich empföhle	empfiehl	empfohlen.	
ich empfände	empfinde	empfunden.	
ich entränne	entrinne	entronnen.	
ich entschliefe	entschlafe, entschlaf	entschlafen.	
ich entspräche	entsprich	entsprochen.	
ich erbliche	erbleiche	erblichen.	m) From bleichen, to whiten, as in the sun, which is regular.
ich erfröre	erfriere	erfroren.	
ich ergriffe	ergreife or ergreif	ergriffen.	n) Used mostly in poetry.
ich erkiefete	erkiefe	erkofen.	o) This verb is seldom used.
ich erkühre (erküre)	erkühre, (erküre)	erkohren (erkoren).	p) Like verlöschen and auslöschen, irregular only when intransitive. Löschen is always transitive and regular.
ich erföffe	erfaufe	erfoffen.	
ich erschölle	erschalle	erschollen.	
ich erschiene	erscheine	erschienen.	
ich erschräke	erschrick	erschrocken.	q) Irregular as intransitive, but regular when transitive.
ich ertränke	ertrinke	ertrunken.	

INFINITIVE.	PRESENT INDICATIVE.	IMP. INDIC.
Erwägen r), to consider,	ich erwäge, ꝛc.	ich erwog
Essen, to eat,	ich esse, du issest, er isset or ißt.	ich aß
Fahen s) (obsolete,) to catch,	ich fahe, du fahest, er fahet.	—
Fahren t), to drive a carriage,	ich fahre, du fährst, er fährt	ich fuhr
Fallen, to fall,	ich falle, du fällst, er fällt	ich fiel
Falten, u), to fold,	ich falte ꝛc.	ich faltete
Fangen, v), to catch,	ich fange, du fängst, er fängt	ich fing
Fechten, to fight,	ich fechte, du fichtst, er ficht	ich focht
Finden, to find,	ich finde, ꝛc.	ich fand
Flechten, to twist,	ich flechte, du flichtst, er flicht	ich flocht
Fliegen w), to fly,	ich fliege, du fliegst, er fliegt	ich flog
Fliehen x), to flee,	ich fliehe, ꝛc.	ich floh
Fließen y), to flow,	ich fließe, ꝛc.	ich floß
Fragen, to ask,	ich frage, du frägst, er frägt	ich frug
Fressen, to devour,	ich fresse, du frissest or frißt	ich fraß
Frieren, to freeze,	ich friere, ꝛc.	ich fror
Gähren z), to ferment,	ich gähre, ꝛc.	ich gohr
Gebären, to bring forth,	ich gebäre, du gebärst (gebierst) er gebärt (gebiert)	ich gebar
Geben a), to give,	ich gebe, du gibst, er gibt	ich gab
Gebieten b), to command,	ich gebiete, ꝛc.	ich gebot,
Gedeihen c), to prosper,	ich gedeihe, ꝛc.	ich gedieh
Gefallen, to please,	ich gefalle, du gefällst, er gefällt	ich gefiel
Gehen d), to go,	ich gehe, ꝛc.	ich ging
Gelingen, to succeed,	es gelingt	es gelang
Gelten e), to be worth, valid,	ich gelte, du giltst, er gilt	ich galt
Genesen, to recover,	ich genese, ꝛc.	ich genaß
Genießen f), to enjoy,	ich genieße, ꝛc.	ich genoß
Gerathen, to hit upon,	ich gerathe, du geräthst, er geräth	ich gerieth
Geschehen, to happen,	es geschieht	es geschah, geschahe
Gewinnen, to gain, to win,	ich gewinne, ꝛc.	ich gewann
Gießen g), to pour,	ich gieße, ꝛc.	ich goß
Gleichen h), to resemble,	ich gleiche, ꝛc.	ich glich
Gleiten i), to glide,	ich gleite, ꝛc.	ich glitt
Glimmen k), to shine,	ich glimme, ꝛc.	ich glomm
Graben, to dig,	ich grabe, du gräbst, er gräbt	ich grub
Greifen, to seize,	ich greife, ꝛc.	ich griff
Haben l), to have,	ich habe, du hast, er hat	ich hatte
Halten, to hold,	ich halte, du hältst, er hält	ich hielt
Hangen m), to hang,	ich hange, du hängst, er hängt	ich hing

IMP. SUBJ.	IMPERATIVE.	PARTICIPLE.	REMARKS.
ich erwöge	erwäge	erwogen.	r) Oftener used regularly.
ich äße	iß	gegessen.	
—	fahe	gefahen.	s) Poetical rarely used: and in the imperfect not at all.
ich führe	fahre	gefahren.	t) Compounds of fahren are irregular, except willfahren.
ich fiele	falle	gefallen.	
ich faltete	falte	gefalten.	u) Irreg. only in participle, for which gefaltet is often used.
ich finge	fange	gefangen.	v) The forms fieng and fienge are obsolete. So also empfieng and empfienge.
ich föchte	ficht	gefochten.	
ich fände	finde	gefunden.	
ich flöchte	flicht	geflochten.	
ich flöge	fliege	geflogen.	w) Fleugst and fleugt present and fleug in the imperative are used only in poetry.
ich flöhe	fliehe or flieh	geflohen.	x) Fleuchst, fleucht and fleuch, poetical.
ich flösse	fließe	geflossen.	y) Fleußest, fleußt and fleuß, poetical.
ich früge	frage	gefragt.	
ich fräße	friß	gefressen.	
ich fröre	friere	gefroren.	
ich göhre	gähre	gegohren.	z) Sometimes regular, gährte.
ich gebäre (gebö͏̈re)	gebäre (gebier)	geboren.	
ich gäbe	gib	gegeben.	a) Some writers prefer giebst, giebt, gieb to gibst, gibt, gib.
ich geböte,	gebiete	geboten.	b) Gebeutst, gebeut, poetical.
ich gediehe	gedeih	gediehen.	c) Gebiegen is but a strengthened adj. form of past part.
ich gefiele	gefalle	gefallen.	
ich ginge	gehe or geh	gegangen.	d) Gieng for ging is antiquated.
es gelänge	gelinge	gelungen.	
ich gälte	gilt	gegolten.	e) Formerly golt, gölte, were used in imp. indic. and subj.
ich genäse	genese	genesen.	
ich genösse	genieße	genossen.	f) Genenßest, geneußt, and imperative geneuß, poetical, seldom used.
ich geriethe	gerathe	gerathen.	
es geschähe	geschehe	geschehen.	
ich gewänne (gewönne)	gewinne	gewonnen.	
ich gösse	gieße	gegossen.	g) Geußest, geußt, and imperative geuß. See genießen;
ich gliche	gleiche	geglichen.	h) Regular as active, to compare,&c. Vergleichen, though active, is irregular.
ich glitte	gleite	geglitten.	i) Geleiten and begleiten are not derived from gleiten, but from leiten, hence regular.
ich glömme	glimme	geglommen.	k) Now more frequently regular.
ich grübe	grabe	gegraben.	
ich griffe	greife	gegriffen.	
ich hätte	habe	gehabt.	l) Handhaben is regular.
ich hielte	halte	gehalten.	
ich hinge	hange	gehangen.	m) Hieng, hienge are old forms. This verb must not be mistaken for hängen, to suspend which is active and regular

INFINITIVE.	PRESENT INDICATIVE.	IMP. INDIC.
Hauen n), to hew,	ich haue, ɛc.	ich hieb
Heben, to heave,	ich hebe, ɛc.	ich hob or hub
Heißen, to be named,	ich heiße, du heißest, er heißt	ich hieß
Helfen, to help,	ich helfe, du hilfst, er hilft	ich half
Keifen o), to chide,	ich keife, ɛc.	ich kiff
Kennen, to know,	ich kenne, ɛc.	ich kannte
Klieben, to cleave,	ich kliebe, ɛc.	ich klob
Klimmen p), to climb,	ich klimme, ɛc.	ich klomm
Klingen, to sound,	ich klinge, ɛc.	ich klang
Kneifen, or Kneipen q), to pinch,	ich kneife, or kneipe, ɛc.	ich kniff or knipp
Kommen, to come,	ich komme, du kommst, er kommt, or du kömmst, er kömmt	ich kam
Können, to be able,	ich kann, du kannst, er kann	ich konnte
Kriechen r), to creep,	ich krieche, ɛc.	ich kroch
Kühren s), to choose,	ich kühre, ɛc.	ich kohr
Laden, to load,	ich lade, du ladest or ladst, er ladet or ladt	ich lud
Lassen t), to let,	ich lasse, du lässest, er lässet (lässt)	ich ließ
Laufen, to run,	ich laufe, du läufst, er läuft	ich lief
Leiden u), to suffer,	ich leide, ɛc.	ich litt
Leihen, to lend,	ich leihe, ɛc.	ich lieh
Lesen, to read,	ich lese, du liesest, er lieset (liest)	ich las
Liegen, to lie down,	ich liege, ɛc.	ich lag
Lügen, to lie,	ich lüge, ɛc.	ich log
Mahlen v), to grind,	ich mahle, du mahlest (mählst), er mahlt (mählt)	ich mahlte (muhl)
Meiden, to avoid,	ich meide, ɛc.	ich mied
Melken w), to milk,	ich melke, du melkst or milkst, er melkt or milkt.	ich molk
Messen, to measure,	ich messe, du missest, er misset or misst	ich maß
Mißfallen, to displease,	ich mißfalle, du mißfällst, er mißfällt.	ich mißfiel
Mißlingen, to go amiss,	es mißlingt.	es mißlang
Mögen, to be able,	ich mag, du magst, ɛc. wir mögen, ɛc.	ich mochte
Müssen, to be obliged,	ich muß, du mußt, er muß, wir müssen, ihr müsset, or mußt, ɛc.	ich mußte
Nehmen, to take,	ich nehme, du nimmst, er nimmt	ich nahm
Nennen, to name,	ich nenne, ɛc.	ich nannte
Pfeifen, to whistle,	ich pfeife, ɛc.	ich pfiff
Pflegen z), to cherish,	ich pflege, ɛc.	ich pflog
Preisen, to praise,	ich preise, ɛc.	ich pries
Quellen y), to gush,	ich quelle, du quillst, er quillt	ich quoll
Rächen z), to avenge,	ich räche, ɛc.	ich rächte (roch)
Rathen to advise,	ich rathe, du räthst, er räth	ich rieth
Reiben, to rub,	ich reibe ɛc.	ich rieb
Reißen, to tear,	ich reiße, ɛc.	ich riß
Reiten a), to ride	ich reite, ɛc.	ich ritt

IMP. SUBJ.	IMPERATIVE.	PARTICIPLE.	REMARKS.
ich hiebe	haue or hau	gehauen.	n) Haute (regular) is used when *cutting wood, carving stone, &c.* are meant.
ich höbe	hebe	gehoben.	
ich hieße	heiße or heiß	geheißen.	
ich hülfe or hälfe	hilf	geholfen.	
ich kiffe	keife or keif	gekiffen.	o) This verb is sometimes used as a regular verb.
ich kennete	kenne	gekannt.	
ich klöbe	kliebe	gekloben.	
ich klömme	klimme	geklommen.	p) Sometimes regular, klimmte.
ich klänge	klinge	geklungen.	
ich kniffe or knippe	kneife or kneipe	gekniffen or geknippen.	q) Kneipte, gekneipt is more frequently used.
ich käme	komm	gekommen.	
ich könnte		gekonnt.	
ich kröche	krieche or kriech	gekrochen.	r) Kreuchst, kreucht, kreuch, obsolete. Only poetically used.
ich köhre	köhre	gekohren.	s) Kühren is antiquated, wählen having taken its place.
ich lübe	labe	gelaben.	
ich ließe	lasse or laß	gelassen.	t) Veranlassen is regular.
ich liefe	laufe or lauf	gelaufen.	
ich litte	leide	gelitten.	u) Verleiden, to disgust, is regular.
ich liehe	leihe	geliehen.	
ich läse	lies	gelesen.	
ich läge	liege	gelegen.	
ich löge	lüge	gelogen.	
ich mahlete (mühle)	mahle	gemahlen.	v) Except past part. gemahlen, no irregular form is in use.
ich miede	meide	gemieden.	
ich mölke	melke	gemolken.	w) Sometimes regular. Milkst, &c., rarely used.
ich mäße	miß	gemessen.	
ich mißfiele	mißfalle	mißfallen.	
ich mißlänge	mißlinge	mißlungen.	
ich möchte	—	gemocht.	
ich müßte	—	gemußt.	
ich nähme	nimm	genommen.	
ich nennete	nenne	genannt.	
ich pfiffe	pfeife or pfeif	gepfiffen.	x) Signifying *to wait on*, or *be accustomed*, it is regular.
ich pflöge	pflege	gepflogen.	y) Quellen, to swell, is regular.
ich priese	preise	gepriesen.	z) The irregular form is no longer used. Where it occurs in former writers it must not be confounded with the same forms from riechen.
ich quölle	quelle	gequollen.	
ich röchte (röche)	räche	gerächt (gerochen).	
ich riethe	rathe	gerathen.	
ich riebe	reibe	gerieben.	
ich risse	reiße	gerissen.	
ich ritte	reite	geritten.	a) Reiten, to ride to, like all compounds of reiten, is irregular; but bereiten, to make ready, from bereit, ready, is regular, like all derivatives.

INFINITIVE.	PRESENT INDICATIVE.	IMP. INDIC.
Rennen b), to run,	ich renne, ꝛc.	ich rannte or rennte
Riechen, to smell,	ich rieche, ꝛc.	ich roch
Ringen, to wrestle,	ich ringe, ꝛc.	ich rang
Rinnen, to run (of fluids),	ich rinne, ꝛc.	ich rann
Rufen c), to call,	ich rufe, ꝛc.	ich rief
Salzen d), to salt,	ich salze, ꝛc.	ich salzte
Saufen, to drink, to tipple,	ich saufe, du säufst, er säuft,	ich soff
Saugen e), to suck,	ich sauge, ꝛc.	ich sog
Schaffen f), to create,	ich schaffe, ꝛc.	ich schuf
Scheiden g), to separate,	ich scheide, ꝛc.	ich schied
Scheinen, to appear,	ich scheine, ꝛc.	ich schien
Schelten, to scold,	ich schelte, du schiltst, er schilt	ich schalt (scholt)
Scheren, to shear,	ich schere, ꝛc.	ich schor
Schieben, to shove,	ich schiebe, ꝛc.	ich schob
Schießen, to shoot,	ich schieße, ꝛc.	ich schoß
Schinden, to flay,	ich schinde, ꝛc.	ich schund
Schlafen, to sleep,	ich schlafe, du schläfst, er schläft	ich schlief
Schlagen h), to beat,	ich schlage, du schlägst, er schlägt	ich schlug
Schleichen, to sneak,	ich schleiche, ꝛc.	ich schlich
Schleifen i), to sharpen,	ich schleife, ꝛc.	ich schliff
Schleißen, to slit,	ich schleiße, ꝛc.	ich schliß
Schliefen, to slip,	ich schliefe, ꝛc.	ich schloff
Schließen, to shut,	ich schließe, ꝛc.	ich schloß
Schlingen, to sling,	ich schlinge, ꝛc.	ich schlang
Schmeißen, to fling,	ich schmeiße, ꝛc.	ich schmiß
Schmelzen k), to melt,	ich schmelze, du schmelzest(schmilzest), er schmelzt (schmilzt)	ich schmolz
Schnauben, to snort,	ich schniebe or schnaube	ich schnob
Schneiden, to cut,	ich schneide, ꝛc.	ich schnitt
Schrauben l), to screw	ich schraube, ꝛc.	ich schraubte (schrob)
Schreiben, to write,	ich schreibe, ꝛc.	ich schrieb
Schreien, to cry,	ich schreie, ꝛc.	ich schrie
Schreiten, to stride,	ich schreite, ꝛc.	ich schritt
Schroten, to bruise, to gnaw,	ich schrote, ꝛc.	ich schrotete
Schwären m), to suppurate,	ich schwäre, ꝛc.	ich schwor
Schweigen, to be silent,	ich schweige, ꝛc.	ich schwieg
Schwellen n), to swell,	ich schwelle, du schwillst, er schwillt,	ich schwoll
Schwimmen, to swim,	ich schwimme, ꝛc.	ich schwamm
Schwinden, to vanish,	ich schwinde, ꝛc.	ich schwand

IMP. SUBJ.	IMPERATIVE.	PARTICIPLE.	REMARKS.
ich rennete	renne	gerannt or gerennt.	b) Rennte and gerennt, seldom used.
ich röche	rieche or riech	gerochen.	
ich ränge	ringe	gerungen.	
ich ränne (rönre)	rinne	geronnen.	
ich riefe	rufe	gerufen.	c) Regular in some writers, but improperly so.
ich salzete	salze	gesalzen.	d) Irregular only in the participle, and in that when used adjectively; as. gesalzene Fische; er hat sie gesalzt.
ich söffe	saufe	gesoffen.	
ich söge	sauge	gesogen.	e) Säugst and säugt are not supported by good usage, but säugen, to suckle, is regular.
ich schüfe	schaffe	geschaffen.	f) In the signification of to procure, to get, it is regular, as also anschaffen, to purchase, to buy; abschaffen, to part with, to dismiss.
ich schiebe	scheibe	geschieben.	g) The active verb scheiben, to part, divide, is regular
ich schiene	scheine	geschienen.	
ich schälte (schölte)	schilt	gescholten.	
ich schöre	schere or schier	geschoren.	
ich schöbe	schiebe	geschoben.	
ich schösse	schieße	geschossen.	
ich schünde	schinde	geschunden.	
ich schliefe	schlafe	geschlafen.	
ich schlüge	schlage	geschlagen.	h) Rathschlagen and berathschlagen, to consult, are regular.
ich schliche	schleiche	geschlichen.	
ich schliffe	schleife or schleif	geschliffen.	i) Regular in all other significations, as, to demolish, or to drag.
ich schlisse	schleiße	geschlissen.	
ich schlöffe	schliefe	geschloffen.	
ich schlösse	schließe	geschlossen.	
ich schlänge	schlinge	geschlungen.	
ich schmisse	schmeiße	geschmissen.	
ich schmölze	schmilz or schmelz	geschmolzen.	k) As an active verb it is regular.
ich schnöbe	schnaube	geschnoben.	
ich schnitte	schneide	geschnitten.	
ich schraubete (schröbe)	schraube	geschraubt. (geschroben).	l) Commonly regular, schraubte, geschraubt.
ich schriebe	schreibe	geschrieben.	
ich schriee	schreie	geschrieeen.	
ich schritte	schreite	geschritten.	
ich schrotete	schrote	geschroten.	Regular now except in the participle, and this is frequently geschrotet.
ich schwöre	schwäre	geschworen.	m) Schwierst &c. in the present is provincial.
ich schwiege	schweige	geschwiegen.	
ich schwölle	schwill or schwelle	geschwollen.	n) Regular, when active.
ich schwämme	schwimme	geschwommen.	
ich schwände	schwinde	geschwunden.	

INFINITIVE.	PRESENT INDICATIVE.	IMP. INDIC.
Schwingen o), to swing,	ich schwinge, ꝛc.	ich schwang or schwung
Schwören, to swear,	ich schwöre, ꝛc.	ich schwor or schwur
Sehen, to see,	ich sehe, du siehst, er sieht	ich sah
Sein, to be,	ich bin, ꝛc.	ich war, ꝛc.
Senden, to send,	ich sende, ꝛc.	ich sandte and sendete
Sieden p), to boil,	ich siede, ꝛc.	ich sott
Singen, to sing,	ich singe, ꝛc.	ich sang
Sinken, to sink,	ich sinke, ꝛc.	ich sank
Sinnen, to think, to muse,	ich sinne, ꝛc.	ich sann
Sitzen, to sit,	ich sitze, ꝛc.	ich saß
Sollen, to be obliged,	ich soll, du sollst, er soll	ich sollte
Spalten q), to split,	ich spalte, ꝛc.	ich spaltete
Speien, to spit,	ich speie, ꝛc.	ich spie
Spinnen, to spin,	ich spinne, ꝛc.	ich spann
Spleißen, to split,	ich spleiße, ꝛc.	ich spliß or spliß
Sprechen, to speak.	ich spreche, du sprichst, er spricht	ich sprach
Sprießen r), to sprout,	ich sprieße, ꝛc.	ich sproß
Springen, to spring,	ich springe, ꝛc.	ich sprang
Stechen, to sting, to prick,	ich steche, du stichst, er sticht,	ich stach
Stecken s), to stick,	ich stecke, ꝛc.	ich steckte or stak
Stehen, to stand,	ich stehe, ꝛc.	ich stand (stund)
Stehlen, to steal,	ich stehle, du stiehlst, er stiehlt	ich stahl
Steigen, ascend,	ich steige, ꝛc.	ich stieg
Sterben, to die,	ich sterbe, du stirbst, er stirbt	ich starb
Stieben t), to fly (as dust),	ich stiebe, ꝛc.	ich stob
Stinken, to stink,	ich stinke, ꝛc.	ich stank
Stoßen, to push,	ich stoße, du stößest, er stößt	ich stieß
Streichen, to stroke,	ich streiche, ꝛc.	ich strich
Streiten, to contend,	ich streite, ꝛc.	ich stritt
Thun, to do,	ich thue, du thust, er thut	ich that
Tragen, to bear,	ich trage, du trägst, er trägt	ich trug
Treffen, to hit,	ich treffe, du triffst, er trifft	ich traf
Treiben, to drive,	ich treibe, ꝛc.	ich trieb
Treten, to tread,	ich trete, du trittst, er tritt	ich trat
Triefen, to drop, to trickle,	ich triefe, ꝛc.	ich troff
Trinken, to drink,	ich trinke, ꝛc.	ich trank
Trügen, to deceive,	ich trüge, du trügst, er trügt	ich trog
Verbergen, to conceal,	ich verberge, du verbirgst, ꝛc.	ich verbarg
Verbieten, to forbid,	ich verbiete, ꝛc.	ich verbot
Verbleiben, to remain,	ich verbleibe, ꝛc.	ich verblieb
Verbleichen, to grow pale,	ich verbleiche, ꝛc.	ich verblich
Verderben u), to perish,	ich verderbe, du verbirbst ꝛc.	ich verdarb
Verdrießen v), to offend,	es verdrießt, ꝛc.	es verdroß
Vergessen, to forget,	ich vergesse, du vergissest, ꝛc.	ich vergaß
Verhehlen, to conceal,	ich verhehle, ꝛc.	ich verhehlte
Verlieren, to loose,	ich verliere, ꝛc.	ich verlor

IMP. SUBJ.	IMPERATIVE.	PARTICIPLE.	REMARKS.
ich schwänge	schwinge	geschwungen.	o) Schwung is less in use than schwang.
ich schwöre or schwüre	schwöre	geschworen.	
ich sähe	siehe	gesehen.	
ich wäre	sei	gewesen.	
ich sendete	sende	gesandt and gesendet.	
ich sötte	siede	gesotten.	p) When active it is mostly regular.
ich sänge	singe	gesungen.	
ich sänke	sinke	gesunken.	
ich sänne (sönne)	sinne	gesonnen.	
ich säße	sitze	gesessen.	
ich sollte	—	gesollt.	
ich spaltete	spalte	gespalten.	q) Irregular only in the participle, and this is sometimes gespaltet when the verb is active.
ich spiee	speie	gespieen.	
ich spänne (spönne)	spinne	gesponnen.	
ich spliße	spleiße	gesplissen.	
ich spräche	sprich	gesprochen.	
ich sprösse	sprieße	gesprossen.	r) This must not be confounded (in the imperfect) with the regular verb sprossen.
ich spränge	springe	gesprungen.	
ich stäche	stich	gestochen.	
ich steckte or stäke	stecke	gesteckt.	s) This verb is commonly regular; when active, always so.
ich stände (stünde)	stehe	gestanden.	
ich stähle (stöhle)	stiehl	gestohlen.	
ich stiege	steige	gestiegen.	
ich stärbe (stürbe)	stirb	gestorben.	
ich stöbe	stiebe	gestoben.	t) So Zerstieben, to be scattered as dust.
ich stänke	stinke	gestunken.	
ich stieße	stoße	gestoßen.	
ich striche	streiche	gestrichen.	
ich stritte	streite	gestritten.	
ich thäte	thue	gethan.	
ich trüge	trage	getragen.	
ich träfe	triff	getroffen.	
ich triebe	treibe	getrieben.	
ich träte	tritt	getreten.	
ich tröffe	trief or triefe	getroffen.	
ich tränke	trinke	getrunken.	
ich tröge	trüge	getrogen.	
ich verbärge	verbirg	verborgen.	
ich verböte	verbiete	verboten.	
ich verbliebe	verbleibe	verblieben.	
ich verbliche	verbleiche	verblichen.	
ich verdärbe (verdürbe)	verdirb	verdorben.	u) Verderben, to destroy (active), is regular.
es verdrösse	—	verdrossen.	v) Verdreußt, &c., nearly obsolete.
ich vergäße	vergiß	vergessen.	
ich verhehlete	verhehle	verhehlt or verhohlen.	
ich verlöre	verliere	verloren.	

INFINITIVE.	PRESENT INDICATIVE.	IMP. INDIC.
Verlöschen, to extinguish,	ich verlösche, du verlöschest or verlischest, er verlöscht or verlischt	ich verlosch
Verschallen w), to die away,	ich verschalle, ꝛc.	ich verscholl
Verschwinden, to disappear,	ich verschwinde, ꝛc.	ich verschwand
Verwirren, to perplex,	ich verwirre, ꝛc.	ich verwirrte
Verzeihen, to pardon,	ich verzeihe, ꝛc.	ich verzieh
Wachsen, to grow,	ich wachse, du wächsest, er wächst	ich wuchs
Wägen or Wiegen z), to weigh,	ich wäge or wiege, ꝛc.	ich wog
Waschen y), to wash,	ich wasche, ꝛc.	ich wusch
Weben z), to weave,	ich webe, ꝛc.	ich wob
Weichen a), to yield,	ich weiche, ꝛc.	ich wich
Weisen, to show,	ich weise, ꝛc.	ich wies
Wenden b), to turn,	ich wende, ꝛc.	ich wendete or wandte
Werben, to sue for,	ich werbe, du wirbst, er wirbt	ich warb
Werden, to become,	ich werde, du wirst, er wird	see L. 32. 4.
Werfen, to throw,	ich werfe, du wirfst, er wirft	ich warf
Winden, to wind,	ich winde, ꝛc.	ich wand
Wissen, to know,	ich weiß, du weißt, er weiß	ich wußte
Wollen, to will,	ich will, du willst, er will	ich wollte
Zeihen, to accuse of,	ich zeihe, ꝛc.	ich zieh
Ziehen c), to draw,	ich ziehe, ꝛc.	ich zog
Zwingen, to force,	ich zwinge, ꝛc.	ich zwang

IMP. SUBJ.	IMPERATIVE.	PARTICIPLE.	REMARKS.
ich verlösche	verlösche or verlisch	verloschen.	
ich verschölle	verschalle	verschollen.	w) But little used, except in the imperfect and participle.
ich verschwände	verschwinde	verschwunden.	
ich verwirrte	verwirre	verwirrt or verworren.	
ich verziehe	verzeihe	verziehen.	
ich wüchse	wachse	gewachsen.	
ich wöge	wäge or wiege	gewogen.	x) Wägen is active, and has wäge in the imperf. subj.: wiegen is neuter, and has wiege. Wiegen, to rock; is regular.
ich wüsche	wasche	gewaschen.	y) Wäschest and wäscht are also used.
ich wöbe	webe	gewoben.	z) Regular except in poetry, or when used figuratively.
ich wiche	weiche	gewichen.	a) Weichen, to soften, to mollify, is regular.
ich wiese	weise	gewiesen.	
ich wendete	wende	gewendet or gewandt.	b) Regular when active.
ich würbe	wirb	geworben.	
ich würde	werde	geworden. L.45.2.	
ich wärfe (würfe)	wirf	geworfen.	
ich wände	winde	gewunden.	
ich wüßte	wisse	gewußt.	
ich wollte	wolle	gewollt.	
ich ziehe	zeihe	geziehen.	
ich zöge	ziehe	gezogen.	c) Zeuchst ꝛc., antiquated, and used only in poetry.
ich zwänge	zwinge	gezwungen.	

VOCABULARY
FOR THE EXERCISES

ABBREVIATIONS.

adj.	adjective.		*pl.*	plural.
adv.	adverb.		*pre.*	preposition.
art.	article.		*prn.*	pronoun.
c.	conjunction.		*v. a.*	active verb.
comp.	comparative.		*v. a. & n.*	active & neuter verb.
f.	feminine gender		*v. aux.*	auxiliary verb.
imp.	imperfect tense.		*v. imp.*	impersonal verb.
int.	interjection.		*v. ir.*	irregular verb.
m.	masculine gender.		*v. n.*	neuter verb.
n.	neuter gender.		*v. r.*	reflexive verb.
p.	participle.			

A.

Aal, *m.* -es, *pl.* -e, eel.

Abend, *m.* -s, *pl.* -e, evening; eve; west; —roth, *n.*—röthe, *f.* evening-red, evening-sky.

Abends, *adv.* in the evening.

Aber, *conj.* but, however, L. 63.

Abfahren, see fahren, P. 180; *v. n. ir.* to set off, set out, depart.

Abmatten, *v. a.* to harass, weary.

Abnehmen, *v. a. & n. ir.* to take off, take down; pluck; perceive, diminish, decrease, decline; see nehmen P. 182.

Abreise, *f.* departure.

Abreisen, *v. n.* to depart, set out.

Absagen, *v. a. & n.* to countermand; refuse, resign; renounce.

Abscheu, *m.* -es, abomination, aversion, detestation.

Abschreiben, *v. a.* see schreiben P. 184, to copy, transcribe.

Absteigen, *v. n. ir.* to descend, dismount, put up. P. 186.

Abweichen, *v. n. ir.* to deviate; digress; vary, depart. P. 188.

Acht, see L. 51. 14

Acht, *f.* care, attention; ban, outlawry; — haben, to attend to; in — nehmen, to take care of; sich in — nehmen, to be on one's guard, to be cautious

Aecht, *adj.* genuine, authentic.

Achtbar, *adj.* respectable, estimable.

Achtel, *n.* -s, *pl.*-, eighth. L. 51.5.

Achten, *v. a.* to regard, attend to; value, deem, esteem; take for

Achtzehn, L.51. 14., eighteen.

Achtzehnte, eighteenth.

Adler, *m.* -s, *pl.* —, eagle.

Adolph, *m.* Adolphus.

Affe, *m.* -n, *pl.* -n, monkey, ape.

Aehnlich, *adj.* like, similar.

Ahorn, *m.* -es, maple.

Albern, *adj.* silly, foolish.

Albrecht, proper name.

Allein, *adv.* alone, only. L. 63.

Aller, all, L. 52.

Allerlei, L. 51. 7.

Als, *conj.* than, but, when, as, like; except, besides; namely.

Also, *adv.* thus, so, in this manner, so far; consequently, therefore. L. 63.

Alt, *adj.* old, ancient, aged.

Aeltern, *pl.* parents.

Amboß, *m.* -es, *pl.* -e, anvil.

Amerika, *n.* America.

Amerikaner, *m.* American.

Amt *n.* -es, *pl.* Aemter, charge, office; employment, business

Amtmann, -es, *pl.* —männer, magistrate, bailiff

An, *pre.* at, on, by, to, unto, with, up, about, against. L. 53.
An'betung, *f.* -, *pl.* -en, adoration.
An'bieten, *v. a. ir.* to offer, proffer.
An'der, (der, die, das Andere), *adj.* second; other. L. 52.
Aen'dern, *v. a.* to alter, change.
Anderthalb', *adj.* one and a half.
An'fang *m.* -es, *pl.* —fänge, beginning, element, origin.
An'fangen, *v. a. ir. & n.* to begin, do, act; open. See fangen, P. 180.
An'gehören, *v. n.* to belong.
An'gehörig, *adj.* belonging to; related to; Angehörige, relatives, relations.
An'geklagte, *m.* -n, *pl.* -n, accused.
An'genehm, *adj.* agreeable, pleasant.
An'geschuldigte, see Angeklagte.
An'griff, *m.* -es, *pl.* -e, attack.
Aengst'lich, *adj.* anxious.
An'haltend, *adj.* constant.
An'hangen, *v. n. ir.* to be attached to, adhere to. P. 180.
An'hängen, *v. a.* to hang on; to adjoin, join; *v. r. fig.* to attach one's self to.
An'klagen, *v. a.* to accuse.
An'klopfen, *v. a.* to fasten by beating; *v. n.* to knock.
An'kommen, *v. n. ir.* to arrive, es kommt auf Sie an, it depends upon you. P. 182.
An'muth, *f.* pleasantness, grace.
An'rücken, *v. a. & n.* to bring near; approach.
An'sehen, *v. a. ir.* to look at.
An'sehnlich, *adj.* considerable, important, of consequence.
An'stalt. *f.* -, *pl.* -en, preparation, institution; Anstalten or Anstalt machen, to make preparations, to prepare.
Anstatt', *pre.* instead of, in lieu.
An'strengend, toilsome.
An'treten, *v. a. ir.* to enter upon; set out. P. 186.
Ant'wort, *f.* -, *pl.* -en, answer

Ant'worten, *v. a.* to answer.
An'vertrauen, *v. a.* to entrust to, confide to.
An'wesend, *adj.* present.
An'ziehen, *v. a. ir.* to draw, put on, attract; interest. P. 188.
Ap'fel, *m.* -s, *pl.* Aepfel, apple.
April', *m.* -s, April.
Ara'ber, *m.* Arab.
Ar'beit, *f.* -, *pl.* -en, work, labor.
Ar'beiten, *v. n.* to work, labor.
Arm, *adj.* poor, indigent.
Arm, *m.* -es, *pl.* -e, arm.
Armee', *f.* -, *pl.* -n, army.
Ar'muth, *f.* -, poverty, want.
Art, *f.* -, *pl.* -en, species, kind, nature; quality; propriety.
Arzenei'. *f.* -, *pl.* -en, medicine.
Arzt, *m.* -es, *pl.* Aerzte, physician doctor.
Ast, *m.* es, *pl.* Aeste, bough, branch.
Atmosphä're, *f.* atmosphere.
Auch, *conj.* also, too, even. L. 63.
Auf, *pre.* on, upon; in, at, to, up; — einmal, at once, all at once; – daß, in order that. L. 54.
Auf'enthalt, *m.* stay; delay.
Auf'fordern, *v. a.* to summon, challenge; ask, invite.
Auf'gehen, *v. n.* to rise; open. See gehen, P. 180.
Auf'halten, *v. a. ir.* to stop, hinder, delay; support; *v. r. ir.* to stay, abide, sojourn; to dwell upon; sich über —, to find fault with, criticize.
Auf'hören, *v. n.* to cease, end.
Auf'lösung, *f.* -, *pl.* -en, dissolution.
Auf'machen, *v. a.* to open, *v. r.* to get up, arise; set out.
Auf'merksam, *adj.* attentive.
Auf'richtig, *adj.* candid, genuine.
Auf'schneiden, *v. a. ir.* to cut up, cut open. P. 184.
Auf'setzen, *v. a.* to set up, put up, put down in writing.
Auf'speichern, *v. a.* to store up.

Auf'stehen, v. a. ir. to arise, get up.
Auf'steigen, v. n. ir. to mount, ascend, rise.
Auf'thun, v. a. ir. to open.
Au'ge, n. -s, pl. -n, eye; bud; —nblick, m. twinkling; moment; —nblicklich, instantaneous; instantly.
Aus, pre. out, out of, from, of; by; on, upon; in; adv. over, out, at an end, finished. L. 54.
Aus'breiten, v. a. to spread, extend.
Aus'dehnen, v. a. & r. to stretch, extend, expand.
Aus'dreschen, v. a. See dreschen, P. 178. to thrash out.
Aus'finden, v. a. See finden, P. 180. to find out.
Aus'geben, v. a. ir. to give out, distribute; disburse, spend.
Aus'gebreitet, adj. extensive.
Aus'gehen, v. n. See gehen P. 180., to go out; go abroad; proceed.
Aus'länder, m. -s, pl. -, foreigner.
Aus'löschen, v. a. to extinguish, quench; expunge, efface.
Aus'reißen, v. a. ir. to pull out, to tear out, to draw out; v. n. ir. to be torn, to tear, to burst; to run away.
Aus'richten, v. a. to do, perform.
Aus'schweifen, v. n. to deviate, to digress.
Au'ßen, adv out, on the outside, without, abroad;
Au'ßer, pre. & conj. out of, without; besides, beside; except, unless, save.
Au'ßerhalb, pre. & adv. abroad, without, out of, beyond.
Äu'ßerst, adj. utmost, extreme, exceeding, last.
Aus'sprechen, v. a. & n. ir. to pronounce, utter; express.
Aus'wandern, v. n. to emigrate.
Aus'wendig, adj. outer, outward, exterior; adv. by heart.
Axt, f. -, pl. Aerte, axe, hatchet

B.

Ba'bington, m. Babington.
Ba'cken, v. a. to bake; dry. P. 178
Bä'cker, m. -s, pl. —, baker.
Bai'er, m. -n. Bavarian.
Bai'ern, n. Bavaria
Bald, adv. soon, early, nearly.
Ball, m. -es, pl. Bälle, ball.
Ballon' m. -s, pl. -s, balloon.
Band' n. -es, pl. Bänder, ribbon, string, (pl. Bände) volume.
Bän'digen, v. a. to tame, break.
Bank, f. pl. Bänke, bench, seat.
Bär, m. -en, pl. -en, bear.
Bau'en, v. a. to build, raise; fig. auf einen —, to rely upon one.
Bau'er, m. -s (-n), pl. -n, peasant.
Baum, m. -es, pl. Bäume, tree.
Bäum'chen, dim. of Baum.
Be'cher, m. -s, pl. —, cup, goblet.
Bedau'ern, v. a. to pity, regret.
Bedeck'en, v. a. to cover, shelter.
Bedien'te, m. -n, pl. n, servant.
Bedür'fen, v. n. ir. to need, want. See dürfen, P. 178.
Bedürf'tig, adj. wanting, destitute.
Befehl', m. -es, pl. -e, command.
Befeh'len, v. a. P. 178; to command.
Befin'den, v. a. ir. to find; think; -, v. r. ir. to be; wie — Sie sich? how do you do?
Beflei'ßigen, v. r. to study, endeavor diligently.
Beflei'ßen, v. r. to be studious of, to study.
Beflis'sen, see befleißen, P. 178.
Bege'ben, v. r. ir. to betake; sich seines Rechts —, to forego one's right.
Bege'hen, v. a. see gehen P. 180., to commit, celebrate.
Begeh'ren, v. a. to desire, demand.
Beglei'ten, v. a. to accompany.
Beglei'ter, m. -s, pl —, attendant.
Begra'ben, v. a. ir. to bury.
Behal'ten, v. a. see halten, P.180. to keep, retain.
Behan'deln, v. a to treat, manage.

Behand'lung, *f.* management.
Behar'ren, *v. n.* to continue, persist, insist, persevere.
Behaup'ten, *v. a.* to affirm; maintain; pretend.
Bei, *pre.* at, near, beside, by, on, upon, to, in; L. 55.
Bei'de, *adj.* both. L. 52. 5.
Bei'kommen, *v. n. ir.* to get at.
Bei'spiel, *n.* -es, *pl.* -e, example, instance; pattern; zum —, for example, for instance.
Bei'ßen, *v. a.* P. 178. to bite.
Bei'stand, *m.* -es, assistance.
Bei'stehen, *v. n. ir.* to assist.
Bei'stimmen, *v. n.* to agree with, assent to.
Bei'wohnen, *v. n.* to be present at, to assist.
Bekla'gen, *v. a.* to commiserate, lament; sich—, to complain.
Belebt', *adj.* animated, living.
Beloh'nen, *v. a.* to reward.
Bemäch'tigen, *v. r.* to seize, take possession of; usurp.
Bemit'leiden, *v. a.* to commiserate, pity.
Benei'den, *v. a.* to envy.
Benö'thigt, in need, in want.
Berau'ben, *v. a.* to rob, plunder.
Bereits', *adv.* already.
Berg, *m.* -es, *pl.* -e, mountain.
Ber'gen, *v. a.* to save; to conceal. P. 178.
Berli'n, *n.* Berlin.
Beschäf'tigen, *v. a.* to employ, busy.
Beschlie'ßen, *v. a. ir.* to determine.
Beschrei'ben, *v. a. ir.* to describe.
Beschul'digen, *v. a.* to accuse.
Besi'tzen, *v. a. ir.* to possess.
Bes'ser, see L. 22. 3.
Bestän'dig, *adj.* constant; durable.
Be'ste, der, die, das, *adj.* best. L. 22.
Beste'hen, *v. a. & n. ir.* to suffer; to be; endure; consist of; insist upon.
Bestel'len, *v. a.* to order, appoint.
Bestim'mung. *f.* —, *pl.* -en, determination; destination; destiny.

Bestra'fen, *v. a.* to punish.
Besuch', *m.* -es, *pl.* -e, visit; frequenting, company.
Besu'chen, *v. a.* to visit, see; frequent; to go to see.
Be'ten, *v. n.* to say a prayer, to pray.
Betheln Gabor, Betheln Gabor, proper name.
Betrach'ten, *v. a.* to look upon, contemplate; consider.
Betra'gen, *v. a. ir.* to amount to, *v. r. ir.* to behave one's self.
Betrübt', *adj.* afflicted, sad.
Betrü'gen, *v. a.* P. 178. to cheat, deceive.
Bett, *n.* -es, *pl.* -en, bed
Bet'teln, *v. n.* to beg, ask alms.
Beu'tel, *m.* -s, *pl.* —, bag, purse.
Bewe'gen, *v. a.* to move; excite.
Bewußt', *adj.* known; conscious of; —sein, *n.* consciousness,
Bezich'tigen, *v. a.* to charge, accuse, convict.
Bezüch'tigen, see bezichtigen.
Bi'ber, *m.* -s, *pl.* —, beaver.
Bie'ber, *adj.* upright, honest, brave; —mann, *m.* man of integrity; gentleman.
Bie'gen, *v. a. ir.* P. 178. to bend, bow, curve; decline.
Bie'ne, *f.* —, *pl.* -n, bee.
Bier, *n.* -es, -s, *pl.* -e, beer.
Bil'den, *v. a.* to form; cultivate, civilize, improve.
Bin'den, *v. a.* to bind, tie. P. 178.
Bin'nen, *pre.* within.
Bir'ne, *f.* —, *pl.* -n, pear.
Bis, *adv. & conj.* till. L. 64. 2.
Bit'ten, *v. a.* to beg, pray, request, entreat, invite. P. 178.
Bit'ter, *adj.* bitter; sharp.
Blank, *adj.* blank, bright, polished.
Bla'sen *v. a.* to blow. P. 178.
Blau, *adj.* blue; -, *n.* -es, blue.
Blech, *n.* -es, *pl.* -e, tin.
Blei, *n.* —, -es, lead.
Blei'stift, *m.* -es, *pl.* -e, **pencil**.

Bleiben, *v. n.* P. 178. to remain; continue; perish.
Blei ern, *adj.* leaden, of lead.
Blind, *adj.* blind.
Blume, *f.* —, *pl.* -n, flower.
Blümchen. L. 18.
Blut, *n.* -es, blood.
Boden, *m.* -s, *pl.* Böden, ground, soil; bottom: loft, garret.
Böhme, *m.* -n, *pl.* -n, Bohemian.
Böse, *adj. & adv.* bad, ill, wicked; hurtful; angry; sore.
Bösewicht, *m.* -es, *pl.* -er, villain.
Bote, *m.* -n, *pl.* -n, messenger.
Böttcher, *f.* -s, *pl.* —, cooper.
Brauchen, *v. a.* to want, need; use.
Brauer, *m.* -s, *pl.* —, brewer.
Brausen, *v. n.* to rush, roar; buzz.
Brav, *adj.* brave, honest.
Brechen, *v. a.* P. 178, to break.
Breit, *adj.* broad; large, wide.
Bremen, *n.* Bremen.
Brennen, *v. a. & n. ir.* P. 178, to burn; scorch, parch; distil; cauterize; brand.
Bresche, *f.* —, *pl.* -n, breach, gap.
Brett, *n.* -es, *pl.* -er, board.
Brief, *m.* -es, *pl.* -e, letter; –papier, L. 18.
Bringen, *v. a.* P. 178. to bring, carry, convey; bear; an sich —, to acquire, get possession.
Brod, *n.* -es, *pl.* -e, bread, loaf.
Brücke, *f.* —, *pl.* -n, bridge.
Bruder, *m.* -s, *pl.* Brüder, brother.
Brüderchen, (*dim. of* Bruder).
Brust, *f.* —, *pl.* Brüste, breast.
Brustnadel, *f.* breastpin.
Buch, *n.* -es, *pl.* Bücher, book; quire; —händler, *m.* book-seller, stationer.
Büchlein, L. 18.
Bürger, *m.* -s, *pl.* —, citizen.

C.

Carthago, *n.* Carthage.
Character, *m.* -s, *pl.* -tere, character.
Chinese, *m.* -n, Chinese.
Cicero, Cicero.
Concert, *n.* -es, *pl.* -e, concert.
Cousine, *f. pl.* -en, cousin.

D.

Da, *adv. & conj.* there, present then, at that time; when, as while, because, since.
Dabei, *adv.* by that, thereby, therewith, thereat, near it, present. L. 24. 14. & 38. 6.
Dach, *n.* -es, -s, *pl.* Dächer, roof.
Dachs, *m.* -ses, *pl.* -se, badger.
Dafür, *adv.* for it, for that, instead of that.
Dagegen, *adv. & conj.* against this, for it, to it, in comparison: in return, in exchange.
Daher, *adv. & adj.* thence, from thence, hence, out of that; therefore.
Dahin, *adv.* thither, there, away, down; gone, past.
Dame, *f.* —, *pl.* -n, lady.
Däne, *m.* -n, Dane.
Damit, *adv. & conj.* therewith with it (this, that), by it, by that, in order.
Dampf, *m.* -es, *pl.* Dämpfe, steam, vapor, smoke, fume; —boot, *m.* steam-boat, steamer.
Dankbar, *adj.* thankful, grateful.
Danken, *v. a. & n.* to thank.
Dann, *adv.* then; thereupon.
Daran, *adv.* thereon, thereat, on it, at it, by it, near it; nahe —, hard by, close to; es liegt nichts —, it is no matter.
Darauf, *adv.* thereon, thereupon, on that, on it, upon it, at that, to that, it, after that.
Daraus, *adv.* thereout, out of that, therefrom, thence, from this, of this.
Darin, *adv.* therein, in that, in this, in it, wherein.
Daß, *conj.* that; — nicht, lest.
Dauern, *v n.* to last, continue, *v. a. & imp.* to grieve, regret.

De'cken, v. a. to cover, screen.
De'gen, m. -s, pl. —, sword.
De'muth, f. —, humility, meekness.
Den'ken, v. a. & n. P. 178. to imagine, fancy; think.
Denn, conj. for, then; than; es sei — daß, unless, if, provided.
Den'noch, conj. yet, nevertheless.
Des'halb, adv. therefore, for this reason, on that account.
Des'senthalben, L. 48. 6.
De'sto, adv. the; — besser, the better; so much the better.
Deutsch, adj. German. L. 23. b.
Deutschland, n. Germany.
Diamant, m. -s, pl. -en. diamond.
Dick, adj. thick, big, large, stout.
Dieb, m. -es, pl. -e, thief.
Die'ner, m. -s, pl. —, servant.
Doch, conj. yet, however, nevertheless; but. L. 65.
Dolch, m. -es, pl. -e, dagger.
Dom, m. -es, pl. -e, dome, cupola; cathedral.
Donau, f. Danube.
Don'nern, v. n. to thunder.
Dop'pelt, adj. double, twofold; adv. doubly, twice.
Dorf, n. -es, pl. Dörfer, village.
Dort, adv. there, yonder; von — aus, from thence, thence; —her, from yonder, thence.
Drei, see L. 51. 14.; —mal, adv. three times. L. 51. 10.
Dre'schen, v. a. P. 178, to thrash.
Drit'tens, L. 51. 11.
Dro'hen, v. n. to threat, threaten, menace.
Druck, m. -es, pl. -e, pressure.
Duf'tend, Duf'tig, adj. vaporous, fragrant.
Dul'dung, f. —, toleration, tolerance.
Dumm, adj. dull, stupid.
Dünn, adj. thin, slender.
Dunst, m. -es, pl. Dünste, vapor, steam.
Durch, pre. through; by means of.

Durchaus', adv. throughout, entirely.
Durch'gehen, see gehen, P. 180, to go through; run away; pass.
Dür'fen, L. 31. & P. 178.
Dur'sten, Dürsten, v. n. & imp. to thirst, be thirsty. L. 44. 2.
Dur'stig, adj. thirsty; eager.
Du'tzend, n. (-es), -s, pl. -e, dozen.

E.

E'ben, adj. & adv. even, level, plain; even, just, exactly, precisely.
E'bene, f. —, pl. -n, plain.
E'del, adj. & adv. noble, precious; —mann, m. nobleman; —müthig, adj. noble, magnanimous.
E'he, adv. before.
E'her, adv. sooner, rather.
Eh're, f. —, pl. -n, honor.
Ehr'lich, adj. honest, faithful.
Ei'che, f. —, pl. -n, oak.
Eich'hörnchen, n. -s, pl. -e, squirrel.
Ei'gen, adj. own; self, proper, peculiar; singular, strange; accurate; —sinnig, adj. capricious, wilful, obstinate.
Ei'genheit, f. —, pl. -en, peculiarity.
Ei'genschaft, f. —, pl. -en, quality.
Ei'genthum, n. -es, property.
Ei'len, v. n. to hasten, hurry.
Ein, einer, eine, eines, eins. L. 25. 3.
Ein'druck, m. -es, pl. -drücke, impression.
Ei'nerlei, L. 51. 12.
Ei'niger, Ei'nige, Ei'niges, L. 52.
Ein'mal, Einmal', time, L. 51. 10.
Ein'sam, adj. solitary, lonely.
Ein'sammeln, v. a. to gather.
Ein'stellen, v. a. to suspend; stop; v. r. to appear.
Ein'tracht, f. unanimity; harmony.
Ein'zeln, adj. single; isolated.
Eis, n. -ses, ice; ice-cream.
Ei'sen, n. -s, iron; —bahn, f. railroad.
Ei'telkeit, f. —, vanity, conceit.
Ei'tern, v. n. to fester.

Elend, *adj.* miserable, wretched.
Elephant, *m.* -en, *pl.* -en, elephant.
Elle, *f.* —, *pl.* -n, ell.
Eltern, s. Aeltern.
Empfangen, *v. a.* P. 178. to receive, take, accept.
Empfehlen, *v. a.* P. 178, to recommend.
Empfinden, *v. a.* P. 178, to feel, perceive; experience.
Empörer, *m.* -s, *pl.* —, rebel.
Ende, *n.* -s, *pl.* -n, end; aim.
Enden, *v. a. & n.* to end, finish.
Endlich, *adv.* at last, finally.
Eng or Enge, *adj.* narrow, tight.
Engel, *m.* -s, *pl.* -, angel; —sbild, *n.* figure or image of an angel.
Engländer, *m.* Englishman.
Englisch, *adj.* English.
England, *n.* England.
Enkel, *m.* -s, *pl.* —, grandson.
Enkelin, *f.* granddaughter.
Entblößt, *adj.* destitute, deprived.
Ente, *f.* —, *pl.* -n, duck.
Entfernen, *v. a.* to remove.
Entgegen, against, opposite. L.55.
Entgehen, *v. n. ir.* to escape.
Entheben, *v. a ir* to exempt from.
Entledigen, *v. a.* to release.
Entrinnen, see rinnen, P. 186, to run away, escape.
Entsagen, *v.n.* to renounce, resign.
Entschlafen, see schlafen, P. 186, to fall asleep; *fig.* to expire.
Entschlagen, *v. r. ir.* to get rid of, divest.
Entschließen, see schließen, P. 186, to resolve, determine.
Entstehen, to arise, originate.
Entweder, *conj.* either.
Entzweien, *v. a.* to disunite, set at variance; *v. r.* to quarrel.
Erbarmen, *v. r.* to pity, have mercy.
Erben, *v. a.* to inherit; —, *v. n.* to devolve by inheritance.
Erbittern, *v. a.* to exasperate.
Erbitterung, *f.* animosity.

Erbstaat, *m.* -es, *pl.* -en, hereditary state.
Erde, *f.* —, *pl.* -n, earth, ground.
Ereignen, *v. r.* to happen, chance.
Ereilen, *v. a.* to overtake, befall.
Erfinden, *v. a. ir.* to invent.
Erfolg, *m.* -es, *pl.* -e, result, issue.
Erfreuen, *v. a.* to gladden; enjoy.
Erfüllen, *v. a.* to fill; do, fulfil.
Ergeben, *v. r. ir.* to surrender, submit; —, *adj.* devoted, addicted, given.
Ergreifen, *v. a.*, (see greifen, P. 180). to seize, catch.
Erhalten, *v. a. & n. ir.* to keep, maintain, save; receive, get.
Erhaltung, *f.* preservation.
Erheben, *v. a. ir.* to raise; levy; —, *v. r. ir.* to rise, rebel.
Erinnern, *v. a.* to remind; —, *v. r.* to remember, recollect.
Erkennen, *v. a. ir.* to perceive; distinguish; recognise.
Erklären, *v. a.* to explain, interpret; define, declare.
Erklärung, *f.* —, *pl.* -en, explanation, interpretation; declaration.
Erklettern, *v. a.*, Erklimmen, *v. a. ir.* to climb, climb up.
Erlauben, *v. a.* to permit, allow.
Erliegen, *v. n. ir.* to succumb, be subdued, sink under.
Ermorden, *v. a.* to murder.
Ermüden, *v. a. & n.* to tire, weary.
Erneuen, *v. a.* to renew, renovate.
Erneuern, s. Erneuen.
Ernst, Ernsthaft, *adj.* earnest, serious, grave, stern.
Ernte, *f.* —, *pl.* -n, harvest, crop.
Erpressung, *f.* —, *pl.* -en, extortion.
Erretten, *v. a.* to save, rescue.
Ersatz, *m.* -es, compensation, amends, restitution.
Erschallen, *v. n.* (see schallen), to sound; spread.
Erscheinen, *v. n.* to appear.
Erschießen, *v. a. ir.* to shoot.
Erschrecken, *v. a.* to frighten; *v. n* P. 180, to be frightened.

Erſt, *adj. & adv.* first; prime; at first; before; only; not till. L.60.
Er'ſtens, *adv.* L. 51. 11.
Ertrin'ken, (see trinken), to be drowned.
Erwäh'nen, *v. a.* to mention.
Erwar'ten, *v. a.* to expect, await.
Erwe'cken, *v. a.* to awaken, rouse.
Erwei'chen, *v. a.* to soften.
Erwei'ſen, *v. a. ir.* to show, evince; do, render.
Erzäh'len, *v. a.* to narrate, tell.
Erzei'gen, *v. a.* to do; confer.
Eſ'ſen, *v. a. & n.* P. 180, to eat.
Eſ'ſig, *m.* -es, -s, vinegar.
Et'was, *pron.* something, L. 52.
Eu'le, *f.* —, *pl.* -n, owl.
Euro'pa, *n.* Europe.
Europä'er, *m.* European.
E'wig, *adj.* eternal, everlasting.

F.

Fä'hig, *adj.* able, apt, fit, capable.
Fah'ren, *v. a.* P. 180, to drive, carry, convey; *v. n. ir.* to ʃve quickly, run, start, rush; go in a carriage; to sail, navigate.
Fall, *m.* -es, *pl.* —, Fälle, fall.
Fal'len, *v. n.* P. 180, to fall; decline; fail.
Falſch'heit, *f.* —, *pl.* -en, falsehood.
Fami'lie, *f.* —, *pl.* -n, family.
Fan'gen, *v. a.* P. 180, to catch, take, seize.
Faß, *n.* -ſſes, *pl.* Fäſſer, cask, barrel, tub, vessel.
Faſt, *adv.* almost, nearly, about.
Faul, *adj.* putrid, lazy, idle.
Faulheit, *f.* —, laziness, idleness.
Februar', *m.* -s, (*pl.* -e), February.
Fech'ten, P. 180, to fight, to fence.
Fe'der, *f.* —, *pl.* -n, feather; pen; spring.
Fe'gen, *v. a.* to sweep; cleanse.
Feh'len, *v. n.* to fail, miss; err, mistake; to be wanting, want, to be deficient; was fehlt Ihnen? what ails you?

Feh'ler, *m.* -s, *pl.* —, fault, error.
Fein, *adj.* fine; delicate; pretty.
Feind'lich, *adj.* hostile, inimical.
Feind'ſeligkeit, *f.* —, *pl.* -en, hostility.
Feld, *n.* -es, *pl.* -er, field, plain; —frucht, *f.* produce of the fields; —herr, *m.* commander-in-chief, general, captain.
Fels, *m.* -ſens, *pl.* -ſen; Fel'ſen, *m.* -s, *pl.* —, rock, cliff.
Fen'ſter, *n.* -s, *pl.* —, window.
Fer'tig, *adj.* ready; done; practised.
Feſ'ſel, *f.* —, *pl.* -n, fetter, chain.
Feſ'ſeln, *v. a.* to fetter, shackle, chain; captivate.
Feſt, *adj. & adv.* fast, fixed, firm.
Fe'ſte, *f.* —, *pl.* -n, fortress, prison.
Feu'er, *n.* -s, *pl.* —, fire.
Fie'ber, *n.* -s, *pl.* —, fever.
Fin'den, *v. a.* P. 180, to find; think; Statt —, to take place.
Fin'ger, *m.* -s, *pl.* —, finger.
Fin'ſter, *adj.* dark, gloomy; sad.
Fi'ſchen, *v. a.* to fish.
Fla'ſche, *f.* —, *pl.* -n, flask, bottle.
Flech'ten, *v. a.* P. 180, to braid.
Fleiſch, *n.* -es, flesh; meat.
Fleiß, *m.* -es, diligence, industry; mit —, intentionally.
Flei'ßig, *adj.* diligent, assiduous.
Flie'gen, *v. n.* P. 180, to fly; hoch —, to soar.
Flie'hen, P. 180, to flee, shun.
Flie'ßen, *v. n.* P. 180, to flow, run.
Floß'graben, *m.* canal.
Flot'te, *f.* —, *pl.* -n, fleet.
Flu'chen, *v. n.* to curse, imprecate.
Fluß, *m.* -ſſes, *pl.* Flüſſe, river, stream; —pferd, *n.* hippopotamus.
Flut, Fluth, *f.* —, *pl.* -en, flood; deluge, inundation; tide.
Folge. *f.* —, *pl.* -, sequel, sequence, consequence.
Fol'gen, *v. n.*, to follow, to succeed, obey.
Folg'lich, *adv.* consequently.
För'dern, *v. a.* to promote.
For'dern, to demand, ask, require; summon.

Forel'le, *f.* —, *pl.* -n, trout.
Fort'schleppen, *v. a.* to drag away.
Fra'gen, *v. a. & n.* to ask, question, interrogate.
Frank'furt, *n.* Frankfort.
Frank'reich, *n* France.
Franzo'se, *m.* -n, Frenchman.
Franzö'sisch, *adj.* French.
Frau, *f.* —, *pl.* -en, woman; wife; lady, madam, mistress.
Fräu'lein, *n.* -s, *pl.* —, Miss, L. 68.
Frei, *adj.* free, exempt; disengaged; vacant, independent; open, public.
Freigebig, *adj.* liberal, generous; —sprechung, *f.* acquittal.
Frei'heit, *f.* liberty, freedom.
Fres'sen, *v. a.* P. 180, to eat; devour; corrode.
Freu'de, *f.* —, *pl.* -n, joy, pleasure.
Freu'en, *v. r.* über etwas, auf etwas, to rejoice in, to be glad; es freuet mich sehr, I am very glad.
Freund, *m.* -es, *pl.* -e, friend.
Freun'din, *f.* -, *pl.* -nen. L. 18.
Freund'lich, *adj.* friendly, affable.
Freund'schaft, *f.* -, *pl.* -en, friendship.
Frie'de, *m.* -ns, (Frieden, *m.* -s), peace.
Friedlich, *adj.* peaceful, peaceable.
Frie'ren, *v. n. & imp. ir.* to freeze, to be chilled; es friert mich, I am cold.
Froh, *adj.* glad, joyful, joyous.
Froh'locken, *v. n.* to exult, shout.
Frucht, *f.* -, *pl.* Früchte, fruit; corn.
Frü'her, formerly.
Früh'ling, *m.* -es, *pl.* -e, spring.
Fuchs, *m.* -ses, *pl.* Füchse, fox.
Fü'gen, *v. a* to join, to unite; *v. r.* to accommodate one's self to, to submit.
Füh'ren, *v. a.* to carry, convey; lead, guide, manage, wear.
Fünf, see L. 51. 14.
Für, *pre.* for; instead of; — und —, for ever and ever. L. 55.
Furcht, *f.* -, fear.
Furcht'bar, *adj.* fearful, dreadful.

Fürch'ten, *v.* to fear, to be afraid, *v. r.* to be afraid of.
Furcht'sam, *adj.* timid, timorous.
Fürst, *m.* -en, *pl.* -en, prince.
Fuß, *m.* -es, *pl.* Füße, foot; bottom, base; standard.
Füt'tern, *v. a. & n.* to line, feed.

G.

Ga'be, *f.* -, *pl.* -n, gift; alms, charity; dose; talent, faculty.
Ga'bel, *f.* -, *pl.* -n, fork.
Galt, *f.* Gelten.
Gans, *f.* -, *pl.* Gänse, goose.
Ganz, whole, all, entire, total; full, perfect, complete; quite.
Gar, L. 65.
Gar'ten, *m.* -s, *pl.* Gärten, garden.
Gärt'ner, *m.* -s, *pl.* -, gardener.
Gast, *m.* -es, *pl.* Gäste, guest; —freund, *m.* guest; host; —mahl, *n.* banquet, entertainment.
Gebäu'de, *n.* -s, *pl.* -, building.
Ge'ben, P. 180, to give; confer.
Geber'den, *v. r.* to make gestures; behave.
Gebie'ten, *v. a.* (see bieten), to command, to order.
Gebie'ter, *m.* -s, *pl.* -, ruler, master.
Gebirge, *n.* -s, *pl.* -, chain of mountains, mountains, *pl.*
Gebot', *n.* -es, *pl.* -e, commandment, precept, order; offer.
Gebrauch', *m.* -es, *pl.* —bräuche, use, custom, usage, practice.
Gebre'chen, *v. n. & imp. ir.* to be wanting, be in want of, want.
Gebüh'ren, *v. n. & r.* to be due, belong to; be fit, become.
Gedan'ke, *m.* -ns, *pl.* -n, thought, idea, notion, meaning; purpose.
Geden'ken, *v. n. ir.* to think of, remember, mention, intend.
Geduld', *f.* -, patience, indulgence.
Gedul'dig, *adj.* patient, indulgent.
Gefahr, *f.* -, *pl.* -en, danger.
Gefähr'lich, *adj.* dangerous.
Gefal'len, (see fallen). to please; *m.* -s, liking, pleasure; favor.

Gefäng'niß. *n.* -ffes, *pl.* -ffe, prison.
Gefühl', *n.* -es, *pl.* -e, feeling, touch, sensation; sensibility.
Ge'gen *pre.* towards, to; against; for; about, near; —theil. *n.* contrary; —über, *pre.* opposite. L.56.
Ge'gend, *f.* -, region, country.
Ge'hen, P. 180, to go, walk, fare, be; wie geht es? how are you? es geht mir wohl, I am well; der Wind geht, the wind blows.
Gehor'chen, *v. n.* to obey.
Gehö'ren, *v. n.* to belong.
Gehor'fam, *adj.* obedient, dutiful; *m.* -s, obedience, duty.
Geist, *m.* -es, *pl.* -er, ghost, spirit; soul; genius.
Geiz, *m.* -es, avarice.
Gei'zig, *adj.* avaricious, covetous.
Gelb, *adj.* yellow.
Geld, *n.* -es, *pl.* -er, money, coin; —beutel, *m.* money purse.
Gelehrt', *adj.* learned, skilled.
Gelin'gen. P. 180, to succeed. L.44.
Gel'ten, P. 180. to be of value.
Gelü'sten, *v. n. & imp.* to desire, long for, lust after, covet.
Gemäß', *adj. & adv.* conformable, suitable, according to.
Gem'se, *f.* -, *pl.* -n, chamois; —njäger, *m.* chamois-hunter.
Gemüth', *n.* -es. *pl.* -er, mind, soul, heart, nature.
Gene'fen, P. 180, to recover.
Genie'ßen, P. 182, *v. a. ir.* to enjoy, taste, eat, drink.
Genug', *adv.* sufficient, enough.
Genü'gen, *v. n.* to suffice, be enough, satisfy, content.
Gera'de, *adj.* straight, right, direct; upright, plain, honest.
Ger'ber, *m.* -s, *pl.* -, tanner.
Gerecht', *adj.* just, righteous.
Gerech'tigkeit, *f.* -, justice.
Gerei'chen, *v. n.* to tend; redound.
Gericht, *n.* -es, *pl.* -e, tribunal; court of justice; sentence; dish.
Gern, *adv.* willingly, gladly, cheerfully, with pleasure.

Ger'ste, *f.* -, barley.
Gesand'te, *m.* -n. *pl.* -n, ambassador.
Geschäf'tig, *adj.* busy; active.
Gesche'hen, P. 182, to happen. chance; to be done.
Geschich'te, *f.* -, *pl.* -n, history, story; —schreiber, *m.* historian.
Geschickt', *adj.* fit, apt, skilful.
Geschmack', *m.* -es, taste.
Geschöpf', *n.* -es, *pl.* -e, creature.
Geschwei'gen, *v. n. ir.* to pass over in silence.
Geschwür', *n.* -es, *pl.* -e, sore, ulcer.
Gesetz', *n.* -es, *pl.* -e, law, decree.
Gestalt', *f.* -, *pl.* -en, figure, form.
Ge'stern, *adv.* yesterday; — früh, yesterday morning; — Abend, last evening.
Gesund', *adj.* sound, healthy.
Getrei'de, *n.* -es, corn, grain.
Getreu', *adj.* faithful, loyal, trusty.
Gewahr', *adj.* perceiving; —werden, to see, perceive.
Gewalt', *f.* -, *pl.* -en, power, force.
Gewalt'fam, *adj.* violent, forcible.
Gewin'nen, P. 182, to win, earn.
Gewiß', *adj.* certain, sure; fixed.
Gewif'fen, *n.* -s, conscience.
Gewöhn'lich, *adj.* usual, common.
Gewohnt', *adj.* used, accustomed.
Gewöl'be, *n.* -s, *pl.* -, vault, arch.
Gewürz', *n.* -es, *pl.* -e, spice; aromatics.
Gie'ßen, P. 182, to pour; spill; cast.
Gif'tig, *adj.* poisonous, venomous.
Glän'zen, *v. n.* to glitter, shine.
Glän'zend, *adj.* bright, glittering.
Glas, *n.* -fes, *pl.* Gläfer, glass.
Gla'fer, *m.* -s, *pl.* -, glazier.
Glatt, *adj.* smooth, even, plain.
Glau'ben, *v. a.* to believe; think.
Gläu'bige. *m. & f.* believer.
Gleich, *adj. & adv.* like, alike; equal; level, plain; straight, just, immediately, presently; —bedeutend, *adj.* synonymous; —gültig, or gleichgültig, *adj.* equivalent, indifferent.

Gleichen, P. 182, to equal, equalize, level; resemble.
Glück', n. -es, luck, fortune.
Glück'lich, adj. happy, fortunate.
Gnä'dig, adj. gracious, merciful.
Gold, n. -es, gold.
Gol'den, adj. golden, made of gold.
Gott, m. -es, pl. Götter, God.
Göt'tin, f. -, pl. -nen, goddess.
Grab, n. -es, pl. Gräber, grave, tomb, sepulchre.
Gra'ben, m. -s, pl. Gräben, ditch, trench; canal.
Gra'ben, P. 182, to dig; cut.
Graf, m. -en, pl. -en, earl, count.
Grän'ze, ꝛc., s. Grenze ꝛc.
Gras, n. -ses, pl. Gräser, grass.
Grau, adj. gray, grizzled.
Gräu'el, m. -s, pl. -, horror, —that, f. atrocious action.
Grau'en, v. n. to turn gray; dawn; v. imp. to have a horror, dread, to be afraid of; n. -s, horror, abhorrence, terror.
Grau'sam, adj. cruel, barbarous.
Greis, adj. gray, hoary; m. -ses, pl. -se, an old man.
Gren'ze, f. -, pl. -n, limit, border.
Gren'zenlos, adj. boundless.
Grieche, m. -n, Greek.
Griechisch, adj. Grecian, Greek.
Grob, adj. coarse; clumsy, gross, rude; —schmied, m. blacksmith.
Grob'heit, f. -, (pl. -en). coarseness, roughness, rudeness.
Groß, adj. great, large, vast, huge; high, tall; eminent, grand; —vater, m. grandfather.
Grün, adj. green, verdant; fresh.
Grund, m. -es, pl. Gründe, ground, bottom; foundation, reason.
Gul'den, m. -s, pl. -, florin.
Gunst, f. -, favor, grace, kindness, affection; permission; pl. -en, zu —en, in favor of.
Gün'stig, favorable, propitious.
Gu'stav, m. Gustavus.
Gut, adj. & adv. good, well, sufficiently; good-natured, kind; n. es, pl. Güter, good; possession, estate, commodity.
Gü'tig, adj. kind, benevolent.

H.

Haar, n. -es, pl. e, hair; wool.
Ha'be, f. property, goods, effects
Ha'ben, v. L. 26, to have, possess.
Ha'bicht, m. -es, pl. -e, hawk.
Ha'der, m. -s, quarrel, brawl.
Ha'fer, m. -s, oat, oats.
Halb, adj. half.
Hälf'te, f. -, pl. -n, half, moiety.
Hals, m. -ses, pl. Hälse, neck; throat.
Hal'ten, P. 180, to hold; keep; support; contain; stop; maintain; manage; value, deem, estimate, think; celebrate, treat.
Ham'burg, n. Hamburg.
Hand, f. -, pl. Hände, hand; —schuh, m. glove, gauntlet.
Han'del, m. -s, pl. Händel, commerce, trade, traffic; bargain; business; affair, action.
Han'deln, v. n. to act; trade, deal.
Hand'werker, m. -s, pl. -, mechanic.
Hanf, m. -es, hemp.
Hanno'ver, Hanover.
Han'gen, P. 182, to hang, dangle.
Hän'gen, to hang, suspend.
Hart, adj. hard; severe, rigorous.
Ha'se, m. -n, pl. -n, hare.
Has'sen, v. a. to hate.
Häß'lich, adj. ugly, wicked.
Hast, f. -, haste.
Hau'en, v. a. P. 182, to hew, cut, strike.
Haupt, n. -es, pl. Häupter, head; chief; — mann, m. captain; — stadt, f. capital, metropolis.
Haus, n. -ses, pl. Häuser, house; household, family; —thier, n. domestic animal.
Häus'chen, L. 18.
He'ben, P. 182, to lift, elevate.
Heer, n. -es, pl. -e, army.
Heil, adj. healed; sound, unhurt; n. -es, welfare, health.

Hei'ligen, v. v. to hallow.
Hein'rich, m. Henry.
Heiß, adj. hot, ardent, torrid.
Hei'ßen, v. a. & n. P. 182, to call, bid; enjoin; to be called, be said; mean, signify; be considered; es heißt, it is said, they say; das heißt, that is to say, that is; wie heißen Sie? what is your name?
Hel'fen, P. 182, to help, assist.
Hell, adj. clear, bright, plain.
Her, adv. hither, hitherward. L. 38.
Heran, adv. on, near, near to; up, upwards. L. 38.
Herauf', adv. up, upwards.
Heraus', adv. out.
Herb, Her'be, adj. harsh, sour, bitter.
Herbei'führen, v. a. to lead near; bring on.
Herbst, m. -es, pl. -e, autumn; harvest.
Her'kommen, v. n. ir. to come here or hither, approach; to proceed.
Herr, m. -en, pl. -en, master; gentleman; lord; sir.
Herr'schen, v. n. to rule, reign, govern, prevail.
Herü ber, adv. over, across. L. 38.
Herun'ter, adv. down. L. 38.
Herz, n. -ens, pl. -en, heart; courage.
Her'zog, m. -es, pl. -e, duke.
Her'zogshut, m. -es, ducal hat.
Heuchelei', f. -, hypocrisy.
Heut, Heu'te, adv. to-day, this day; — zu Tage, now-a-days.
Hie'ben, see hauen, P. 182.
Hier, adv. here; in this world; —her, adv. hither, here.
Hilfe, f. -, pl. -n. aid, help, succor, assistance, relief.
Hilf'los, adj. helpless.
Him'mel, m. -s, pl. -, heaven, heavens, pl., sky; zone, climate.
Hin, adv. thither, away, gone. L. 38
Hinab', adv. down, down there (s. herunter, hinunter). L. 38.
Hinauf', adv. up, up there. L. 38.
Hinaus', adv. out, out there.

Hin'gehen, v. n. ir. to go to; pass.
Hin'ter, pre. & adv. behind, after, back, backwards; —stube, f. back-room; —theil, n. hind-part; stern.
Hinü'ber, adv. over, across, beyond. L. 38.
Ho'bel, m. -s, pl. -, plane.
Hoch, adj. high, lofty; sublime.
Hof, m. -es, pl. Höfe, yard, courtyard; farm; manor, court.
Hof'fen, v. a. to hope, expect.
Hoff'nung, f. -, pl. -en, hope, expectation.
Höf'lich, adj. polite.
Höf'lichkeit, f. -, pl. -en, courteousness, civility; politeness.
Hol'länder, m. Dutchman.
Holz, n. -es, pl. Hölzer, wood; timber.
Hö'ren, v. a. & n. to hear, give ear.
Hübsch, adj. & adv. pretty, fair.
Huf, m. -es, pl. -e, hoof.
Hü'gel, m. -s, pl. -, hillock, hill.
Huhn, n. -es, pl. Hühner, fowl.
Hül'fe, f. Hilfe.
Hülf'los, see hilflos.
Hügel'chen, L. 18.
Hund, m. -es, pl. -e, dog.
Hun'dert, see L. 51. 14.
Hünd'chen, L. 18.
Hun'gerig, adj. hungry.
Hun'gern, v. n. & imp. to hunger to be hungry; starve. L. 42.
Hut, m. -es, pl. Hüte, hat, bonnet.
Hyä'ne, f. -, pl. -n, hyena.

J (Vocal).

Im, L. 15. 4.
Im'mer, adv. always, ever.
In, pre. into, in; at, within, to, of. L. 56.
Indem', while, when, because, since.
In'nerhalb, pre. within.
In'sel, f. -, pl. -n, island, isle.
Interessant', adj. interesting.
Interes'se, n. -s, pl. -n, interest.
Island, n. -es, Iceland.
Italie'nisch, adj. Italian

J (Consonant).

Ja, *adv.* yes, ay, yea; L. 65.
Ja'gen, *v. a. & n.* to chase, hunt; in die Flucht —, to put to flight.
Jä'ger, *m.* -s. *pl.* -, hunter.
Jahr, *n.* -es, *pl.* -e, year.
Jah'reszeit, *f.* season.
Januar', *m.* -s, January.
Je, *adv.* ever, always; —nachdem, according as.
Je'dermann, every body.
Jedoch', however, nevertheless
Je'tzig. *adj.* present, now.
Jetzt, *adv.* now, at present.
Joch, *n.* -es, *pl.* -e, yoke; bow
Johann', *m.* John.
Joseph, *m.* Joseph.
Ju'de, *m.* -n. *pl.* -n, jew.
Ju'gend, *f.* youth.
Ju'li, Ju'lius, *m.* -, July.
Jung, *adj.* young; new, recent.
Jüngling, *m.* -es, *pl.* -e, youth, lad.
Ju'piter, Jupiter.
Ju'wele, *f.* -, *pl.* -n, jewel; —nhänd= ler, *m.* jeweller.

K.

Kaf'fee, *m.* -s, coffee.
Kai'ser, *m.* -s, *pl.* -, emperor.
Kai'serin, *f.* -, *pl.* -nen, empress.
Kalb, *n.* -es, *pl.* Kälber, calf.
Kalt, *adj.* cold, chill, frigid.
Kameel', *n.* -es, *pl.* -e, camel.
Kame'rad, *m.* -en, comrade.
Kamm, *m.* -es, *pl.* Kämme, comb.
Kampf, *m.* -es, *pl.* Kämpfe, combat.
Kanin'chen, *n.* -s, *pl.* -, rabbit.
Kan'ne, *f.* -, *pl.* -n, can, jug.
Kano'ne, *f.* -, *pl.* -n, cannon; —nschuß, *m.* —nschußweite, *f.* cannon-shot.
Kan'zel. *f.* -, *pl.* -n, pulpit, chair.
Kapell'e or Capelle *f.* chapel.
Karl, *m.* Charles.
Kä'se, *m.* -s, *pl.* -, cheese.
Ka'tze, *f.* -, *pl.* -n, cat.
Kau'fen. *v. a.* to buy, purchase
Kauf'mann, *m.* -es, *pl.* -leute, merchant.

Kaum, *adv.* scarce, scarcely.
Kei'chen, *v. n.* to pant, gasp.
Kel'le. *f.* -, *pl.* -n, trowel.
Kel'ler, *m.* -s, *pl.* -, cellar, cave.
Ken'nen, *v. a.* P. 182, to know, be acquainted with: — lernen, to become acquainted with.
Ker'ker, *m.* prison, dungeon.
Ket'te, *f.* -, *pl.* -n, chain.
Keu'chen, s. Keichen.
Kind. *n.* -es, *pl.* -er, child; infant.
Kind'lein, *dim.* of Kind.
Kir'che, *f.* -, *pl.* -n, church.
Kir'sche, *f.* -, *pl.* -n, cherry.
Kis'sen, *n.* cushion, pillow.
Kla'gen, *v. n.* to complain, lament.
Kleid, *n.* -es, *pl.* -er, garment, dress, garb, gown.
Klein, *adj.* little, small, trifling.
Klei'nigkeit. *f.* -, *pl.* -en, trifle.
Klet'tern, *v. n.* to climb, scramble,
Klug, *adj.* prudent, ingenious. wise, judicious, skilful.
Klug'heit, *f.* -, prudence, judiciousness, wit, wisdom.
Kna'be, *m.* -n, *pl.* -n, boy, lad.
Knäb'chen, L. 18.
Knecht, *m.* -es, *pl.* -e, servant, slave.
Knie'en, Kni'en, *v. n.* to kneel.
Knopf, *m.* -es, *pl.* Knöpfe, button.
Knos'pe, *f.* -, *pl.* -n, bud, eye.
Koch, *m.* -es, *pl.* Köche, cook.
Kof'fer, *m.* -s, *pl.* -, coffer, trunk.
Kohl, *m.* -es, cabbage.
Kohl'e, *f.* -, *pl.* -n, charcoal; coal
Kom'men, P. 182, to come; get to, arrive at.
Kö'nig, *m.* -es, *pl.* -e, king; —reich, *n.* kingdom.
Kö'nigin. *f.* -, *pl.* -nen, queen.
Kö'niglich, *adj.* royal, kingly.
Kön'nen, L. 31.
Koral'le, *f.* -, *pl.* -n, coral.
Korb, *m.* -es, *pl.* Körbe, basket
Körb'chen, L. 18.
Korn, *n.* -es, *pl.* Körner, grain; corn
Kör'per, *m.* -s, *pl.* -, body.
Kraft, *f.* -, *pl.* Kräfte, strength, force, vigor, faculty, power.

Kraft, *pre.* by virtue of, L. 48.
Krank, *adj.* sick, ill, diseased.
Krank'heit, *f.* -, *pl.* -en, disease, illness.
Kranz, *m.* -es, *pl.* Kränze, garland, wreath; crown, circle, society.
Kra'tzen, *v. a. & n.* to scratch.
Kreuz, *n.* -es, *pl.* -e, cross, crucifix; —zug, *m.* crusade.
Krie'chen, P. 182, to creep, crawl.
Krieg, *m.* -es, *pl.* -e, war.
Krie'ger, *m.* -s, *pl.* -, warrior.
Kriegs'zug, *m.* campaign.
Krokodil' *n.* -es, *pl.* -e, crocodile.
Kro'ne, *f.* -, *pl.* -n, crown, coronet; head; top (of a tree).
Kü'che, *f.* -, *pl.* -n, kitchen.
Kühl, *adj.* cool, fresh; cold.
Kühn, *adj.* bold, hardy, dauntless.
Kum'mer, *m.* -s, sorrow, grief.
Kun'de, *f.* -, *pl.* -n, knowledge, information; news, notice; *m.* -n, *pl.* -n, customer.
Kunst, *f.* -, *pl.* Künste, art, artifice; skill.
Künst'ler, *m.* -s, *pl.* -, artist.

L.

Lä'cheln, *v. n.* to smile.
La'chen, *v. n.* to laugh, smile.
Lä'cherlich, *adj.* ridiculous.
Lachs, *m.* -ses, *pl.* -se, salmon.
La'ge, *f.* -, *pl.* -n, situation, site, position; attitude.
La'ger, *n.* -s, *pl.* -, couch, bed; camp.
La'gern, *v. a.* to lay down; store; encamp; to lie down.
Lahm, *adj.* lame; halt, halting.
Lamm, *n.* -es, *pl.* Lämmer, lamb.
Lämm'chen, *dim. of* Lamm. L. 18.
Lam'pe, *f.* -, *pl.* -n, lamp.
Land, *n.* -es, *pl.* Länder (Lande), land; ground, soil; country; —straße, *f.* high-road, highway.
Lang, *adj.* long, tall; during; —muth, *f.* long-sufferance; —weilig, *adj.* tedious, tiresome.
Lan ge, *adv.* long, a long while.

Lang'sam, *adj.* slow, dull, heavy.
Längst, *adv.* long ago, long since.
Las'sen, L. 31. & P. 182.
Last, *f.* -, *pl.* -en, load, burden; —thier, *n.* beast of burden.
La'sterhaft, *adj.* vicious, wicked.
Lä'stig, *adj.* burdensome, troublesome.
Lauf, *m.* -es, *pl.* Läufe, run, course.
Lau'fen, P. 182, to run.
Laut, *m.* -es, *pl.* -e, sound, tone.
Le'ben, *v. n.* to live; *n.* -s, life; vivacity.
Le'der, *n.* -s, *pl.* -, leather.
Le'dern, *adj.* leathern.
Le'dig, *adj.* empty, void, vacant; free, unmarried.
Le'gen, *v. a.* to lay, to put, to place.
Lehr'reich, *adj.* instructive.
Leh'ren, *v. a.* to teach, instruct.
Leh'rer, *m.* -s, *pl.* -, teacher, instructor, professor, master.
Lehr'ling, *m.* -es, *pl.* -e, apprentice.
Leib, *m.* -es, *pl.* -er, body.
Leicht, *adj.* light; easy; fickle.
Leid, *adj.* sorrowful, troublesome; es ist mir —, es thut mir —, I am sorry for it.
Lei'den, P. 182, to suffer, endure, bear, tolerate; — mögen, to like; *n.* -s, *pl.* -e, suffering; misfortune.
Lei'hen, *v. a.* P. 182, to lend.
Leipzig, *n.* Leipsic.
Ler'che, *f.* -, *pl.* -n, lark; larch-tree.
Ler'nen, *v. a. & n.* to learn; kennen —, to become acquainted with; auswendig —, to learn by heart.
Le'sen, *v. a. & n.* P. 182, to read; gather.
Letzt, *adj.* last, ultimate, final.
Leuch'ter, *m.* -s, *pl.* -, candlestick.
Leu'te, *pl.* people, persons.
Licht, *adj.* light, clear, bright; *s.* light, candle.
Lieb, *adj.* dear, beloved; pleasing; meine Liebe, my dear; es ist mir —, I am glad.

Liebe, *f.* -, love, affection.
Lieben, *v. a. & n.* to love.
Lieber, *adv.* rather, sooner, better.
Liebling, *m.* -es, *pl.* -e, favorite, darling.
Lied, *n.* -es, *pl.* -er, song, air.
Liegen, P. 182, to lie; be situated.
Lilie, *f.* -, *pl.* -n, lily.
Linde, *f.* -, *pl.* -n, linden-tree.
Link. *adj.* left; left-handed.
Lob, *n.* -es, praise; commendation.
Loben, *v. a.* to praise, commend.
Loch, *n.* -es, *pl.* Löcher, hole.
Lohn, *m. & n.* -es, *pl.* Löhne, reward, wages, *pl.* hire; pay, salary.
Lord, *m.* lord.
Löwe, *m.* -n, *pl.* -n, lion.
Luft, *f.* -, *pl.* Lüfte; air; breeze; atmosphere.
Luftballon, *m.* air-balloon.
Lügen, P. 182, to lie, tell a lie.
Lust, *f.* -, *pl.* Lüste, pleasure, joy, enjoyment, delight; inclination, fancy, desire.
Lüsten, f. Gelüsten. L. 44. 4.
Lützen, *n.* Lutzen.

M.

Machen, *v. a.* to make, do, fabricate, produce; represent; was — Sie! how do you do? how are you?
Macht, *f.* -, *pl.* Mächte, might, force.
Mächtig. *adj.* mighty, powerful; einer Sprache — sein to be master of a language.
Mädchen, *n.* -s, *pl.* -, maiden, girl.
Magdeburg. *n.* Magdeburg.
Mager, *adj* meager, lean; dry.
Mahlen, P. 182, to grind.
Mährchen, *n.* -s, *pl.* -, tale, legend.
Mai, *m.* -es, May.
Mal. *n.* -es, *pl.* -e, time, bout. L. 51.
Maler, *m.* -s, *pl.* -, painter.
Malta, Malta.
Man, one, they, people. L. 30. 3.
Mancher, Manche, Manches, *pre.* many a, many a one; Manche,

pl. many, some, several; Manches, many things.
Mandel, *f.* -, *pl.* -n, almond.
Mann, *m.* -es, *pl.* Männer, man; husband.
Mannsfeld, *m.* Mansfield.
Mantel. *m.* -s, *pl.* Mäntel, cloak.
Maria, Maria, Mary.
Markt, *m.* -es, *pl.* Märkte, market, mart, market-place.
Mäßig, *adj.* moderate, temperate.
Mast, *m.* -es, *pl.* -en, mast.
Matrose, *m.* -n, *pl.* -n, sailor.
Maurer, *m.* -s, *pl.* -, mason.
Maximilian, *m.* Maximilian.
Meer, *n.* -es, *pl.* -e, sea, ocean.
Meereswoge, *f.* wave, billow.
Mehl, *n.* -es, flour, meal; dust.
Mehr, *adj. & adv.* more. L. 22, 3.
Mehrere, *adj. pl.* several.
Meiden, P. 182, to avoid; shun.
Meinen, *v. a. & n.* to think, suppose.
Meinung, *f.* -, *pl.* -en, opinion, meaning; intention; mind.
Meißel, *m.* -s, *pl.* -, chisel.
Meist, *sup.* most, mostly. L. 22, 3.
Meister, *m.* -s, *pl.* -, master.
Melden, *v. a.* to announce, notify.
Mensch, *m.* -en, man; person.
Messen, P. 182, to measure; survey; compare.
Messer, *n.* -s, *pl.* -, knife.
Metall, *n.* -es, *pl.* -e, metal.
Milch, *f.* -, milk.
Minden, *n.* Minden.
Minister, *m.* -s, *pl.* -, minister.
Mißlingen, Mißlingen, *v. n.* P. 182, to go amiss, to fail.
Mißverstehen, stehen, P. 184, to misunderstand.
Mit, *pre.* with, by, at, upon, under, to.
Mittel. *n.* -s, *pl.* middle, medium; mean, means, expedient; remedy.
Mitten, *adv.* in the midst, in the middle of, in the heart of amidst.

Mo'de, *f.* -, *pl.* -n, mode, fashion.
Mö'gen, L. 31. & P. 182.
Mög'lich, *adj.* possible, visible; practicable.
Mo'nat, *m.*-es, *pl.*-e, month; moon.
Mond, *m.* -es, *pl.* -e, (-en), moon; month.
Mor'gen, *m.* -s, *pl.* -, morning; morn; Orient, East; *adv.* to-morrow; — früh, to-morrow morning.
Mü'de, *adj.* weary, tired, fatigued.
Mül'ler, *m.* -s, *pl.* -, miller.
Mün'chen, *n.* Munich.
Mun'ter, *adj.* awake; brisk, active.
Musik', *f.* -, *pl.* Mu'siken, music.
Mus'kel, *m.* -s, *pl.* -n, muscle.
Müs'sen, L. 31. & P. 182.
Muth, *m.* -es, courage, spirit; mood.
Mut'ter, *f.* -, *pl.* Mütter, mother.

N.

Nach, *pre.* after, behind, in, at, to, for, towards; upon; according to. L. 57.
Nach'bar, *m.* -s, *pl.* -n, neighbor.
Nachdem', *conj.* after, when.
Na'chen, *m.* -s, *pl.* -, boat, skiff.
Nach'folger, *m.* -s, *pl.* -, successor.
Nach'lässig, *adj.* negligent, careless, slovenly; inattentive.
Nach'richt, *f.* -, *pl.* -en, account, advice, intelligence, information, notice, tidings.
Nächst, *pre. & adv.* next, next to, closest; lately.
Näch'ste, L. 22, 3.; *m.* -n, *pl.* -n, neighbor, fellow-creature.
Nacht, *f.* -, *pl.* Nächte, night.
Nach'tigall, *f.* -, *pl.* -en, nightingale.
Na'gel, *m.* -s, *pl.* Nägel, nail; pin, peg.
Na'hern, *v. a. & r.* to bring near; approach, draw near.
Na'me, *m.* -ns, *pl.* -n, name; title; renown, reputation.

Nas'horn, *n.* rhinoceros.
Nation, *f.* -, *pl.* -en, nation.
Ne'bel, *m.* -s, *pl.* -, mist; fog.
Ne'ben, *pre.* by, near, beside, besides, by the side of, next to, close to, with.
Nebst, *pre.* together with, with, besides, including.
Neffe, *m.* -n, *pl.* -n, nephew.
Neh'men, P. 182, to take; receive
Neid, *m.* -es, envy, jealousy.
Nei'disch, *adj.* envious; grudging,
Nei'gung, *f.* -, *pl.* -en, inclination, proneness, disposition.
Nein, *adv.* no.
Nen'nen, P. 182, to name, denominate; call.
Nerv, *m.* -en, *pl.* -en, nerve; —enfieber, *n.* nervous fever.
Nest, *n.* -es, *pl.* -er, nest.
Neu, *adj.* new; fresh; recent, modern; aufs Neue, von Neuem, anew, afresh, again.
Neu'lich, *adj.* lately, recently.
Neun, L. 51. 14.
Neun'zig, see L. 51. 14.
Nicht, *adv.* not. L. 66.
Nichts, *pr.* nothing, naught.
Nie, *adv.* never, at no time.
Nie'der, *adj.* low, lower, nether, inferior; mean; *adv.* low, down, downwards.
Nie'derlage, *f.* -, *pl.* -en, defeat, overthrow; depot, warehouse.
Nie'derländer, *m.* Hollander.
Nie'derwerfen, L. 188, to throw down, prostrate.
Nie'mand, *pre.* nobody, no one
Noch, L. 66.
Nor'weger, *m.* Norwegian.
No'te, *f.* -, *pl.* -n, note.
Noth, *adj.* needful, necessary; es thut —, it is necessary; *f.* -, *pl.* Nöthen, need; distress; calamity.
Nur, *adv.* only, solely, but, ever
Nuß, *f.* -, *pl.* Nüsse, nut.
Nütz'lich, *adj.* useful, profitable.

O.

Ob, *conj.* whether, if; L. 58, als —, as if; *pre.* on, on account of; beyond.

Oberon, *m.* Oberon.

Obgleich, *conj.* though, although, notwithstanding.

Obst, *n.* -es, fruit, fruits; fruitage.

Ochs, Ochse, *m.* -fen, *pl.* -fen, ox; bull.

Oesterreich, *n.* Austria.

Oder, Oder, (river).

Oder, *conj.* or; or else; either, or.

Ofen, *m.* -s, *pl.* Oefen, stove.

Oeffnen, *v. a. & r.* to open.

Oft, *adv.* oft, often, frequently.

Oheim, *m.* -es, *pl.* -e, uncle.

Ohne, *pre. & adv.* without.

Oel, *n.* -es, *pl.* -e, oil.

Oper, *f.* -, *pl.* -n, opera.

Ordentlich, *adj.* orderly, regular.

Ort, *m.* -es, *pl.* -e, (Oerter), place.

Ost, *m.* -es, East.

Osten, *m.* -s, East.

Ostindien, *n.* East India.

P.

Paar, *n.* -es, *pl.* -e, pair, couple; a few.

Papier, *n.* -es, *pl.* -e, paper.

Paradiesvogel, *m.* bird of paradise.

Paris, *n.* Paris.

Paß, *m.* -sses, *pl.* Pässe, pass, passage, passport.

Passen, *v. n.* to fit, suit.

Peinigen, *v. a.* to torment, rack.

Perle, *f.* -, *pl.* -n, pearl.

Pest, *f.* -, *pl.* -en, pestilence, plague.

Pfaffe, *m.* -n, *pl.* -n, priest, parson.

Pfeffer, *m.* -s, pepper.

Pfeifen, P. 182, to pipe; whistle.

Pferd, *n.* -es, *pl.* -e, horse.

Pfirsiche, *f.* -, *pl.* -n, peach.

Pflanzen, *v. a.* to plant, set; *n.* -s, planting.

Pflaume, *f.* -, *pl.* -n, plum.

Pflegen, *v. a.* to take care of, nurse; attend to; *v. n.* to be accustomed, indulge.

Pflicht, *f.* -, *pl.* -en, duty; obligation.

Pflücken, *v. a.* to pluck, pick.

Pflug, *m.* -es, *pl.* Pflüge, plough.

Philipp, *m.* Philip.

Pinsel, *m.* -s, *pl.* -, paint-brush, pencil.

Plan, *m.* -es, *pl.* Pläne, plan, design.

Poliren, *v. a.* to polish.

Post, *f.* -, *pl.* -en, post, post-office; stage; intelligence, news.

Potsdam, *n.* Potsdam.

Prag, *n.* Prague.

Prahlen, *v. n.* to boast, brag.

Praktisch, practical.

Preisen, P. 182, to praise, commend; call.

Preßburg, *n.* Presburg.

Presse, *f.* -, *pl.* -n, press; dilemma.

Pressen, *v. a.* to press; oppress.

Preußen, *n.* Prussia.

Prinz, *m.* -en, *pl.* -en, prince.

Prometheus, *m.* Prometheus.

Protestant, *m.* -en, *pl.* -en, protestant.

Protestantisch, *adj.* protestant.

Pult, *n.* -es, *pl.* -e, desk.

Putzmacherin, *f.* milliner.

Q.

Quell, *m.* -s, *pl.* -en, source; well, fountain.

Quelle, *f.* -, *pl.* -n, well (f. Quell), spring, fountain.

R.

Rabe, *m.* -n, *pl.* -n, raven.

Rache, *f.* -, vengeance, revenge.

Rächen, *v. a.* to revenge, avenge: *v. r.* to revenge one's self, take vengeance.

Rang, *m.* -es, rank, order, rate, dignity, quality; row.

Rast, *f.* -, *pl.* -en, rest, repose; -los, *adj.* restless.

Rath, *m*. -es, counsel, advice; means, expedient; consultation, deliberation; court, council.
Ra'then, P. 182, to counsel, advice; guess.
Raubthier, *n*. beast of prey.
Rau'ben, *v. a.* to rob, prey, pillage.
Räu'ber, *m*. -s, *pl*. -, robber.
Rau'chen, *v. a. & n.* to smoke.
Raum, *m*. -es, *pl*. Räume, room, space.
Rech'nung, *f*. -, *pl*. -en, bill, calculation; account, computation.
Recht, *adj. & adv.* right; just; true, real; in right condition, legitimate; rightly, well, very.
Recht, *n*. -es, *pl*. -e, right; claim, title; privilege, immunity; law, justice.
Re'de, *f*. -, *pl*. -n, speech; harangue, oration; discourse; eine — halten, to make a speech.
Red'lichkeit, *f*. honesty, candor.
Reformation', *f*. -, *pl*. -en, reformation.
Re'gel, *f*. -, *pl*. -n, rule, principle.
Re'gen, *m*. -s, *pl*. -, rain; shower.
Regent', *m*. -en, *pl*. -en. regent.
Regiment', *n*. -s, *pl*. -er, regiment; government, power.
Rei'ben, P. 182, to rub, grate.
Reich, *adj*. rich, wealthy, opulent; *n*. -es. *pl*. -e, empire, realm.
Reichs'fürst, *m*. prince of the empire.
Reich'thum, *m*. -es, *pl*. -thümer, riches, *pl*. wealth.
Reif, *adj*. ripe, mature.
Rei'fen, *v. n.* to grow ripe, ripen; *v. imp*. to rime.
Rei'he, *f*. -, *pl*. -n, row; rank, file; range; order, series; turn.
Rein, *adj*. clean; pure; clear; innocent.
Rei'se, *f*. -, *pl*. -, journey, voyage.
Rei'sen, *v. n.* to travel, journey.
Rei'ten, P. 182, to ride, go on horseback.
Rei'ter, *m*. -s, *pl*. -, horseman.

Rei'zend, *adj*. charming.
Religion', *f*. -, *pl*. -en, religion.
Renuthier, *n*. rein-deer.
Republik', *f*. -, *pl*. -en, republic.
Rich'ter, *m*. s-, *pl*. -, judge, magistrate.
Rie'se, *m*. -n, *pl*. -n, giant.
Rie'senschlange, see Schlange, boaconstrictor.
Ring, *m*. -es, *pl*. -e, ring.
Rock, *m*. -es, *pl*. Röcke, coat.
Rom, Rome.
Rö'misch, roman.
Ro'se, *f*. -, *pl*. -n, rose.
Roth. *adj*. red.
Rubin', *m*. -es, *pl*. -e, ruby.
Ru'dolph, *m*. Rudolph.
Rück'zug, *m*. -es, *pl*. -züge, retreat.
Ru'fen, P. 184, to call, cry.
Ru'he, *f*. -. rest, repose, quiet; tranquillity, peace; sleep.
Ru'hig, *adj*. quiet, peacable.
Ruhm, *m*.-es. glory, renown, fame.
Rüh'men, *v. a.* to praise, glorify, extol; *v. r*. to glory in, boast of.
Rund, *adj*. round, rotund, circular.
Ruß'land, *n*. -s, Russia.
Rus'se, *m*. -n, Russian.

S.

Sa'che, *f*. -, *pl*. -n, thing, matter; affair, concern; business.
Sach'se, *m*. -n, Saxon.
Sach'sen, *n*. Saxony.
Sa'gen, *v. a. & n.* to say, tell; speak.
Salat', *m*. -es, *pl*. -e, salad.
Salz, *n*. -es. *pl*. -e, salt.
Sam'meln, *v. a.* to collect, gather.
Sam'met, *m*. -es, velvet.
Sammt, *pre*. together with.
Sand, *m*. -es, sand.
Sand'faß, *n*. sand-box.
Sanft, *adj*. soft, gentle, smooth, mild; —muth, —müthigkeit, *f* gentleness, mildness.
Sän'ger, *m*. -s, *pl*. -, singer.
Sardi'nien, *n*. Sardinia.

Sattel, m. -s, pl. Sättel, saddle.
Sattler, m. -s, pl. -, saddler.
Satz, m. -es, pl. Sätze, leap, jump; sediment; position, thesis; point; sentence, period; stake.
Saufen, P. 184, to drink (of beasts).
Scene, f. -, pl. -n, scene.
Schaden, v. n. to hurt, harm, damage, injure.
Schaf, n. -es, pl. -e, sheep.
Schaffen, P. 184, to create, call into existence, make, produce.
Schämen, v. r. to be ashamed.
Schande, f. -, shame, disgrace.
Scharf, adj. sharp; severe, strict.
Schatten, m. -s, pl. -, shadow, shade; phantom.
Schatz, m. -es, pl. Schätze, treasure.
Schätzen, v. a. to value, esteem.
Schau, f. -, show, view; review.
Schaufel, f. -, pl. -n, shovel.
Schäumen, v. a. to skim; v. n. to foam, froth.
Scheere, s. Schere.
Scheinen, P. 184, to shine; appear, seem.
Schelten, P. 184, to scold, chide.
Schenken, v. a. to pour, fill; give, make a present.
Schere, f. -, pl. -n, scissors, shears.
Scheren, P. 184, to shave (the beard); shear.
Schicken, v. a. & n. to send, dispatch.
Schießen, P. 184, to shoot; discharge; dart, rush.
Schiff, n. -es, pl. -e, ship, vessel; nave (of a church).
Schild, m. -es, pl. -e, shield, coat of arms; n. -es, pl. -er, signboard, sign; —kröte, f. turtle, tortoise.
Schinden, v. a. P. 184, to flay, skin.
Schlachtbank, f. slaughtering-bench; shambles.
Schlachten, v. a. to slaughter, kill.

Schlachtthier, n. fattened animal, animal whose flesh is used for food.
Schlafen, v. n. P. 184, to sleep, rest.
Schlag, m. -es, pl. Schläge, blow, stroke; kind, sort, stamp; apoplexy.
Schlagen, P. 184, to beat, strike, slay; coin; warble.
Schlange, f. -, pl. -n, serpent, snake.
Schlau, adj. sly, crafty, cunning.
Schlecht, adj. bad, base, mean.
Schleichen, P. 184, to sneak, slink; move slowly.
Schleifen, P. 184, to grind, polish, furbish.
Schließen, P. 184, to shut, lock, close; conclude.
Schlimm, adj. ill, bad, evil; sad; arch; sore; unwell.
Schloß, n. -sses, pl. Schlösser, lock; castle.
Schlüssel, m. -s, pl. -, key.
Schmach, f. ignominy, disgrace, blemish, outrage.
Schmecken, v. a. & n. to taste.
Schmeichelhaft, adj. flattering.
Schmelzen, P. 184, to melt, dissolve.
Schmerz, m. -es, pl. -en, pain, ache; fig. affliction, grief.
Schmied, m. -es, pl. -e, smith.
Schmieden, v. a. to forge; fetter, chain.
Schnee, m. -s, snow.
Schneiden, P. 184, to cut.
Schneider, m. -s, pl. -, tailor.
Schnell, adj. quick, swift, sudden.
Schon, adv. already; even.
Schön, adj. beautiful, fine, fair.
Schonen, v. a. to spare, save.
Schöpfung, f. -, pl. -n, creation.
Schreibpapier, n. writing-paper.
Schreiben, P. 184, to write.
Schreien, P. 184, to cry scream.
Schreiten, P. 184, to stride, step, stalk.
Schrift, f. -, pl. -en, writing; writ.

Schuh, m. -es, pl. -e, shoe.
Schuld, f.-, pl. -en, guilt; debt.
Schul'dig, adj. guilty; indebted.
Schul'digkeit, f -, pl.-en, duty, due; obligation.
Schu'le, f. -, pl. -n, school.
Schü'ler, m. -s, pl. —, scholar.
Schutz, m. -es, protection, guard.
Schwa'ben, n. Suabia.
Schwach, adj. weak, feeble, imbecile; faint.
Schwan, m. -es, pl. Schwäne, swan.
Schwan'ken, v. n. to stagger, fluctuate, waver; hesitate.
Schwarz, adj. black; dark.
Schwa'tzen' Schwä'tzen, v. n. to talk, prattle, prate, chatter.
Schwe'ben, v. n. to wave, to hang; to be suspended.
Schwe'de, m. -n, Swede.
Schwe'den, n. Sweden.
Schwebisch, Swedish.
Schwein, n. -es, pl. -e, swine, hog, pig.
Schwel'len, v. a. to swell, make swell, raise; v. n. P. 184, to swell, rise; heave.
Schwer, adj. heavy; difficult, hard; —muth, f. melancholy, sadness.
Schwer'lich, adv. hardly, scarcely.
Schwert, n. -es, pl. er, sword.
Schwe'ster, f. -, pl. -n, sister.
Schwie'rig, adj. hard, difficult.
Schwimm'vogel, m. swimming-bird.
Schwim'men, P. 184, to swim.
Schwö'ren, P. 186, to take an oath; swear; vow.
Schwur, n. -es, pl. Schwüre, oath.
Sclave ic., s. Sklave.
Sechs, see L. 51. 14.
Sech'zig, see L. 51, 14.
See'le, f. -, pl. -n, soul.
Se'geln, v. a. & n. to sail.
Se gen, m. -s, pl. -, blessing, benediction; bliss.
Se'hen, P. 186, to see, look, view, behold.

Sehr, adv. very, much, greatly, extremely, very much.
Sei'den, adj. silken.
Sei'fe. f. -, pl. -n, soap.
Sein, L. 32.
Sei'ne, Seine (river).
Seit, adv. & pre. since. L. 58.
Seitdem', adv. since.
Sei'te, f.-. pl. -n, side; page.
Selbst, pre. & adv. self, even. L. 29. 6.
Sel'ten, adj. rare, scarce, seldom.
Senf, m. -es, mustard.
Se'tzen, v. a. to set, put, place; v. n. to leap, pass over; v. r. to sit down; perch.
Seuf'zen, v. n. to sigh, groan.
Sie'ben, see L. 51. 14.
Sieg, m. -es, pl. -e, victory; —reich, adj. victorious, triumphant.
Sin'gen, P. 186, to sing, chant.
Sin'ken, P. 186, to sink.
Sinn, m. -es, pl. -e, sense; mind; intention; meaning, acceptation.
Sit'te, f. -, pl. -n, custom, manner; Sitten, pl. manners, morals.
Si'tzen, P. 186, to sit; to be imprisoned; fit.
Sklave, m. -n, pl. -n, slave.
Smaragd', m. -es, pl. -en, emerald.
So, adv. & conj. so, thus. L. 66.
So'fa, n. -s, pl. -s. sofa.
Sogar', adv. even; so much.
Sohn, m. -es, pl. Söhne, son.
Soldat', m. -en, pl. -en, soldier.
Söld'ner, m. -s, pl. -, mercenary.
Sol'len, L. 31.
Som'mer, m. -s, pl. -, summer.
Son'der, pre. without.
Son'dern, L. 16. 3.
Son'ne, f.-, pl. -n, sun; —schein, m. sunshine; —schirm, m. parasol.
Son'nig, adj. sunny, sun-shiny.
Sonn'tag, m. -es, pl. -e, Sunday.
Sonst, adv. else, otherwise, in other respects; besides, more-

ore.; at other times, formerly.
L. 67.
Sepha, f. Sefa.
Sor'ge, f. -, pl. -n, care, concern, sorrow; — tragen, to take care.
Sorg'fältig, adj. solicitous, careful
Spal'ten, v. a. & n. to split.
Spa'nisch, adj. Spanish.
Spa'nien, n. Spain.
Spa'zieren, v. n. to walk; — gehen, to take a walk. L. 35.
Spazier'gang, m. walk.
Speer, m. -es, pl. -e, spear, lance.
Spei'se, f. -, pl. -n, food; dish; meal.
Sper'ling, m. -es, pl. -e, sparrow.
Sphä're, f. -, pl. -n, sphere.
Spie'gel, m. -s, pl. -, looking-glass.
Spie'len, v. a. & n. to play; act.
Spin'nen, P. 186, to spin.
Spiz, spizig, adj. pointed.
Spi'ze, f. -, pl. -n, point, head.
Spi'zig, adj. pointed, sharp.
Spot'ten, v. a. to mock, deride.
Spra'che, f. -, pl. -n, language.
Spre'chen, P. 186, to speak, talk.
Sprich'wort, n. -es, pl. —wörter, proverb, adage, saying.
Sprin'gen, P. 186, to leap, spring.
Staar, m. -es, pl. -e, starling.
Staat, m. -es, pl. -en, state; —secretär, m. secretary of state.
Stadt, f. -, pl. Städte, town, city.
Stahl, n. -es, pl. Stähle, steel.
Stamm, m. -es, pl. Stämme, stock, trunk, stem, stalk; race, family.
Stand, m. -es, pl. Stände, stand, standing, position; state, estate.
Stark, adj. strong, stout, robust.
Stär'ke, f. -, pl. -en, strength, force.
Starr, adj. stiff; numb, benumbed; inflexible, obstinate; staring.
Statt, f. -, place, stead; —finden, to take place; pre. & adv. instead of.
Staub, m. -es, dust, powder; sich aus dem — machen, to run away
—wolke, f. cloud of dust.

Stechen, v. a. & n. P. 186, to sting, prick.
Ste'hen, P. 186, to stand, remain, stop; es steht bei Ihnen, it depends upon you; es steht ihm gut, that becomes him well.
Steh'len, P. 186, to steal, pilfer.
Stei'gen, P. 186, to mount, ascend, descend. See L. 38. 4.
Steil' adj. steep.
Stein, m. -es, pl. -e, stone, rock; chessman, man, pawn.
Stel'le, f. -, pl. -n, place, stand spot; situation; office.
Ster'ben, P. 186, to die, decease.
Sterb'lich, adj. mortal; desperate.
Stern, m. -es, pl. -e, star.
Stim'me, f. -, pl. -n, voice.
Stock, m. -es, pl. Stöcke, stick, cane.
Stolz, adj. proud, haughty. m. -es, pride, haughtiness, arrogance.
Stra'fe, f. -, pl -n, punishment, correction, penalty, fine.
Strauß, m. -es, pl. Sträuße, ostrich.
Streit, m. -es, combat, fight; —süchtig, adj. litigious, contentious.
Strei'ten, P. 186, to fight, contend, litigate.
Streng, adj. rough, strict, rigorous, severe, rigid, hard.
Strom, m. -es, pl. Ströme, stream, torrent; flood; current.
Stück, n. -es, pl. -e, piece, head.
Studi'ren, v. a. to study.
Stuhl, m. -es, pl. Stühle, chair, stool, seat, pew.
Stun'de, f. -, pl. -n, hour, lesson.
Sturm, m. -es, pl. Stürme, storm, alarm, tumult; assault.
Stür'zen, v. a. & n. to throw, precipitate; overthrow; fall, rush.
Su'chen, v. a. to seek, search, look for; try.
Sud, m. -es, south.
Sü'den, m. -s, south.
Süß, adj. sweet; **fresh.**

T.

Ta'del, *m.* -ß, fault, blame.
Ta'deln, *v. a.* to blame, censure.
Tag, *m.* -es, *pl.* -e, day; —löhner, *m.* day-laborer.
Täg'lich, Tagtäg'lich, *adj.* daily.
Talent', *n.* -es, *pl.* -e, talent.
Tan'ne, *f.* -, *pl.* -n, fir, fir-tree; pine.
Tan'te, *f.* -, *pl.* -n, aunt.
Tan'zen, *v. a. & n.* to dance.
Tap'fer, *adj.* valiant, brave, gallant.
Ta sche, *f.* -, *pl.* -n, pocket; —ntuch, *n.* pocket-handkerchief.
Tas'se, *f.* -, *pl.* -n, cup, saucer, dish.
Taub, *adj.* deaf; *fig.* empty.
Tau'be, *f.* -, *pl.* -n, dove, pigeon.
Tau'chen, *v. a. & n.* to dive, duck, dip, immerge, plunge.
Tau'cher, *m.* -ß, *pl.* -, diver.
Täu'schen, *v. a.* to delude, deceive, disappoint, cheat.
Tau'send, L. 51. 14.
Tell, *m.* Tell.
Tep'pich, *m.* -es, *pl.* -e, carpet.
Teu'fel, *m.* -ß, *pl.* -, devil.
Thal, *n.* -es, *pl.* Thäler, vale, valley.
Tha'ler, *m.* -ß, *pl.* -, thaler.
That, *f.* -, *pl.* -en, deed, action, fact.
Thee, *m.* -ß, tea.
Theresia, *f.* Therese.
Theu'er, *adj.* dear, costly.
Thier, *n.* -es, *pl.* -e, animal, beast.
Thor'heit, *f.* -, *pl.* -en, folly.
Thö'richt, *adj.* foolish, silly.
Thun, P. 186, to do, perform, act; es thut nichts, it is no matter, es thut Noth, it is necessary; es thut mir leid, I am sorry; weh —, to hurt.
Thür, *f.* -, *pl.* -en, door.
Ti'ber, Tiber.
Tief', *adj.* deep, low; profound; high.
Tie'ger, Ti'ger, *m.* -es, *pl.* -, tiger.

Til'ly, *m.* -ß, Tilly.
Tin'te, *f.* -, *pl.* -n, ink; tint; —nfaß, ink-stand.
Tisch, *m.* -es, *pl.* -e, table; board.
Tisch'ler, *m.* -ß, *pl.* -, cabinet-maker.
To'ben, *v. n.* to rage, to din.
Toch'ter, *f.* -, *pl.* Töchter, daughter.
Tod, *m.* -es, death, disease.
Todt, *adj.* dead; lifeless.
Tod'tengruft, *f.* vault for the dead.
Ton, *m.* -es, *pl.* Töne, sound, tone; accent; stress, fashion.
Trä'ge, *adj.* idle, lazy, slothful.
Tra'gen, P. 186, to bear, carry, wear; produce, yield; suffer; support.
Trau'en, *v. n.* to trust, confide in, have confidence in.
Trau'ern, *v. n.* to be in mourning; grieve, to be afflicted.
Trau'rig, *adj.* sad, sorrowful.
Tref'fen, P. 186, to hit; strike; hit off; befal, meet.
Trei'ben, P. 186, to drive; put in motion; perform; float along.
Tre'ten, P. 186, to tread, step; move.
Treu, *adj.* faithful, trusty, true.
Treu'e, *f.* -, fidelity, faithfulness.
Trin'ken, P. 186, to drink.
Tro'cken, *adj.* dry, arid; barren; cold.
Tro'ja, *n.* Troy.
Trom'mel, *f.* -, *pl.* -n, drum.
Trö'sten, *v. a.* to comfort, console.
Trö'ster, *m.* -ß, *pl.* -, comforter.
Tro'tzen, *v. n.* to dare, brave, defy.
Tuch, *n.* -es, *pl.* Tücher, cloth; handkerchief, neckcloth.
Tu'gend, *f.* -, *pl.* -en, virtue.
Tür'ke, *m.* -n, Turk.

U.

Ue'bel, *adj. & adv.* evil, ill, bad, badly; wrong; sick sickly; — wollen, to bear a grudge.
Ue'ben, *v. a.* to exercise, practise; execute, do.
Ue'ber, *pre. & adv.* over, above. L.59.

Ue'berdrüſſig, *adj.* tired, wearied, satiated, disgusted.

Ueberei'lung, *f.* -, *pl.* -en, precipitation, hastiness; error committed from hurry.

Ue'berführen, *v. a.* to lead over; transport; Ueberfüh'ren, *v. a.* to convict, convince. L. 40, 2.

Uebergeʹben, *v. a. ir.* to surrender, deliver; *v. r.* to surrender; retch, vomit.

Ueberle'gen, *adj.* superior.

Ue'bermorgen, *adv.* day after tomorrow.

Ue'bermüthig, *adj.* haughty, insolent.

Uebernach'ten, *v. n.* to pass, or spend the night.

Uebernehʹmen (see nehmen, P.182), to receive, accept; undertake.

Ueberzeuʹgen, *v. a.* to convince.

Ueberzeuʹgung, *f.* -, *pl.* -en, conviction.

Ueberzie'hen, *v. a. ir.* to cover; *fig.* to invade.

Ue'bung, *f.* -, *pl.* -en, exercise, exercising; practising, practice.

U'fer, *n.* -s, *pl.* -, shore, coast, bank.

Uhr, *f.* -, *pl.* -en, clock, watch; wie viel — iſt es? what time is it? L. 54, Note.

Um, *pre. adv. & conj.* about, round, near; at, for, by; past. L. 60.

Um — willen, L. 48, 5.

Um'bringen, *v. a.* to kill, murder.

Umhinʹ, *adv.* about; ich kann nicht —, I cannot forbear; I cannot help. L. 31.

Um'kommen, *v. n. ir.* to perish, die.

Umſonſtʹ, *adv.* gratis, without pay, for nothing; in vain, vainly, to no purpose; without cause.

Um'ſtand, *m.* -es, *pl.* -ſtände, circumstance; condition.

Un'angenehm, *adj.* unpleasant, disagreeable.

Un'aufmerkſam, *adj.* inattentive.

Un'bändig, *adj.* indomitable, unmanageable, intractable.

Und, *conj.* and.

Un'dankbar, *adj.* ungrateful.

Un'eingedenk, *adj.* unmindful.

Un'ermeßlich, *adj.* immeasurable, immense, vast.

Unermüd'lich, *adj.* indefatigable.

Un'erträglich, Unerträg'lich, *adj.* intolerable, insufferable, insupportable.

Un'gar, *m.* -n, Hungarian.

Un'gariſch, *adj.* Hungarian.

Un'garn, *n.* Hungary.

Un'geduld, *f.* -, impatience.

Un'gemach, *n.* -es, discomfort, fatigue, adversity, calamity.

Un'gewohnt, *adj.* unaccustomed.

Un'glück, *n.* -es, misfortune; disaster; adversity, calamity.

Un'glücklich, *adj.* unlucky, unhappy, unfortunate; disastrous.

Un'höflich, *adj.* uncivil, impolite.

Univerſitätʹ, *f.* -, *pl.* -en, university.

Un'kraut, *n.* -es, weed, tare.

Un'möglich, *adj.* impossible.

Un'recht, *adj.* wrong; unjust; *n.* -es, wrong; injustice.

Un'ſchuldig, *adj.* innocent, guiltless.

Un'ſicher, *adj.* insecure, unsafe; uncertain, dubious.

Un'ſichtbar, *adj.* invisible.

Unſterblich, *adj.* immortal.

Un'ter, *pre.* under; below, beneath; among, amongst, between, betwixt, amid, amidst. L. 61.

Unterdrü'cken, *v. a.* to oppress.

Un'tergehen, *v. n. ir.* to go down; set; perish.

Unternehʹmen, *v. a.* to undertake, attempt.

Unterre'dung, *f.* -, *pl.* -en, conference, conversation, discourse.

Un'terſchied *m.* -es, *pl.* -e, difference, distinction.

Un'terthan, *adj.* subject to, de-

pendent; *m.* -en, *pl.* -en, subject.
Unterwer'fen, *v. a. ir.* to submit, subdue.
Un'treu, *adj.* unfaithful, faithless.
Un'vergeßlich, *adj.* memorable not capable of being forgotten.
Un'verstand, *m.* -es, want of judgment, want of sense, want of wit.
Un'wissenheit, *f.* -, ignorance.
Unzähl'bar, *adj.* innumerable.
Unzähl'lig, see Unzählbar.
Un'zufrieden, *adj.* discontent, discontented, dissatisfied.
Ur'sache, *f.* -, *pl.* -n, cause, reason.
Ur'theil, *n.* -es, *pl.* -e, judgment, decision, sentence, verdict.

V.

Va'ter, *m.* -s, *pl.* Väter, father.
Bene'dig, *n.* Venice.
Verach'ten, *v. a.* to despise, scorn.
Verän'derung, *f.* -, *pl.* -en, change, alteration, variation.
Verbin'den, *v. a. ir.* to bind up, tie up; unite, join; oblige.
Verbot', *n.* -es, *pl.* -e, prohibition.
Verbre'chen, *n.* -s, *pl.* -, crime.
Verbre'cher, *m.* -s *pl.* -, criminal.
Verbrin'gen, *v. a. ir.* to spend, consume.
Verbün'dete, *m.* -n, ally.
Verdacht', *m.* -es, suspicion.
Verdäch'tig, *adj.* suspected, suspicious.
Verder'ben, P. 186, to corrupt, render unfit, spoil.
Verdie'nen, *v. a.* to gain; earn; merit, deserve.
Verdienst', *m.* -es, gain, profit; *n.* -es *pl.* -e, merit, desert.
Verdienst'voll, *adj.* meritorious.
Verdient', *adj.* merited, deserved.
Verdrie'ßen, *v. imp.* P. 186, to grieve, cause disgust, trouble.
Vered'lung, *f.* *pl.* -en, improvement.
Vereh'ren, *v. a.* to honor, venerate; revere; adore.

Verei'nigen, *v. a.* to unite.
Verei'nigt, united.
Verei'nigung, *f.* -, *pl.* -en, union, association, alliance, agreement.
Verfah'ren, *v. n. ir.* to deal, proceed.
Verseh'len, *v. a.* to miss, fail.
Vergan'gen, *adj.* gone, past; last.
Verge'hen, *v. n. ir.* to pass away, vanish; decay; perish.
Verges'sen, P. 186, to forget.
Vergnügen, *n.* -s, *pl.* -, pleasure, diversion.
Verhaf'ten, *v. a.* to arrest, imprison.
Verhaßt, *adj.* hated, hateful.
Verhin'dern, *v. a.* to hinder, prevent, impede, cross.
Verkau'fen, *v. a.* to sell, vend.
Verkehr', *m.* -es, intercourse, commerce, traffic, communication.
Verlan'gen, *v. a. & n.* to ask, demand; desire, long for; es verlangt mich zu wissen, I long to know; *n.* -s, desire, demand.
Verlas'sen, *v. a. ir.* to leave, forsake; *v. r. ir.* auf einen —, to rely upon, depend on; *adj.* destitute, abandoned.
Verle'gen, to misplace; to publish; *adj.* embarassed, puzzled, confused.
Verle'genheit, *f.* -, *pl.* -en, embarrassment, perplexity, difficulty.
Verlei'ten, *v. a.* to mislead, misguide; seduce.
Verlie'ren, P. 186, to lose.
Ver'lust, *m.* -es, *pl.* -e, loss; damage.
Vermei'den, *v. a. ir.* to avoid, shun.
Vermö'gen, *v. a. & n. ir.* to be able, to have the power; einen zu etwas —, to prevail upon one to do; *n.* -s, ability, power, faculty, property, wealth.
Vernunft', *f.* -, reason; sense.
Vernünf'tig, *adj.* rational, reasonable; sensible, judicious, discreet.

Verpflich'ten, *v. a.* to bind by duty or oath ; to oblige.
Verrath', *m.* -es, treason.
Verrä'ther, *m.* -s, *pl.* -, traitor.
Versa'gen, *v. a. & n.* to deny, refuse ; miss fire, fail.
Versam'meln, *v. a. r.* to assemble, meet, congregate.
Verschal'len, *v. n. ir.* to cease sounding, die away.
Verschwen'derisch, *adj.* prodigal, lavish, profuse, wasteful.
Verschwin'den, *v. n. ir.* to disappear, vanish.
Verspre'chen, *v. a. ir.* to promise.
Verstän'dig, *adj.* sensible, intelligent, judicious.
Verste'hen, *v. a. & n. ir.* to understand ; apprehend, mean.
Verstel'lung, *f.* -, *pl.* -en, dissimulation.
Versu'chen, *v. a.* to try, attempt, experience ; taste ; tempt.
Verthei'digen, *v. a.* to defend.
Vertrei'ben, *v. a. ir.* to drive away, chase, expel.
Verwan'dte, *m. & f.* -n, *pl.* -n, relation, kin, kinsman.
Verwerflich, *adj.* blamable, objectionable, exceptionable.
Verwun'den, *v. a.* to wound.
Verzei'hen, (see zeihen, P. 188), to pardon, forgive, excuse.
Verzei'hung, *f.* pardon.
Vet'ter, *m.* -s, *pl.* -n, cousin.
Vieh, *n.* -es, beast, brute, cattle ; —händler, *m.* dealer or trader in cattle.
Viel, *ad. & adv.* much, many, a great deal ; —mehr, *adv. & conj.* more, much more ; rather.
Vielleicht', *adj.* perhaps, possibly, may be.
Vier, L. 51, 14 ; —mal, L. 51, 10.
Vier'tel, L. 51. 5.
Vierzehn, L. 51, 14.
Vierzig, L. 51, 14.
Vo'gel, *m.* -s, *pl.* Vögel, bird, fowl.
Vö'gelchen, L. 18.

Vogt, *m.* -es, *pl.* Vögte, bailiff, steward ; prefect ; constable, beadle.
Volk, *n.* -es, *pl.* Völker, people, nation.
Voll, *adj.* full, whole ; entire.
Vollen'den, *v. a.* to end, finish, accomplish ; perfect.
Vollkommen, Vollkom'men, *adj.* perfect, accomplished ; complete.
Von, *pre.* of, from, by, on, upon. L. 61.
Vor, *pre.* before ; from, of, ago, since ; in preference to L. 61.
Vor'dertheil, *n.* forepart ; head.
Vor'gestern, *adv.* day before yesterday.
Vor'haben, *v. a. ir.* to design, intend, purpose.
Vo'rig, *adj.* former, last.
Vor'mund, *m.* -es, *pl.* -münder, guardian.
Vor'setzen, *v. a.* to set before place or put before ; prefix.
Vor'stellung, *f.* -, *pl.* -en, presentation ; representation ; remonstrance.
Vor'theil, *m.* -es, *pl.* -e, advantage, profit, gain, interest.

W.

Waa're, *f.* -, *pl.* -n, ware, merchandise, commodity, goods.
Wa'chen, *v. n.* to be awake, watch, guard.
Wachsen, P. 188, to grow, increase.
Wachs'thum, *m. & n.* -es, growth ; increase, vegetation.
Waffen, *pl.* arms, weapons.
Wa'gen, *m.* -s, *pl.* -, wagon, carriage, chariot ; coach.
Wag'ner, *m.* -s, *pl.* -, wagon-maker.
Wahr, *adj.* true, genuine.
Wäh'rend, *pre. & conj.* during, while.
Wahr'heit, *f.* -, *pl.* -en, truth, verity.

Wald, m. -es, pl. Wälder, forest, wood; —horn, n. French-horn, bugle horn.
Wallenstein, m. Wallenstein.
Wand, f. -, pl. Wände, wall; side.
Wandern, v. n. to wander.
Wann, adv. when; dann und —, now and then, some times.
Warm, adj. & adv. warm, hot.
Waschtisch, m. washstand.
Warten, v. a. & n. to stay, attend to; nurse; wait.
Warum', adv. why, wherefore.
Was, pre. what. L. 10, 2.
Waschen, v. a. & n. P. 188, to wash.
Wasser, n. -s, pl. Wasser, water.
Weben, v. a. P. 188, to weave; work.
Wechsel, m. -s, pl. -, vicissitude, change; bill of exchange.
Wecken, v. a. to wake, to awake.
Weder, conj. neither.
Weg, m. -es, pl. -e, way, passage, walk, road; manner, means.
Wegen, pre. because of, on account of, for, by reason of.
Wegfliegen, v. n. ir. to fly away.
Weglaufen, v. n. ir. to run away.
Wegnehmen, v. a. to take away.
Weh, adj. & conj. sore, painful; — thun, to ache, pain; hurt.
Weich, adj. soft, tender, weak.
Weide, f. -, pl. -n, willow.
Weigern, v. a. & r. to refuse, deny, decline.
Weil, adv. & conj. while, during, as, as long as, when; because, since.
Wein, m. -es, pl. -e, wine; vine.
Weinen, v. n. to weep, cry.
Weise, adj. wise, sage.
Weise, f. -, pl. -n. mode, manner, way, fashion, method; melody, tune.
Weisheit, f. -, wisdom, prudence.
Weiß, adj. white; clean.
Weit, adj. & adv. distant, remote, far, far off, afar; wide, large.
Weizen, m. -s, wheat.

Welle, f. -, pl. -n, wave, billow.
Welt, f. -, pl. -en, world.
Weltberühmt, adj. far-famed.
Weltmeer, n. ocean.
Wenig, adj. & adv. little, few, some; ein —, a little.
Wenigstens, adv. at least, at the least.
Wenn, adv. & conj. if, in which case, when, whenever.
Werden, v. n. ir. L. 32, 3, to become, grow, turn, be, prove; happen.
Werfen, P. 188, to throw, cast.
Werk. n. -es, pl. -e, work; action, deed; workmanship; building.
Weser, f. Weser.
Weserstrom, m. Weser-river, river Weser.
Wider, pre. against, contrary to, in opposition to.
Widerstand, m. -es, resistance.
Widerstehen, v. a. n. ir. to resist, withstand.
Widerstreben, v. n. to strive against, struggle against.
Widrig, adj. contrary, adverse; repugnant, loathsome.
Wie, adv. & conj. how, as. L. 67, 3.
Wiedehopf, m. -es, pl. -e, lapwing.
Wiederschein, m. reflection.
Wiedersehen, v. a. ir. to see again.
Wiege, f. -, pl. -n, cradle.
Wien, n. Vienna.
Wiese, f. -, pl. -n, meadow.
Wieviel'ste, L. 51, 13.
Wild, adj. wild, savage; fierce.
Wille, m. -ns, will, mind, design, purpose.
Wind, m. -es, pl. -e, wind, air.
Winden, P. 188, to wind, wring, twist; v. r. ir. to wind, writhe.
Winter, m. -s, pl. -, winter.
Wirklich, adj. actual, real, true.
Wirth, m. -es, pl. -e, host, landlord, innkeeper; master of the house.
Wissen, P. 188, to know, have knowledge of.

Wo, *odv.* where.
Woche, *f.* -, *pl.* -n, week.
Wohin', *adv.* whither, what way.
Wohl. *adv.* well; indeed; probably; L. 67; —thätig, *adj.* beneficent, charitable.
Wohnen, *v. n.* to lodge, dwell, abide, reside.
Wolf, *m.* -es, *pl.* Wölfe, wolf.
Wolke, *f.* -, *pl.* -n, cloud.
Wölkchen, *dim. of* Wolke.
Wolle, *f.* -, wool.
Wollen, L. 31.
Wonach', whereafter, after which.
Worauf', *adv.* whereon, whereupon, on which.
Worin'. *adv.* wherein, whereinto, in which, in what.
Wornach', *s.* Wonach.
Wort, *n.* -es. *pl.* -e (Wörter), word; expression, term, parole.
Wörterbuch, *n.* -es, *pl.* —bücher, dictionary, lexicon, vocabulary.
Wundarzt, *m.* surgeon.
Würdig, *adj.* worthy, deserving.
Würdigen, *v. a.* to deign, vouchsafe ; value, estimate.
Wurm, *m.* -es, *pl.* Würmer, worm.
Würze, *f.*-, *pl.*-n, seasoning, spice.
Wüste, *f.* -, *pl.* -n, desert.
Wüthen, *v. n.* to rage, chafe, foam, rave.

Z.

Zehen, see zehn. L. 51, 14.
Zeigen. *v. a.* to show, point out.
Zeit, *f.*-, *pl.*-en, time, season; tide.
Zeitung, *f.* -, *pl.* -en, news, tidings. *pl.*; newspaper, gazette.
Zerbrechen. *v. a. & n. ir.* to break to pieces, fracture ; sich den Kopf —, to rack one's brains.
Zerstören, *v. a.* to destroy ; demolish.
Zertreten, *v. a. ir.* to crush by treading on, tread down.
Ziehen, *v. a. & n. ir.* to draw; pull ; cultivate ; to go, march, migrate.

Ziel, *n* -es, *pl.*-e, term, limit ; aim, butt, scope.
Ziemlich, *adj.* pretty, tolerable, middling ; near.
Zimmer, *n.* -s, *pl.* -, room, appartment ; —mann, *m.* carpenter.
Zittern, *v. n.* to tremble, quake.
Zu, *pre. & adv.* at, by, to, for, in, on. L. 62.
Zucker, *m.* -s, sugar.
Zuflucht, *f.* -, refuge, shelter, recourse.
Zufrieden, *adj.* content, contented, satisfied.
Zugehören, *v. n.* to appertain, belong to.
Zugthier, draught animal.
Zukommen, *v. n. ir.* to come to, approach ; *v. imp.* to belong to; become.
Zuletzt', *adv.* at last, lastly, after all, finally.
Zumachen, *v. a.* to shut, close.
Zürnen, *v. n.* to be angry.
Zurück', *adv.* back, backward.
Zusammenziehen, *v. a. ir.* to draw together ; contract.
Zutragen, *v. a. ir.* to carry to, to bring ; *v. r. ir.* to happen, chance, come to pass.
Zuvorkommen, *v. n. ir.* to anticipate ; prevent, obviate.
Zuweilen, *adv.* sometimes.
Zuwider, *pre. & adv.* contrary to, against ; offensive.
Zwanzig. L. 51, 14.
Zwanzigste, L. 51, 14.
Zwar, *conj.* certainly, it is true, to be sure, indeed.
Zwei. L. 51 ;—mal, *adv.* twice.
Zweite, L. 51, 14.
Zwiefach, L. 51.
Zwingen. P. 188, to constrain, force, compel.
Zwischen, *pre. p.* between, betwixt, among, amongst.
Zwo. *s.* Zwei.
Zwölf, see L. 51, 14.

A.

Able, fähig, geschickt, see können, L. 31.
Above, oben, über.
Accompany, begleiten.
Accomplish, ausführen, ausrichten.
According, nach, gemäß, zufolge,
— as, je nachdem.
Account, die Rechnung; on — of, wegen; auf Abschlag.
Accuse, anflagen, beschuldigen.
Achieve, vollenden, erwerben.
Acquaintance, die Bekanntschaft; der Bekannte.
Acquainted, bekannt, vertraut, kundig.
Across, kreuzweise, über, querüber.
Act, handeln, sich benehmen.
Action, die Handlung.
Adapt, sich schicken.
Adherent, anhängend; Anhänger.
Advice, der Rath; Nachricht.
Advise, rathen.
Affair, das Geschäft, die Sache.
Afraid, furchtsam, bange, to be —, fürchten.
After, nach, nachdem; —noon, der Nachmittag.
Ago, vor.
Again, wieder, noch einmal.
Against, wider, gegen.
Agreeable, angenehm.
Ail, schmerzen; what ails you? was fehlt Ihnen?
Aim, das Ziel, der Zweck, die Absicht; zielen.
All, alles, ganz; überhaupt, L. 10. 9.
Allow, erlauben, gestatten, lassen.
Almost, fast, beinahe.
Alone, allein.
Already, bereits, schon.
Also, auch, gleichfalls.
Although, obgleich.
Always, immer, stets.
America, (das) Amerika.
American, amerikanisch, Amerikaner.
Among, unter, zwischen.
Anchor, der Anker.
Ancient, alt.
Angry, zornig, ärgerlich, böse.

Animal, das Thier.
Another, ein anderer; noch einer.
Answer, die Antwort; antworten.
Anvil, der Amboß.
Any, —body, Jemand, L. 52. 6.
—thing, etwas.
Any one, Jemand, irgend Jemand.
Ape, der Affe.
Apple, der Apfel.
Appear, erscheinen.
Arab, der Araber.
Arm, der Arm.
Army, die Armee, das Kriegsheer.
Around, herum; um, umher.
Arrival, die Zukunft.
Arrive, ankommen.
Artist, der Künstler.
As, als, da, weil, wie, so.
Ashamed (to be), sich schämen.
Asleep, eingeschlafen.
Assist, beistehen, helfen.
Assistance, der Beistand, die Hilfe.
At, zu, an, bei, in, auf, über, vor, aus, mit, gegen; — all, L. 10. 9.
Attendant, der Begleiter, die Begleiterin.
Attentive, aufmerksam.
August, der August.
Aunt, die Muhme, Tante.
Australia, Australien.
Austria, Oestreich or Oesterreich.
Autumn, der Herbst.
Avail, helfen, nützen, sich bedienen.
Avoid, meiden, vermeiden.
Away, weg, fort.
Axe, die Art, das Beil.

B.

Bad, schlecht, böse, schädlich.
Baker, der Bäcker.
Ball, der Ball, das Tanzfest.
Barley, die Gerste.
Barrel, das Faß, die Tonne.
Basket, der Korb.
Battle, die Schlacht.
Bavaria, Bayern.
Bavarian, der Bayer, baierisch.
Bear, der Bär; ertragen, gebären.
Beast, das Thier; — of burden Lastthier; — of prey, Raubthier

Beat, schlagen, klopfen.
Beautiful, schön.
Beaver, der Biber.
Because, weil, deßwegen.
Become, werden, sich schicken, geziemen.
Bed, das Bett.
Bee, die Biene.
Beef, das Rindfleisch.
Beer, das Bier.
Before, vor, bevor, ehe; vorn, vorher, bereits, früher.
Beggar, der Bettler.
Begin, beginnen, anfangen.
Behavior, das Betragen.
Behind, hinter, hinten, zurück.
Being, das Dasein, Wesen.
Believe, glauben.
Belong, gehören, angehören.
Below, unter.
Bench, die Bank.
Beneath, unter.
Benefactor, der Wohlthäter.
Benevolent, wohlwollend, wohlthätig.
Beside, Besides, neben, außer; außerdem; to be — one's self, außer sich sein.
Besiege, belagern.
Between, zwischen, unter.
Beyond, über, jenseits, außer, hinaus.
Bird, der Vogel.
Birth, die Geburt, Herkunft.
Bite, beißen.
Bitter, bitter.
Black, schwarz; dunkel; —smith, der Grobschmied.
Blame, tadeln; der Tadel.
Bleat, blöken.
Blessing, der Segen; die Wohlthat.
Blind, blind.
Blue, blau.
Boast, groß thun, prahlen, sich rühmen.
Bohemian, der Böhme.
Book, das Buch.
Boot, der Stiefel.
Bough, der Ast.

Boundless, grenzenlos, unbegrenzt.
Boy, der Knabe.
Braid, flechten, weben.
Branch, der Zweig, Ast.
Brave, tapfer, brav; edel.
Bread, das Brod.
Break, brechen, zerbrechen.
Breastpin, die Brustnadel.
Bremen, Bremen.
Brewer, der Brauer.
Bridge, die Brücke.
Bring, bringen.
Broad, breit, weit, groß.
Brother, der Bruder; — in law, der Schwager.
Brunswick, Braunschweig.
Bud, die Knospe, das Auge.
Burdensome, lästig.
Burn, brennen.
Bury, begraben.
But, aber, sondern, außer, nur, als.
Buy, kaufen.
By, von, durch, zu, nach, mit, für, neben, bei, auf.

C.

Cabinetmaker, der Tischler.
Cage, der Käfig.
Call, rufen, nennen.
Camel, das Kameel.
Can, die Kanne; können, im Stande sein.
Candle, das Licht, die Kerze; —stick, der Leuchter.
Cane, der Stock, das Rohr.
Cap, die Kappe, Mütze.
Capable, fähig, tüchtig.
Captain, der Hauptmann, Kapitain.
Care, die Sorge, Sorgfalt; to take —, Sorge tragen; pflegen.
Careful, vorsichtig, behutsam.
Carlsruhe, Karlsruhe.
Carpenter, der Zimmermann.
Carriage, der Wagen.
Cat, die Katze.
Catch, fangen, ergreifen.
Cattle, das Vieh.
Cause, die Ursache, Sache; verursachen, bewirken.

Certain, gewiß, zuverlässig; gewißlich.
Chain, die Kette; fesseln.
Chair, der Stuhl, Sessel.
Chamois, die Gemse.
Charge, übertragen, setzen.
Charm, bezaubern, reizen.
Charming, reizend.
Cheat, betrügen.
Cheese, der Käse.
Child, das Kind.
Chisel, der Meißel.
Christian, der Christ.
Church, die Kirche.
Circumstance, der Umstand, die Lage.
Citizen, der Bürger.
City, die Stadt.
Climb, klimmen, klettern; ersteigen.
Cloak, der Mantel.
Clock, die Wanduhr.
Cloth, das Zeug, Tuch.
Cloud, die Wolke.
Coat, der Rock.
Coblenz, Coblenz.
Coffee, der Kaffee.
Cold, kalt, frostig; die Kälte.
Cologne, Köln.
Colonel, der Oberst.
Color, Farbe.
Come, kommen. P. 182, gelangen.
Command, der Befehl, befehlen, gebieten.
Commerce, der Handel, Verkehr.
Commit, begehen.
Companion, der Gefährte, Gesellschafter.
Company, die Gesellschaft, der Besuch.
Compel, nöthigen, zwingen.
Complain, sich beklagen.
Complete, vollständig; gänzlich, ganz.
Conceal, verbergen.
Concert, das Concert.
Conduct, die Aufführung, das Betragen.
Conqueror, der Eroberer.
Conscious, bewußt.

Consequent, folgend; folglich.
Consider, bedenken, achten; halten
Consumption, die Auszehrung.
Contented, zufrieden.
Contradict, widersprechen.
Convict, überführen.
Convince, überzeugen.
Cook, der Koch, die Köchin.
Copy, abschreiben.
Cost, kosten.
Count, Graf; zählen.
Country, das Land.
Courage, der Muth, die Tapferkeit.
Course, der Lauf; of —, natürlich, ohne Zweifel.
Cousin, der Vetter, die Cousine.
Cover, decken, bedecken.
Cow, die Kuh.
Crawl, kriechen, schleichen.
Creep, kriechen.
Crime, das Verbrechen.
Crocodile, das Krokodill.
Cruel, grausam, unmenschlich.
Crutch, die Krücke.
Custom, der Gebrauch, die Sitte.
Cut, der Schnitt, schneiden, hauen.

D.

Dagger, der Dolch.
Dane, der Däne.
Danger, die Gefahr.
Dangerous, gefährlich.
Danube, die Donau.
Daughter, die Tochter; — in law, die Schwiegertochter.
Day, der Tag; to-day, heute; — before yesterday, vorgestern.
Dead, todt.
Deaf, taub.
Deal, der Theil; a great —, sehr viel.
Dear, theuer, werth.
Death, der Tod.
Deceive, betrügen, hintergehen, täuschen.
Decrease, abnehmen, schwinden.
Deed, die That.
Deep, tief.
Defeat, überwinden, schlagen.
Defend, vertheidigen.

Deficient, mangelhaft; he is —in, es mangelt ihm an. L. 44.
Defy, Trotz bieten, trotzen; verschmähen.
Deliberate, berathschlagen, sich besinnen.
Demand, die Forderung; das Verlangen.
Demosthenes, Demosthenes.
Departure, die Abreise.
Deprive, berauben, um ... bringen.
Description, die Beschreibung.
Desert, verlassen, weglaufen.
Deserve, verdienen.
Desk, das Pult.
Destiny, das Verhängniß.
Destitute, entblößt, hilflos.
Determine, bestimmen; sich entschließen.
Devoted, ergeben.
Diamond, der Diamant.
Die, der Stempel; die Würfel; sterben; umkommen.
Difficult, schwer, schwierig.
Dig, graben.
Dignity, die Würde, der Rang; das Amt.
Diligent, fleißig, emsig.
Discontented, unzufrieden.
Disease, die Krankheit.
Ditch, der Graben.
Do, thun, machen; verrichten; sich befinden.
Dog, der Hund.
Domestic, häuslich; —animal, das Hausthier.
Door, die Thüre.
Down, unten, nieder, hinab, hinunter, herunter.
Dozen, das Dutzend.
Draught animal, das Zugthier.
Draw, ziehen; zeichnen.
Dresden, Dresden.
Drink, der Trank, das Getränk; saufen, trinken.
Drive, treiben.
Drum, die Trommel.
Duck, die Ente.
Dutch, holländisch, die Holländer.

Due, gebührend, angemessen.
Duke, der Herzog.
During, während.
Duty, die Pflicht, Schuldigkeit.

E.

Eagle, der Adler.
Earn, verdienen, gewinnen.
Earth, die Erde.
Easy, —ily, leicht, ruhig, frei.
Eat, essen, fressen.
Eel, der Aal.
Egg, das Ei.
Either, einer von beiden; entweder.
Elephant, der Elephant.
Ell, die Elle.
Eloquence, die Beredtsamkeit.
Else, anders, sonst.
Emerald, der Smaragd.
Emigrate, auswandern.
Emperor, der Kaiser.
Encamp, sich lagern.
Endeavor, sich bemühen, sich bestreben; streben.
Enemy, der Feind.
Engage, bestellen, miethen.
England, England.
English, die Engländer, englisch.
Englishman, der Engländer.
Enjoy, sich erfreuen, genießen.
Enough, genug, hinlänglich.
Entire, ganz, vollständig.
Envious, neidisch.
Envy, beneiden.
Error, der Irrthum, Fehler.
Escape, entrinnen, entkommen.
Europe, Europa.
European, der Europäer; europäisch.
Even, eben; gerade; sogar; selbst.
Evening, der Abend, die Abendzeit.
Ever, je, jemals; immer.
Every, L. 8. & 52. b.; —where, allenthalben, überall.
Evil, übel, böse.
Except, außer, bis auf.
Exhortation, die Ermahnung.
Exile, die Verbannung.
Expect, erwarten.
Experience, erfahren.
Extensive, ausgedehnt, ausgebreitet.

Exterior, das Aeußere.
Eye, das Auge; Oehr.

F.

Fail, fehlen; unterlassen.
Faithful, treu, redlich.
Fall, der Fall; fallen; to – asleep, einschlafen, entschlafen.
Far, entfernt, fern.
Fast, fest; geschwind, schnell.
Fat, fett.
Father, der Vater; — in law, der Schwiegervater; —land, das Vaterland.
Fatigue, die Ermüdung, v. ermüden.
Fault, der Fehler, die Schuld, P. 84.
Favor, die Gunst.
Favorable, günstig.
Fear, die Furcht; v. fürchten.
Feel, fühlen; empfinden.
Feeling, das Gefühl.
Few, wenig; a —, einige.
Field, das Feld.
Fifty, fünfzig.
Fight, fechten, streiten.
Final, -ly, endlich.
Find, finden, antreffen.
Fine, fein, schön.
Fire, das Feuer.
First, L. 51, 14.
Fish, der Fisch; fischen.
Fit, passen.
Flatter, schmeicheln, liebkosen.
Flatterer, der Schmeichler.
Flattering, schmeichelhaft, schmeichelnd.
Flee, fliehen.
Fleet, schnell, flink; die Flotte.
Florin, der Gulden.
Flour, das Mehl.
Flow, fließen, strömen.
Flower, die Blume; Blüthe.
Flute, die Flöte.
Fly, die Fliege; fliegen; fliehen.
Foam, der Schaum; schäumen.
Follow, folgen, nachfolgen.
Fool, der Thor, Narr.
Foolish, thöricht, närrisch.
Foot, der Fuß; on —, zu Fuß.

For, für, nach, mit, wegen, um ... willen, an, aus, während, auf, zu, denn.
Foreign, ausländisch, fremd.
Foreigner, der Ausländer.
Forest, der Forst, Wald.
Forget, vergessen. P. 186.
Formerly, früher, ehemals.
Fortunate, glücklich.
Four, L. 51, 14.
Fox, der Fuchs.
Fragrant, duftend, wohlriechend.
France, Frankreich.
Frankfort, Frankfurt.
Free, befreien, frei.
Freedom, die Freiheit.
French, französisch; die Franzosen.
Frenchman, der Franzose.
Friend, der Freund, die Freundin.
Frighten, erschrecken.
From, von, aus.
Fruit, die Frucht, das Obst; -tree, der Obstbaum.
Funeral, das Begräbniß, — procession, der Leichenzug.
Future, die Zukunft; zukünftig.

G.

Gallant, tapfer, brav.
Garden, der Garten.
Gather, sammeln, lesen.
General, allgemein; der Feldherr, General.
Generally, gewöhnlich; im Allgemeinen.
Generous, großmüthig; freigebig.
Gentleman, Herr, der gebildete, feine Mann.
German, deutsch.
Germany, Deutschland.
Get, erhalten, bekommen; kommen; gelangen; gerathen; lassen; to — rid of, los werden; to — at, beikommen.
Giant, der Riese.
Girl, das Mädchen.
Give, geben, schenken.
Glad, froh, heiter, zufrieden; to be —, sich freuen.

Glass, das Glas; der Spiegel.
Glazier, der Glaser.
Glittering, glänzend, schimmernd.
Glove, der Handschuh.
Go, gehen. P. 180.
God, Gott.
Gold, das Gold; golden; —smith, der Goldschmied.
Gone, weg, fort.
Good, gut.
Goods, die Güter, Waaren.
Goose, die Gans.
Govern, regieren; lenken; beherrschen.
Gracious, gnädig, gütig.
Gradual, -ly, nach und nach; stufenweise.
Grain, das Korn, Getreide.
Grandfather, der Großvater.
Grass, das Gras.
Grateful, dankbar.
Gray, grau.
Great, groß.
Greek, der Grieche.
Green, grün; frisch; unreif.
Grind, mahlen.
Grow, wachsen.
Guilty, schuldig.

H.

Half, halb.
Hamburg, Hamburg.
Hammer, der Hammer.
Hand, die Hand.
Hang, hangen; behängen.
Hanover, Hannover.
Happen, sich ereignen, geschehen.
Happy, glücklich.
Harbor, der Hafen.
Harburg, das Harburg.
Hard, hart; schwer.
Hardly, kaum, schwerlich.
Hare, der Hase.
Hasten, eilen.
Hat, der Hut; —maker, der Hutmacher.
Hate, hassen, verabscheuen.
Hateful, verhaßt, gehässig.
Hatter, der Hutmacher.

Hay, das Heu.
He, er; derjenige.
Headache, das Kopfweh.
Healthy, gesund.
Hear, hören.
Heart, das Herz, Gemüth; by —, auswendig.
Heavy, schwer.
Help, die Hilfe; helfen, see können, L. 31.
Hemp, der Hanf.
Here, hier, hierher.
Hero, der Held.
Hers, der, die, das ihrige.
High, hoch.
Hill, der Hügel.
Him, ihm, dem, ihn, den.
Himself, selbst, sich.
Hippopotamus, das Nilpferd, Flußpferd.
History, die Geschichte.
Hit, schlagen; treffen.
Hold, halten.
Hole, das Loch, die Höhle.
Home, nach Hause; at —, zu Hause.
Honest, ehrlich, rechtschaffen.
Honor, die Ehre; ehren.
Hope, die Hoffnung; hoffen.
Horse, das Pferd, Roß; on —back, zu Pferde.
Hotel, der Gasthof.
House, das Haus.
How, wie, auf welche Art.
However, wie auch, aber.
Human, menschlich.
Hundred, hundert.
Hungary, Ungarn.
Hungarian, der Ungar; ungarisch.
Hungry, hungrig; he is —, es hungert ihn, or ihn hungert.
Hunter, der Jäger.
Husbandman, der Landmann.
Hyena, die Hyäne.
Hypocrisy, die Heuchelei.

I.

I, ich; I say! hören Sie doch! Hören Sie einmal.
Ice, das Eis.

Idle, müßig, träge.
Idolish, abgöttisch.
If, wenn, falls.
Ignorant, unwissend.
Immediate, gleich, augenblicklich, sogleich.
Immigrant, der Einwanderer.
Impardonable, unverzeihlich.
Impression, der Eindruck.
In, in; bei, an, zu, auf, mit, unter, nach, über, herein, hinein.
Inattentive, unaufmerksam, unachtsam.
Indolence, Trägheit.
Indolent, lässig, träge.
Industrious, fleißig.
Industry, der Fleiß.
Inhabitant, der Einwohner.
Injure, schaden, beleidigen, beeinträchtigen.
Injurious, ungerecht, nachtheilig.
Ink, die Tinte.
Innocence, die Unschuld.
Inquire, sich erkundigen, fragen.
Insist, bestehen.
Instead of, statt, anstatt.
Instructive, belehrend, lehrreich:
Interesting, anziehend, interessant.
Into, in.
Iron, das Eisen; eisern.
Irresistible, unwiderstehlich.
Italian, italienisch.

J.

Joy, die Freude.
Judge, richten, beurtheilen; der Richter.
June, der Juny or Juni.
Just, gerecht, rechtschaffen; eben.
Justice, die Gerechtigkeit.

K.

Kind, die Gattung, Art. What kind of, L. 10, adj. gütig, freundlich.
King, der König.
Kingdom, das Königreich.
Kitchen, die Küche.
Knife, das Messer.
Know, wissen, kennen.

L.

Labor, die Arbeit.
Laborer, der Arbeiter; Taglöhner.
Lady, die Frau, Dame.
Lamb, das Lamm.
Lame, lahm.
Lamp, die Lampe.
Land, das Land.
Language, die Sprache.
Large, groß, weit, breit.
Last, letzt.
Late, spät; —ly, neulich.
Laugh, das Lachen, Gelächter; lachen.
Law, das Gesetz.
Lay, legen.
Lazy, faul, träge.
Lead, führen.
Leader, der Führer.
Learn, lernen, erfahren.
Learned, gelehrt.
Least, at —, wenigstens.
Leather, das Leder; ledern.
Legend, das Mährchen; die Sage.
Leipsic, Leipzig.
Lend, leihen.
Less, kleiner, weniger.
Lesson, die Lektion, Stunde.
Let, lassen.
Letter, der Buchstabe; Brief.
Liberty, die Freiheit, at —, see dürfen, L. 31.
Lie, die Lüge; lügen.
Lie, liegen.
Life, das Leben.
Light, das Licht; to come to —, ans Tageslicht kommen.
Lighten, leuchten, blitzen.
Like, gleich, ähnlich; gefallen; the —, dergleichen; he would — to, er möchte gern.
Lily, die Lilie.
Line, die Linie, Zeile; füttern.
Lion, der Löwe.
Little, klein; gering, wenig.
Live, leben; wohnen.
Lock, das Schloß; zuschließen schließen.

Long, lang, lange.
Look, das Ansehen haben; aussehen.
Lose, verlieren.
Loud, —ly, laut.
Love, die Liebe; lieben.
Low, niedrig; brüllen.

M.

Magdeburg, Magdeburg.
Magistrate, die Obrigkeit, der Amtmann.
Maine, der Main.
Make, machen, verrichten, lassen.
Man, der Mensch; Mann.
Mannheim, Mannheim.
Many, viel, L. 52; —a, mancher.
March, der März.
Mark, das Zeichen.
Market, der Markt.
Mason, der Maurer.
Master, der Meister; Herr; — of a language, einer Sprache mächtig.
Matter, die Sache; what is the —? was gibt es?
May, der Mai.
May, mögen, können, dürfen.
Mayence, Mainz.
Mean, gemein, schlecht; das Mittel; by means of, vermittelst.
Measure, das Maß; messen.
Meat, das Fleisch.
Mechanic, der Handwerker.
Meditate, überlegen, nachdenken, erwägen.
Meet, to go to — entgegen gehen; treffen; begegnen.
Meissen, Meißen.
Melt, schmelzen.
Memory, das Gedächtniß.
Mention, erwähnen.
Merchant, der Kaufmann.
Metal, das Metall.
Miller, der Müller.
Milliner, die Putzmacherin.
Mind, das Gemüth; der Sinn.
Mindful, aufmerksam; eingedenk.
Mine, mein, meinige. L. 25.
Minute, die Minute.

Miser, der Geizhals.
Miserable, elend, erbärmlich.
Miss, das Fräulein.
Miss, missen; verfehlen.
Mistake, der Irrthum; sich irren; fehlen.
Misunderstand, falsch verstehen, mißverstehen.
Money, das Geld, die Münze.
Month, der Monat.
Moon, der Mond.
More, das Mehr; mehr.
Morning, der Morgen.
Most, meist.
Mother, die Mutter.
Mountain, der Berg.
Much, viel; sehr.
Munich, München.
Murder, ermorden.
Music, die Musik.
Must, müssen. L. 31.
Mustard, der Senf.
My, mein, meine. L. 9, 2.

N.

Napoleon, Napoleon.
Nation, die Nation, das Volk.
Near, nahe, beinahe, fast; bei.
Need, bedürfen, nöthig haben.
Neighbor, der Nachbar, Nächste, die Nachbarin.
Neither, L. 52, 10, weder; auch nicht; — ... nor, weder ... noch.
Nephew, der Neffe.
Nest, das Nest.
Never, nie, niemals.
Nevertheless, nichtsdestoweniger, dessenungeachtet, dennoch).
New, neu; frisch.
News, die Neuigkeit, Nachricht.
Next, nächst, folgend.
Night, die Nacht.
Nightingale, die Nachtigall.
Nile, der Nil.
Ninth, neunte.
No, nein; nicht; kein.
Nobleman, der Edelmann.
Nobody, Niemand. L. 10, 8.

None, keiner, keine, keines.
Nor, noch; auch nicht. L. 66.
Not, nicht. L. 66.
Nothing, nichts.
Now, nun, jetzt, soeben.

O.

Oak, die Eiche.
Oats, der Hafer.
Obedience, der Gehorsam.
Obedient, gehorsam.
Obey, gehorchen.
Objection, die Entgegensetzung; der Einwurf; Vorwurf; to have no —, nichts dagegen haben.
Oblige, verpflichten, verbinden, see müssen, L. 31.
Obtain, erhalten, erlangen.
Occur, vorkommen, sich ereignen.
Oder, die Oder.
Oelper, Oelper, *proper name*.
Of, von, wegen, vermittelst; — course, natürlich, es versteht sich.
Offend, beleidigen.
Often, oft, öfters.
Oil, das Oel.
Old, alt.
On, an, auf, in, bei, zu, mit, unter, vor, über, von, weg, weiter, fort, gegen; zufolge.
Only, einzig; allein, nur; erst.
Opera, die Oper.
Opinion, die Meinung.
Oppose, sich widersetzen.
Opposite, gegenüber.
Oppress, unterdrücken.
Oppressor, der Unterdrücker.
Or, oder.
Ostrich, der Strauß.
Other, der, die, das andere; every — day, einen Tag um den andern; —wise, anders, sonst.
Out, aus, draußen; – of, aus, außer.
Over, über, auf, hinüber, herüber, vorüber, vorbei; allzu, zu sehr, weit, breit; überhin, durch; vor.
Owe, schuldig sein, verdanken.
Ox, der Ochs.

P.

Page, die Seite, Blattseite.
Painter, der Maler.
Painting, das Gemälde.
Pair, das Paar.
Palace, der Palast.
Paper, das Papier; papieren.
Paradise, das Paradies.
Parents, die Eltern.
Paris, Paris.
Part, der Theil.
Pass, der Paß; to — by, vorbeigehen.
Past, vergangen, vorbei.
Patience, die Geduld.
Patient, geduldig; der Kranke, Patient.
Patriotism, die Vaterlandsliebe.
Peaceful, friedsam.
Peach, die Pfirsiche.
Pear, die Birne.
Peasant, der Landmann, Bauer.
Pen, die Feder, Schreibfeder.
Pencil, der Pinsel; Bleistift.
People, das Volk, die Leute; bevölkern.
Pepper, der Pfeffer.
Perfect, vollkommen.
Perform, verrichten, vollziehen, ausführen.
Perhaps, vielleicht.
Perish, umkommen; zu Grunde gehen.
Persuade, überreden.
Physician, der Arzt.
Piece, das Stück.
Pine, die Fichte, Tanne.
Pink, die Nelke.
Pity, das Mitleiden; it is a —, es ist Schade; bemitleiden, bedauern.
Plan, der Plan, Entwurf.
Plane, die Fläche; der Hobel.
Play, spielen, scherzen.
Pleasant, —ly, angenehm.
Please, gefallen; ergötzen.
Pleasure, das Vergnügen.
Plow, der Pflug.
Plum, die Pflaume.

Point, der Punkt; to be ipon the -, im Begriffe sein.
Polite, fein. artig, höflich.
Poor, arm, dürftig, mager.
Possess, to — one's-self of a thing, sich einer Sache bemächtigen.
Possession, der Besitz.
Potato, die Kartoffel.
Pound, Pfund.
Pour, gießen; einschenken.
Poverty, die Armuth.
Power, die Macht, Gewalt, Kraft.
Powerful, —ly, mächtig.
Practical, praktisch.
Praise, das Lob; loben, preisen.
Prefer, vorziehen.
Presence, die Gegenwart, Anwesenheit.
Press, die Presse.
Pretty, hübsch, nett, ziemlich.
Prey, der Raub.
Price, der Preis; Werth.
Prince, der Prinz; Fürst.
Principle, der Grundsatz.
Prison, das Gefängniß.
Probable, wahrscheinlich.
Procession, der Aufzug; die Procession.
Promise, das Versprechen; versprechen, geloben.
Pronounce, aussprechen.
Proper, eigen; schicklich.
Proud, stolz; trotzig.
Prudence, die Klugheit; Vorsichtigkeit.
Prussia, Preußen.
Pulpit, die Kanzel.
Punish, bestrafen.
Purse, der Beutel.
Put, stellen; legen.

Q.

Quarrel, zanken, streiten.
Quarter, das Viertel.
Question, die Frage; Streitfrage.
Questionable, zweifelhaft.
Quire, das Buch. L. 47. 3.

R.

Rabbit, das Kaninchen.
Rain, der Regen; regnen.
Raise, heben, aufheben.
Rapid, schnell, geschwind.
Rather, lieber.
Read, lesen.
Really, wirklich, in der That.
Reason, die Vernunft; Ursache; der Grund.
Receive, empfangen, erhalten.
Recognize, erkennen.
Recommend, empfehlen.
Recover, gesund werden; genesen.
Red, roth.
Redound, zurückfließen; gereichen.
Refuse, ausschlagen, sich weigern.
Regard, ansehen.
Reindeer, das Rennthier.
Relation, der, die Verwandte.
Remain, bleiben.
Remedy, das Hilfsmittel.
Remember, sich erinnern. P 126.
Renounce, entsagen.
Renowned, berühmt.
Resemble, gleichen; ähnlich sein.
Reside, wohnen.
Resist, widerstehen.
Respect, achten, schätzen, hochachten.
Return, zurückkehren, zurückgeben, zurückschicken.
Revolution, die Umwälzung, Revolution.
Reward, vergelten, belohnen.
Rhine, der Rhein.
Rhinoceros, das Nashorn.
Ribbon, das Band.
Rich, reich.
Ride, reiten, fahren.
Ridicule, lächerlich machen; sich über ... aufhalten.
Ring, der Ring; Kreis; Klang.
Ripe, reif, zeitig.
Ripen, reifen.
River, der Fluß; Strom.
Road, die Straße.
Rob, rauben, berauben.
Roof, das Dach.
Room, der Raum, die Stube, das Zimmer.
Rose, die Rose.

Ruby, der Rubin.
Rude, —ly, roh, rauh, grob.
Rule, die Regel; Herrschaft.
Run, laufen, rennen, rinnen; — away, durchgehen.
Russian, der Russe; russisch.
Rye, der Roggen; das Korn.

S.

Sacrifice, das Opfer.
Sad, traurig, betrübt.
Saddle, der Sattel.
Saddler, der Sattler.
Sail, das Segel.
Sailor, der Matrose.
Sake, L. 48. 6.
Salmon, der Lachs.
Salt, das Salz.
Same, derselbe, dieselbe, dasselbe; the very —, der nämliche.
Satisfy, befriedigen.
Save, retten, erretten.
Saxon, der Sachse; sächsisch.
Saxony, Sachsen.
Say, sagen.
Scholar, der Schüler; Gelehrte; die Schülerin.
School, die Schule.
Scold, schelten.
Sea, die See, das Meer.
Season, die Jahreszeit; rechte Zeit.
Season of the year, die Jahreszeit.
Seat, der Sitz, Stuhl; setzen.
Secret, das Geheimniß.
See, sehen.
Seem, scheinen.
Seize, ergreifen.
Self, selbst.
Sell, verkaufen.
Send, senden, schicken; to — for, holen lassen.
Sense, der Sinn, Verstand.
Servant, der Diener.
Several, verschiedene, mehrere.
Shall, sollen, werden.
Sharp, —ly, scharf.
Sharpen, schärfen, schleifen, zuspitzen.
Sheep, das Schaf.
Shine, scheinen, leuchten.

Ship, das Schiff.
Shoe, der Schuh; das Hufeisen. —maker, der Schuhmacher.
Shoot, schießen.
Short, kurz.
Shovel, die Schaufel.
Show, zeigen.
Sick, krank, unwohl.
Side, die Seite, on this —, diesseits, on the other —, jenseits.
Sight, das Gesicht; out of —, aus den Augen.
Silk, die Seide; seiden.
Silly, einfältig, albern.
Silver, das Silber.
Similar, ähnlich.
Since, seitdem, vorher, weil, da.
Sing, singen.
Sister, die Schwester; —inlaw, die Schwägerin.
Sit, sitzen, passen.
Six, sechs.
Sixteenth, L. 51. 14.
Skillful, geschickt.
Slander, verleumden.
Slaughter, schlachten.
Slave, der Sclave.
Sleep, der Schlaf; schlafen.
Slow, langsam.
Small, klein, gering.
Smile, lächeln.
Smith, der Schmied, Schmid, Schmidt.
Smoke, der Rauch; rauchen.
Smooth, glatt.
Snow, der Schnee; schneien.
So, so.
Sofa, das Ruhebett, Sopha.
Soft, weich, sanft; leise.
Soldier, der Soldat.
Some, L. 52, 6; —body, jemand; —thing, etwas; —times, zuweilen, manchmal; —where, irgendwo.
Son, der Sohn.
Song, der Gesang; das Lied.
Soon, bald, früh.
Sorry, traurig, betrübt; I am —, es thut mir leid.
Soul, die Seele, der Geist.

Speak, sprechen, reden.
Spear, der Spieß, Speer, die Lanze.
Speech, Rede.
Spendthrift, der Verschwender.
Spin, spinnen; drehen.
Split, spalten.
Spring, der Sprung; die Quelle; Frühling; springen.
Squirrel, das Eichhörnchen.
Stable, der Stall.
Stand, der Stand, die Stelle; stehen.
Starling, der Staar.
Start, fahren; abreisen.
State, der Staat; —'s-man, der Staatsmann.
Stay, der Aufenthalt; bleiben.
Stead, die Stelle. L. 48. 7.
Steal, stehlen.
Steel, der Stahl; stählen; stählern. L. 23, 9.
Steep, steil.
Still, still, ruhig; noch. L. 66.
Sting, stechen.
Stone, der Stein.
Stop, hemmen; anhalten; aufhören; sich aufhalten.
Story, die Geschichte; das Mährchen.
Stove, der Ofen.
Stranger, der Fremde, Unbekannte.
Stream, der Strom.
Strength, die Stärke.
Strike, schlagen, stoßen, hauen.
Strong, stark, kräftig, derb.
Struggle, sich sträuben, kämpfen; — against, widerstreben.
Study, studiren, nachdenken.
Stupid, dumm; albern.
Subject, der Unterthan; unterthan.
Submit, sich unterwerfen, sich gefallen lassen.
Succeed, nachfolgen; gelingen.
Suffer, leiden.
Suffering, das Leiden, leidend.
Sugar, der Zucker.
Summer, der Sommer.
Summon, auffordern.
Sun, die Sonne.
Superior, überlegen, vorzüglicher.
Sure, sicher, gewiß.

Surrender, sich ergeben.
Suspect, in Verdacht haben.
Swan, der Schwan.
Swell, schwellen, aufschwellen.
Swim, schwimmen.
Sword, das Schwert.

T.

Table, die Tafel; der Tisch.
Tailor, der Schneider.
Take, nehmen; machen; to — off, abnehmen.
Talk, sprechen, plaudern.
Tall, groß, hoch.
Tanner, der Gerber.
Taste, der Geschmack.
Tea, der Thee.
Teach, lehren, unterrichten.
Teacher, der Lehrer, die Lehrerin.
Tear, die Thräne.
Tedious, langweilig.
Tell, zählen, erzählen.
Term, der Termin.
Terms, die Bedingung.
Than, als, denn.
That, daß.
The, der, die, das, je..., desto..., um so; — more, — better, je mehr, desto besser.
Thee, dir, dich; of —, deiner.
Their, ihr, ihre.
Them, ihnen, sie.
Themselves, sie selbst, sich selbst.
There, da, dort, daselbst, dahin; es; —fore, daher, darum; also.
They, sie.
Thief, der Dieb.
Thing, das Ding, die Sache.
Think, denken, meinen, glauben; to — of, gedenken.
Third, dritte; das Drittel.
Thirst, der Durst.
Thirty, L. 51, 14.
Though, obschon, obgleich.
Thousand, tausend.
Thrash, dreschen.
Threat, die Drohung.
Threaten, drohen.
Three, drei

Thresh, *see* Thrash.
Through, durch.
Throw, werfen.
Thunder, donnern, wettern.
Thus, so, also, auf diese Art.
Thyself, du selbst, selbst, dich, dir.
Tiber, die Tiber.
Tiger, der Tiger.
Till, bis.
Time, die Zeit.
Tired, müde, überdrüssig.
To, zu, um, an, auf, mit, nach, für, gegen; bis; — and fro, hin und her.
To-day, heute.
To-morrow, morgen.
Tongs, die Zange.
Too, zu, allzu; auch.
Toothache, das Zahnweh.
Town, die Stadt; to —, nach der Stadt.
Traitor, der Verräther.
Travel, reisen.
Traveler, der Reisende.
Treat, behandeln.
Tree, der Baum; Stamm.
Tremble, zittern.
Trouble, die Unruhe; der Verdruß, Kummer.
Trout, die Forelle.
True, wahr, treu.
Trunk, der Koffer; Stamm.
Trust, trauen, vertrauen, sich verlassen.
Truth, die Wahrheit.
Try, prüfen, versuchen.
Turk, der Türke.
Turn, Reihe, P. 83; drehen; drechseln.
Twelve, L. 51, 14.
Twenty, zwanzig.
Twice, zweimal.
Two, L. 51, 14.
Tyrant, der Tyrann, Wütherich.

U.

Unaccustomed, ungewohnt.
Uncle, der Oheim, Onkel.
Under, unter, unten; nieder; untergeordnet.
Understand, verstehen, begreifen; see können, L. 31.
Unfavorable, ungünstig.
Unfortunate, unglücklich.
Unhappy, unglücklich.
Unite, vereinigen.
United, vereinigt.
Unjust, —ly, ungerecht.
Unpardonable, unverzeihlich.
Unpleasant, unangenehm.
Until, bis.
Unwell, unwohl.
Up, auf, aufwärts, hinauf, herauf, empor.
Upon, auf, an, über, bei, aus, in, nach, zufolge.
Useful, nützlich.

V.

Valiant, tapfer, brav.
Value, der Werth.
Vanity, die Eitelkeit.
Velvet, der Sammet.
Very, sehr.
Vest, die Weste.
Vex, plagen, quälen, verdrießen.
Vice, das Laster.
Vienna, Wien.
Village, das Dorf.
Villain, der Schelm, Spitzbube.
Vinegar, der Essig.
Visit, der Besuch; besuchen.
Voice, die Stimme.
Volume, der Band.

W.

Wagon, der Wagen; —maker, der Wagner.
Wait, warten.
Walk, der Gang, Weg, Spaziergang; gehen.
Wall, die Wand, Mauer.
Want, das Bedürfniß; to be in —, benöthigt sein, nöthig haben; Mangel leiden an ...
War, der Krieg.
Warm, warm.
Wash, waschen; —stand, der Waschtisch.

Watch, die Uhr, Taschenuhr.
Wave, die Welle, Woge.
Way, der Weg.
We, wir.
Weak, schwach.
Wealth, der Wohlstand, Reichthum.
Wear, tragen, anhaben.
Weather, das Wetter.
Weave, weben.
Wedding, die Hochzeit.
Week, die Woche.
Weep, weinen, beweinen.
Well, wohl, gut.
Were, waren.
What, was, welcher; welch ein; was für ein; wie viel; L. 10.
Whatever, was nur, was auch immer.
Wheat, der Waizen.
When, wenn, wann, als, da.
Where, wo, wohin.
Whether, ob.
Which, welcher, welche, welches.
While, indem, während.
Whistle, die Pfeife; pfeifen.
White, weiß.
Who, wer, welcher; der, die; –ever, wer auch immer.
Whole, ganz.
Why, warum, L. 10, 5.
Wicked, gottlos.
Will, der Wille; wollen, L. 31.

Win, gewinnen.
Window, das Fenster
Windy, windig.
Wine, der Wein.
Winter, der Winter.
Wise, weise, verständig.
Wish, der Wunsch; wünschen, see wollen, L. 31.
With, mit, nebst, sammt, bei, auf, für, an, durch.
Without, außer, ohne.
Wolf, der Wolf.
Woman, das Weib, die Frau.
Wood, das Holz.
Wooden, hölzern.
Wool, die Wolle.
Word, das Wort.
Work, die Arbeit; das Werk; arbeiten.
World, die Welt, Erde.
Worm, der Wurm.
Worst, schlechteste, ärgste.
Worth, der Werth; werth, würdig.
Write, schreiben.
Writing, die Schrift.
Wrong, unrecht, falsch.

Y.

Year, das Jahr.
Yellow, gelb.
Yesterday, gestern.
Yet, doch, dennoch, noch.
Young, jung; frisch.

ADDENDA.

Begegnen, to meet.
Bereiten, to prepare.
Bieten, to offer.
Bist, art, are. See L. 32. 2.
Darbieten, to offer, extend.
Dereinst, once, in future.
Farbe, *f.* color.
Feind, *m.* -es, enemy; *adj.* hostile.

Gebildet, *adj.* cultivated, educated.
Herrlich, *adj.* glorious, excellent
Raub, *m.* robbing, plunder.
Schwinden, to disappear.
Verständlich, *adj.* intelligible.
Zange, *f.* tongs.

www.ingramcontent.com/pod-product-compliance
Lightning Source LLC
Chambersburg PA
CBHW021810230426
43669CB00008B/702